Mental Health Tribunals

Other titles available from Law Society Publishing:

Advising Mentally Disordered Offenders (2nd edn)
Carolyn Taylor and Julia Krish, with Dr Frank Farnham

Assessment of Mental Capacity (3rd edn)
British Medical Association and the Law Society

Mental Capacity (2nd edn)
Nicola Greaney, Fenella Morris and Beverley Taylor

Titles from Law Society Publishing can be ordered from all good bookshops or direct (telephone 0870 850 1422, email **lawsociety@prolog.uk.com** or visit our online shop at **bookshop.lawsociety.org.uk**).

MENTAL HEALTH TRIBUNALS

Law, Policy and Practice

Philip Fennell, Penny Letts and Jonathan Wilson

The Law Society

Whilst all reasonable care has been taken in the preparation of this publication, neither the publisher nor the authors can accept any responsibility for any loss occasioned to any person acting or refraining from action as a result of relying upon its contents.

The views expressed in this publication should be taken as those of the authors only unless it is specifically indicated that the Law Society has given its endorsement.

Legislation in Appendices A, B and D and the Practice Direction in Appendix C are Crown Copyright and reproduced here with the permission of the Controller of HMSO. Appendix H is reproduced with the kind permission of the Mental Health Lawyers Association.

ISBN-13: 978-1-85328-735-0

Published in 2013 by the Law Society
113 Chancery Lane, London WC2A 1PL

Typeset by Columns Design XML Ltd, Reading
Printed by CPI Group (UK) Ltd, Croydon, CR0 4YY

FSC
www.fsc.org
MIX
Paper from
responsible sources
FSC® C013604

The paper used for the text pages of this book is FSC® certified. FSC (the Forest Stewardship Council®) is an international network to promote responsible management of the world's forests.

Contents

Foreword

I first represented a client at a Mental Health Review Tribunal in 1979, when the relevant law was the Mental Health Act 1959; there were no second opinion doctors, Mental Health Act Commission or Care Quality Commission and of course no Human Rights Act. The concepts of patients' rights, mental health survivors and patient advocacy were more or less unheard of, and non-means tested aftercare for detained patients had not yet come in.

Tribunal reports could be, and frequently were, withheld from patient applicants in their entirety, so they were often outside the door for much of the hearing, whether or not they were represented. There was no requirement for the medical member to outline his or her conversation with the applicant at the pre-hearing interview, and as it was not necessary for tribunals to give detailed reasons for their decisions the prospect of challenging a decision was really very low indeed.

Well, those days are long gone and the law, and society, now recognise the extreme vulnerability of people who are not only mentally disordered but also detained or deprived of their liberty. But it is not enough to have good laws, they also need to be understood if the rights of the individual are to be properly protected.

To be an effective representative, or even to be an effective tribunal member, you not only need to understand the relevant law on tribunals but also much wider issues; you need to know something about psychiatry and psychology, medication and treatment, risk assessment and risk management. And mental health professionals also need to understand the law if they are to be effective witnesses at tribunals.

This book, written by three well-known experts in mental health law, psychiatry and tribunals, contains everything those participating in tribunals could possibly need to know. It not only explains the law and procedure of Mental Health Tribunals but also describes their history; common mental disorders and how to treat them; the criteria for detention and discharge; the ways of challenging decisions and, specifically for legal representatives, how a case should be run.

The book is helpfully set out into subject areas, within which the combined expertise of the authors provides a comprehensive and readable account of the relevant issues. Much mental health law is notoriously opaque in its drafting, and the authors' lucid unpacking of the statutes is a pleasure to read.

I will use this book frequently, and recommend it to both newcomers to the field, who will receive an education, and old hands, who will enjoy refreshing their knowledge at this source.

Lucy Scott-Moncrieff
President of the Law Society
March 2013

Preface

The First-tier Tribunal (Mental Health) in England and the Mental Health Review Tribunal for Wales play a vital constitutional role in upholding the human rights of people who suffer from mental disorder. They have evolved from the original Mental Health Review Tribunals for England and Wales, established under the Mental Health Act 1959 to provide an independent review of the need for compulsory powers in an individual case. The tribunals provide a forum where a person can seek review of the lawfulness of detention on grounds of mental disorder, as required by art.5(4) of the European Convention on Human Rights (ECHR). They also provide a forum where a person may seek to uphold the right to respect for private life under ECHR, art.8 by seeking review of the lawfulness of a community treatment order or guardianship.

This book is intended to provide a guide to the operation of Mental Health Tribunals which will be of use to tribunal members and staff, to those representing patients or responsible authorities before the tribunals, to professionals appearing before the tribunal such as approved mental health professionals, approved clinicians and nursing staff, and indeed to anyone who wishes to understand the operation of Mental Health Tribunals in England and Wales.

The book will be of particular value for those who represent patients at tribunal hearings. The importance of such representation was underlined by Brook LJ in *R* v. *Legal Aid Board, ex p. Duncan* [2000] EWHC Admin 294, at [571]–[572]:

> Mental health law is difficult enough today. Reading the report of a psychiatrist, identifying its areas of weakness, commissioning evidence from the appropriate expert to challenge it, and representing a client at a tribunal requires expert professional skills born, as we have said, of education and practical experience. It is not like going down to the magistrates' court as a duty solicitor, arduous though those duties are.
>
> In the fairly near future the demands made on skilled solicitors in this field are going to increase exponentially.

Changes which the judge had in mind included the pending implementation of the Human Rights Act 1998, and the proposed legislation which led to the Mental Capacity Act 2005 and Mental Health Act (MHA) 2007. To these can now be added the Tribunals, Courts and Enforcement Act 2007 which was enacted as a result of the 2001 Leggatt Report on the review of tribunals. All of these, in combination, have greatly increased the complexity of mental health law and practice.

The amendments introduced by MHA 2007 to the Mental Health Act (MHA) 1983 began a process of divergence between the laws of England and Wales. Each jurisdiction now has its own separate regulations and tribunal rules; each has its own Code of Practice; each has its own tribunal; and, now, the introduction of the Mental Health (Wales) Measure 2010 adds 50 new sections to MHA 1983 as it applies in Wales, including 17 new rule-making powers. This book addresses the relevant law and procedure as they apply in both England and Wales.

The first part of this book provides some background to Mental Health Tribunals: Chapter 1 deals with the human rights context in which mental health legislation operates, and Chapter 2 examines the origins and role of Mental Health Tribunals in England and Wales. Chapter 3 sets out the definition of mental disorder and describes the main forms of mental disorder which may lead to the use of compulsory powers.

The second part of the book considers the legal framework within which the tribunals operate. Chapter 4 considers non-offender patients, setting out the relevant detention powers and the routes by which detention may be ended (including not only applications and references to the tribunal but also discharge by other routes). Chapter 5 deals similarly with offender patients, considering the relevance of mental disorder at the time of the offence, the trial, the sentencing and thereafter in custody. Chapter 6 considers community care services generally, then examines the process for admission to and discharge from guardianship and community treatment orders. Chapters 7 and 8, in relation to unrestricted and restricted patients respectively, discuss the tribunals' various powers and duties. These chapters include a detailed consideration of the meaning of the various statutory criteria for compulsion.

The third part deals with the rules and the operation of the tribunals, structured in a rough chronological order. Chapter 9 deals with pre-hearing procedures (including, in particular, case management and directions). Chapter 10 summarises the requirements for statements and reports both in England and in Wales, and deals with disclosure of various types of documents in the context of tribunal proceedings. Chapter 11 deals with procedures relating to the hearing itself, including the approach to evidence and the typical order of events. Chapter 12 explains the procedures for challenging a decision, whether review by the First-tier Tribunal in England, or appeal or judicial review hearings in the Upper Tribunal or Administrative Court.

The final part is a practical guide for representatives, in particular those who represent patients. Chapter 13, on tribunal representation, introduces the Law Society's Mental Health Accreditation Scheme and the various sources of conduct and ethical guidance, before setting out the 'the life of a tribunal file' from introduction to the client to consideration of the written reasons. The final chapter summarises the provisions of the Legal Aid Standard Civil Contract 2010 as they apply to mental health cases.

It should be noted that the Legal Services Commission (from April 2013 the Legal Aid Agency) has given formal notice that membership of the Law Society's Mental Health Accreditation Scheme will be mandatory for all staff carrying out representation at Mental Health Tribunals. This book should assist those preparing for accreditation or re-accreditation to that scheme, as well as in their practice as tribunal representatives.

As with any law book, the information on law and procedure and some of the documents reproduced in the appendices are likely to change over time. Regular updates on legislation and case law relating to Mental Health Tribunals are available on the Mental Health Law Online website at **www.mentalhealthlaw.co.uk**.

Philip Fennell
Jonathan Wilson
Penny Letts
March 2013

About the authors

Philip Fennell is a professor of Law at Cardiff University. He was the specialist legal adviser to the Joint-Parliamentary Scrutiny Committee on the Draft Mental Health Bill 2004, and to the Parliamentary Joint Committee on Human Rights for the Committee's scrutiny of the 2006 Bill. Philip has written widely on mental health law, including as contributor and editor of *Principles of Mental Health Law and Policy* (Oxford University Press, 2010) and author of *Mental Health: Law and Practice* 2nd edition (Jordan Publishing, 2011).

Penny Letts is a policy consultant, trainer and member of the Administrative Justice and Tribunals Council. She was formerly Law Society policy advisor on mental health and disability, a specialist adviser to the Joint Parliamentary Committee on the Draft Mental Capacity Bill and a Mental Health Act Commissioner. Penny wrote a major part of the *MCA 2005 Code of Practice*, was general editor of *Assessment of Mental Capacity* 3rd edition (Law Society, 2010) and contributor to *Atkins Court Forms on Mental Health Tribunals* (LexisNexis, 2009). She is also editor of Jordans' *Elder Law Journal* and co-author of *Court of Protection Practice* (Jordan Publishing, annual publication).

Jonathan Wilson is a practising solicitor specialising in mental health and capacity law, and a member of the Law Society's Mental Health Accreditation Scheme. He is a committee member of the Mental Health Lawyers Association (MHLA) and designed the MHLA's accreditation scheme training course which has been approved by the Law Society. Jonathan also runs the Mental Health Law Online website and CPD programme (**www.mentalhealthlaw.co.uk**) and is author of its regular updates and Annual Review.

Acknowledgements

We owe a huge debt of gratitude to John Horne, Teaching Fellow at Northumbria University's School of Law, who provided extremely helpful comments on various drafts of every chapter and gave enormous support and encouragement throughout the project.

Many other people helped us by providing comments on drafts or answering our questions, including: Richard Jones, Carolyn Kirby, Richard Charlton, Ian Campbell, Nick Lewis, Chris Curran, Dr Pamela Taylor, Dr Rosemarie Cope, Anthony Harbour, Oliver Toop, Camilla Parker, Angela Truell and members of the Secretariat at HM Courts and Tribunals Service (Mental Health) and the Mental Health Review Tribunal for Wales.

Acknowledgements

Table of cases

Table of statutes

Table of statutory instruments

Abbreviations

AAC	Administrative Appeals Chamber
AC	approved clinician
AJTC	Administrative Justice and Tribunals Council
AMHP	approved mental health professional
ASW	approved social worker
BNF	British National Formulary
CAMHS	Child and Adolescent Mental Health Service
CCG	Clinical Commissioning Group
CJA 2003	Criminal Justice Act 2003
CPA	Care Programme Approach
CPN	community psychiatric nurse
CQC	Care Quality Commission
CRPD	United Nations Convention on the Rights of Persons with Disabilities
CTO	community treatment order
DH	Department of Health
DoLS	Deprivation of Liberty Safeguards
DPA 1998	Data Protection Act 1998
ECHR	European Convention on Human Rights
ECT	electro-convulsive therapy
ECtHR	European Court of Human Rights
HESC	Health, Education and Social Care
HMCTS	Her Majesty's Courts and Tribunals Service
HRA 1998	Human Rights Act 1998
HSH	high secure hospital
IMCA	independent mental capacity advocate
IMHA	independent mental health advocate
IPP	indeterminate sentence for public protection
LAA	Legal Aid Agency
LSC	Legal Services Commission
LSSA	local social services authority
MAPPA	Multi-Agency Public Protection Arrangements
MCA 2005	Mental Capacity Act 2005
MHA 1959	Mental Health Act 1959

MHA 1983	Mental Health Act 1983
MHA 2007	Mental Health Act 2007
MHCS	Mental Health Casework Section (National Offender Management Service)
MHLA	Mental Health Lawyers Association
MHRT	Mental Health Review Tribunal
MHRT Rules 1983	Mental Health Review Tribunal Rules 1983
MHT	Mental Health Tribunal
MoJ	Ministry of Justice
NICE	National Institute of Clinical Excellence
NR	nearest relative
PACE	Police and Criminal Evidence Act 1984
PCT	Primary Care Trust
RC	responsible clinician
RMO	responsible medical officer
SCT	supervised community treatment
SOAD	second opinion appointed doctor
STJ	salaried tribunal judge
TCEA 2007	Tribunals, Courts and Enforcement Act 2007
UT	Upper Tribunal
VLO	Victim Liaison Officer

CHAPTER 1

Mental health detention: law, policy and international human rights

1.1 HUMAN RIGHTS AND MENTAL HEALTH LEGISLATION

Mental health law and policy have a profound effect on human rights, particularly the right to liberty and the right to physical integrity. Mentally disordered people are entitled to the protection of general human rights instruments such as the UN Universal Declaration of Human Rights 1948, the International Covenant on Civil and Political Rights 1966, the UN Convention on the Rights of the Child 1989, the European Convention on Human Rights 1950, and the Charter of Fundamental Rights of the European Union 2000. Protection of individual human dignity is a fundamental requirement of all international human rights instruments,[1] and is a pervasive issue in upholding rights to autonomy, to liberty, to protection of physical integrity, and to protection against inhuman or degrading treatment.

Most states maintain laws authorising detention and treatment without consent of people suffering from mental disorder who pose a risk to themselves or to others. This chapter outlines the development of current law and policy relating to detention under the two English statutes which authorise detention on grounds of mental disorder: the Mental Health Act (MHA) 1983; and the Mental Capacity Act (MCA) 2005. The case law of the European Court of Human Rights has had a profound influence on the content of these Acts. Since this book deals with Mental Health Tribunals (in England, the First-tier Tribunal (Mental Health) (referred to in this book as the Mental Health Tribunal (MHT)) and in Wales the Mental Health Review Tribunal (MHRT) for Wales), the main focus will be on MHA 1983. Patients detained under MCA 2005 have no rights to challenge detention before a tribunal, their recourse being to ask for review by the supervisory body authorising the deprivation of their liberty or by the Court of Protection.

In terms of impact on law and policy in the United Kingdom, the European Convention on Human Rights is the most important human rights instrument. The

---

[1] The UN Universal Declaration of Human Rights 1948, art.1 states 'All human beings are born free and equal in dignity' and art.3 states 'Everyone has the right to life liberty and security of the person'. The Charter of Fundamental Rights of the European Union 2000, art.1 reaffirms that 'Human dignity is inviolable. It must be respected and protected'.

Human Rights Act (HRA) 1998 requires domestic courts, so far as it is possible to do so, to read and give effect to primary and subordinate legislation in a way which is compatible with Convention rights (HRA 1998, s.3), and to take into account the Strasbourg jurisprudence in determining any question which has arisen in connection with a Convention right (HRA 1998, s.2). Where a superior court (the High Court or any court above) considers that a provision of the UK statute is incompatible with a Convention right, it may make a declaration of incompatibility (HRA 1998, s.4(2)). This operates as a signal to the responsible minister to introduce legislation to rectify the incompatibility, which may be done by primary legislation or by Order in Council (HRA 1998, s.10).[2] HRA 1998, s.6 places a duty on all public authorities (which includes all courts and tribunals, and any person or body certain of whose functions are of a public nature) to act compatibly with Convention rights.[3]

1.2 CONVENTION RIGHTS AND DETENTION ON GROUNDS OF UNSOUNDNESS OF MIND

Article 5(1) of the European Convention on Human Rights (ECHR) provides that no one shall be deprived of his liberty unless this is done in accordance with a procedure prescribed by law, and is necessary in a democratic society on one of a number of grounds. One of those grounds, listed in art.5(1)(e), is unsoundness of mind. In order for a non-emergency detention on grounds of unsoundness of mind to comply with art.5, reliable evidence of a true mental disorder must be presented to a competent authority.

1.2.1 Grounds for detention

In *Winterwerp* v. *The Netherlands* (1979) 2 EHRR 387, the European Court of Human Rights (ECtHR) laid down three minimum substantive and procedural requirements for lawful detention of persons of unsound mind ('the *Winterwerp* criteria') (see also *Van der Leer* v. *Netherlands* (1990) 12 EHRR 567):

1. Except in emergency cases, the individual must reliably be shown to be of unsound mind. This has been held to entail the establishment of a true mental disorder on the basis of objective medical expertise.
2. The mental disorder must be of a kind or degree justifying compulsory confinement.

---

[2] See e.g. the Mental Health Act 1983 (Remedial) Order 2001, SI 2001/3712 introduced to rectify the incompatibility between MHA 1983, ss.72(1) and 73(1) and ECHR, art.5 identified in *R (H)* v. *Mental Health Review Tribunal North and East London Region and Secretary of State for Health* [2002] QB 1, [2001] 3 WLR 512.
[3] The public authority has a defence if it could not have acted differently because of primary legislation or if it was acting to enforce primary or subordinate legislation which cannot be read or given effect in a manner consistent with Convention rights.

3.   The validity of continued confinement depends on the persistence of such a mental disorder. This implies that it is for those carrying out the detention to satisfy themselves at intervals that the criteria for detention continue to be met.

In *X v. Finland* [2012] ECHR 1371, the decision to continue the applicant's involuntary confinement, after the initial care order, was made by the head physician of the hospital after having obtained a medical observation statement by another physician of the same establishment.[4] In the Finnish system the medical evaluation is made by two physicians of the same psychiatric hospital in which the patient is detained. The court held that:

> The patients do not therefore have a possibility to benefit from a second, independent psychiatric opinion. The Court finds such a possibility to be an important safeguard against possible arbitrariness in the decision-making when the continuation of confinement to involuntary care is concerned. In this respect the Court also refers to the CPT's [European Committee for the Prevention of Torture] recommendation that the periodic review of an order to treat a patient against his or her will in a psychiatric hospital should involve a psychiatric opinion which is independent of the hospital in which the patient is detained.

The patient must be able to initiate review of detention. In *X v. Finland* [2012] ECHR 1371, at [170] the ECtHR drew attention to the fact that, under Finnish law, the renewal is initiated by the domestic authorities, and noted that:

> A patient who is detained in a mental hospital does not appear to have any possibilities of initiating any proceedings in which the issue of whether the conditions for his or her confinement to an involuntary treatment are still met could be examined. The Court has found in its earlier case-law that a system of periodic review in which the initiative lay solely with the authorities was not sufficient on its own. In the present case this situation is aggravated by the fact that in Finland a care order issued for an involuntary hospitalisation of a psychiatric patient is understood to contain also an automatic authorisation to treat the patient, even against his or her will. A patient cannot invoke any immediate remedy in that respect either.

The court held that there was a breach of art.5(1)(e) in that Finnish law did not provide adequate protection against arbitrariness. Patients must have the right to initiate a challenge against renewal of detention.

Detention must also be a proportionate response in all the circumstances to manage the risk posed by the patient. The ECtHR has held that detention of an individual is such a serious measure that it is only justified where other, less severe, measures have been considered and found to be insufficient to safeguard the

---

[4]   In England and Wales regulations prevent both medical recommendations coming from doctors on the same team, or who are in a line management relationship with each other: Mental Health (Conflicts of Interest) (England) Regulations 2008, SI 2008/1205; Mental Health (Conflicts of Interest) (Wales) Regulations 2008, SI 2008/2440 (W.213). See also Department of Health, *Code of Practice on the Mental Health Act 1983* (2008) chapter 7; Welsh Government, *Mental Health Act 1983 Code of Practice for Wales* (2008) chapter 3.

individual or public interest which might require the person concerned to be detained (*Litwa* v. *Poland* (2001) 33 EHRR 53).

The Convention case law on ECHR, art.5 establishes that if someone is to be detained on grounds of unsoundness of mind the detention must take place in a hospital, clinic or similar institution (*Aerts* v. *Belgium* (1998) 20 EHRR 50, at [46]), and that failure to give adequate treatment for mental disorder to a prisoner may breach the prohibition on inhuman or degrading treatment in art.3 (*Dybeku* v. *Albania* (41153/06), judgment of 18 December 2007).

1.2.2 Review of lawfulness of detention

ECHR, art.5(4) requires that anybody deprived of his liberty must be able to obtain speedy access to a court or tribunal to review the lawfulness of their detention (including whether the *Winterwerp* criteria are met), and the court must have the power to order discharge if detention is not lawful (*X* v. *United Kingdom* (1981) 4 EHRR 188, 1 BMLR 98 (ECtHR)).

1.2.3 Mental Health Act 1983: compliance with Convention rights

The powers of detention under MHA 1983 comply with the *Winterwerp* requirements in that they require objective medical evidence in the form of medical recommendations to be presented to a competent authority: the managers of the NHS or private hospital receiving the patient in the case of a non-offender patient or a criminal court in the case of an offender patient. That medical evidence must state that the patient is suffering from mental disorder of a nature or degree warranting assessment or/and treatment in hospital, or in relation to admission for treatment, the mental disorder is of a nature or degree which makes it appropriate for the patient to receive treatment which can only be provided if the person is detained. Detention must be necessary for the person's own health or safety or for the protection of other people. Hence, the requirements are met that the objective medical evidence must certify unsoundness of mind of a kind or degree warranting the confinement, and that the confinement is a proportionate response. The requirements of art.5(4) and the ruling in *X* v. *United Kingdom* are met in that patients subject to detention have the right to apply for discharge to the Mental Health Tribunal which has a duty to order release from detention if not satisfied that the *Winterwerp* criteria are met in the patient's case.

In September 2004, the Committee of Ministers of the Council of Europe adopted Recommendation (2004)10 of the Committee of Ministers to Member States concerning the protection of the human rights and dignity of persons with mental disorder, particularly those subject to involuntary placement or involuntary treatment. This Recommendation emphasises the need for decisions to detain or treat without consent to be based on objective medical expertise and that treatment must have a therapeutic purpose. The 'therapeutic purpose' requirement is reflected in MHA 1983, s.145(4) (added by the Mental Health Act (MHA) 2007) which provides that: 'Any reference in this Act to medical treatment, in relation to mental disorder, shall be construed as a reference to medical treatment the purpose of which is to alleviate, or prevent a worsening of, the disorder or one or more of its symptoms or manifestations.'

Similar principles are set out by the World Health Organization in the *WHO Resource Book on Mental Health, Human Rights and Legislation* (2005) which, as the subtitle 'Stop Exclusion, Dare to Care' suggests, goes beyond enjoining protection of the right to liberty and personal integrity and seeks to promote the right to independence, social integration and participation in the life of the community.

1.3 MENTAL HEALTH LAW REFORM

1.3.1 Drivers for reform

There are three principal drivers of mental health law and policy (see House of Lords and House of Commons Joint Pre-Parliamentary Scrutiny Committee, *Report on the Draft Mental Health Bill* (HL Paper 79(1), HC Paper 95(1), Session 2004–2005), paras.18–22):

(a) reducing stigma and promoting social inclusion;
(b) management of risk to the public and to sufferers themselves; and
(c) protection of human rights.

Although there have been various policy initiatives seeking to promote social inclusion and reduce stigma,[5] since the 1990s mental health policy in England and, to a lesser extent, Wales has been dominated by risk management and concerns about homicides and suicide and self-harm by mentally disordered people. These fears had a profound impact on mental health law and policy and have produced continuing tensions between public safety and social inclusion. Two inquiries were particularly prominent in driving the risk management agenda. The first was the *Report of the Inquiry into the Care and Treatment of Christopher Clunis*, concerning a schizophrenia sufferer who killed Jonathan Zito, which found inadequate risk assessment, failure to provide adequate supervision, and no proper after-care plan (J.H. Ritchie, D. Dick and J.R. Lingham *et al.*, *Inquiry into the Care and Treatment of Christopher Clunis* (London, HMSO, 1994)[6]). The response to *Clunis* was a steady increase of controls over patients in the community, culminating in the introduction of the community treatment order by MHA 2007. The second was the *Report of the Independent Inquiry into the Care and Treatment of Michael Stone.*

---

[5] Department of Health, *National Service Framework for Mental Health: Modern Standards and Service Models* (2000); Welsh Assembly, *Government Strategy Document for Adult Mental Health Services in Wales: Equity, Empowerment, Effectiveness, Efficiency* (2001). The National Service Frameworks for England have now been replaced by Department of Health, *New Horizons: a Shared Vision for Mental Health*, available at **www.dh.gov.uk/en/Publicationsandstatistics/Publications/PublicationsPolicyAndGuidance/DH_109705**.

[6] See also J.W. Coid, 'The Christopher Clunis Inquiry' (1994) 18 *The Psychiatrist* 449.

Stone suffered from psychopathic disorder and who was convicted in 1996 of killing Lyn and Megan Russell (South East Coast Strategic Health Authority, 2006). The *Stone* case was used in support of removing the so-called 'treatability test', the precondition of detention of people with personality disorder and mental impairment, that medical treatment in hospital must be likely to alleviate or prevent deterioration in the patient's condition.

The process of reforming MHA 1983 was long drawn out, beginning with the report of the Richardson Committee in 1999 (Department of Health, *Report of the Expert Committee: Review of the Mental Health Act 1983* (1999)), followed in 2000 by a two-volume White Paper, *Part 1: The New Legal Framework* and *Part 2: High Risk Patients* (Cm 5016–1 and Cm 5016–2 (2000)), and a Draft Bill in 2002 jointly produced by the Department of Health (DH) and the Home Office.[7] The Government identified the following flaws in MHA 1983 (Cm 5016–l (2000), para.1.15):

> The 1983 Act ... fails to address the challenge posed by a minority of people with mental disorder who pose a significant risk to others as a result of their disorder. It has failed properly to protect the public, patients or staff. Severely mentally ill patients have been allowed to lose contact with services once they have been discharged into the community. Such patients have been able to refuse treatment in the community. And it is the community as well as those patients which has paid a heavy price. We also need to move away from the narrow concept of treatability which applies to certain categories of mental disorder in the 1983 Act. New legislation must be clearly framed so as to allow all those who pose a significant risk of serious harm to others as a result of their mental disorder to be detained in a therapeutic environment where they can be offered care and treatment to manage their behaviour.

Although the 2002 Bill drew criticism from all the key stakeholders, this was rejected by the Department of Health and the Home Office in their document *Improving Mental Health Law: Towards a New Mental Health Act* (2004) which accompanied a new Draft Mental Health Bill in 2004. The 2004 Bill was introduced in substantially the same form as the 2002 version, and was subject to strong criticism by the Joint Pre-Parliamentary Scrutiny Committee. Initially, the Government expressed determination to proceed with the 2004 Bill, but later it opted to introduce an amending measure rather than a comprehensive new statute.[8] One of the main reasons for this decision appears to have been concern that the Mental Health Tribunal would be unable to carry out the new task proposed for it of authorising rather than reviewing detention.

---

[7] See P. Fennell, 'Joined Up Compulsion: the White Paper on Reform of the Mental Health Act 1983' (2001) *Journal of Mental Health Law* (June) 5.

[8] House of Lords and House of Commons Joint Pre-Parliamentary Scrutiny Committee, *Report on the Draft Mental Health Bill* (HL Paper 79(1), HC Paper 95(1), Session 2004–2005); see also P. Fennell, 'Protection! Protection! Protection! The Government's Response to the Joint Parliamentary Scrutiny Committee on the Mental Health Bill 2004' (2005) *Journal of Mental Health Law* (November) 1.

1.3.2 Mental Health Act 2007: changes to Mental Health Act 1983

Ultimately, the Mental Health Bill 2006 was passed as MHA 2007, which substantially amended MHA 1983. The tribunal's role of reviewing rather than authorising detention remains unaltered. MHA 2007 introduced a broader definition of mental disorder ('any disorder or disability of the mind'), abolished the treatability test, replacing it with a test that appropriate treatment must be available, and established new powers of supervised community treatment (known as community treatment orders (CTOs)). MHA 2007 also created the statutory roles of approved mental health professional (AMHP) (to replace the approved social worker (ASW)), responsible clinician (RC) (to replace the responsible medical officer (RMO)), as well as the completely new roles of approved clinician (AC) and independent mental health advocate (IMHA).

Although the reform process was largely driven by a desire to manage the risk posed by mentally disordered people both to their own welfare and safety and to public safety, the Government has always been concerned to pursue this agenda in a manner which complies with the European Convention on Human Rights. Convention compliance has been a major issue in mental health law since the 1981 decision of the ECtHR in *X* v. *United Kingdom*, which had a major influence on MHA 1983 and the extension of the jurisdiction of Mental Health Review Tribunals (MHRTs).

1.3.3 Mental Health Act 2007: changes to Mental Capacity Act 2005

In 2004 the European Court of Human Rights delivered its ruling in *HL* v. *United Kingdom* (2004) 40 EHRR 761, that a procedure prescribed by law must be followed where a mentally disordered person is subject without consent to a degree of control over their residence, treatment and movement which reaches a degree and intensity sufficient to amount to a deprivation of liberty. HL lacked capacity to consent to admission and was not objecting, and so had been admitted informally without resort to the procedures prescribed by MHA 1983. The ECtHR held that this breached art.5(1)(e) of ECHR, that HL was detained, and his lack of objection was not relevant to the question whether he had been deprived of his liberty (para.90):

> The right to liberty in a democratic society is too important for a person to lose the benefit of Convention protection simply because he has given himself up to detention, especially when it is not disputed that that person is legally incapable of consenting to, or disagreeing with, the proposed action.

To comply with the ruling, MHA 2007 amended the Mental Capacity Act 2005, introducing procedures to authorise the deprivation of liberty of people lacking capacity to consent to admission to a hospital or care home. MCA 2005 allows detention in a hospital or care home of people who suffer from mental disorder and who lack capacity in relation to the decision to receive in-patient care. Detention must be necessary in the person's own best interests. The provisions authorising detention under MCA 2005 (s.4 and Scheds.A1 and 1A) are known as the Deprivation of Liberty Safeguards (DoLS) (see **4.2**). A person may be deprived of liberty by an urgent or a standard authorisation or by a decision of the Court of Protection. A standard authorisation is granted by a supervisory authority which must review the need for deprivation of liberty, if requested to do so by the person detained, their representative or the managing authority of the hospital or care home (MCA 2005, Sched.A1, para.95). The Court of Protection also has jurisdiction to review the lawfulness of deprivations of liberty (MCA 2005, s.21A).

1.4   UNITED NATIONS CONVENTION ON THE RIGHTS OF PERSONS WITH DISABILITIES

The European Convention on Human Rights has clearly had a great influence on mental health legislation, and on the reforms introduced in 2007. However, in 2008, the United Nations Convention on the Rights of Persons with Disabilities (CRPD) came into force, and the CRPD has important implications for mental health legislation. The United Kingdom ratified the CRPD in 2009 and the European Union (EU) ratified it with regard to those powers within its competence in 2010. The CRPD is enforced by a compulsory reporting system, as is standard in all UN human rights treaties, as well as through an optional petition system (CRPD, arts.35 and 36).

Article 34 of the Convention establishes the Committee on the Rights of Persons with Disabilities ('Disability Rights Committee') and other provisions set out its competences with regard to supervising compliance with the Convention. Key among these competences is the quasi-judicial function under the petition system set out in the Optional Protocol (which came into force in 2006). Article 1 of the Optional Protocol states that '[a] State Party to the present Protocol recognizes the competence of the Committee on the Rights of Persons with Disabilities to receive and consider communications from or on behalf of individuals or groups of individuals subject to its jurisdiction who claim to be victims of a violation by that State Party of the provisions of the Convention'. The United Kingdom ratified the Optional Protocol in 2009.

'Persons with disabilities' are defined inclusively rather than exhaustively in art.1, by way of a description rather than a definition: 'Persons with disabilities include those who have long-term physical, mental, intellectual or sensory impairments which in interaction with various barriers may hinder their full and effective participation in society on an equal basis with others.' This clearly includes people whom ECHR, art.5 describes as 'persons of unsound mind', people who are described in UK mental health legislation as suffering from 'mental disorder' (see e.g. MHA 1983, s.1, where mental disorder is defined as 'any disorder or disability of the mind'), or to use the term preferred by psychiatric service users and survivors, those who are subject to 'psycho-social disability'.

1.4.1 Application of CRPD to UK mental health law

There has already been one English case, *AH* v. *West London Mental Health Trust and Secretary of State for Justice* [2011] UKUT 74 (AAC), where the Upper Tribunal used CRPD, art.13 to reinforce a particular interpretation of ECHR, art.6. Under CRPD, art.13, ratifying states agree to ensure 'effective access to justice for persons with disabilities on an equal basis with others'. The case concerned the right to a public hearing before the Mental Health Tribunal to review the lawfulness of psychiatric detention. Rule 38 of the Tribunal Rules creates a presumption that hearings will be held in private, but a patient may request a public hearing (see further **9.6.1**). Lord Justice Carnwath held that (at [22]):

> article 6 of the European Convention on Human Rights (re-enforced by article 13 of the CRPD) requires that a patient should have the same or substantially equivalent right of access to a public hearing as a non-disabled person who has been deprived of his or her liberty, if this article 6 right to a public hearing is to be given proper effect. Such a right can only be denied a patient if enabling that right imposes a truly disproportionate burden on the state.

Although this example might suggest a mainly supporting or complementary role for the CRPD in relation to rights arising under ECHR, there can be no doubting the truth of the oft-repeated assertion that the application of the CRPD to persons with psychosocial disabilities creates what has been described as a 'paradigm shift'[9] away from the more traditional human rights-based approach to mental health legislation exemplified in the case law of the European Court of Human Rights.[10]

1.4.2 The 'paradigm shift'

The CRPD starts from the premise that marginalisation and segregation on grounds of disability are per se unlawful. As Wachenfeld puts it, ECHR, in art.5(1)(e), starts from the opposite premise, and 'endorses the concept that it is permissible to marginalise certain people considered a medical threat to society' (*The Human Rights of the Mentally Ill in Europe* (Copenhagen, Danish Centre for Human Rights, 1992), p.128). ECHR thus makes permissible the deprivation of liberty of persons bearing infectious diseases, persons of unsound mind, alcoholics, drug addicts and vagrants, without the need to prove any wrongdoing on their part. The following passage from *Guzzardi* v. *Italy* Series A, No. 39, 6 November 1980, at [98] is often quoted as the rationale of art.5(1)(e):

---

[9]   See T. Minkowitz, 'Abolishing Mental Health Laws to Comply with the Convention on the Rights of Persons with Disabilities' in B. McSherry and P. Weller (eds), *Rethinking Rights-Based Mental Health Laws* (Oxford, Hart Publishing, 2010), pp.151–77.

[10]   See e.g. P. Fennell, 'The Third Way in Mental Health Policy: Negative Rights, Positive Rights and the Convention' (1999) 26 *Journal of Law and Society* 103; P. Fennell, 'Convention Compliance, Public Safety and the Social Inclusion of Mentally Disordered People' (2005) 32 *Journal of Law and Society* 90; and P. Fennell, 'Human Rights, Bioethics and Mental Disorder' in (2008) 27 *Medicine and Law: Special Edition on Bioethics and Human Rights* 95.

The reason why the Convention allows the latter individuals, all of whom are socially maladjusted, to be deprived of their liberty is not only that they have to be considered as occasionally dangerous for public safety, but also that their own interests necessitate their detention.

The fundamental assumption of the ECHR 'paradigm' vis-à-vis mental disorder is faith in medical science and medical ethics, backed up by judicial scrutiny of the medical evidence. Article 14 of the CRPD appears to pose a direct challenge to this approach, by purportedly proscribing any legislation which allows detention on grounds of unsoundness of mind. Article 14(1) requires states parties to ensure that persons with disabilities, on an equal basis with others:

> (a) [e]njoy the right to liberty and security of person; (b) [a]re not deprived of their liberty unlawfully or arbitrarily, and that any deprivation of liberty is in conformity with the law, and that the existence of a disability shall in no case justify a deprivation of liberty.

The key phrase here is 'the existence of a disability shall in no case justify a deprivation of liberty'. Australia has entered a 'declaration of its understanding' that 'the Convention [CRPD] allows for compulsory assistance or treatment of persons, including measures taken for the treatment of mental disability, where such treatment is necessary, as a last resort and subject to safeguards'.[11] The trenchant interpretation offered by the Office of the United Nations High Commissioner for Human Rights in the 2009 *Thematic Study on Enhancing Awareness and Understanding of the Convention on the Rights of Persons with Disabilities* (UN Doc. A/HRC/10/48 (26 January 2009)) makes clear, however, just how the CRPD shifts the premise upon which decisions concerning the deprivation of liberty should be based (at para.48):

> Prior to the entrance into force of the Convention, the existence of a mental disability represented a lawful ground for deprivation of liberty and detention under international human rights law. The Convention radically departs from this approach by forbidding deprivation of liberty based on the existence of any disability, including mental or intellectual, as discriminatory. Article 14, paragraph 1(b), of the Convention unambiguously states that 'the existence of a disability shall in no case justify a deprivation of liberty'. Proposals made during the drafting of the Convention to limit the prohibition of detention to cases 'solely' determined by disability were rejected.[12] As a result, unlawful detention encompasses situations where the deprivation of liberty is grounded in the combination between a mental or intellectual disability and other elements such as dangerousness, or care and treatment. Since such measures are partly justified by the person's disability, they are to be considered discriminatory and in violation of the

---

[11] Notwithstanding the nomenclature used, such statements are reservations as defined by art. 2(1)(d) of the Vienna Convention on the Law of Treaties (1969) 1155 UNTS 331.

[12] During the third session of the Ad Hoc Committee on what was then entitled a 'Comprehensive and Integral International Convention on the Protection and Promotion of the Rights and Dignity of Persons with Disabilities', proposals were made to add the word 'solely' to then draft art.10, para.1(b), so it would read 'any deprivation of liberty shall be in conformity with the law and in no case shall be based solely on disability'. This amendment was not adopted. The Convention's *travaux préparatoire* are available at **www.un.org/disabilities/default.asp?id=153**.

prohibition of deprivation of liberty on the grounds of disability, and the right to liberty on an equal basis with others prescribed by article 14.

Accordingly, any mental health legislation authorising the 'institutionalization of persons with disabilities on the grounds of their disability without their free and informed consent must be abolished' (para.49). This necessarily entails repeal of provisions authorising detention for the person's own care and treatment, as well as preventive detention on grounds of danger to self or others, 'in all cases in which such grounds of care, treatment and public security are linked in legislation to an apparent or diagnosed mental illness'. The Thematic Study emphasises that this was not to say that 'persons with disabilities cannot be lawfully subject to detention for care and treatment or to preventive detention' (para.49). What it does require, however, is that 'the legal grounds upon which restriction of liberty is determined must be de-linked from the disability and neutrally defined so as to apply to all persons on an equal basis'.

This raises a serious ethical and legal issue, particularly in countries which are parties to ECHR, since the list of grounds on which a person may lawfully be deprived of liberty in art.5 is exhaustive, and does not permit preventive detention except where the person falls within one of the categories in art.5(1)(e). Any domestic legislation in a Council of Europe Member State which allows preventive detention 'de-linked' from objective evidence of a true mental disorder would be likely to fall foul of ECHR, art.5. Moreover, anyone who is detained on grounds of unsoundness of mind must be detained in a hospital, clinic, or similar institution (*Aerts* v. *Belgium* (1998) 29 EHRR 50).

The UN Committee on the Rights of Persons with Disabilities has already applied the approach adopted in the Thematic Study in its report on Tunisia (see *Summary Record, Tunisia*, UN Doc. CRPD/C/5/SR.4 (2011), para.18). Tunisian legislation provides that a person suffering from a mental disorder may be involuntarily admitted to hospital when: it is not possible to obtain the consent of the person concerned because of his disorder; the person concerned requires urgent medical attention; and the mental state of the person concerned poses a threat to his own health or that of others (see *Tunisia, Initial Report on Implementation of the International Convention on the Rights of Persons with Disabilities*, UN Doc. CRPD/C/TUN/1 (14 July 2010), para.104). With regard to CRPD, art.14 and Tunisian legislation, the Committee expressed concern at the fact 'that having a disability, including an intellectual or psychosocial disability, can constitute a basis for the deprivation of liberty under current legislation'. It was recommended to Tunisia that it 'repeal legislative provisions which allow for the deprivation of liberty on the basis of disability, including a psychosocial or intellectual disability'. The Committee further recommended 'that until new legislation is in place, all cases of persons with disabilities who are deprived of their liberty in hospitals and specialized institutions be reviewed and that the review also include a possibility of appeal' (see *Concluding Observations of the Committee on the Rights of Persons with Disabilities: Tunisia*, UN Doc. CRPD/C/TUN/CO/1 (13 May 2011), paras.24–25). Assuming that the Committee maintains the approach it has adopted toward art.14 in assessing the compliance of other states parties, there is a conflicting treaty obligation for those states parties to the CRPD who are also parties to ECHR.

The CRPD as an unincorporated treaty has limited impact on domestic UK law. If an individual wished to be treated in accordance with, for example, CRPD, art.14 and in a manner that conflicts with the approach of ECHR, art.5 and sought to challenge a public authority which refused to do such treatment, a court would have to uphold the public authority's deference to what art.5 requires of it. Assuming all domestic remedies are exhausted, and the other admissibility criteria set out in art.2 of the Optional Protocol are satisfied, the individual can challenge the public authority's decision by referring the matter to the Disability Rights Committee. The Committee will follow the CRPD and is likely to find the United Kingdom in violation of its treaty obligations.

1.4.3   Compliance with ECHR or CRPD?

The reforms introduced by MHA 2007 were strongly influenced by the need to comply with ECHR, but clearly risk falling foul of CRPD, art.14, as interpreted by the UN institutions. Both MCA 2005 and MHA 1983 (as amended) have special regimes of powers to provide for the detention of persons suffering from mental disorder. Both are aimed at compliance with ECHR, art.5. Both are in breach of CRPD, art.14 as interpreted by the UN Disability Rights Committee. The United Kingdom has not entered reservations to the CRPD to take account of the conflict between ECHR, art.5 and CRPD, art.14. As public authorities are bound to comply with the requirements of ECHR, art.5, the United Kingdom is open to the risk that a communication will be lodged so as to use the petition system to seek redress before the Disability Rights Committee. The United Kingdom will then have to try and reconcile its obligations, if it can, and if not, then accept that it will have to be in breach of either ECHR or the CRPD.

Although the CRPD represents a radical approach to the rights of people with psychosocial disabilities, by comparison with ECHR, it has a number of shortcomings. First, due to the nature of the petition and reporting systems under the CRPD, they cannot provide effective protection against arbitrary detention. Furthermore, abandoning reliance on objective medical evidence of a true mental disorder – which is of a nature or degree warranting confinement as the basis for preventive detention on grounds of risk to self or others – is a major shift in approach. Though the current arrangements afford extensive discretion to psychiatrists and both national courts and the ECtHR are reluctant to question clinical judgment (see *Herczegfalvy* v. *Austria* (1992) 15 EHRR 437), the safeguards of medical expertise and medical ethics are not lightly to be dismissed without some credible alternative.

Moreover, the European Union is party to the CRPD and may at some point ratify the Optional Protocol. The Union's approach to any such matters where it exercises its competence may also be found to be in breach of the CRPD as the Union under both its Charter of Fundamental Rights and the European Court of Justice's jurisprudence will play close attention to Council of Europe standards. As Philip Fennell and Urfan Khaliq put it (in 'Conflicting or Complementary Obligations? The UN Disability Rights Convention, the European Convention on Human Rights and English Law' (2011) 6 *European Human Rights Law Review* 662, at 674):

> It is thus not beyond the realms of possibility that the EU States, such as the United Kingdom, might be obliged to give effect to the CRPD in domestic law through the prism of European Union law and find themselves having to try and reconcile EU obligations with the European Convention and the CRPD. Faced with hard choices between the contravention of EU law, the ECHR and the CRPD, or even just the ECHR and the CRPD, the one whose contravention incurs the least political and probably legal costs is the latter.

The most likely use of the CRPD in domestic courts and tribunals is as an aid to construction of ECHR. We have already seen how Carnwath LJ in *AH* v. *West London Mental Health Trust and Secretary of State for Justice* [2011] UKUT 74 (AAC) used CRPD, art.13 to reinforce an interpretation of ECHR, art.6 that a public hearing should be granted.

However, in *R (NM)* v. *London Borough of Islington, Northamptonshire County Council and the Parole Board* [2012] EWHC 414 (Admin), Sales J acknowledged that there had been some cases where the ECtHR had given some weight to the CRPD, but rejected the argument that CRPD, art.19, which requires states to recognise the equal right of people with disabilities to live in the community, should be taken into account in interpreting ECHR, art 5. The argument was that ECHR, art.5 and CRPD, art.19 entitled a prisoner who had a hearing coming up before the Parole Board to be treated as a person 'appearing to be in need of community care services' and therefore entitled to an assessment of his needs under s.47 of the National Health Service and Community Care Act 1990. Sales J rejected this contention. Although he did not rule out that arts.19 and 26 of the CRPD might be used as aids to interpretation of ECHR, art.5 and s.47 of the National Health Service and Community Care Act 1990, the judge held that even if they could they would not assist the claimant ([98]–[112], esp. [108]).

The position before a Mental Health Tribunal is slightly different. *Johnson* v. *United Kingdom* (1997) 27 EHRR 296 establishes that where a court (or tribunal) reviewing the lawfulness of detention finds that a person is no longer suffering from mental disorder, it is not under an obligation to discharge immediately, but may order discharge subject to the provision of after-care support. If this happens, art.5(4) requires that the court must have the power to ensure that discharge is not unreasonably delayed. In *Johnson*, the patient had been subject to a deferred conditional discharge, so that the tribunal decided that he was entitled to discharge. In *R (B)* v. *Camden London Borough Council* [2005] EWHC 1366 (Admin), Stanley Burnton J held that:

> A detained patient who is the subject of a deferred conditional discharge decision of a tribunal, which envisages his conditional discharge once after-care services are in place, is a person who 'may be in need of such services', since if such services are available to

him he will be discharged and immediately need them. Whether a patient who may reasonably be considered to be liable to have such an order made in an impending tribunal hearing [is a person who 'may be in need of such services'] is an issue I do not have to decide in the instant case, but I incline to the view that he is.

1.5 CONCLUSION

The aim of this chapter has been to demonstrate how important it is for Mental Health Tribunals and those appearing before them to be aware of the developing human rights context within which mental health legislation operates, of the relevance of arguments based on the European Convention on Human Rights, and the potential impact of the UN Convention on the Rights of Persons with Disabilities.

CHAPTER 2

The origins and role of Mental Health Tribunals

This chapter gives a brief overview of the origins of Mental Health Tribunals in England and Wales and describes the development of the current tribunal structure for dealing with applications and references for the review of, and discharge from, compulsory powers under MHA 1983.

2.1 MENTAL HEALTH REVIEW TRIBUNAL IN ENGLAND AND WALES

The Mental Health Review Tribunal (MHRT) was originally established under the Mental Health Act (MHA) 1959 as an independent body which examined the legal justification for the continued detention of a patient for treatment in hospital or other mental health unit. Such a tribunal was recommended by the Royal Commission of 1954–57, chaired by Lord Percy and tasked with reviewing the existing law relating to mental illness and mental deficiency. The Royal Commission (*Report of the Royal Commission on the Law relating to Mental Illness and Mental Deficiency* (Cmnd 169, HMSO, 1957)) made clear that (pp.150–51):

> these review tribunals would not be acting as an appellate court of law to consider whether the patient's mental condition at the time when the compulsory powers were first used had been accurately diagnosed by the doctors signing the recommendations, or whether there had been sufficient justification for the use of compulsory powers at the time, nor to consider whether there was some technical flaw in the documents purporting to authorize the patient's admission ... The review tribunal's function would be to consider the patient's mental condition at the time when it considers his application, and to decide whether the type of care which has been provided by the use of compulsory powers is the most appropriate to his present needs, or whether any alternative form of care might now be more appropriate, or whether he could now be discharged from care altogether.

Thus, the changes brought about by MHA 1959 removed the need for judicial certification before the use of compulsory powers of detention and replaced it with new entitlements for patients to seek periodic review of the need for detention after the event. In 1973, the Aarvold Report (*Report of the Review of Procedures for the Discharge and Supervision of Psychiatric Patients subject to Special Restrictions*

(Cmnd 0191, HMSO, 1973)), which reviewed the procedures for the discharge and supervision of psychiatric patients subject to special restrictions, summarised the fundamental role of MHRTs as (para.35):

> a safeguard for the liberty of the individual and to ensure against unjustified detention in hospital.

Research into the working of the MHRT under MHA 1959 (see Jill Peay, 'Mental Health Review Tribunals: Just or Efficacious Safeguards?' (1981) 5 *Law and Human Behaviour* 161) found considerable defects in both the legal framework and the operation of tribunals themselves. In addition, the decision of the European Court of Human Rights (ECtHR) in *X* v. *United Kingdom* (1981) 4 EHRR 181[1] found the law to be in breach of art.5(4) of the European Convention on Human Rights (ECHR). The Mental Health Act 1983 was intended to counter many of the criticisms of MHRTs, to bring the law into line with ECHR and to result in 'significant improvements' in the tribunal system (see DHSS, *Reform of Mental Health Legislation* (Cmnd 8405, HMSO, 1981)).

The improvements brought about by MHA 1983 and subordinate or related legislation included the following:

- measures to ensure that patients are informed of their rights of appeal;
- rights of patients admitted for assessment to apply to the tribunal and to have a tribunal hearing within seven days of their application;
- public funding for legal representation of patients at the MHRT;
- automatic reference to the tribunal of patients who do not apply of their own accord;
- reducing the periods of detention for patients compulsorily admitted by the criminal courts, thus increasing the frequency of patients' entitlement to a review of detention by the MHRT;
- rights of restricted patients to apply to the tribunal and increased powers of the tribunal to discharge patients under (then) Home Office restrictions;
- improved rules on tribunal procedures aimed at ensuring consistency in the conduct of hearings and in decision-making.

Despite those improvements, a number of research reports (e.g. Jill Peay, *Tribunals on Trial* (Oxford, Clarendon Press, 1989); Stephen Blumenthal and Simon Wessely, *The Pattern of Delays in MHRTs* (HMSO, 1994); Elizabeth Perkins, *Decision Making in Mental Health Review Tribunals* (Policy Studies Institute, 2003)), as well as the ongoing monitoring of the (then) Council of Tribunals (as illustrated by the comments in successive *Annual Reports of the Council on Tribunals* since 1986), identified significant failings in the operation of the MHRT. In *Mental*

---

[1] The ECtHR held that under ECHR, art.5(4) a detained patient, including a restricted patient, has the right of periodic access to a judicial body to determine the justification for continued detention: a tribunal with only advisory powers, and no power to discharge the patient (as was the case pre-MHA 1983 in respect of restricted patients), did not constitute a judicial body.

Health Review Tribunals: Special Report (Cm 4740, TSO, 2000), the Council on Tribunals summarised its main concerns, citing in particular the tribunal's lack of independence from its sponsoring Department of Health, and highlighted inadequate resources as the main cause of the continuing problems within the MHRT.

2.2 THE LEGGATT REPORT AND BEYOND: IMPLICATIONS FOR THE MHRT

2.2.1 Leggatt review of tribunals

In 2000, Sir Andrew Leggatt was appointed by the Lord Chancellor to conduct a wide-ranging review of tribunals in order to bring tribunals and administrative justice into the then Government's proposals for modernising the justice system overall. The Leggatt Report (*Tribunals for Users: One System, One Service* (TSO, 2001)) made over 300 recommendations aimed at making tribunals 'independent, coherent, professional, cost-effective and user-friendly' (para.1). In particular, it recommended that tribunals should be rationalised and brought together in a single, coherent tribunal system administered by an agency reporting to the Lord Chancellor.

2.2.2 Tribunals, Courts and Enforcement Act 2007

Leggatt's vision finally came into fruition in England (and in Scotland and Wales in relation to non-devolved tribunals only) with the Tribunals, Courts and Enforcement Act (TCEA) 2007, which came into effect in November 2008.[2] Section 3 of that Act provides for a First-tier Tribunal and an appellate Upper Tribunal. They are presided over by the Senior President of Tribunals (TCEA 2007, s.3(4)). All tribunals which are part of the unified system were administered by the Tribunals Service, an agency of the Ministry of Justice, which in April 2011 became part of Her Majesty's Courts and Tribunals Service (HMCTS). HMCTS now deals with the administration of the First-tier and Upper Tribunals.

Jurisdictions joining the First-tier Tribunal were allocated to a chamber designed to reflect the commonality of work of tribunals in that chamber (TCEA 2007, s.7). Each chamber has a Chamber President. Each tribunal consists of its judges and other members. Judges of the First-tier Tribunal are guaranteed judicial independence under the Constitutional Reform Act 2005 (TCEA 2007, s.1).

In respect of mental health cases, the Health, Education and Social Care (HESC) Chamber exercises powers under MHA 1983 which were previously exercised by the MHRT.[3] The Chamber's powers in these cases only apply to England – there is

---

[2] For an excellent and comprehensive review of the reformed tribunal structure and the operation of tribunals in England, see Edward Jacobs, *Tribunal Practice and Procedure* (2nd edn, Legal Action Group, 2011).
[3] Functions under MHA 1983 have been transferred to it: First-tier Tribunal and Upper Tribunal (Chambers) Order 2008, SI 2010/2655, art.4(i). The HESC Chamber also considers appeals previously dealt with by the Special Educational Needs and Disability Tribunal, the Care Standards Tribunal and the Primary Lists Tribunal.

still a Mental Health Review Tribunal for Wales, established under MHA 1983 and operating under functions devolved to the National Assembly for Wales (MHA 1983, s.65(1) and National Assembly for Wales (Transfer of Functions) Order 1999, SI 1999/672, art.2, Sched.1). So, although the term 'mental health review tribunal' is still sometimes used, the MHRT in England ceased to exist on 3 November 2008 and was replaced by the First-tier Tribunal (Health, Education and Social Care Chamber) (Mental Health), known as the First-tier Tribunal (Mental Health) or (used for shorthand in this book) the Mental Health Tribunal (MHT) (see Transfer of Tribunals Functions Order 2008, SI 2008/2833). The tribunal in Wales is now referred to as the Mental Health Review Tribunal for Wales (MHRT for Wales). The MHT in England and the MHRT for Wales are referred to throughout MHA 1983 as 'the appropriate tribunal' (see MHA 1983, Part V and Transfer of Tribunals Functions Order 2008, SI 2008/2833).

The mental health jurisdiction of the First-tier Tribunal (the MHT) is administered by HMCTS and the administration is undertaken by HMCTS-MH staff at the Secretariat offices based in Leicester. All Secretariat staff are civil servants and are completely independent of the hospital authorities. The Welsh Assembly has responsibility for the MHRT for Wales and administration is carried out at the Secretariat office in Cardiff.

The Upper Tribunal (Administrative Appeals Chamber) hears appeals on a point of law from both the MHT in England and the MHRT for Wales.

2.2.3 Mental Health Act 2007

At the same time as implementation of TCEA 2007 in November 2008, MHA 2007 also came into force, primarily bringing about amendments to MHA 1983. These included changes to the definition of mental disorder (see **Chapter 3**) and to the criteria for detention, renewal and mandatory tribunal discharge, as well as the introduction of supervised community treatment for patients who had previously been detained for treatment in hospital. These changes also had a significant impact on the work of Mental Health Tribunals.

Under MHA 1983 (as amended by MHA 2007), the appropriate tribunal (in either England or Wales) to which the patient must apply (or be referred) therefore depends, for those liable to be detained, on the location of the hospital in which they are detained; for those subject to supervised community treatment, it depends on the location of the responsible hospital; and for those subject to guardianship or for conditionally-discharged patients, it depends on where they reside (MHA 1983, s.77(3), (4)).

2.3 ROLE AND FUNCTIONS OF MENTAL HEALTH TRIBUNALS

2.3.1 Role of Mental Health Tribunals

Most patients requiring treatment for mental disorder in a National Health Service or independent hospital are informally admitted and are free to leave at any time (MHA 1983, s.131(1)). Mental Health Tribunals are concerned only with those patients who are liable to be compulsorily detained in hospital, subject to compulsory guardianship, subject to supervised community treatment (under a community treatment order) or subject to conditional discharge.

The principal function of Mental Health Tribunals is to review, on the application of the patient, the legal justification for a patient's continued detention, guardianship or supervised community treatment at the time of the hearing and to determine whether the statutory criteria justifying the use of compulsory powers continue to be met. The tribunal must also determine whether or not a patient should be discharged when other persons (such as the responsible clinician, the hospital managers appointed to act on behalf of the detaining authority or the Secretary of State for Justice in respect of restricted patients) have not exercised their powers to discharge the patient (MHA 1983, s.23)[4] and the patient has not applied to the tribunal of his or her own accord, through either unwillingness or lack of capacity. This process is known as the 'automatic reference procedure'.[5] The tribunal must also make a determination when the patient's nearest relative (who has the right to apply in certain circumstances) has applied for the patient to be discharged.

In *R* v. *Canons Park Mental Health Review Tribunal, ex p. A* [1994] 1 All ER 481, Mr Justice Sedley (as he then was) said that the tribunal is (at 490):

> a body charged with reviewing the operative decisions of the responsible authorities to detain the patient, and its functions are to reappraise the patient's condition at the time of the hearing and in the light of its findings do one of three things – to direct discharge as of right, to direct discharge in the exercise of its discretion, or to do neither.

It should be noted that the tribunal has no discretion to direct the discharge of a restricted patient where the statutory grounds for detention continue to be met. Also, the tribunal has no power to consider the validity of the original admission giving rise to the use of MHA 1983 powers or to investigate the circumstances that led to the use of compulsory powers in respect of the patient (as recommended by the Percy Commission (see **2.1**) and confirmed in *R* v. *East London and the City Mental Health Trust, ex p. Brandenburg* [2003] UKHL 58, [2004] All ER 400, at [9(3)]). If a person wishes to challenge the validity of the original decision to detain,

---

[4] The Secretary of State for Health may also, in limited circumstances, discharge a patient, see MHA 1983, s.23(3) and (3A). The Secretary of State for Justice has his/her own powers to discharge restricted patients under s.42(2).

[5] 'Reference' means a reference under MHA 1983, ss.67(1), 68(1), (2), 71(1), (2), 75(1). Both the Secretary of State for Health (under s.67) and the Secretary of State for Justice (under ss.71 and 75) also have powers (and in some circumstances, duties) to refer cases to the tribunal, as described in **Chapters 4** and **5**.

or the renewal of detention, this must be done through an application to the court for judicial review of the decision in question or, where there is evidence of irregularities such that lawful justification for the detention is lacking, by writ of habeas corpus. However, in relation to the tribunal's role, evidence as to the circumstances leading to the use of compulsory powers may be relevant to the tribunal in considering the patient's current mental condition and in determining whether the statutory criteria are met at the time of the hearing.

2.3.2 Burden and standard of proof

Until 2001, the patient had to establish that he was no longer suffering from mental disorder justifying his continuing detention, but following the implementation of HRA 1998, the court held that this was incompatible with the patient's rights under ECHR, art.5 (*R (H)* v. *MHRT North and East London Region* [2001] EWCA Civ 415). The Government introduced a Remedial Order (Mental Health Act 1983 (Remedial) Order 2001, SI 2001/3712) placing the onus on the detaining authority to establish the presence of mental disorder of a nature or degree to justify continued detention of the patient (MHA 1983, ss.72 and 73). Whether this amounts to placing the burden of proof before a Mental Health Tribunal on those arguing for the continued use of compulsory powers under MHA 1983 is the subject of continued legal debate, given the 'inquisitorial' nature of the tribunal's role in determining whether the statutory grounds continue to be met.[6]

The standard of proof is the civil standard on the balance of probabilities. The Court of Appeal (*R (N)* v. *MHRT Northern Region* [2005] EWCA Civ 1605) has held that in the Mental Health Tribunal (at [103]):

> it [is] likely that the tribunal's task will be made easier if, instead of dividing up the issues into matters that are susceptible to proof to a defined standard and those that are not, it approaches the entire range of issues by reference to the standard of proof on the balance of probabilities, whilst recognising that in practice the standard of proof will have a much more important part to play in the determination of disputed issues of fact than it will generally have in matters of judgment as to appropriateness and necessity.

2.4 CONSTITUTION AND MEMBERSHIP OF MENTAL HEALTH TRIBUNALS

While there are similarities in the constitution and membership of the First-tier Tribunal (Mental Health) in England and the MHRT for Wales, since they are both based on the framework previously established under MHA 1983, the legal authorities for each jurisdiction are now separate and are therefore described separately below.

---

[6] For an examination of the concept of the burden of proof in the context of Mental Health Tribunals, see J. Cooper and H. Davis, 'Is there a Burden of Proof in Mental Health Cases?' (2011) *Journal of Mental Health Law* 5.

2.4.1 First-tier Tribunal (Mental Health)

In England, when deciding how the First-tier Tribunal should be constituted in mental health cases, the Senior President of Tribunals must have regard to the provisions of MHA 1983 that applied before the functions of the tribunal were transferred (see First-tier Tribunal and Upper Tribunal (Composition of Tribunal) Order 2008, SI 2008/2835, art.2). Under those provisions, the Mental Health Tribunal is composed of three panels consisting of:

1.   tribunal judges (mainly fee-paid lawyers, but a number of full-time salaried tribunal judges (STJs) have been appointed);
2.   medical members (mostly fee-paid consultant psychiatrists (some retired from practice) with one full-time salaried medical member); and
3.   members with experience in administration, knowledge of social services or having other suitable qualifications or experience (referred to as specialist lay members, all fee-paid).

The legislation also sets out the qualifications of those eligible for appointment as (non-judge) members of the First-tier Tribunal (see TCEA 2007, s.4, Sched.2, para.2; Qualifications for Appointment of Members to the First-tier Tribunal and Upper Tribunal Order 2008, SI 2008/2692). The Senior President has issued a Practice Statement confirming the continuance of these arrangements for the composition of tribunals in mental health cases (*Composition of Tribunals in relation to matters that fall to be decided by the Health, Education and Social Care Chamber on or after 3 November 2008* (Tribunals Service, 30 October 2008)). Appointments to the panels are made by the Lord Chancellor, following a selection process leading to recommendations for appointment by the Judicial Appointments Commission (the selection process is set out in Constitutional Reform Act 2005, ss.86–93). In the case of panels 2 and 3, the Judicial Appointments Commission must consult with the Secretary of State for Health.

Separate selection processes are carried out for the appointment of the President and Deputy Presidents of the Health, Education and Social Care Chamber (TCEA 2007, s.7, Sched.4). The President of the Health, Education and Social Care Chamber acts as President of the First-tier Tribunal (Mental Health) and may delegate some of his/her functions to the Deputy President. The selection of members to deal with any particular proceeding, or class of proceeding, is made by the President or by another member of the tribunal nominated by him/her. In practice, however, HMCTS staff carry out the task of appointing panel members for a hearing under powers delegated to them (Tribunal Procedure (First-tier Tribunal) (Health, Education and Social Care Chamber) Rules 2008, SI 2008/2699 ('English Rules'), rule 4).

The jurisdiction of a tribunal to deal with any proceedings may be exercised by any three or more of its members, including at least one from each panel. A judge always chairs the tribunal (First-tier Tribunal and Upper Tribunal (Composition of Tribunal) Order 2008, SI 2008/2835, arts.2, 6, 7). If the case concerns a restricted patient, the judge chairing the tribunal must be one approved for that purpose by the Lord Chancellor (art.2). This requirement was intended to ensure that those presiding over tribunals in cases of patients who have been convicted of serious offences have 'substantial judicial experience of the criminal courts'. Until recently, the judge chairing a case involving a restricted patient was a circuit judge or a recorder, but the Lord Chancellor has now approved some salaried judges of the First-tier Tribunal to hear restricted cases.

2.4.2 Mental Health Review Tribunal for Wales

As with the First-tier Tribunal (Mental Health) in England, the MHRT for Wales is composed of three panels consisting of (MHA 1983, s.65(2), Sched.2, para.1):

1. legal members;
2. medical members; and
3. members with experience in administration, knowledge of social services or having other suitable qualifications or experience (known as lay members).

Appointments to these panels are made by the Lord Chancellor, following a selection process leading to recommendations for appointment by the Judicial Appointments Commission. In the case of panels 2 and 3, the Judicial Appointments Commission must consult with the Secretary of State for Health. In exercising his functions in relation to Wales, the Lord Chancellor must consult with Welsh Ministers (National Assembly for Wales (Transfer of Functions) Order 1999, SI 1999/672, art.5, Sched.2).

The jurisdiction of a tribunal to deal with any proceedings may be exercised by any three or more of its members, including at least one from each panel. A legal member always acts as the chair (called the 'president' in Wales) of the tribunal. One of the legal members is appointed by the Lord Chancellor to be Chairman of the MHRT for Wales.[7]

The selection of members to deal with any particular proceeding, or class of proceeding, is made by the Chairman of the MHRT for Wales or by another member of the tribunal nominated by him/her. The Chairman has power to issue directions dealing with any matter which is preliminary or incidental to a hearing (Mental Health Review Tribunal for Wales Rules 2008, SI 2008/2705 ('Welsh Rules'), rule 4), presumably including the power to delegate to staff the function of appointing the panel for a hearing. If the Chairman is among those selected, s/he will chair the tribunal; if not, s/he nominates another legal member to be the president.

---

[7] The prospective amendment under Mental Health Act 2007, s.38(2) making provision for the appointment of a President of the MHRT for Wales has not yet been brought into force, so there is currently one Chairman of the MHRT for Wales and each individual panel for a hearing is presided over by the legal member, known as the 'president'.

2.4.3 Disqualification of members (England and Wales)

A member is not qualified to serve as a member of a tribunal to consider an application or reference where (First-tier Tribunal and Upper Tribunal (Composition of Tribunal) Order 2008, SI 2008/2835, art.2; Welsh Rules, rule 11(1)):

(a) s/he is a member or an officer of the responsible authority or of the registration authority concerned in the proceedings; or

(b) s/he is a member or an officer of a National Health Service Trust (England) or Local Health Board (Wales) which has the right to discharge the patient; or

(c) s/he appears to have a conflict of interest or bias of opinion in respect of the patient or has recently treated the patient in a professional medical capacity.

A member will not be disqualified because s/he was a member of a tribunal which heard a previous application or reference concerning the patient (*R* v. *Oxford Mental Health Review Tribunal, ex p. Mackman* (1986) *The Times*, 2 June). Similarly, the court has held that a 'fair-minded and informed observer' (the test for apparent bias set out in *Porter and others* v. *Magill* [2002] 2 AC 357, at [103]), having taken into account all the facts of the case, would not conclude that there was a real possibility of bias on the part of a tribunal judge who had previously sentenced the patient to a hospital order with restrictions under MHA 1983 (*R (M)* v. *Mental Health Review Tribunal* [2005] EWHC 2791 (Admin)).

In *R (PD)* v. *West Midlands and North West Mental Health Review Tribunal* [2004] EWCA Civ 311, a patient challenged the legality of the tribunal's decision not to discharge him from detention in hospital, on the ground that the medical member was a consultant psychiatrist employed by the detaining authority. The doctor had never worked in the hospital where the patient was detained and did not know the patient or any of the clinical team treating him. The Court of Appeal found that in this case, the argument that there was apparent bias was founded on an analysis of case precedent rather than the apprehension of a fair-minded and informed observer, who would have been satisfied that there was no real possibility of bias, having taken account of the facts of this particular case.

2.4.4 Role of the medical member

The role of the medical member in Mental Health Tribunals warrants particular attention. The medical member has a dual role: in addition to being a decision-maker with the other tribunal members, s/he is also required to examine the patient in private in advance of the hearing and take any other necessary steps in order to form an opinion of the patient's mental condition (English Rules, rule 34(1); Welsh Rules, rule 20). The tribunal rules for both England and Wales (see **2.5**) require the examination (known as the 'preliminary' examination or interview) to be carried out 'so far as practicable' – this is to cover the situation where a patient refuses to co-operate with the examination, making it not 'practicable'. The medical member must, in any event, examine the patient's medical records and take other steps (such as consulting with staff or carers) to be able to form an opinion.

In practice, the detail of the preliminary examination and investigation is shared in private with the other two panel members prior to the commencement of the hearing. In *R (S)* v. *MHRT* [2002] EWHC 2522 (Admin), the court rejected an application for judicial review on the grounds of incompatibility of this process with the patient's rights under ECHR, art.5(4). It was held that, so long as the medical member expresses only a *provisional* view, which is then subject to hearing all the other evidence before the tribunal, there will be no prejudice. Therefore, provided the patient and his/her representative are alerted to the evidence and views of the medical member in sufficient detail, and sufficiently early in the proceedings to enable them to challenge or otherwise deal with them, there would be no breach of art.5(4) (*R (H)* v. *MHRT for North and East London* [2001] EWCA Civ 415 (Crane J)) (see further **9.7**).

In *R (RD)* v. *Mental Health Review Tribunal* [2007] EWHC 781 (Admin), the medical member examined the patient and, at the outset of the hearing, the tribunal president gave an account of the medical member's interview with RD reporting a 'preliminary view' that, while the patient appeared ready for transfer from high to medium security, he was not yet ready for discharge and 'would appear to need the regime of a secure unit rather than community living' (at [13]). The president said that this was 'a very preliminary view, subject to anything we hear today'. RD argued that while it was legitimate for the medical member to communicate an opinion about the patient's mental state, it was not legitimate for her to communicate an opinion as to whether he should be discharged. Munby J rejected this argument stating that (at [19]):

> The communication by the medical member of her 'very preliminary' view was manifestly lawful, notwithstanding that it went to the ultimate issue and not merely to the question of RD's mental condition. There is nothing in rule 11 [MHRT Rules 1983] to disable the medical member from doing what she (like the other members of the Tribunal) would otherwise plainly be entitled to do, namely to discuss all aspects of the case with the other members of the Tribunal before the hearing and to express to them her preliminary views either on the case as a whole or on any particular aspect of the case, just as there is nothing in rule 11 to disable the medical member (like the other members of the Tribunal) from expressing to the parties at the outset of the hearing her preliminary views either on the case as a whole or on any particular aspect of the case. The contrary, in my judgment, is simply unarguable.

This means that a 'preliminary view' may be expressed not only on the patient's mental state but also, as long as it is made very clear that it is a preliminary view, on the question of whether the patient should be discharged.

A pilot study into patients' experiences of the First-tier Tribunal (Mental Health) carried out by the Administrative Justice and Tribunals Council and the Care Quality Commission found that many patients did not understand the purpose of the preliminary medical examination or its relevance to the tribunal hearing (*Patients' Experiences of the First-tier Tribunal (Mental Health): Report of a Joint Pilot*

Project (2011), pp.18–20). The MHT in England subsequently prepared an information leaflet for patients explaining the preliminary interview and its role in the tribunal process which is sent directly to patients with the letter acknowledging receipt of the application or reference to the tribunal.[8]

At the time of writing, the MHT in England is considering requesting a change in the tribunal procedure rules (see **2.5**) to remove the requirement for a preliminary examination in all cases, but no specific details have been announced. Readers must be alert to the possibility of changes in the role of the medical member in the future.

2.4.5 CAMHS panel

Following a commitment made by Baroness Ashton, then Minister for Constitutional Affairs, during the parliamentary debate on the Mental Health Bill 2007 that 'no child should appear before the tribunal unless he has been seen or supported in some way by someone with the [relevant] expertise' (*Hansard,* HL Deb., col. 744 (17 January 2007)), the MHT in England established the Child and Adolescent Mental Health Service (CAMHS) panel. The purpose of the panel is to ensure that where a child or young person who is detained (or is subject to another order under MHA 1983) applies, or has their case referred to a tribunal, 'wherever possible' at least one of the tribunal members appointed to deal with the case has special expertise relevant to the care and treatment of children and young people. Specialist training is provided for members appointed to the CAMHS panel. For the purposes of the CAMHS panel, any person under the age of 18 at the time of the application or reference is treated as a child.

There is no statutory obligation to appoint a member of the CAMHS panel to hear every case involving a child, only a commitment to do so 'wherever possible', and in furtherance of the overriding objective (see **2.5.1**) which requires 'using any special expertise of the tribunal effectively' (English Rules, rule 2(2)(d); Welsh Rules, rule 3(2)(c)). While HMCTS is able to appoint a member of the CAMHS panel in the vast majority of cases, cases may still go ahead without a CAMHS member if no one from the panel is available to sit. There is no CAMHS panel for MHRT for Wales.

2.5 PROCEDURAL RULES, PRACTICE DIRECTIONS AND PRACTICE STATEMENTS

2.5.1 Tribunal rules

The procedure for the hearing of both applications and references to a Mental Health Tribunal is governed:

---

[8] HMCTS, *Your Interview with the Tribunal Doctor: Information for Patients* (Mental Health Tribunal, Form T129), available at **http://hmctsformfinder.justice.gov.uk/courtfinder/forms/t129-eng.pdf**.

(a)   in England, by the Tribunal Procedure (First-tier Tribunal) (Health, Education and Social Care Chamber) Rules 2008, SI 2008/2699 (referred to as the
'English Rules') made by the Tribunal Procedure Committee under powers
transferred by the Lord Chancellor;[9]

(b)   in Wales, by the Mental Health Review Tribunal for Wales Rules 2008, SI
2008/2705 (referred to as the 'Welsh Rules') made by the Lord Chancellor
(MHA 1983, s.78).

The overriding objective of both sets of Rules (English Rules, rule 2; Welsh Rules,
rule 3) is to enable the tribunal to deal with cases fairly and justly (and in Wales,
efficiently and expeditiously). Fairly and justly includes:

(a)   dealing with the case in ways which are proportionate to the importance of the
case, the complexity of the issues, the anticipated costs and the resources of
the parties (note: this factor is not specified in the Welsh Rules; however, since
the list of what is entailed by the overriding objective is inclusive rather than
exclusive, the MHRT in Wales may consider that this element is part of
dealing with cases 'fairly, justly, efficiently and expeditiously');

(b)   avoiding unnecessary formality and seeking flexibility in the proceedings;

(c)   ensuring, so far as practicable, that the parties are able to participate fully in
the proceedings;

(d)   using any special expertise of the tribunal effectively; and

(e)   avoiding delay, so far as compatible with proper consideration of the issues.

The tribunal must seek to give effect to the overriding objective when it exercises
any power under the Rules, or interprets any rule or Practice Direction. Parties[10] are
required to assist the tribunal to further the overriding objective and (in England) to
co-operate with the tribunal generally. This requirement is not specified in the
Welsh Rules, as it was felt that placing an obligation on a detained patient to
co-operate with the tribunal was undesirable. The Upper Tribunal has given guidance on furtherance of the overriding objective, emphasising the expectation that
legal representatives will try to agree matters without the need for the tribunal to
make a ruling (*Dorset Healthcare NHS Foundation Trust* v. *MH* [2009] UKUT 4
(AAC), at [13]):

> Those provisions therefore impose an express obligation upon the parties to assist in the
> furtherance of the objective of dealing with cases fairly and justly, which includes the
> avoidance of unnecessary applications and unnecessary delay. That requires parties to
> cooperate and liaise with each other concerning procedural matters, with a view to
> agreeing a procedural course promptly where they are able to do so, before making any
> application to the tribunal. This is particularly to be expected where parties have legal

---

[9]   Under TCEA 2007, ss.22(2), 36(1), Sched.6, Part 1. The 2008 Rules have subsequently been
amended by SI 2009/1975, SI 2010/43, SI 2010/2653, SI 2011/651 and SI 2012/500.

[10]   A 'party' is defined as: the patient, the responsible authority, the Secretary of State for Justice (if
the patient is a restricted patient), the Secretary of State for Health or Welsh Ministers (in a reference
seeking approval under MHA 1983, s.86), and any other person who starts a mental health case by
making an application (English Rules, rule 1(3); Welsh Rules, rule 1(2)).

representation. Parties should endeavour to agree disclosure issues without the need for the tribunal to make a ruling. However, even where a direction from the tribunal may be required (for example, where a responsible authority holding medical records requires an order for the disclosure of medical records to overcome issues of confidentiality or arising from the Data Protection Act, or where there are genuine issues as to how most appropriately to proceed), it will assist the tribunal to further the overriding objective if the parties can identify any directions they are able to agree, subject to the approval of the tribunal. Where they are unable to agree every aspect, this liaison will at least have the advantage of crystallising their positions, and more clearly identifying the issue(s) upon which the tribunal will have to rule. We stress that, in the context of an urgent application in the mental health jurisdiction, this liaison between the parties must not lead to any avoidable delay.

Both the First-tier Tribunal in England and the MHRT for Wales have considerable case management powers under the Rules (English Rules, rule 5; Welsh Rules, rule 5), in particular to ensure that cases may be dealt with 'speedily' in compliance with ECHR, art.5(4) and in furtherance of the overriding objective of dealing with cases fairly and justly.

2.5.2 Practice Directions

In England, the Senior President of Tribunals may give directions as to the practice and procedure of the First-tier Tribunal provided the Lord Chancellor consents (the powers relating to the giving of directions are set out in TCEA 2007, s.23). A Chamber President may also give directions as to the practice and procedure of the chamber over which he presides with the agreement of both the Lord Chancellor and the Senior President of Tribunals. Practice Directions may include variation and revocation of existing directions.

For mental health cases in England, detailed requirements for the content of the statements and reports to be provided to the First-tier Tribunal are set out in a Practice Direction issued by the Senior President of Tribunals (Practice Direction: *First-tier Tribunal Health Education and Social Care Chamber: Statements and Reports in Mental Health Cases*, effective from 6 April 2012, supplemented by Guidance Booklet T124, *Reports for Mental Health Tribunals* (HMCTS, April 2012)). This includes the content of clinical, social circumstances and nursing reports as required in accordance with rule 32, which must be up to date and prepared specifically for the tribunal. In Wales, the Schedule to the Welsh Rules specifies slightly different requirements for the content of statements and reports (see **Chapter 10** for details of the requirements in both England and Wales).

In England, the Senior President has also issued Practice Directions on the conduct of cases in the First-tier Tribunal involving children, vulnerable adults and sensitive witnesses (Practice Direction: *First-Tier and Upper Tribunal 'Child, Vulnerable Adult and Sensitive Witnesses'*, 30 October 2008) and on the use of the Welsh language in tribunals in Wales (Practice Direction: *First-Tier and Upper Tribunal 'Use of the Welsh Language in Tribunals in Wales'*, 30 October 2008) which apply to both the First-tier and the Upper Tribunal.

2.5.3 Practice Statements and other guidance

In England, the Senior President of Tribunals may also issue Practice Statements concerning such matters as the composition of tribunals, the delegation of functions to staff and the arrangements for the neutral citation of decisions or written reasons of the First-tier Tribunal and Upper Tribunal.[11] There are no equivalent provisions for the MHRT for Wales other than those set out in the Rules.

The Chamber President or Deputy Chamber President may also issue practice guidance to assist judges and members of the First-tier Tribunal in England and those appearing before them. In the mental health jurisdiction, in addition to the guidance on report writing for Mental Health Tribunals, guidance notes have been issued on the procedures for handling relevant representations from the victims of patients; the role of independent mental health advocates (IMHAs) in First-tier Tribunal hearings; and on the terms and conditions for the observation of tribunal hearings (which are usually held in private). In addition HMCTS has issued a specification for the minimum requirements for the rooms made available by hospitals for use by Mental Health Tribunals.[12]

2.5.4 Duties under the Equality Act 2010

All tribunals provide a service to those applying to them and are also carrying out a public function. Tribunals are therefore subject to the duty to make reasonable adjustments under s.20 of the Equality Act 2010, aimed to make sure that disabled people can use the service to the same standard, or as close as it is reasonably possible to get to the standard, usually offered to non-disabled people. The definition of a disability is a mental or physical impairment that has a substantial and long-term adverse effect on the person's ability to carry out normal day-to-day activities (Equality Act 2010, s.6(1)). This will apply to many people appearing before a Mental Health Tribunal on account of their mental health problems, but some may also have physical disabilities for which adjustments may need to be made.

The duty to make reasonable adjustments under s.20 is anticipatory, which means that the tribunal must consider in advance (and on an ongoing basis) what disabled people with a range of impairments might reasonably need to access the tribunal, such as people who have a visual impairment, a hearing impairment, a mobility impairment or a learning disability. As well as providing physical aids and adaptations, or providing the support of an advocate, consideration must also be given to providing information in an accessible format. In England, the Practice Direction on the conduct of cases in the First-tier Tribunal involving children,

---

[11] All Practice Directions and Statements are available on the Justice website at **www.justice.gov.uk/tribunals/practice**.
[12] All guidance notes are available at **www.justice.gov.uk/tribunals/mental-health/hearings**.

vulnerable adults and sensitive witnesses (see **2.5.2**) provides an example of reasonable adjustments that may be made for disabled witnesses appearing at the tribunal.

2.6 MECHANISMS FOR REVIEW AND APPEAL

The mechanisms for the review of a tribunal's decision in mental health cases and the procedures relating to applications for permission to appeal differ in England and Wales. These are summarised separately below and further details are given in **Chapter 12**.

2.6.1 England

In order to appeal against a decision of the First-tier Tribunal, permission must first be obtained. On receiving an application for permission to appeal a tribunal's decision (English Rules, rule 46(1), (2)),[13] the First-tier Tribunal must first consider whether to review the decision. It cannot review a decision unless it is satisfied that there was an error of law in the tribunal's decision (English Rules, rule 47(1)). It must also take into account the overriding objective.

The tribunal also has power to review a decision on its own initiative (TCEA 2007, s.9(2)(a)). The Explanatory Notes to TCEA 2007 describe in the following terms the purpose of the First-tier Tribunal's jurisdiction to review its own decisions (para.100):

> Sections 9 and 10 provide powers for the First-Tier and Upper Tribunals to review their own decisions without the need for a full onward appeal and, where the tribunal concludes that an error was made, to re-decide the matter. This is intended to capture decisions that are clearly wrong, so avoiding the need for an appeal. The power has been provided in the form of a discretionary power for the Tribunal so that only appropriate decisions are reviewed. This contrasts with cases where an appeal on a point of law is made, because, for instance, it is important to have an authoritative ruling.

Although it has been held that there is nothing unfair in a decision being reviewed by the First-tier judge who originally made it (*AA* v. *Cheshire and Wirral Partnership NHS Foundation Trust* [2009] UKUT 195 (AAC) at [27]), in practice the review is usually undertaken by the principal judge of the First-tier Tribunal (Mental Health) or by one of the salaried judges.

If the First-tier Tribunal reviews the decision itself, it can do any of the following (TCEA 2007, s.9(4)–(6)):

- correct accidental errors in the decision or record of the decision;
- amend reasons given for the decision;

---

[13] An application must identify the decision of the tribunal to which it relates; identify the alleged error or errors of law in the decision; and state the result the party making the application is seeking: English Rules, rule 46(5).

- set the decision aside, in which case it must then either re-decide the matter concerned (in practice, it will usually do this by giving directions for a fresh hearing in front of a differently constituted First-tier panel), or refer the matter to the Upper Tribunal for the re-decision;
- take no further action.

If the First-tier Tribunal decides not to review the decision, or reviews the decision and decides to take no action in relation to the decision, or part of it, the tribunal must consider whether to give permission to appeal to the Upper Tribunal in relation to the decision or that part of it. Important rulings on points of law should be referred to the Upper Tribunal, which, as a court of record, can lay down authoritative precedents (*R (RB)* v. *First-Tier Tribunal (Review)* [2010] UKUT 160 (AAC)).

If the tribunal refuses permission to appeal it must send to the parties, with the record of its decision, a statement of its reasons for such refusal and notification of the right to make an application to the Upper Tribunal for permission to appeal, how to apply and the time within which such application must be made.

In addition to seeking permission to appeal, there are other ways of applying for correction, setting aside or review of a tribunal decision. For example, where there have been clerical mistakes or other accidental slips or omissions in a tribunal decision, an application may also be made to the First-tier Tribunal for the decision to be corrected (English Rules, rule 44). Where there has been some procedural irregularity in the proceedings (for example, a relevant document was not received by the tribunal or by a party or their representative), an application can be made for the decision to be set aside (English Rules, rule 45). The tribunal may treat any such application for correction, setting aside or review, or an application for permission to appeal against a decision, as an application for any other one of those things (English Rules, rule 50).

2.6.2 Wales

There is no statutory provision for the MHRT for Wales to review a decision, only to decide whether to give permission to appeal to the Upper Tribunal (Welsh Rules, rule 30).

An application for permission to appeal must be made to the MHRT for Wales in writing and must identify the decision of the tribunal to which it relates; identify the alleged error or errors of law in the decision; and state the result the party making the application is seeking. The tribunal must send to the parties a record of its decision whether or not to grant permission to appeal.

If the tribunal refuses permission to appeal it must send with the record of its decision a statement of its reasons for such refusal and notification of the right to make an application to the Upper Tribunal for permission to appeal, how to apply and the time within which such application must be made.

2.6.3 Appeals to the Upper Tribunal (England and Wales)

The Upper Tribunal hears appeals on a point of law of decisions from Mental Health Tribunals in both England and Wales and may also deal with judicial review of their decisions. The Upper Tribunal is a newly created court of record with jurisdiction throughout the United Kingdom, established under the Tribunals, Courts and Enforcement Act 2007. The Upper Tribunal consists of High Court judges and other specialist judges. The Upper Tribunal is divided into three chambers.

The main functions of the Upper Tribunal are to hear appeals from the decisions of First-tier Tribunals (TCEA 2007, s.11); to exercise powers of judicial review in certain circumstances (TCEA 2007, s.15); and to deal with enforcement of decisions, directions and orders made by tribunals (TCEA 2007, s.25). The procedure of the Upper Tribunal is regulated by the Tribunal Procedure (Upper Tribunal) Rules 2008, SI 2008/2698. Any party to a case in the First-tier Tribunal has the right to appeal to the Upper Tribunal (with the permission of the First-tier Tribunal or the Upper Tribunal) on a point of law arising from the First-tier Tribunal's decision (TCEA 2007, s.11).

The Administrative Appeals Chamber (AAC) of the Upper Tribunal hears appeals and exercises judicial review over the decisions of the First-tier Tribunal (Mental Health) and the MHRT for Wales. The High Court in England and Wales, the Court of Session in Scotland, and the High Court in Northern Ireland all have power to transfer judicial review applications to the Upper Tribunal. For England and Wales, the Lord Chief Justice has the power to issue directions transferring classes of judicial review to the Upper Tribunal.

In the first case which came before the Upper Tribunal, guidelines were set out as to the precedential authority to be given to various constitutions of the AAC (*Dorset Healthcare NHS Foundation Trust* v. *MH* [2009] UKUT 4 (AAC) at [37]):

(i)   Judges of the Upper Tribunal in the AAC speak with equal authority. All their decisions may be cited to the Upper Tribunal, First-tier Tribunals and other tribunals from which appeals to the AAC come and the appropriate decision-making authorities. Where they decide questions of legal principle they must be followed by the appropriate decision-making authorities and the tribunals below in cases involving the application of that principle, unless they can be distinguished. It should be borne in mind that similarity in underlying facts does not automatically give rise to similarity in the principle to be applied and questions of fact should not be elevated into questions of legal principle.

(ii)   If confronted with decisions which conflict, the appropriate decision-making authority and tribunals below must prefer the decision of a Three-Judge Panel of the AAC or a Tribunal of Commissioners to that of a single judge or Commissioner.

(iii)   In so far as the AAC is concerned, on questions of legal principle, a single judge shall follow a decision of a Three-Judge Panel of the AAC or Tribunal of Commissioners unless there are compelling reasons why he should not, as, for instance, a decision of a superior court affecting the legal principles involved. A single judge in the interests of comity and to avoid confusion on questions of legal principle normally follows the decisions of other single judges. It is recognised however that a slavish adherence to this could lead to the perpetuation of error and he is not bound to do so.

Appeals against decisions of the Upper Tribunal lie to the Court of Appeal.

Further details of the mechanisms for challenging tribunal decisions are set out in **Chapter 12**.

2.7 CONCLUSION

This chapter has given a brief overview of the origins of Mental Health Tribunals and provides an introduction to the structure, functions and procedures of the current tribunal systems in England and Wales for the hearing of mental health cases. **Chapters 3** to **8** set out in detail the relevant legal provisions relating to patients subject to MHA 1983 powers and the powers and duties of Mental Health Tribunals in dealing with applications and references affecting such patients. **Chapters 9** to **14** focus on tribunal practice and procedures and provide guidance for representatives of patients in relation to applications to and hearings before Mental Health Tribunals.

CHAPTER 3

The definition of mental disorder and the criteria for compulsion

This chapter considers the legal definition of mental disorder and the criteria for the use of compulsory powers under MHA 1983. A diagnosis of mental disorder in itself is not sufficient to justify the use of compulsory powers. Further grounds for detention or compulsory treatment must be fulfilled; for example, assessment and/or treatment under detention or a community treatment order (CTO) must be necessary in the interests of the patient's own health or safety or for the protection of others. It is also a requirement of detention for treatment or a CTO that appropriate treatment must be available. If a tribunal is not satisfied that any one or more of these criteria for compulsion are met, it must discharge the patient.

The chapter also includes descriptions of the main forms of mental disorder which may lead to detention or the use of compulsory powers, and sets out the medications which may be used to treat those disorders, with or without the patient's consent.

3.1 DEFINITION OF MENTAL DISORDER

The Mental Health Act 1983 applies to the 'reception, care and treatment of mentally disordered patients' (s.1(1)). A person cannot be detained or subject to community powers under MHA 1983 unless they are suffering from mental disorder. Mental disorder means 'any disorder or disability of the mind' (s.1(2)), which is as broad as the term 'unsoundness of mind' used in ECHR, art.5. For detention on grounds of unsoundness of mind to be lawful under art.5(1)(e) there must be objective medical evidence of a true mental disorder of a kind or degree warranting detention (*Winterwerp* v. *The Netherlands* (1979) 2 EHRR 387). Article 5(1)(e) cannot be taken to permit the detention of a person simply because his views deviate from the norms prevailing in a particular society (para.37). The English Code of Practice (Department of Health, *Mental Health Act 1983 Code of Practice* (2008)) says this (para.3.6):

Difference should not be confused with disorder. No-one may be considered to be mentally disordered solely because of their political, religious or cultural beliefs, values or opinions, unless there are proper clinical grounds to believe that they are the symptoms or manifestations of a disability or disorder of the mind. The same is true of a person's involvement, or likely involvement, in illegal, anti-social or 'immoral' behaviour. Beliefs, behaviours or actions which do not result from a disorder or disability of the mind are not a basis for compulsory measures under the Act, even if they appear unusual or cause other people alarm, distress or danger.

There are two international diagnostic manuals used by psychiatrists: the American Psychiatric Association's *Diagnostic and Statistical Manual of Mental Disorders* (4th edn, Washington, 1994) (DSM-IV-TR), which is soon to be published in a revised version as DSM-V, and the World Health Organization's *International Classification of Diseases* (Geneva, 1992) (ICD-10), also soon to be revised as ICD-11. Both distinguish between social deviance and mental disorder. ICD-10 states that:

> Disorder is used to imply the existence of a clinically recognizable set of symptoms or behaviour associated in most cases with distress and with interference with personal functions. Social deviance alone, without personal dysfunction, should not be included in mental disorder as defined here.

The Government did not wish to be tied down by the need for a disorder to appear in the pages of an international diagnostic manual in order to be a true mental disorder. In the parliamentary debates on the 2006 Bill, the Minister of State, Rosie Winterton MP, said it 'cannot be said that something that is not in any classification is not a mental disorder' (Public Bill Committee, Mental Health Bill 2006, col.16). However, the English Code of Practice emphasises that 'Relevant professionals should determine whether a patient has a disorder or disability of the mind in accordance with good clinical practice and accepted standards of what constitutes such a disorder or disability' (English Code of Practice, para.3.2; similar wording appears in the Welsh Code of Practice, *Mental Health Act 1983 Code of Practice for Wales* (2008), para.2.8). It is also important to remember that the existence of a disorder which appears in the pages of the ICD or DSM is not sufficient of itself to establish liability to detention or compulsory powers. In all cases, the disorder must be of 'a nature or degree' warranting or making compulsion appropriate, and some disorders (for example, learning disability and addiction) can only give rise to the use of compulsory powers in limited circumstances.

3.2 CLINICALLY RECOGNISED MENTAL DISORDERS

The English Code of Practice contains the following non-exhaustive list of clinically recognised conditions which could fall within the concept of mental disorder (English Code of Practice, para.3.3; and see Welsh Code of Practice, para.2.10):

- affective disorders, such as depression and bipolar disorder;
- schizophrenia and delusional disorders;
- neurotic, stress-related and somatoform disorders, such as anxiety, phobic disorders, obsessive compulsive disorders, post-traumatic stress disorder and hypochondriacal disorders;
- organic mental disorders such as dementia and delirium (however caused);
- personality and behavioural changes caused by brain injury or damage (however acquired);
- personality disorders;
- mental and behavioural disorders caused by psychoactive substance use;
- eating disorders, non-organic sleep disorders and non-organic sexual disorders;
- learning disabilities;
- autistic spectrum disorders (including Asperger's syndrome);
- behavioural and emotional disorders of children and adolescents.

The Mental Health Act 2007 Explanatory Notes give the following examples of 'clinically recognised mental disorders' (para.17):

> [M]ental illnesses such as schizophrenia, bipolar disorder, anxiety or depression, as well as personality disorders, eating disorders, autistic spectrum disorders and learning disabilities. Disorders or disabilities of the brain are not regarded as mental disorders unless (and only to the extent that) they give rise to a disability or disorder of the mind as well.

Hence, a brain injury or a brain tumour may cause a mental disorder or a mental disability.

3.3 PART IV OF THE MENTAL HEALTH ACT 1983

The mental illnesses mentioned in the above quotation from MHA 2007 Explanatory Notes may be treated with medication, or in the case of depressive illnesses by medication or electro-convulsive therapy (ECT). MHA 1983, Part IV (entitled 'Consent to Treatment') contains provision for these treatments to be given to certain groups of detained patients without their consent subject to a second opinion (MHA 1983, ss.58, 58A, 62, 63). It also provides (in s.57) that psychosurgery or surgical hormone implants for the reduction of male sex drive may not be given to a patient unless the patient is certified by a panel of three independent people appointed by the Care Quality Commission to be capable of consenting and to have consented to it, and the medical member of that panel has certified that it is appropriate for the treatment to be given (MHA 1983, s.57). Before considering the characteristics of the mental illnesses listed above, it is important to consider the provisions which exist to enable detained patients to be given treatment for mental disorder without their consent.

Following the changes introduced by MHA 2007, the responsible clinician (RC) replaced the responsible medical officer (RMO) as the person having overall responsibility for the patient's case (MHA 1983, s.34(1)). However (unlike RMOs) RCs need not be medically qualified, provided they have undergone the required training to be an approved clinician (AC) approved by the Secretary of State (or Welsh Ministers) to act for the purposes of MHA 1983. In cases where the RC is not medically qualified, responsibility for the patient's medical treatment for the purposes of MHA 1983, Part IV may be delegated to another AC who is medically qualified and has the appropriate rights concerning the prescription of drugs, etc.

3.3.1 Medicines for mental disorder

Medicines for mental disorder generally require either the patient's consent or a second opinion. Patients liable to be detained under the powers authorising detention for longer than 72 hours (except for patients remanded for assessment under MHA 1983, s.35, or conditionally-discharged restricted patients) may be given medicines for mental disorder without their consent, subject to the second opinion procedure in s.58 (MHA 1983, ss.56 and 58). Before becoming entitled to a second opinion a detained patient may be given medicine for mental disorder for up to three months from the first time that medicine was given during that period of detention. If the patient is consenting, the AC in charge of the patient's medical treatment must certify that the patient is capable and has consented, and must give a brief description of the treatment consented to on statutory Form T2 (in Wales Form CO2). The Codes of Practice require the AC to indicate on the form the drugs prescribed by the classes described in the British National Formulary (BNF), the method of their administration, and the dose range, indicating the dosages if they are above the BNF limit (English Code of Practice, para.24.17; Welsh Code of Practice, para.17.29).

If the patient is (a) incapable of understanding the nature, purpose and likely effects of the drug treatment, or (b) capable but refuses it, the treatment can only be given if there is a certificate from a second opinion appointed doctor (SOAD) confirming (a) or (b) above, and stating that it is appropriate for the treatment to be given (England Form T3, Wales Form CO3).[1] The SOAD must authorise the treatment to be given without the patient's consent in terms of BNF categories.

The BNF is not the only prescribing guide available to doctors, but it has played an important part in the second opinion process. It is published jointly by the British Medical Association and the Royal Pharmaceutical Society and updated biannually. It is a very useful reference work for a tribunal representative to acquire.[2] It describes the effects and side-effects of each drug, specifying recommended maximum dosage levels. The BNF is intended for the guidance of doctors, pharmacists and others who have the necessary training to interpret the information it provides. Each category (for example 4.2.1 anti-psychotic drugs, 4.2.2 depot

---

[1] References to forms are to the forms in the Mental Health (Hospital, Guardianship and Treatment) (England) Regulations 2008, SI 2008/1184, Sched.1 and the Mental Health (Hospital, Guardianship, Community Treatment and Consent to Treatment) (Wales) Regulations 2008, SI 2008/2439 (W.212), Sched.1.

[2] For all Legal Aid mental health contracts, the supervisor must 'maintain access . . . to medical reference publications which must cover categorisation of mental illnesses; and classification of psychiatric medication' (Legal Services Commission Standard Civil Contract Specification (2010), para.9.14).

anti-psychotics, 4.2.3 anti-manic drugs) includes a large number of different drugs, so this method of describing treatment confers considerable scope for the AC in charge of a patient's treatment to change medication within categories, or to give more than one drug within the same category at the same time.

3.3.2 Electro-convulsive therapy (ECT)

ECT is the passing of a current of electricity through the front part of the brain sufficient to produce a convulsion. The patient is first anaesthetised and then given a muscle relaxant in order to minimise the possibility of physical damage during the convulsion. ECT is usually given in a course of 6 to 12 sessions administered once or twice weekly. It is used particularly as a treatment of severe depression, or depression where anti-depressant medication has not worked, or where the patient's condition is serious and there is not time to wait for medication to take effect. ECT may also be used in the treatment of mania, and Healey argues that 'It is now clear that ECT is as specific and as effective as lithium in the treatment of mania' (David Healey, *Psychiatric Drugs Explained* (5th edn, London, Churchill Livingstone, 2009), p.93).

The administration of ECT is governed by MHA 1983, s.58A, which provides that, subject to the possibility of ECT being given in an emergency under s.62, it may not be given unless one of three circumstances applies:

1. the patient is over 18, has consented, and either the AC in charge of treatment or a SOAD certifies that the patient is capable of understanding the nature, purpose and likely effects of the treatment;

2. the patient is under 18, has consented, and a SOAD has certified both:

    (a) that the patient is capable of understanding the nature, purpose and likely effects and has consented; and
    (b) that it is appropriate for the treatment to be given;

3. a SOAD has certified that the patient is not capable of understanding the nature, purpose and likely effects of ECT but it is appropriate for the treatment to be given, and giving it would not conflict with a valid and applicable advance decision refusing it, or a decision by someone holding a lasting power of attorney, a deputy or the Court of Protection.

As with medicines, the AC in charge of treatment must certify that an adult patient is capable and has consented (Mental Health (Hospital, Guardianship and Treatment) (England) Regulations 2008, SI 2008/1184, Sched.1, Form T4; Mental Health (Hospital, Guardianship, Community Treatment and Consent to Treatment) (Wales) Regulations, SI 2008/2439 (W.212), Sched.1, Form CO4). If the patient is under 18 the certificate of capacity and consent must come from a SOAD, who must go on to certify that it is appropriate for the treatment to be given (Form T5

(England); Form CO5 (Wales)). ECT may no longer be given without consent outside the above circumstances unless it is an emergency covered by s.62(1A) (see below).

3.3.3 Emergency treatment

MHA 1983, s.62 is intended to allow treatment to be given if a second opinion cannot be arranged sufficiently speedily to cope with an emergency, while at the same time protecting patients against hazardous or irreversible treatments. It applies whether or not the patient is capable of understanding the nature, purpose or likely effects of the treatment. Section 62(1) states that the second opinion procedures in ss.57 and 58 do not apply to any treatment:

(a) which is immediately necessary to save the patient's life; or

(b) which (not being irreversible) is immediately necessary to prevent a serious deterioration of his condition; or

(c) which (not being irreversible or hazardous) is immediately necessary to alleviate serious suffering by the patient; or

(d) which (not being irreversible or hazardous) is immediately necessary and represents the minimum interference necessary to prevent the patient from behaving violently or being a danger to himself or to others.

The National Institute of Clinical Excellence (NICE) has produced a recommended list of medications to achieve 'rapid tranquilisation' which includes Lorazepam, a strong sedative, Haloperidol, an old-style antipsychotic, and Olanzapine, a more modern 'atypical anti-psychotic' designed to have fewer Parkinsonian side-effects than the old style anti-psychotics (*Violence: The Short Term Management of Disturbed/Violent Behaviour in In-Patient Psychiatric Settings* (Clinical Guideline 25, February 2005), pp.47–59) (see **3.5**).

Section 62(1A) provides that ECT may be given without prior compliance with s.58A if immediately necessary on grounds (a) to save life, or (b) not being irreversible, to prevent serious deterioration in the patient's condition. ECT is not regarded as an irreversible treatment.

3.3.4 Other treatments which may be given without consent

MHA 1983, s.63 provides that:

> The consent of a patient shall not be required for any medical treatment given to him for the mental disorder from which he is suffering, not being a form of treatment to which section 57, 58 or 58A above applies, if the treatment is given by or under the direction of the approved clinician in charge of the treatment.

Case law (discussed below) has made it clear that force-feeding patients suffering from anorexia nervosa or other eating disorders can be treatment for mental disorder covered by s.63. In *Re KB (Adult) (Mental Patient: Medical Treatment)* (1994) 19 BMLR 144, at [146], Ewbank J said that 'relieving symptoms was just as much part of treatment as relieving the underlying cause'. *B* v. *Croydon Health Authority* [1995] 1 All ER 683 (CA) differed from *Re KB* in that the patient suffered from a borderline personality disorder rather than anorexia, but the Court of Appeal held that s.63 applied to treatment directed at the symptoms or sequelae of mental disorder just as much as to treatment directed to remedying B's underlying personality disorder which caused her compulsion to harm herself by not eating. Self-harm by starvation was a symptom of the underlying disorder. In *R* v. *Collins and Ashworth Hospital Authority, ex p. Brady* [2000] Lloyd's Rep. Med. 355, the court held that it would be lawful under s.63 to force-feed a patient on hunger strike. The pursuit of the hunger strike was held to be a manifestation of his histrionic personality disorder which led him to embark on dramatic conflicts with authority. MHA 1983, s.145(4) (confirming that the purpose of medical treatment under the Act is to alleviate, or prevent a worsening of, the disorder or one or more of its symptoms or manifestations) was introduced by MHA 2007 partly to reflect the judicial pronouncements in *B* v. *Croydon* and *ex p. Brady* (see **3.11.2**).

Since these cases were decided, in *X* v. *Finland* [2012] ECHR 1371, the European Court of Human Rights held (at [220]) that in order for an interference with the right of physical integrity such as forced medication (or presumably forcible feeding) to comply with art.8(2), the law must guarantee proper safeguards against arbitrariness and the patient must have 'a remedy available whereby s/he could require a court to rule on the lawfulness, including proportionality, of the forced administration of medication and to have it discontinued.' We must await a case where consideration may be given to whether judicial review of decisions to treat under s.63 are adequate to meet requirement.

Having considered the possibilities to give treatment without consent under MHA 1983, we now turn to consider the main forms of mental disorder which may lead to detention or the imposition of a CTO.

3.4 AFFECTIVE OR MOOD DISORDERS

The two principal affective or mood disorders are (i) depression and (ii) bipolar disorder (which is also sometimes referred to as manic depressive illness or manic depressive psychosis).

3.4.1 Depressive disorders

Depression may range from a state of mild sadness to a disorder of psychotic proportions accompanied by delusions or hallucinations.[3] A major depressive episode will usually manifest itself in persistent depressed mood in the absence of a precipitant event, or if there is a precipitant event, the response will be out of all

---

[3] The term 'psychotic' indicates the presence of hallucinations, delusions, abnormalities of behaviour, such as gross excitement and overactivity, marked psychomotor retardation (slowing of physical or emotional reactions), disorganised speech or disorganised or catatonic behaviour.

proportion to the magnitude of the event. A depressive episode will involve loss of interest or pleasure in nearly all usually enjoyed activities, negative thinking, reduced energy, decreased self-esteem and confidence, and may be accompanied by feelings of worthlessness or guilt which may reach delusional proportions. There may be thoughts of suicide or self-harm, or in severe cases the person may be beyond communication or refusing food and fluids. Other common features include unintended weight loss or gain, decreased libido, increase or decrease in the time spent sleeping, early morning waking, agitation or psychomotor retardation. The greater the number and intensity of symptoms, the more severe the disorder. In severe cases, sometimes called psychotic depression, delusions and hallucinations may occur, for example, somatic delusions (the idea that some part of the body is abnormal in function or appearance).

Anti-depressant medication

Some commonly prescribed antidepressants are listed below. Tricyclic anti-depressants are prescribed less frequently than selective serotonin re-uptake inhibitors (SSRIs), and monamine oxidase inhibitors (MAOIs) are rarely given.

Table 3.1 SSRIs (BNF 4.3.3)

Drug	UK trade name
Citalopram	Cipramil
Escitalopram	Cipralex
Fluoxamine	Faverin
Fluoxetine	Prozac
Paroxetine	Seroxat
Sertraline	Lustral
Venlafaxine	Effexor

Table 3.2 Tricyclic anti-depressants (BNF 4.3.1)

Drug	UK trade name
Amitryptiline Hydrochloride	Tryptizol/Lentizol
Clomipramine	Anafranil
Dosulepin Hydrochloride	Prothiaden
Doxepin	Sinequan
Imipramine Hydrochloride	Tofranil
Lofepramine	Gamanil/Lomont
Nortryptiline	Allegron
Trimipramine	Surmontil

Drug	UK trade name
Mianserin Hydrochloride	Mianserin
Trazodone	Mollpaxin

Table 3.3   MAOIs (BNF 4.3.2)

Drug	UK trade name
Phenelzine	Nardil
Isocarboxazid	Isocarboxazid
Moclobemide	Mannerix/Aurorix
Tranylcypromine	Tranylcypromine

3.4.2   Bipolar disorder

Bipolar disorder (also known as manic depressive illness or manic depressive psychosis) is a form of affective (mood) disorder where the sufferer experiences swings in mood or affect between profound depression and elation. The elated state may be described as hypomania or mania, hypomania being a lesser degree of mania. Hypomania involves mild elevation of mood with increased energy and activity. The person may be extremely talkative, over familiar and may show increased sexual energy. Mania is where the person's mood has been elevated out of keeping with their circumstances for at least one week and is so severe as to disrupt ordinary social and work activities more or less completely. Symptoms may include rapid fire speech, grandiosity, irritability, hyperactivity, recklessness with money and decreased need for sleep. Bipolar illness may entail manic episodes of four to five months followed by depressions lasting six months or more, there may be only manic episodes, or the illness may involve more rapid cycling (ICD-10, F30–39, Mood (Affective) Disorders, 112). Bipolar illness may be accompanied by psychotic features, for example, grandiose delusional beliefs such as being chosen for an important mission or possessing special powers or abilities.

Medication for bipolar disorder

Lithium Carbonate is often used as a treatment for bipolar illness and as a mood stabiliser in the prevention of further episodes of mania and depression. Healey notes that 'In practice antipsychotics are the first line of treatment for mania. In part this stems from the pressing need to contain the behaviour of individuals with mania, and moderate to large doses of anti-psychotics do this relatively quickly' (David Healey, *Psychiatric Drugs Explained* (5th edn, London, Churchill Livingstone, 2009), p.89). This may then be followed up by treatment with Lithium Carbonate or another mood stabiliser.

Table 3.4 Anti-manic drugs (BNF 4.2.3)

Drug	UK trade name
Lithium Carbonate	Liskonum
Carbamazepine	Tegretol
Sodium Valproate	Epilim

Table 3.5 Anti-epileptic drugs sometimes used as mood stabilisers (BNF 4.8.1)

Drug	UK trade name
Lamotrigine	Lamictal
Gabapentin	Neurontin

3.5 PSYCHOTIC ILLNESS

3.5.1 Schizophrenia

The most common psychotic illness is schizophrenia which, together with schizo-typal and other delusional disorders, is grouped in ICD-10, F20–29. These disorders are characterised by 'fundamental and characteristic distortions of thinking and perception, and by inappropriate or blunted affect (mood)' (ICD-10, 86). The characteristic distortions include auditory and visual hallucinations, delusions, attaching grossly disproportionate importance to minor and irrelevant matters, and developing an unshakable belief in the importance of bizarre ideas. As ICD-10 vividly describes it (ICD-10, 86–87):

> The disturbance involves the most basic functions that give a normal person a feeling of individuality, uniqueness and self-direction. The most intimate thoughts, feelings, and acts are often felt to be known to or shared by others, and explanatory delusions may develop, to the effect that natural or supernatural forces are at work to influence the afflicted individual's behaviour or thoughts.

Symptoms of schizophrenia are often characterised as either positive or negative. The positive symptoms of schizophrenia include delusions, hallucinations, and strange speech and behaviour. Negative symptoms include flat emotional response, withdrawal, apathy, loss of interest in personal hygiene and appearance, or not wanting to leave the house or socialise or converse with others. Many people without a diagnosis of schizophrenia may also experience such negative symptoms from time to time, but they are commonly present for those with schizophrenia.

Paranoid schizophrenia is the most common type of schizophrenia in most parts of the world. Its classic symptoms include delusions of persecution, exalted birth, special mission, bodily change or jealousy, hallucinatory voices that threaten the patient or give commands, or auditory hallucinations without verbal form. There may also be hallucinations of smell or taste, or of sexual or other bodily sensations. The person may speak in a disorganised way and use neologisms (made up words), or express magical thinking or odd beliefs. There are also generalised deficits in cognitive functioning and impaired insight. Schizoaffective disorders are diagnosed when both schizophrenic and affective symptoms (either depression or mania) are present at the same time or within a few days of each other during the same episode of illness.

Anti-psychotic medication

There are two groups of anti-psychotic drugs. The so-called 'first generation' anti-psychotics have a high incidence of extra-pyramidal Parkinsonian symptoms (tremor and stiffness), akathisia (restlessness), drowsiness and tardive dyskinesia (movements of the face and less often of the arms and legs). Second generation (atypical) anti-psychotics are less likely to cause Parkinsonian side-effects but are more likely to cause weight gain and type 2 diabetes. There is little difference in terms of effectiveness between the two groups of drugs, with the exception of Clozapine which is often used when there has been little or no response to other anti-psychotics. This drug can affect the bone marrow and for this reason regular blood tests are required. NICE issued a clinical guideline on core interventions in schizophrenia in 2009 (*Core Interventions in the Treatment and Management of Schizophrenia in Adults in Primary and Secondary Care* (NICE Clinical Guideline 82, March 2009)). The Royal College of Psychiatrists has issued guidance on high dose anti-psychotics.[4]

Table 3.6   First generation (typical) anti-psychotics (BNF 4.2.1)

Drug	UK trade name
Chlorpromazine	Largactil
Trifluoperazine	Stelazine
Sulpiride	Sulpitil/Dolmatil/Sulparex
Haloperidol	Haldol/Serenace/Dozic

Table 3.7   Second generation (atypical) anti-psychotics (BNF 4.2.1)

Drug	UK trade name
Amisulpiride	Solian
Aripiprazole	Abilify
Clozapine	Clozaril
Olanzapine	Zyprexa

---

[4]   Available at **www.rcpsych.ac.uk/files/pdfversion/CR138.pdf**.

Drug	UK trade name
Palperidone	Invega
Quetiapine	Seroquel
Risperidone	Risperdal
Sertindole	Serdolect
Zotepine	Zoleptil

A depot is an intramuscular injection which lasts in the system for two to four weeks.

Table 3.8 Depot anti-psychotics

Drug	UK trade name
Flupentixol Decanoate	Depixol
Fluphenazine Decanoate	Modecate
Haloperidol Decanoate	Haldol
Olazapine Embonate	ZypAdhera*
Pipotiazine Palmitate	Depixol
Zuclopenthixol Decanoate	Clopixol
Risperidone	Risperdal Consta*
Paliperidone	Xeplion*

* Second generation (atypical) depot anti-psychotics

Anti-Parkinsonian (anti-muscarinic) drugs

Drugs used to treat the Parkinsonian side-effects of anti-psychotics include Procyclidine, Orphenadrine and Trihexyphenidol (Benzhexol).

3.5.2   Stress-related and anxiety disorders

Both ICD-10 and DSM-IV include stress-related and anxiety disorders (ICD-10, F40–48; DSM-IV, 393). These include post-traumatic stress disorder, phobic anxiety disorders such as agoraphobia, social phobias, animal phobia, examination phobia, other anxiety disorders manifested in panic attacks, or disorders where patients repeatedly present physical symptoms requesting medical investigations, in spite of repeated negative findings and reassurance from doctors. It is rare for patients with anxiety disorders to be detained under mental health legislation, their affliction rarely being of a nature or degree warranting detention. Obsessive compulsive disorder can on occasion produce disabling effects to the requisite nature or degree justifying detention for the person's own health. Here, obsessive thoughts enter the patient's head again and again. This causes anxiety and results in ceaseless repetition of compulsive acts or ritualised behaviour in an attempt to reduce anxiety levels.

3.6   DEPENDENCE ON ALCOHOL OR DRUGS

MHA 1983, s.1(3) provides that dependence on alcohol or drugs is not considered to be a disorder or disability of the mind for the purposes of MHA 1983. Although dependence on alcohol or drugs appears in the diagnostic manuals as a mental disorder, and drug or alcohol addiction is a separate ground of detention under ECHR, art.5(1)(e), the effect of s.1(3) (MHA 2007 Explanatory Notes, para.26) is that:

> no action can be taken under the 1983 Act in relation to people simply because they are dependent on alcohol or drugs (including opiates, psycho-stimulants or some solvents), even though in other contexts their dependence would be considered clinically to be a mental disorder.

The exclusion refers to dependence, so it would appear that extreme intoxication is not prevented from being a mental disorder by this provision, the Government's view being that although the persistent use of alcohol or drugs is not a mental disorder 'the effects of such use may be' (MHA 2007 Explanatory Notes, para.25). The English Code of Practice stresses that other mental disorders relating to the use of alcohol or drugs are not excluded, and these include withdrawal state with delirium or associated psychotic disorder, organic mental disorders associated with prolonged abuse of drugs or alcohol, and even severe acute intoxication (drunkenness), provided all the relevant criteria are met (English Code of Practice, para.3.11).

The exclusion does not mean that addicts are excluded entirely from the scope of MHA 1983. A person may have a mental disorder which is completely unrelated to their dependence on alcohol or drugs. Excess consumption of alcohol or drugs may cause recognised forms of mental illness such as Korsakoff's Syndrome, drug induced psychoses, delirium consequent on withdrawal, or depression. MHA 2007 Explanatory Notes also point out that the exclusion does not mean that (para.27):

> people may never be treated without consent under the 1983 Act for alcohol or drug dependence. Like treatment for any other condition which is not itself a mental disorder, treatment for dependence may be given under the 1983 Act if it forms part of treatment for a condition which is a mental disorder for the purposes of the 1983 Act . . .

This might occur where the dependence is a consequence, or is exacerbating the effects, of the mental disorder and treatment may therefore be given under MHA 1983, s.63 (*B* v. *Croydon Health Authority* [1995] 1 All ER 683 (CA)).

3.7 LEARNING DISABILITY AND AUTISTIC SPECTRUM DISORDERS

3.7.1 Learning disability

The term currently favoured in the United Kingdom to describe people with intellectual impairment is 'learning disability'. This reflects a move away from medical models of illness towards recognition of learning disability as a developmental disability, and away from treatment in hospitals towards an emphasis on care at home or in small residential units, integrated into the community, where the skills of residents can be developed and their individuality can be better respected. The new MHA 1983, s.1(4) defines learning disability as 'a state of arrested or incomplete development of the mind which includes significant impairment of intelligence and social functioning'.

People with learning disabilities (without any additional mental disorder) are ineligible for detention for treatment under s.3, or under the offender provisions in MHA 1983, Part III, unless their learning disability is associated with abnormally aggressive or seriously irresponsible conduct on their part (known as 'the conduct requirement', see **3.7.3**). The same applies to reception into guardianship or subjection to a community treatment order.

This limitation was introduced in relation to learning disability in MHA 1983. Lord Rix, President of Mencap, explained to the House of Lords during the debates on the 2006 Bill that these words represented the 'best compromise we could then reach between the Government's position that people with a learning disability should come under the scope of the Act, and my position that people with a learning disability are not ill and should not be treated as if they were' (*Hansard*, HL Deb., vol. 687, col. 662 (28 November 2006)).

People with learning disabilities who have no additional mental disorder and who do not meet the conduct requirement are not completely excluded from the powers of detention under MHA 1983. They may be subject to the doctor's or the nurse's holding power (s.5), admission for assessment under s.2, emergency admission for assessment under s.4, they may be removed from a public place to a place of safety by a police officer under s.136, and a warrant may be granted under s.135 to enter premises to remove them to a place of safety.

Diagnosis of learning disability is based on a combination of 'arrested or incomplete development of the mind' and 'significant impairment of intelligence and social functioning'. The English Code of Practice states that a person with arrested or incomplete development of mind is one 'who has experienced a significant impairment of the normal process of maturation of intellectual and social development that occurs during childhood and adolescence'. This means that the 'features which qualify as a learning disability' should have been 'present prior to adulthood'. The Code emphasises that (English Code of Practice, para.34.4; see also Welsh Code of Practice, para.34.9):

For the purposes of the Act, learning disability does not include people whose intellectual disorder derives from accident, injury or illness occurring after they completed normal maturation (although such conditions do fall within the definition of mental disorder in the Act).

In relation to the 'significant impairment' component, the Code of Practice requires assessment to be 'reliable and careful', acknowledging that 'It is not defined rigidly by the application of an arbitrary cut-off point such as an IQ of 70'. Some IQ tests can disadvantage people whose education has been interrupted, or people whose first language is not English, and verbal tests may disadvantage people with communication problems. Standardised IQ tests, although an important indicator, do not determine the question whether a person is suffering from arrested or incomplete development of mind, or of its level of severity, and a full social assessment is required.

In *Meggary* v. *Chief Adjudications Officer* (1999) *The Times*, 11 November, Simon Brown LJ said that intelligence includes not just understanding and intellect but also 'the qualities of insight and sagacity', and that 'in the case of an autistic child those qualities may well be lacking and, to the extent that they are, there will be a functional impairment which overlaps both limbs …, i.e. both intelligence and social functioning'. The words 'impairment of intelligence' and 'social function-ing', and whether they are significant are 'not terms of art', but 'ordinary English words' and the significance or severity of the impairment is to be measured 'against the standard of normal persons', not by comparison with other people with learning disabilities (*R* v. *Hall (John Hamilton)* (1988) 86 Cr. App. R 159, 162 (Parker LJ)).

3.7.2 Autistic spectrum disorders

An issue which caused controversy in the debates leading to MHA 2007 was whether autistic disorder was a learning disability or another form of mental disorder. The essential features of autistic disorder according to the DSM-IV are the presence of markedly abnormal or impaired development in social interaction, communication or awareness of others, leading to gross and sustained impairment in reciprocal social interaction, and failure to develop peer relationships. The English Code of Practice states that autistic spectrum disorders occur 'from early stages in development in which the person shows marked difficulties with social communication, social interaction and social imagination. They may be preoccu-pied with a particular subject of interest' (English Code of Practice, para.34.19; Welsh Code of Practice, paras.34.14–34.17). The English Code stresses that 'These disorders are developmental in nature and are not mental illnesses in themselves' (English Code of Practice, para.34.20).

The English Code notes that although it is possible for someone on the autistic spectrum to meet the conditions for treatment under the Act without having any other form of mental disorder, even without abnormally aggressive or seriously irresponsible behaviour, 'this is likely to happen only very rarely' (English Code of Practice, para.34.18). Moreover (para.34.8):

Compulsory treatment in a hospital setting is rarely likely to be helpful for a person with autism, who may be very distressed by even minor changes in routine and is likely to find detention in hospital anxiety provoking. Sensitive, person-centred support in a familiar setting will usually be more helpful.

The Code stresses that 'These disorders are developmental in nature and are not mental illnesses in themselves', but goes on to say that 'it should be borne in mind that people with autistic spectrum disorders may also have co-morbid mental disorders, including mood disorders and, occasionally, personality disorders' (para.34.20).

3.7.3 Conduct requirement

In *R* v. *Trent Mental Health Review Tribunal, ex p. Ryan* [1992] COD 157, Nolan LJ said that whether conduct amounts 'to seriously irresponsible or abnormally aggressive behaviour' raised 'questions other than of a purely clinical nature'. The English Code states that factors to be taken into account in determining whether there is abnormally aggressive behaviour 'may include' (English Code of Practice, para.34.8; and see Welsh Code of Practice, para.34.10):

- when such aggressive behaviour has been observed, and how persistent and severe it has been;
- whether it has occurred without a specific trigger or seems out of proportion to the circumstances that triggered it;
- whether, and to what degree, it has in fact resulted in harm or distress to other people, or actual damage to property;
- how likely, if it has not been observed recently, it is to recur; and
- how common similar behaviour is in the population generally.

Such conduct on the part of the person need not be current nor have been particularly recent. The requirement will be met if the learning disability has been associated with such conduct in the past and if there is a real risk that, if treatment in hospital is discontinued, that conduct will manifest itself in the future (*Lewis* v. *Gibson* [2005] EWCA Civ 587, [2005] MHLR 309, at [31] (Thorpe LJ)). (See also *R (P)* v. *Mental Health Review Tribunal (East Midlands and North East Region)* [2002] EWCA Civ 697, at [23]–[26] (Pill LJ), where the abnormally aggressive conduct requirement was met even though the last example was the index offence in 1992, which had been a particularly ferocious and violent homicide.)

In assessing whether there is 'seriously irresponsible conduct' factors may include (English Code of Practice, para.34.9):

- whether behaviour has been observed that suggests a disregard or an inadequate regard for its serious or dangerous consequences;
- how recently such behaviour has been observed and, when it has been observed, how persistent it has been;
- how seriously detrimental to the patient, or to other people, the consequences of the behaviour were or might have been;

- whether, and to what degree, the behaviour has actually resulted in harm to the patient or the patient's interests, or in harm to other people or to damage to property; and
- if it has not been observed recently, how likely it is to recur.

In *Re F (Mental Health Act: Guardianship)* [2000] 1 FLR 192 (CA), the issue was whether a learning disabled 17-year-old was eligible for Mental Health Act guardianship. She was said to be exhibiting seriously irresponsible conduct by wanting to return to a home where she had suffered neglect and possible sexual abuse. The Court of Appeal held that guardianship could not be used since the urge to return to one's home and family is 'almost universal' and therefore she was not behaving seriously irresponsibly. In *Newham London Borough Council* v. *S (Adult: Court's Jurisdiction)* [2003] EWHC 1909 (Fam), Wall J held that guardianship could not be used to remove S to residential care from the care of her father who was having serious difficulty coping with her, because 'the only example of "seriously irresponsible conduct" on S's part was her total lack of road sense and a tendency to rush into the road without looking' (at [11]). However, this line of argument was not accepted in *R (GC)* v. *Managers of the Kingswood Centre of Central and North West London NHS Foundation Trust* (CO/7784/2008) (unreported, Administrative Court, 2008), where a patient with a learning disability who had a compulsion to pick up litter, even if that litter was in the road, was found to be acting in an irresponsible manner, causing risk to herself and others.

Although people with learning disabilities who do not satisfy the conduct requirement cannot be detained under MHA 1983, s.3, or be subject to guardianship, they may be deprived of their liberty under MCA 2005 Deprivation of Liberty Safeguards (MCA 2005, ss.4A, 16, Scheds.A1 and 1A) if they lack capacity and detention in a hospital or care home is in their best interests (see **4.2**). The conduct requirement does not apply in relation to deprivation of liberty under MCA 2005.

3.8 PERSONALITY DISORDER

Until MHA 2007 reforms, a person with a personality disorder could only be detained under MHA 1983 if they had a diagnosis of 'psychopathic disorder', meaning 'a persistent disorder or disability of mind (whether or not including significant impairment of intelligence) which *resulted in* abnormally aggressive or seriously irresponsible conduct' (emphasis added). Personality disorder is a type of unsoundness of mind within the meaning of ECHR, art.5(1)(e) (*Koniarska* v. *United Kingdom* (Application 33670/96), Decision of 12 October 2000 (ECtHR); *Reid* v. *United Kingdom* (2003) 37 EHRR 9 (ECtHR)). It is also a mental disorder for the purposes of MHA 1983, s.1(2) but the requirement of abnormally aggressive or seriously irresponsible conduct no longer applies in relation to this category of disorder.

Personality disorders are grouped together in ICD-10, F60–69 'Disorders of Adult Personality and Behaviour', and defined as (ICD-10, 200):

Clinically significant conditions and behaviour patterns which tend to be persistent and are characteristic of an individual's characteristic lifestyle and mode of relating to self and others. They are deeply ingrained and enduring behaviour patterns, manifesting themselves as inflexible responses to a broad range of personal and social situations. They represent either extreme or significant deviations from the way the average individual in a given culture perceives, thinks, feels, and particularly relates to others.

The DSM-IV lists the following diagnostic features of personality disorder (DSM-IV, 633):

An enduring pattern of inner experience and behaviour that deviates markedly from the individual's culture. This is manifested in two or more of the following areas:

(1)   cognition (ie ways of perceiving and interpreting self, other people and events)
(2)   affectivity (ie the range, intensity, lability and appropriateness of emotional response)
(3)   interpersonal functioning
(4)   impulse control.

The enduring pattern must be inflexible and pervasive across a wide range of personal and social situations, and must lead to clinically significant distress or impairment in social, occupational or other important areas of functioning. The pattern must also be stable and of long duration and its presence must be traceable back at least to adolescence or early adulthood.

Although the conduct requirement has been removed in relation to the detention of people with a diagnosis of personality disorder, their disorder must still be of a nature or degree warranting or making detention appropriate (see **3.10**).

3.9   REMOVAL OF THE SEXUAL DEVIANCY EXCLUSION

One of the prime concerns behind MHA 2007 reforms was to remove obstacles to using the powers of detention under MHA 1983 to protect society against sex offenders, in particular those leaving prison at the end of determinate sentences and assessed as posing a high risk of re-offending. MHA 1983 had provided that no one could be treated as mentally disordered by reason only of sexual deviancy, and this posed a problem when it came to detaining patients on grounds of paedophilia, which is one of the paraphilias (fetishistic disorders), or on grounds of a personality disorder which manifests itself only in sexual deviancy. Removal of the sexual deviancy exclusion has meant that sex offenders, and persons who are at risk of sex offending because of paraphilia or personality disorder, are now detainable under MHA 1983.

3.10 NATURE OR DEGREE OF MENTAL DISORDER

Whether mental disorder is of the relevant nature or degree warranting assessment in hospital or making detention appropriate depends on whether the relevant admission criteria (necessity for the patient's own health or safety or for the protection of others, and availability of appropriate treatment) are met. The disorder must be of a nature or degree making it appropriate for the person to receive treatment in hospital. The terms 'nature or degree' are disjunctive – one is sufficient – for example, mental disorder may be of a nature warranting detention even if its symptoms are not currently of a degree to make detention necessary (*R* v. *Mental Health Review Tribunal for the South Thames Region, ex p. Smith* [1999] COD 148 (QBD)). As MHA 2007 Explanatory Notes state (para.31), 'nature' refers to the particular mental disorder from which the patient is suffering, its chronic nature, its prognosis, and the patient's previous response to receiving treatment for disorder. 'Degree' refers to the current manifestation of the patient's disorder. In *CM* v. *Derbyshire Healthcare NHS Foundation Trust and Secretary of State for Justice* [2011] UKUT 129 (AAC), Judge Levenson held that (at [12], following *Smirek* v. *Williams* [2000] MHLR 38 (CA); *R* v. *MHRT, ex p. Moyle* [2000] Lloyd's LR 143):

> If the nature of a patient's illness is such that it will relapse in the absence of medication, then whether the nature is such as to make it appropriate for him to be liable to be detained in hospital for medical treatment depends on an assessment of the probability that he will relapse in the near future if he were free in the community and on whether the evidence is that without being detained in hospital he will not take the medication.

The judge found no evidence of past non-compliance with medication while released from hospital (although there was evidence of forgetting appointments), and that the First-tier Tribunal was continuing the appellant's detention for the purposes of addressing his drug taking and chaotic lifestyle. Judge Levenson held that the First-tier Tribunal's decision must be set aside because there was 'no real evidence to support its view that non-compliance with medication and the risk of consequent relapse in the near future would probably occur', and that on the facts, 'continued detention for the purposes of avoiding a chaotic lifestyle or drug taking or the absence of drug counselling is not permitted by law' ([25] and [27]).

Winterwerp v. *The Netherlands* also established that detention must be a necessary and proportionate response to the patient's circumstances. Other less restrictive measures must have been considered and found to be insufficient to safeguard the individual or public interest, leaving no alternative to detention (*Litwa* v. *Poland* (2001) 33 EHRR 53, (2000) 63 BMLR 199 (ECtHR), at [78]).

3.11 TREATABILITY AND THE AVAILABILITY OF APPROPRIATE TREATMENT

Under MHA 1983, the 'treatability test' applied to people with psychopathic disorder or mental impairment: to detain or renew detention of these patients, it had to be certified that medical treatment was likely to alleviate or prevent deterioration in the patient's condition, which would be hard to do if the patient was resolutely not co-operating. This might happen if a person with a personality disorder refused to engage with psychological treatment. Treatment might be available and appropriate but unlikely to make any difference if the patient refused to participate. However, treatment was defined in the original MHA 1983, s.145 by a non-exhaustive list: '"medical treatment" includes nursing and also includes care, habilitation and rehabilitation under medical supervision'. Because of the breadth of this concept, which includes nursing and care, it was difficult for this argument to succeed in the courts (see *Reid* v. *Secretary of State for Scotland* [1999] 2 AC 512 (HL)). Regardless of the position in the courts, the Government's concern was that psychiatrists were frequently viewing risky patients as not detainable on grounds of their untreatability.

3.11.1 Appropriate treatment

MHA 2007 abolished the treatability test, replacing it with the requirement that appropriate treatment must be available to the patient, 'appropriate treatment' meaning 'medical treatment which is appropriate in his case, taking into account the nature and degree of the mental disorder and all other circumstances of his case' (MHA 1983, s.3(4)).

The Government's position was that abolishing treatability did not infringe ECHR. This was based on *Reid* v. *United Kingdom* (2003) 37 EHRR 9, where the European Court of Human Rights (ECtHR) said that art.5(1)(e) imposed no requirement that detention in a mental hospital was conditional on the illness or condition being of a nature or degree amenable to medical treatment. The court held that (para.51):

> Confinement under Art. 5(1)(e) may be necessary not only where a person needs therapy, medication or other clinical treatment to cure or alleviate his condition, but also where the person needs control and supervision to prevent him, for example, causing harm to himself or other persons.

The Joint Committee on Human Rights conceded that there was nothing in ECHR to prevent abolition of the treatability test. They also noted art.17(1)(iii) of Council of Europe Recommendation No. (2004)10 of the Committee of Ministers to Member States concerning the human rights and dignity of persons with mental disorder, which requires that detention has a 'therapeutic purpose'. This is broadly defined (in art.2(3)) as 'including prevention, diagnosis, *control*, cure or treatment' (emphasis added).

3.11.2 Availability of appropriate treatment and preventive detention

The Mental Health Act 2007 altered the concept of medical treatment in MHA 1983, s.145(1) so that it now 'includes nursing', and also includes 'psychological intervention and specialist mental health habilitation, rehabilitation and care'. A new s.145(4) was added, which provides that 'Any reference in this Act to medical treatment, in relation to mental disorder, shall be construed as a reference to medical treatment the purpose of which is to alleviate, or prevent a worsening of, the disorder or one or more of its symptoms or manifestations'. Instead of treatment having to be likely to alleviate or prevent deterioration in the patient's condition, it must have a therapeutic purpose, but not necessarily a demonstrated therapeutic effect. It is a condition of detention under s.3 and a condition of a community treatment order, that appropriate treatment must be available for the patient.

The Codes of Practice give guidance on the appropriate medical treatment test, and seek to distinguish between nursing and specialist day-to-day care in a safe and secure therapeutic environment and mere preventive detention. The English Code states (English Code of Practice, paras.6.16–6.17; and see Welsh Code of Practice, paras.4.15–4.16):

> Appropriate medical treatment does not have to involve medication or individual or group psychological therapy – although it very often will. There may be patients whose particular circumstances mean that treatment may be appropriate even though it consists only of nursing and specialist day-to-day care under the clinical supervision of an approved clinician, in a safe and secure therapeutic environment.
> Simply detaining someone – even in a hospital – does not constitute medical treatment.

The distinction between preventive detention and treatment has been raised in two cases since MHA 2007, involving patients with personality disorder who appealed against tribunal decisions refusing discharge. In *MD* v. *Nottinghamshire Health Care NHS Trust* [2010] UKUT 59 (AAC), [2010] AACR 34, MD refused to engage in psychotherapy, arguing that he was entitled to discharge in that one of the conditions of detention (the availability of appropriate treatment) was no longer met. The tribunal declined to discharge because MD had a psychopathic personality disorder, was at risk of violent re-offending, and, taking a long-term view, 'appropriate positive psychotherapeutic treatment is available here' (at [25]). Alternatively, the tribunal concluded that the patient had been (at [26]):

> engaging in and benefiting from the specialist nursing care and 'milieu' therapy on the ward . . . nursing and specialist day to day care under clinical supervision of an approved clinician, in a safe and secure therapeutic environment with a structured regime . . . the language of Code paragraph 6.16.

In the Upper Tribunal, Judge Jacobs held that the distinction between containment and treatment and the definition of 'available' and 'appropriate' were 'matters of fact and judgment for the tribunal ... [which] is an expert body and ... has to use that expertise to make its findings and exercise its judgment' (at [48]). The line between treatment and containment would only be crossed 'if there was no prospect of the patient progressing beyond milieu' (at [35]) and then treatment would no longer be appropriate, but the facts found by the tribunal showed that the patient had not reached that position as 'there was the potential for the milieu to benefit the patient in both the short and longer term'. To say the least this is not a rigorous standard, since the concept of 'milieu therapy' has not been further defined.

In *DL-H* v. *Devon Partnership NHS Trust and Secretary of State for Justice* [2010] UKUT 102 (AAC), the patient also refused to engage. Judge Jacobs acknowledged that since attempts to get the patient to engage can be treatment under s.145(1), there is 'a danger that a patient for whom no appropriate treatment is available may be contained for public safety rather than detained for treatment' (at [32]). The solution lay in the tribunal's duty to 'investigate behind assertions, generalisations and standard phrases', to address the question of whether the patient could be persuaded to engage, and to make an individualised assessment of the precise treatment that can be provided. However, as long as the tribunal goes through a thorough inquisitorial process and gives adequate reasons for its findings, it would seem to be open to the tribunal to find that, even if the only present treatment is 'milieu' nursing and care, as long as it can find some prospect that the patient may progress beyond milieu and engage with other therapies, then appropriate treatment will be available.

3.12 CONCLUSION

This chapter has explained the legal concept of mental disorder which applies to detention and the use of compulsory community powers under MHA 1983. The role of the tribunal and the representative is to consider whether, at the time of the hearing, the patient continues to suffer from a mental disorder of a nature or degree warranting or making compulsion appropriate, and whether the other criteria for compulsion are met.

CHAPTER 4

Non-offender patients: detention, discharge and review

This chapter considers the powers to detain non-offender patients in Part II of MHA 1983, the powers to remove a patient to a place of safety under ss.135 and 136, and the entitlement of patients detained under Part II and their relatives to apply for a tribunal hearing or to have their case referred to the tribunal.

The Mental Health Act 1983 Codes of Practice applying in England and Wales, respectively (Department of Health, *Mental Health Act 1983 Code of Practice* (2008); Welsh Government, *Mental Health Act 1983 Code of Practice for Wales* (2008)), both state that approved mental health professionals (AMHPs) and doctors must always consider alternative ways to detention for providing the care and treatment needed, and patients should only be detained under MHA 1983 if there is no effective alternative (English Code of Practice, para.4.13; Welsh Code of Practice, para.2.27). The main alternatives are care at home or in the community; informal admission to hospital; or application of the Deprivation of Liberty Safeguards (DoLS) in MCA 2005. The circumstances where the DoLS may be used as an alternative to detention under MHA 1983 are governed by MCA 2005, Sched.1A discussed further below (see **4.2**).

4.1 INFORMAL ADMISSION

MHA 1983 is based on the principle that, wherever possible, patients should be admitted to hospital on an informal basis, and that powers of compulsion should be used as a last resort (MHA 1983, s.131(1)):

> Nothing in this Act shall be construed as preventing a patient who requires treatment for mental disorder from being admitted to any hospital or registered establishment in pursuance of arrangements made in that behalf and without any application, order or direction rendering him liable to be detained under this Act . . .

Approximately 60 per cent of all admissions to hospital are informal (NHS Information Centre, Fifth Report from Mental Health Minimum Dataset Returns (London, Health and Social Care Information Centre, 2011)). The Codes state that informal admission is usually appropriate when a patient who has the capacity to do so consents to admission to hospital. However, they also point out that this is not an absolute rule. It does not apply if the patient presents a clear danger to self or others, and also where reliable evidence of past experience indicates a strong likelihood that they will change their mind about informal admission with resulting risk to their own health or safety or to that of other people (English Code of Practice, paras.4.9–4.12; Welsh Code of Practice, paras.2.28–2.29). The English Code warns that the threat of detention must not be used to induce a patient to consent as it is likely to invalidate any apparent consent (para.4.12).

Informal patients are in theory free to leave hospital at any time (they need not seek permission from their doctor, approved clinician, or anyone else). However, the doctor's or nurse's holding power under MHA 1983, s.5 may be invoked to prevent an informal patient from leaving hospital (see **4.4**). The English Code states that 'Patients should not be admitted informally with the sole intention of then using the holding power' (para.12.7) and also advises that (para.2.45):

> [Informal] patients should be made aware of their legal position and rights. Local policies and arrangements about movement around the hospital and its grounds must be clearly explained to the patients concerned. Failure to do so could lead to a patient mistakenly believing that they are not allowed freedom of movement, which could result in an unlawful deprivation of their liberty.

A patient may be deprived of liberty by detention under MHA 1983, or by use of the Deprivation of Liberty Safeguards under MCA 2005, which are considered briefly below.

4.2 DEPRIVATION OF LIBERTY SAFEGUARDS

The Deprivation of Liberty Safeguards (DoLS) in MCA 2005, Sched.A1 were introduced in 2009 to comply with the ruling of the European Court of Human Rights (ECtHR) in *HL* v. *United Kingdom* (2004) 40 EHRR 761, that a patient who lacked capacity to consent to admission but was not resisting admission was entitled to the protection of ECHR, art.5. Therefore any admission in circumstances amounting to a deprivation of liberty had to be carried out in accordance with a procedure prescribed by law, and art.5(4) required that the person had to be able, either themselves or through a proxy, to challenge detention before a court with the power to order discharge.

The DoLS procedures were introduced under MCA 2005 rather than under MHA 1983 because there was strong pressure to avoid using the allegedly stigmatising procedures of the Mental Health Act to detain people who lack capacity solely because of learning disability or mental illnesses associated with old age. The DoLS procedures differ from MHA 1983 detention in that MCA 2005 deprivation of liberty may take place in a hospital *or* a care home, and the person must lack capacity in relation to the question whether or not he should be accommodated in the hospital or care home for the purpose of being given the relevant care or treatment (MCA 2005, Sched.A1, para.15).

If the decision to use the DoLS is made, the 'managing authority' of the hospital or care home where the incapacitated person is or is about to be deprived of his liberty will be responsible for requesting authorisation for deprivation of liberty from 'the supervisory body'.[1] There are two types of DoLS authorisation: a standard authorisation for up to 12 months, renewable (Sched.A1, para.24), or an urgent authorisation. An urgent authorisation for up to seven days (extendable only once) may be granted by the managing authority to itself, but it must apply for a standard authorisation at the same time (Sched.A1, para.69).

The supervisory body will then arrange for assessments to be carried out to determine whether the six qualifying requirements are met in the case of the person who is to be made subject to the DoLS authorisation. These are as follows:

- The person must be over 18.
- The person is suffering from mental disorder. A person with a learning disability who does not have abnormally aggressive or seriously irresponsible conduct may be deprived of liberty under the DoLS procedure. The exclusions in relation to addiction to alcohol or drugs do not apply to the DoLS procedure (Sched.A1, paras.13, 14).
- The person lacks capacity in relation to the question whether or not he should be accommodated in the relevant hospital or care home for the purpose of being given the relevant care or treatment (Sched.A1, para.15).
- The person must be eligible in accordance with MCA 2005, Sched.1A. The grounds of ineligibility include that the person is already detained under MHA 1983, s.2 or s.3 or is 'within the scope of the 1983 Act', i.e. an application under s.2 or s.3 could be made in respect of him (see below).
- It must be necessary in the person's best interests to be a detained resident in order to prevent harm to himself, and detention must be a proportionate response to (a) the likelihood of the person suffering harm, and (b) the seriousness of that harm (Sched.A1, para.16).
- There must be no refusals. The 'no refusals' requirement will be met unless (a) the person has, when capable, made a valid advance decision refusing some or all of the treatment which would be provided if the authorisation were to be granted; or (b) the proposed placement of the person in a hospital or care home would conflict with a valid decision of an attorney or a deputy appointed by the court (Sched.A1, para.17).

In relation to the eligibility requirement, the provisions of MCA 2005, Sched.1A are highly complex. As a general rule, where the intention is to provide treatment for mental disorder rather than physical disorder in circumstances amounting to a

---

[1]   In England the supervisory body for hospitals is the Primary Care Trust (but this will transfer to the relevant local authority when PCTs are abolished in 2013). In Wales it is the National Assembly for Wales. In both jurisdictions the supervisory body for care homes is the local authority. MCA 2005, Sched.A1, paras.171–172.

deprivation of liberty, MHA 1983 should be used. (For a more detailed discussion of eligibility, see P. Fennell, *Mental Health: Law and Practice* (2nd edn, Bristol, Jordans, 2011), paras.6.83–6.85.) Although the decision as to which legal framework to use is a judgment for the professionals concerned, they must bear in mind the comments of Charles J in *GJ* v. *A Foundation Trust, A Primary Care Trust and the Secretary of State for Health* [2009] EWHC 2972 (Fam), that the deeming provisions in Sched.1A are:

> strong pointers in favour of the conclusions that (a) the MHA 1983 is to have primacy when it applies, and (b) the medical practitioners referred to in ss.2 and 3 of the MHA 1983 cannot pick and choose between the two statutory regimes as they think fit having regard to general considerations (e.g. the preservation or promotion of a therapeutic relationship with [the patient]) that they consider render one regime preferable to the other.

Patients subject to the DoLS procedures are not entitled to a tribunal hearing. Their safeguards are via the supervisory body and the Court of Protection. The supervisory body must appoint a representative for a person in respect of whom a standard authorisation has been issued (MCA 2005, Sched.A1, para.139). The role of the representative is to maintain contact with the person and to support and represent them in matters relating to their deprivation of liberty, which may include asking the supervisory body to review the authorisation (MCA 2005, Sched.A1, para.95) or applying to the Court of Protection under MCA 2005, s.21A to seek termination or variation of a standard or an urgent authorisation. The supervisory body is also required by MCA 2005, s.39D to instruct an independent mental capacity advocate (IMCA) to help the person or their representative to exercise their rights.

4.3 CHILDREN: INFORMAL ADMISSION AND ADMISSION BY PARENTAL CONSENT

There is no minimum age limit for detention or subjection to a community treatment order (CTO) under MHA 1983, although no one under 16 may be subject to guardianship under the Act. There are some differences in the law, depending on the age of the child and their ability to make decisions for themselves.

4.3.1 16- or 17-year-olds

Young people aged 16–17 with capacity can make their own arrangements for informal admission to hospital notwithstanding that one or more other people have parental responsibility for them (MHA 1983, s.131(2)–(3)). If a 16- or 17-year-old patient does not consent to informal admission it may not be carried out on the basis of the consent of someone with parental responsibility. If admission to hospital for treatment for mental disorder is necessary in the case of refusal, it will have to be carried out under MHA 1983, Part II, assuming the criteria for detention are met.

4.3.2 Children under 16

Hospitals are likely to be reluctant to admit children under 16 without the consent of someone with parental responsibility, although under common law a child under 16 can consent to treatment and care if he has the necessary maturity and understanding to be capable of consenting (*Gillick* competence; *Gillick* v. *West Norfolk and Wisbech Health Authority* [1986] AC 112). If a child is *Gillick* competent and refusing admission, they should not be admitted on parental consent but instead formal detention should be considered (see also *Storck* v. *Germany* (2005) 43 EHRR 96). If someone under 16 lacks *Gillick* competence, the English Code of Practice advises that (English Code of Practice, paras.36.45–36.46; see also Welsh Code of Practice, chapter 33):

> it will usually be possible for a person with parental responsibility to consent on their behalf to their informal admission . . . Before relying on parental consent in relation to a child who is under 16 and who is not Gillick competent, an assessment should be made of whether the matter is within the zone of parental control.

However, in *RK* v. *BCC* [2011] EWCA Civ 1305 (at [14]) the Court of Appeal held that while an adult may exercise parental responsibility to authorise others to impose restrictions on the liberty of the child, restrictions so imposed must not amount to a deprivation of liberty. Detention engages the art.5 rights of the child and a parent may not authorise the detention of a child.

The 'zone of parental control' is not a term used in family law. Its use in the English Code is intended to assist in identifying the circumstances when parental consent may be relied upon as authority to admit or treat without consent where the patient is under 16, or is 16 or 17 and lacks capacity to consent. The English Code says there are two key questions when deciding whether a particular decision is in the zone of parental control (para.36.10):

- firstly, is the decision one that a parent would be expected to make, having regard both to what is considered to be normal practice in our society and to any relevant human rights decisions made by the courts?; and
- secondly, are there no indications that the parent might not act in the best interests of the child or young person?

The Code recommends that the following factors should be considered (para.36.12):

- the nature and invasiveness of what is to be done to the child (including the extent to which the child's liberty will be curtailed) – the more extreme the intervention, the more likely it will be that it falls outside the zone;
- whether the child is resisting – treating a child that is resisting needs more justification;
- general social standards in force at the time as to the sorts of decisions it is acceptable for parents to make – anything that goes beyond the kind of decisions parents routinely make will be more suspect;

- the age and maturity of the child – the greater this is, the more likely it will be that it should be the child who is taking the decision; and
- the extent to which a parent's interest may conflict with those of the child – this may suggest the parent will not act in the child or young person's best interests.

The zone of parental responsibility applies not only to decisions to admit the child to hospital in circumstances not amounting to a deprivation of liberty, it also potentially applies to parental consent for the child to receive treatment, but this should be confined to non-invasive treatments where the child is not resisting (see *Storck* v. *Germany* (2006) 43 EHRR 96). Patients admitted informally do not have the right to apply to the tribunal for discharge.

4.3.3 Specific statutory duties applicable to children

There are several specific statutory duties which apply to children admitted to a psychiatric hospital, whether informally or under powers of detention. MHA 1983, s.131A places a duty on hospital managers to ensure that the hospital environment of a child patient is 'suitable having regard to his age (subject to his needs)'. MHA 1983, s.140 requires Primary Care Trusts (to be replaced in 2013 by clinical commissioning groups) and Health Authorities to notify the local social services authorities in their area of the hospitals administered by them or otherwise available to them where:

arrangements are from time to time in force:

(a)   for the reception of patients in cases of special urgency;
(b)   for the provision of accommodation or facilities designed so as to be specially suitable for patients who have not attained the age of 18 years.

MHA 1983, s.116 places a duty on each local authority, where a child who is in their care under a care order is admitted to a hospital, independent hospital or care home, to arrange for visits to be made to the child on their behalf. This duty applies whether the admission is 'for treatment for mental disorder or for any other reason'. The local authority is also required to take such other steps in relation to child patients while in the hospital or care home, as would be expected to be taken by their parents.

Sections 85 and 86 of the Children Act 1989 require that when a child is provided with accommodation for a period of three months by any Health Authority, NHS Trust, local education authority, independent hospital or residential care home, the body or the proprietors of the relevant private hospital or home must notify the appropriate local authority. That local authority is then under a duty to take steps to ensure that the child's welfare is safeguarded.

All NHS bodies and the services they contract for have a duty under s.11 of the Children Act 2004 to carry out their functions having regard to the need to safeguard and promote the welfare of children.

Having considered informally admitted patients, those admitted under the DoLS procedures, and children admitted by parental consent, none of whom is entitled to apply to the Mental Health Tribunal, we now turn to consider the powers to detain non-offender patients under MHA 1983 and the opportunities available to challenge detention.

4.4 HOLDING POWERS

(MHA 1983, s.5; English Code of Practice, chapter 12; Welsh Code of Practice, chapter 8)

An application for compulsory admission to hospital may be made notwithstanding that the patient is already an in-patient receiving treatment in hospital for either a physical or a mental disorder. A patient who initially consents to admission but later seeks to leave hospital may be prevented from doing so by means of the holding powers under MHA 1983, s.5(2) or (4), which empower doctors or (where the patient is receiving treatment for mental disorder) approved clinicians or nurses to keep an informal patient in hospital so that an application for compulsory admission can be made. 'In-patient' means any person who is receiving in-patient treatment in a hospital, except a patient who is already liable to be detained under s.2, 3 or 4 of the Act, or who is a supervised community treatment (SCT) patient. This means that if someone subject to SCT has been recalled to hospital and chooses to stay beyond the 72-hour limit consequent to the recall, they may not be detained under s.5(2) or (4) (MHA 1983, s.5(6)). 'In-patient' also includes patients who are in hospital by virtue of a deprivation of liberty authorisation under MCA 2005 (English Code of Practice, para.12.6).

The English Code of Practice states that 'Patients should not be admitted informally with the sole intention of then using the holding power' (para.12.7).

4.4.1 Doctor's and approved clinician's holding power

(MHA 1983, s.5(2); English Code of Practice, 12.2–12.20; Welsh Code of Practice, 8.8–8.18)

Maximum duration of detention: 72 hours from the time when a report is furnished to the person delegated by the hospital managers to receive such reports, or from the time it is put in the hospital's internal mail system.

Criteria: The doctor or approved clinician (AC) in charge of the patient's treatment (or their nominated deputy) must consider that an application ought to be made for compulsory admission under MHA 1983, Part II.

Procedural requirements: The doctor or AC should have personally examined the patient (English Code of Practice, para.12.9; Welsh Code of Practice, para.8.13), and must furnish a report to the hospital managers that an application under Part II ought to be made (Mental Health (Hospital, Guardianship and Treatment) (England) Regulations 2008, SI 2008/1184, reg.4(1)(g) and Form H1; Mental Health (Hospital, Guardianship, Community Treatment and Consent to Treatment) (Wales) Regulations 2008, SI 2008/2439 (W.212), reg.4(1)(g) and Form HO12).

Section 5(2) confers a holding power on the registered medical practitioner or AC in charge of the treatment of an in-patient in any hospital, not necessarily a psychiatric one. If the patient is receiving in-patient treatment for a physical disorder, the person in charge of treatment and therefore entitled to exercise the power in s.5(2) will be a doctor. It is only where a patient is receiving in-patient treatment for mental disorder that they will have an AC. The AC may be a doctor, but the role may also be exercised by a chartered psychologist, a first level nurse, an occupational therapist or a social worker, provided they have acquired the status by demonstrating the prescribed competencies and undertaking an approved AC training course.[2] Doctors or ACs may nominate one, but not more than one, doctor or AC to act for them in their absence (MHA 1983, s.5(3), (3A)). The English Code states that 'Doctors and approved clinicians may leave instructions with ward staff to contact them (or their nominated deputy) if a particular patient wants or tries to leave. But they may not leave instructions for their nominated deputy to use section 5, nor may they complete a section 5 report in advance to be used in their absence'. The Welsh Code provides that 'entries into notes which appear to limit the discretion of the doctor/approved clinician or deputy must be avoided (for example "For section 5(2) if he tries to leave")', but the doctor or AC in charge 'may make an entry to the effect that the use of powers under section 5(2) should be considered if the patient tries to leave' (English Code of Practice, para.12.17; Welsh Code of Practice, para.8.31).

Effect: The holding power ceases when an application under MHA 1983, Part II is made, or when a decision is made by the doctor or AC that no assessment needs to be undertaken, or following assessment a decision is made not to make an application for compulsory admission (English Code of Practice, paras.12.5, 12.19; Welsh Code of Practice, paras.8.5, 8.17). A patient detained under s.5(2) is not subject to the provisions of MHA 1983, Part IV relating to consent to treatment and treatment without consent (MHA 1983, s.6(3)(b)).

Eligibility to apply to the tribunal: Although the Department of Health *Reference Guide to the Mental Health Act 1983* (London, 2008), p.138 refers to patients detained under the 72-hour power of detention in s.4 as having a right to apply for a tribunal hearing, patients subject to the holding power do not. Horne questions whether this is ECHR compliant, but points out that the basis of the distinction appears to be that s.5 patients 'are being "held" for a decision as to whether or not to move onto a s.2 or a s.3, whereas s.4 patients are already being detained "for assessment" and that therefore they are immediately "covered" by s.66' (J. Horne, *Mental Health Tribunals Workbook* (Newcastle, University of Northumbria, 2012), p.35).

---

[2] Mental Health Act 1983 Approved Clinician (General) Directions 2008, issued under National Health Service Act 2006, ss.7, 8 and 273, available at **www.dh.gov.uk**; Mental Health Act 1983 Approved Clinician (Wales) Directions 2008, issued under the National Health Service (Wales) Act 2006, ss.12, 13 and 203.

4.4.2 Nurse's holding power

(MHA 1983, s.5(4); English Code of Practice, 12.21–12.34; Welsh Code of Practice, 8.19–8.31)

Maximum duration of detention: Six hours from the moment the nurse makes the necessary record (English Code of Practice, para.12.24; Welsh Code of Practice, para.8.24).

Criteria: It appears to a nurse registered with the Nursing and Midwifery Council in the field of practice of mental health or learning disability nursing (Mental Health (Nurses) (England) Order 2008, SI 2008/1207; Mental Health (Nurses) (Wales) Order 2008, SI 2008/2441 (W.214)) that:

(a)   the patient is suffering from mental disorder to such a degree that it is necessary for his or her health or safety or for the protection of others that s/he be immediately restrained from leaving hospital; and

(b)   it is not practicable to secure the immediate attendance of a practitioner (or clinician) for the purpose of furnishing a report under s.5(2).

Procedural requirements: The nurse must record in writing on the relevant statutory form the fact that the above criteria are satisfied (Mental Health (Hospital, Guardianship and Treatment) (England) Regulations 2008, SI 2008/1184, reg.4(1)(h) and Form H2; Mental Health (Hospital, Guardianship, Community Treatment and Consent to Treatment) (Wales) Regulations 2008, SI 2008/2439 (W.212), reg.4(1)(h) and Form HO13). The form must be sent as soon as possible to the hospital managers, and a record should be made in the notes of the use of the power, the reasons, and the time of expiry (MHA 1983, s.5(5); English Code of Practice, para.12.31; Welsh Code of Practice, para.8.24).

This power can only be used where a patient is receiving treatment as an in-patient for mental disorder. It cannot be used on a general hospital ward where a patient is receiving treatment for physical disorder. The decision to invoke the power is the personal decision of the nurse, who cannot be instructed to exercise the power by anyone else (English Code of Practice, para.12.25; Welsh Code of Practice, para.8.21).

Effect: The power authorises detention for up to six hours or until the earlier arrival of a doctor or AC who can exercise the holding power under s.5(2). If the doctor or AC then uses that holding power, the maximum period of 72 hours runs from when the nurse first made the record detaining the patient under s.5(4). A patient detained under s.5(4) is not subject to the provisions of MHA 1983, Part IV relating to consent to treatment and treatment without consent (MHA 1983, s.56(3)(b)). There is no right of appeal to a tribunal.

4.5 DETENTION IN A PLACE OF SAFETY

(MHA 1983, ss.135–136; English Code of Practice, chapter 10; Welsh Code of Practice, chapter 7)

Magistrates have two separate powers under MHA 1983, s.135 to grant warrants authorising entry on private premises, either to remove a vulnerable person to a place of safety or to retake patients who have escaped from lawful custody under the Mental Health Acts of England, Wales, or Scotland (see **4.5.2**). Section 136 empowers a police constable to remove a person who appears to him to be suffering from mental disorder from a public place to a place of safety (see **4.5.3**). The purpose of removal to a place of safety is to enable the person to be assessed by an approved mental health professional (AMHP) and a doctor. In *R (Sessay)* v. *South London and Maudsley NHS Foundation Trust and the Commissioner of Police for the Metropolis* [2011] EWHC 2617 (QB), an agreed declaration was made that MCA 2005, ss.5 and 6 allowing restraint to be used to carry out an act of care or treatment on an adult who lacks capacity to consent 'do not confer on police officers authority to remove persons to hospital or other places of safety for the purposes set out in sections 135 and 136 of the Mental Health Act 1983'. In that case, the claimant's removal from her home to hospital by the police was unlawful and breached her rights under ECHR, arts.5 and 8 (Supperstone J, at [4] and [54]).

4.5.1 Place of safety

A place of safety is defined in s.135(6) as residential accommodation provided by a local social services authority, a hospital, a police station, independent hospital or care home for mentally disordered persons, or any other suitable place the occupier of which is willing temporarily to receive the patient. The Codes of Practice (English Code of Practice, para.10.21; Welsh Code of Practice, paras.7.18–7.20) and Home Office Circular 007/2008 *Police Stations as Places of Safety*, para.2.2 contain guidance in similar terms. The English Code provides that:

> A police station should be used as a place of safety only on an exceptional basis. It may be necessary to do so because the person's behaviour would pose an unmanageably high risk to other patients, staff or users of a healthcare setting. It is preferable for a person thought to be suffering from a mental disorder to be detained in a hospital or other healthcare setting where mental health services are provided (subject, of course, to any urgent physical healthcare needs they may have).

In formulating local policy, regard is to be had to the impact different types of place of safety may have on the person and on the outcome of the assessment.

In *MS* v. *United Kingdom* [2012] ECHR 804, the ECtHR found a breach of ECHR, art.3 because of conditions in the police cell where MS was held and because of the delay in admitting him to hospital to receive treatment for his disturbed mental state.

The English Code of Practice states that social services authorities, hospitals, NHS commissioners, police forces and ambulance services should ensure that they have a clear and jointly agreed policy for use of ss.135 and 136, as well as the operation of agreed places of safety within their localities. Staff in each agency must be properly trained and understand their responsibilities to provide prompt assessment and, if appropriate, admission to hospital (para.10.16). The Royal College of Psychiatrists has produced standards on the use of s.136, which the (former) Mental Health Act Commission recommended should 'inform local policies' (see Royal College of Psychiatrists, *Standards on the Use of Section 136 of the Mental Health Act 1983* (College Report CRI49, September 2008); Mental Health Act Commission, *Coercion and Consent: Thirteenth Biennial Report 2007–2009* (2009), para.2.131).

A person who has been removed to one place of safety under s.135 or s.136 may be transferred to another one (or more) within the 72-hour time limit. Hence a person may initially be detained in a police cell but be removed to a hospital for further assessment, still within the authority of s.136. The 72-hour period runs from arrival at the first place of safety (MHA 1983, ss.135(3A)–(3B), 136(3)–(4)).

4.5.2 Removal from private premises to a place of safety

Maximum duration of detention: 72 hours from arrival at the first place of safety. The authority to detain a person under s.135(1) ends as soon as (a) an application under MHA 1983, Part II has been made, or other arrangements have been made for the person's treatment or care; or (b) it has been decided to make no application in respect of them under Part II of the Act or to make other arrangements for their treatment or care. This means that where a doctor has completed an examination of the person prior to the arrival of the AMHP and concludes that the person is not mentally disordered, the person can no longer be detained and must immediately be released. If the doctor considers that the patient is suffering from mental disorder, but that compulsory admission is not appropriate, the person should still be seen by an AMHP to consider what other arrangements for treatment and care may be made (English Code of Practice, para.10.31; Welsh Code of Practice, para.7.10).

Criteria: The criteria for removal under s.135(1) are that an AMHP has reasonable cause to suspect that a person believed to be suffering from mental disorder (a) has been or is being ill-treated, neglected or kept otherwise than under proper control; or (b) is living alone and unable to care for himself.

The criteria for removal under s.135(2) are that a constable or other person authorised to retake a patient who is liable to be taken or retaken has reasonable cause to believe that (a) the patient is to be found on specified premises; and (b) admission to those premises has been refused or that a refusal of such admission is apprehended.

Procedural requirements: A warrant under s.135(1) may be granted where information has been laid on oath before a magistrate by an AMHP stating that the above criteria are met. The magistrate may then issue a warrant authorising a police officer (provided s/he is accompanied by an AMHP and a doctor, MHA 1983, s.135(4)) to enter the private premises identified on the warrant, using force if necessary, and, 'if thought fit', to remove a person to a place of safety with a view to the making of an application under Part II, or of other arrangements for his treatment or care. The Codes of Practice suggest that local authorities should issue guidance to AMHPs on how and when to use the power to apply for a warrant under s.135(1) (English Code of Practice, para.10.7; Welsh Code of Practice, para.7.3). When acting on a s.135(1) warrant, the police officer must be accompanied by an AMHP and a doctor, and the English Code of Practice states that it 'may be helpful if the doctor who accompanies the police officer is approved for the purposes of section 12(2) of the Act', adding that 'Following entry . . ., the AMHP and doctor between them should, if feasible, carry out [on the premises] a preliminary assessment of the person to determine whether they need to be assessed further for an application under the Act or for other arrangements for care or treatment' (paras.10.3–10.4).

A warrant under s.135(2) may be granted when a constable or other person with a power to retake a patient lays information on oath before a magistrate stating that the s.135(2) criteria are met. The English Code of Practice lists the groups of patients who are considered to be absent without leave for the purposes of MHA 1983, s.18, which include detained patients who have left hospital without leave being authorised under s.17; those who failed to return from authorised leave; SCT patients who failed to attend hospital or who absconded after being recalled; conditionally-discharged patients who have been recalled; or guardianship patients absent without permission from where they are required to live (para.22.2). The police are also empowered to retake patients who escape from a place of safety or any place where they are in lawful custody, or who escape while being taken and conveyed (MHA 1983, s.138).

Effect: Patients detained in a place of safety under s.135 are not subject to the provisions of MHA 1983, Part IV relating to consent to treatment and treatment without consent (MHA 1983, s.56(3)(b)).

Eligibility to apply to the tribunal: Patients detained in a place of safety under s.135 do not have a right to apply for review of their detention before a tribunal.

4.5.3 Police constable's power to remove from a public place to a place of safety

Maximum duration of detention: 72 hours from arrival at the first place of safety. The authority to detain a person under s.136 ends as soon as (a) an application under MHA 1983, Part II has been made, or other arrangements have been made for the person's treatment or care; or (b) it has been decided to make no application under Part II of the Act or make other arrangements for their treatment or care. This means that where a doctor has completed an examination of such a person prior to the arrival of the AMHP and concludes that the person is not mentally disordered, the person can no longer be detained and must immediately be released. If the doctor considers that the patient is suffering from mental disorder, but that compulsory admission is not appropriate, the person should still be seen by an AMHP to consider what other arrangements for treatment and care may be made (English Code of Practice, para.10.31; Welsh Code of Practice, para.7.10).

Criteria: It appears to a constable (meaning any police officer) that a person is suffering from mental disorder and is in immediate need of care or control, and the constable thinks it is necessary in that person's interests or for the protection of others to take that person to a place of safety.

Procedural requirements: If a constable finds a person who appears to be mentally disordered in 'a place to which the public have access' and the above criteria are met, that person can be removed to a place of safety. The person need not be diagnosed by a doctor as mentally disordered; the constable need only have a reasonable belief that the patient suffers from mental disorder. The purpose of removal is to enable the person to be examined by a doctor and interviewed by an AMHP and for any necessary arrangements for his treatment or care to be made. The power is exercisable only in 'a place to which the public have access', and the English Code notes that it does not matter whether access is 'by payment or otherwise' (para.10.12).

The Police and Criminal Evidence Act (PACE) 1984 preserves the power to remove under s.136(1) as a power of arrest, which allows PACE 1984, s.32 to apply, empowering a police officer to search a person at a place other than a police station (PACE 1984, ss.26, 32, Sched.2). Where an individual has been arrested by the police under s.136 he is entitled to have another person informed of his arrest and whereabouts, and where he is detained in a police station as the place of safety he has a right of access to legal advice. Code of Practice C issued under PACE 1984 ('PACE Code C') governs the detention, treatment and questioning of persons by police officers, and applies to people removed to a police station under s.136.

Effect: Patients detained in a place of safety under s.136 are not subject to the provisions of MHA 1983, Part IV relating to consent to treatment and treatment without consent (MHA 1983, s.56(3)(b)).

Eligibility to apply to the tribunal: Patients detained in a place of safety under s.136 do not have a right to apply for review of their detention before a tribunal.

4.6   EMERGENCY ADMISSION FOR ASSESSMENT

(MHA 1983, s.4; English Code of Practice, chapter 5; Welsh Code of Practice, 5.5–5.12)

Maximum duration: 72 hours from the time of the admission, unless the second medical recommendation required by MHA 1983, s.2 is furnished to the managers within that period. The effect of a conversion from detention under s.2 to detention under s.4 is that the 28-day authority to detain under s.2 is deemed to have begun to run from the time of admission under s.4.

Criteria:

1.   The patient must be suffering from mental disorder of a nature or degree which warrants his detention in hospital for assessment or for assessment followed by medical treatment for at least a limited period; and

2.   the patient ought to be detained in the interests of his health or safety or for the protection of other persons; and

3.   it must be of urgent necessity that the patient is admitted for assessment and that full compliance with the provisions for admission for assessment under s.2 would involve undesirable delay.

Procedural requirements: An application by an AMHP or by the patient's nearest relative supported by one medical recommendation, which should, if practicable, be given by a doctor who has previous acquaintance with the patient. The doctor need not be approved under MHA 1983, s.12 as having special experience in the diagnosis or treatment of mental disorder. The applicant must have seen the patient personally within the previous 24 hours, and the authority to take and convey the patient to hospital extends for no longer than 24 hours from the time when the medical examination was carried out or the application made, whichever is the earlier (MHA 1983, ss.4(5), 6(1)(b), and 11(5)). The applicant must certify that the admission is of urgent necessity and that compliance with s.2 would involve undesirable delay. The medical recommendation must give information clarifying the nature of the emergency, requiring the doctor to estimate the delay which would be involved if the full requirements of s.2 were to be complied with, and to specify the harm to the patient or to other people which might result from such delay (see Mental Health (Hospital, Guardianship and Treatment) (England) Regulations 2008, SI 2008/1184 and Mental Health (Hospital, Guardianship, Community Treatment and Consent to Treatment) (Wales) Regulations 2008, SI 2008/2439 (W.212)). The Codes state that s.4 should never be used for administrative convenience. In determining whether there is a genuine emergency, the applicant and doctor should have evidence of (English Code of Practice, paras.5.5–5.6; Welsh Code of Practice, paras.5.6–5.7):

- an immediate and significant risk of mental or physical harm to the patient or to others; or
- danger of serious harm to property; or
- a need for physical restraint of the patient.

The English Code makes clear the responsibility of NHS Commissioners to ensure that doctors are available to respond to requests for assessment in a timely manner, and that if AMHPs find themselves having to consider making emergency applications because of difficulties in securing a second doctor, they should report that fact to the local social services authority on whose behalf they are acting (paras.5.7–5.8).

Effect: An application under s.4 may be converted into a full s.2 application authorising up to 28 days' detention by the furnishing of the required second medical opinion within the 72-hour period. In such a case, the 28 days' detention permitted under s.2 begins from the time the patient was admitted under s.4. Patients admitted under s.4 are not subject to the provisions of MHA 1983, Part IV, which relate to consent to treatment, until the second medical recommendation has been furnished and received by the hospital managers (MHA 1983, s.56(3)(a)).

Eligibility to apply to the tribunal: An application under s.4 is an application for admission for assessment. Patients admitted for assessment have the right to apply to a tribunal within the first 14 days of detention for assessment (MHA 1983, s.66(1)(a), (2)(a)). A patient may therefore make an application to the tribunal during the currency of the 72 hours' detention permitted by s.4. If the second medical recommendation is not furnished, the application to the tribunal will lapse, because the patient is no longer liable to be detained for assessment.

4.7 ADMISSION FOR ASSESSMENT

(MHA 1983, s.2; English Code of Practice, 4.1–4.8; Welsh Code of Practice, chapter 5)

Maximum duration: 28 days, non-renewable (*R* v. *Wilson, ex p. Williamson* [1996] COD 42).

Criteria:

1. The patient must be suffering from mental disorder of a nature or degree which warrants his detention in hospital for assessment or for assessment followed by medical treatment for at least a limited period; and
2. the patient ought to be detained in the interests of his health or safety or for the protection of other persons.

Procedural requirements: An application by an AMHP or by the patient's nearest relative (NR), either of which must be supported by two medical recommendations. Applications by nearest relatives are extremely rare. Indeed, the English Code of Practice strongly suggests that an application by an AMHP is preferable (para.4.28):

> An AMHP is usually a more appropriate applicant than a patient's nearest relative, given an AMHP's professional training and knowledge of the legislation and local resources, together with the potential adverse effect that an application by the nearest relative might have on their relationship with the patient.

Local social services authorities (LSSAs) have a duty, at the request of an NR, to send an AMHP to interview the patient and to consider the case with a view to making an application for admission (MHA 1983, s.13(4)). If, in such a case, the AMHP does not make an application, the NR must be given written reasons for this in a letter which 'should contain, as far as possible, sufficient details to enable the nearest relative to understand the decision while at the same time preserving the patient's right to confidentiality' (English Code of Practice, para.4.80).

The application: The applicant must personally have seen the patient within the 14-day period prior to the application (MHA 1983, s.11(5)). An AMHP who makes an application must interview the patient in a suitable manner and satisfy himself that detention in hospital is in all the circumstances the most appropriate way of providing the care and treatment which the patient needs (MHA 1983, s.13(2)).

The AMHP must take all reasonable steps to inform the NR of the application either before it is made or within a reasonable time thereafter, and must inform the NR of the NR's power to discharge the patient under s.23(2) (MHA 1983, s.11(3)). The NR cannot block a patient's detention under s.2.

In the rare circumstance where the NR makes the application, the hospital managers must inform the responsible LSSA, which must arrange for a social worker to interview the patient and report on his social circumstances. This provision is intended to ensure that in every case of admission for assessment or treatment, there is a social circumstances report available to the managers and the tribunal (MHA 1983, s.14).

Medical recommendations: The application must be supported by medical recommendations given by two doctors, one of whom must be approved by the Secretary of State for Health as having special experience in the diagnosis or treatment of mental disorder. If practicable one recommendation should be given by a doctor who has had previous acquaintance with the patient (MHA 1983, s.12(2)).[3] The English Code states that 'it is preferable that a doctor who does not have previous acquaintance with the patient be approved under section 12 of the Act' (para.4.74). The two doctors must have examined the patient either together or within five clear days of each other (i.e. if the first examination was on Wednesday, the second must take place by the following Tuesday) (MHA 1983, s.12(1)).

Regulations deal with the issue of conflict of interest which preclude an AMHP from making an application or a doctor from giving a medical recommendation. The regulations specify the circumstances where a conflict may arise as the result of financial reasons, business reasons, professional reasons or by reason of personal relationship (Mental Health (Conflicts of Interest) (England) Regulations 2008, SI 2008/1205; Mental Health (Conflicts of Interest) (Wales) Regulations 2008, SI 2008/2440 (W.213)).

Effect: Patients detained under s.2 may be given treatment for mental disorder without their consent subject to the provisions of MHA 1983, Part IV. Leave of absence from hospital must be authorised by the responsible clinician (under s.17).

Eligibility to apply to the tribunal: A patient detained under s.2 has the right to apply to the tribunal for discharge once within the first 14 days following admission, which is extended until the next day on which the tribunal office is open if the

---

[3] The forms for the medical recommendations are set out in Mental Health (Hospital, Guardianship and Treatment) (England) Regulations 2008, SI 2008/1184 and Mental Health (Hospital, Guardianship, Community Treatment and Consent to Treatment) (Wales) Regulations 2008, SI 2008/2439 (W.212).

tribunal office is closed on the fourteenth day (MHA 1983, s.66(1)(a), (2)(a)).[4] The hearing must take place within seven days of the tribunal receiving the application (Tribunal Procedure (First-tier Tribunal) (Health Education and Social Care Chamber) Rules 2008, SI 2008/2699 ('English Rules'), rule 37(1)); MHRT for Wales Rules 2008, SI 2008/2705 ('Welsh Rules'), rule 24(1)).

4.8 ADMISSION FOR TREATMENT

(MHA 1983, s.3; English Code of Practice, chapter 4; Welsh Code of Practice, chapter 5)

Maximum duration: Six months, renewable for a further six months and then renewable for periods of 12 months at a time (MHA 1983, s.20(1), (2)).

Criteria:

1. The patient must be suffering from mental disorder of a nature or degree which makes it appropriate for the patient to receive medical treatment in a hospital; and

2. it must be necessary in the interests of the patient's health or safety or for the protection of other persons that he should receive such treatment and it must be the case that the treatment cannot be provided unless he is detained under this section; and

3. treatment must be available for the patient which is 'appropriate in his case, taking into account the nature and degree of the mental disorder and all other circumstances of his case'.

The requirement in (2), that the treatment which the patient needs cannot be provided unless he is detained under s.3, was considered in *R* v. *Hallstrom, ex p. W (No. 2)* [1986] 2 All ER 306, where McCullough J said that (at 315b):

> Admission for treatment under s. 3 is intended for those whose mental condition is believed to require a period of treatment as an in-patient. It may be that such patients will also be thought to require a period of out-patient treatment thereafter, but the concept of 'admission for treatment' has no applicability to those whom it is intended to admit and detain for a purely nominal period, during which no necessary treatment will be given.

---

[4] In *R (Modaresi)* v. *Secretary of State for Health* [2011] EWCA (Civ) 1359, the Court of Appeal considered rule 32 of the Tribunal Procedure (First-tier Tribunal) (Health, Education and Social Care Chamber) Rules 2008, SI 2008/2699 ('English Rules') which provided that such an application 'must be . . . (c) sent or delivered to the tribunal so that it is received within the time specified in the Mental Health Act 1983'. The Court of Appeal held that para.12 of the Rules applied, which provided that 'If the time specified by these Rules . . . ends on a day other than a working day, the act is done in time if it is done on the next working day'.

Procedural requirements: An application by an AMHP or (rarely) by the patient's nearest relative, either of which must be supported by two medical recommendations (MHA 1983, s 11(1)).[5] The provisions relating to making an application in relation to admission for assessment (see **4.7**) also apply to admission for treatment except that when applying under s.3, the AMHP must consult the NR; but the requirement to consult the NR does not apply if it appears that to do so would not be reasonably practicable (English Code of Practice, paras.4.59–4.60)[6] or would involve unreasonable delay. Detention under s.3 may not take place if the NR objects (MHA 1983, s.11(4)), although an application to displace an NR who objects unreasonably to the patient's admission under s.3 may be made to the county court under s.29. Where the patient is already detained under s.2 and it is proposed to detain him/her under s.3 but the NR is thought to be unreasonably objecting, detention under s.2 is automatically extended while displacement proceedings are taken in the county court and will continue until those proceedings are concluded.

The provisions relating to medical recommendations are fuller than those which apply to admission for assessment (see **4.7**); each recommendation must state the grounds of the doctor's opinion and each must state whether there are other methods of dealing with the patient and, if so, why these are not appropriate (Mental Health (Hospital, Guardianship and Treatment) (England) Regulations 2008, SI 2008/1184, and Mental Health (Hospital, Guardianship, Community Treatment and Consent to Treatment) (Wales) Regulations 2008, SI 2008/2439 (W.212)). The recommendations must also identify where the 'appropriate medical treatment' is available.

Effect: MHA 1983, Part IV applies to patients detained under s.3, which means they may be given treatment for mental disorder without their consent in circumstances set out in ss.58, 58A, 62 and 63. Detention is renewable under s.20 by the responsible clinician (RC) furnishing a report to the hospital managers. The RC may grant leave to the patient under s.17 and has the power to discharge the patient under s.23. MHA 1983, s.117 places a duty jointly on Health Authorities and social services authorities, in co-operation with relevant voluntary agencies, to provide after-care services for patients who have been detained in hospital for treatment under s.3 and who cease to be detained and leave hospital. Patients are entitled to s.117 community care services free of charge (*R* v. *Manchester City Council, ex p. Stennett* [2002] UKHL 34, [2002] 4 All ER 124 (HL)). Patients who are liable to be detained under s.3 are eligible to be placed on a community treatment order under

---

[5] The forms are set out in Mental Health (Hospital, Guardianship and Treatment) (England) Regulations 2008, SI 2008/1184 and Mental Health (Hospital, Guardianship, Community Treatment and Consent to Treatment) (Wales) Regulations 2008, SI 2008/2439 (W.212).

[6] The word 'practicable' was interpreted in *R (E)* v. *Bristol City Council* [2005] EWHC 74 (Admin) as having to take account of the wishes, health and wellbeing of the patient. Bennett J counselled caution before removing the important role of the NR on grounds of practicability. However, the relative should not be consulted if it were likely to be detrimental to the patient or an infringement of their right to respect for private life under ECHR, art.8.

MHA 1983, ss.17A–17G (MHA 1983, s.17A(2)). Patients' rights to community care and compulsory community powers are discussed further in **Chapter 6**.

Eligibility to apply to the tribunal: A patient detained under s.3 has the right to apply to the tribunal for discharge once within the first six months following admission, once in the following six months, and thereafter once in each 12-month period for which the detention is renewed (MHA 1983, s.66(1)(b), (2)(b), and s.66(1)(f), (2)(f)). Patients who are transferred from guardianship to hospital may apply within six months of the transfer, and once during each period where detention is renewed. In such cases the renewal date is six months from the date of acceptance of the original guardianship application (MHA 1983, s.66(1)(e), (2)(e) and s.19(2)(d)). Patients detained under s.3 are eligible for tribunal review of their case on their own application or in certain circumstances that of their nearest relative, or on a reference by the hospital managers or the Secretary of State for Health (discussed at **4.13** and **4.14**).

4.9 ADMISSION UNDER MENTAL HEALTH ACT 1983, S.2 OR S.3?

In ECHR terms, for detention under either s.2 or s.3, the patient must be suffering from mental disorder of a kind or degree warranting confinement. Beyond that the criteria are subtly but significantly different. A key difference between the scope of the respective sections is that a patient with a learning disability may not be detained under s.3 unless the disorder is associated with abnormally aggressive or seriously irresponsible conduct on his part (see **3.7.1**). For other patients, the English Code states that 'An application for detention can be made under either section' (para.4.25) and sets out the criteria for deciding which section to use.

Section 2 should be used if the full extent of the nature and degree of the person's condition is unclear, or if there is a need to carry out an in-patient assessment in order to formulate a treatment plan or to assess whether the patient will accept treatment on a voluntary basis following admission. Admission for assessment may also be used where a patient is known to the service but there is a need to carry out a new in-patient assessment in order to reformulate a treatment plan, or to reach a judgment about whether the patient will accept treatment on a voluntary basis.

Use of s.3 is recommended if the patient is already detained under s.2 (which cannot be renewed) or the nature and current degree of the patient's mental disorder, the essential elements of the treatment plan to be followed and the likelihood of the patient accepting treatment on a voluntary basis are already established (English Code of Practice, paras.4.25–4.27).

The Welsh Code states that a decision on which procedure to use should not be influenced in favour of s.2 by the fact that detention for assessment will bring quicker access to a tribunal, or that the patient's nearest relative objects to admission and may therefore block detention under s.3, or be influenced in favour of s.3 by the fact that the power to impose supervised community treatment is only available for patients detained for treatment (para.5.3).

4.10 POWERS TO DISCHARGE PATIENTS DETAINED UNDER MENTAL HEALTH ACT 1983, PART II

4.10.1 Responsible clinician's power of discharge

(MHA 1983, s.23(2); English Code of Practice, 29.15–29.17; Welsh Code of Practice, 12.26–12.28)

Hospital managers must ensure that patients detained for assessment or treatment are allocated an appropriate responsible clinician (RC), defined as the approved clinician (AC) with overall responsibility for the patient's case (MHA 1983, s.34). The RC has the power under MHA 1983, s.23(2) to discharge a patient from detention under Part II by order in writing. In *R (Wirral Health Authority and Wirral Borough Council)* v. *Dr Finnegan and DE* [2001] EWHC (Admin) 312, [2001] MHLR 66, Scott Baker J observed (at [68]) that:

> There are no statutory criteria governing the exercise of this power. Its exercise is wholly within the [RC's] discretion subject . . . to the usual restrictions of lawfulness and so forth . . . If . . . exercised for reasons based on error of law it is subject to challenge by judicial review.

Before the decision is taken to discharge, the RC is responsible for ensuring, in consultation with the other professionals concerned, that the patient's needs for health and social care are fully assessed and the care plan addresses them (English Code of Practice, para.27.10; Welsh Code of Practice, para.31.9). The RC is also responsible for ensuring that a proper assessment is made of risks to the patient or other people and that plans, services and support are available to manage those risks. Consideration should be given to the after-care needs of the patient under s.117, and whether a patient being discharged from detention meets the criteria for guardianship or a CTO (discussed in **Chapter 6**).

In *Winterwerp* v. *The Netherlands,* the ECtHR held that the validity of continued confinement depends on the continued existence of mental disorder of a nature or degree warranting compulsion. In *R (C)* v. *Mental Health Review Tribunal and South West Region* [2000] MHLR 220, at [20], Scott Baker J held that the RC has a continuing duty to consider whether the admission criteria remain satisfied. The English Code of Practice also stresses that RCs must keep under review the appropriateness of exercising the discharge power (para.29.16):

> Because responsible clinicians have the power to discharge patients, they must keep under review the appropriateness of using that power. If, at any time, responsible clinicians conclude that the criteria which would justify renewing a patient's detention or extending the patient's SCT (as the case may be) are not met, they should exercise their power of discharge. They should not wait until the patient's detention or SCT is due to expire.

The English and the Welsh regulations require that an RC's order for discharge must, as soon as practicable after it is made, be sent to the hospital managers (Mental Health (Hospital, Guardianship and Treatment) (England) Regulations

2008, SI 2008/1184, rule 18; Mental Health (Hospital, Guardianship, Community Treatment and Consent to Treatment) (Wales) Regulations 2008, SI 2008/2439 (W.212), rule 7).

4.10.2 Nearest relative's power of discharge

(MHA 1983, s.23; English Code of Practice, 29.18–29.23; Welsh Code of Practice, 23.9)

MHA 1983, s.26(1) provides that 'relative' means any of the following persons:

(a)   husband, wife or civil partner;
(b)   son or daughter;
(c)   father or mother;
(d)   brother or sister;
(e)   grandparent;
(f)   grandchild;
(g)   uncle or aunt;
(h)   nephew or niece.

Subject to some exceptions, the 'nearest relative' (NR) is generally the person who appears first on this list and, if there is more than one relative falling within the same category, the eldest takes priority. The definition of 'husband', 'wife' or 'civil partner' includes a person with whom the patient has been living as husband or wife or civil partner for not less than six months, although such a person cannot take precedence over a husband, wife or civil partner unless there has been a separation or desertion. Any person who has resided with the patient for five years or more or is caring for the patient is counted as a relative (MHA 1983, s.26).[7] A relative who ordinarily resides with or cares for the patient will take precedence over any other relative, even a spouse (s.26(4)). If the patient is ordinarily resident in the United Kingdom and the person who would be the NR is ordinarily resident abroad, that person is ineligible to be NR by virtue of s.26(5)(a). This exclusion does not apply in a case where the patient him or herself is ordinarily resident abroad.

The NR of a child who is in care is determined in accordance with MHA 1983, s.27 whereby the NR will be the local authority unless the patient is married, in which case it will be the spouse. If the child is subject to guardianship under s.5 of the Children Act 1989, MHA 1983, s.28 applies, and the NR will be the guardian. No spouse can take precedence. If a child is a ward of court an application for compulsory admission requires the leave of the court, as does any application by the NR to the tribunal.

MHA 1983, s.132(4) requires the managers of any hospital or mental nursing home where a patient is detained to take 'such steps as are practicable' to inform the person appearing to be the NR of the patient's rights under the Act, and of his or her

---

[7]   In *Re D (Mental Patient: Habeas Corpus)* [2000] 2 FLR 848 (CA), the Court of Appeal held that the words 'caring for' have their ordinary meaning, and that although care need not have been provided over a long period, it must be more than minimal and must have a quality of continuity.

powers and duties under the Act. This duty applies unless the patient has requested that the relative not be informed of the fact that the admission has taken place. If the patient lacks capacity to request that the information should not be copied to the NR, the information should be provided, unless either the patient has, while capable, refused to allow the information to be imparted, or to do so would be likely to harm the patient. (See *R (E)* v. *Bristol City Council* [2005] EWHC 74 (Admin), [2005] MHLR 83 where it was held for the purposes of MHA 1983, s.11(4) that it would not be 'reasonably practicable' to consult the NR if it would cause harm to the patient and therefore breach his or her rights under ECHR, art.8.)

The NR may authorise another person to perform the functions of NR under the Act. The authority may be revoked at any time (Mental Health (Hospital, Guardianship and Consent to Treatment) (England) Regulations 2008, SI 2008/1184, reg.24 which allows the NR to grant or revoke, in writing, authority to exercise the functions of the NR).

The NR has the power to direct discharge from detention of a patient who is admitted for assessment or for treatment, and to discharge a patient from a CTO (MHA 1983, s.23(2)(a)). Where the NR wishes to discharge a detained or a community patient, not less than 72 hours' notice must be given in writing to the hospital managers. The RC may then, within that period, forward to the managers a 'barring certificate', if he or she considers that the patient, if discharged, would be likely to act in a manner dangerous to self or others. The NR must be informed that the barring certificate has been issued. Its effect is that the discharge order made by the NR is of no effect, and no further discharge order may be made within the six-month period beginning with and including the date of its issue (MHA 1983, s.25; see *Zoan* v. *Rouamba* [2000] 2 All ER 620 (CA)). If the patient is detained under MHA 1983, s.3 (but not s.2), the NR can make an application to the tribunal within 28 days of notification of the issue of the barring certificate, with the tribunal itself subsequently being obliged to apply the 'dangerousness' test (MHA 1983, ss.66(1)(g) and (2)(d) and s.72(1)(b)(iii)).

4.10.3   Hospital managers' power of discharge

(MHA 1983, s.23; English Code of Practice, chapter 31; Welsh Code of Practice, chapter 27)

MHA 1983, s.23 gives hospital managers the power to discharge unrestricted patients from detention. The Codes of Practice provide detailed guidance on the managers' power of discharge. Managers have a duty to ensure that all patients are aware that they may seek discharge by this route, and that they are aware of the distinction between this and their right to a Mental Health Tribunal hearing.

Managers may undertake a review at any time at their discretion. Managers must consider holding a review when they receive a request from a patient or when the RC issues a barring certificate opposing a nearest relative's application for the patient's discharge. They might decide that it is inappropriate to hold a review where one has been held recently and there is no evidence that the patient's condition has changed or where a tribunal hearing either is due soon or has been held recently (English Code of Practice, paras.31.11–31.13; Welsh Code of Practice, paras.27.9–27.13). Managers have a statutory duty to decide whether to exercise their discretion to discharge from detention when the RC submits a report renewing detention. Therefore, a review must be held on renewal, whether or not the patient objects.

The Codes distinguish between contested renewal cases where the patient or NR is disputing the need for detention or SCT, and uncontested cases where they are not. However, the English Code acknowledges that (para.31.40):

> It is for hospital managers to decide whether to adopt a different procedure in uncontested cases. Some hospitals, as a matter of policy, do not differentiate between contested and uncontested cases.

With uncontested cases, the Codes advise that the patient should be interviewed by a single member of the panel if requested, or if the panel think it appropriate. Otherwise managers' panels may consider the case on the papers, but should hold a full hearing if they think there is reason to believe the patient may wish to be discharged, or if there are *prima facie* grounds for thinking that the decision to renew detention or SCT may not be correct (English Code of Practice, paras.31.41–31.42; Welsh Code of Practice, para.27.30). If the panel agrees that the patient should not be discharged the review can be concluded and the outcome recorded in the patient's records. With contested cases the recommended procedure mirrors that of the tribunal, with the crucial difference that the managers do not have the benefit of a medical member of the decision-making panel. For this reason managers are advised not to form clinical assessments of their own, and where there is any divergence of view between the managers and the RC about whether the patient reaches the clinical grounds for continued detention, especially in relation to risk assessment, the panel should consider an adjournment for further professional advice (English Code of Practice, para.31.35; Welsh Code of Practice, para.27.28).

Where a patient is liable to be detained for assessment or for treatment in an independent hospital, the Secretary of State for Health (or Welsh Ministers) has a power of discharge (see **4.14**). If the patient is being cared for pursuant to a contract with an NHS body, the managers of that body have the power of discharge (MHA 1983, s.23(3) and (3A)). The English Code suggests that, where detained patients are placed in an independent hospital under a contract with an NHS Trust, the Trust committee which is appointed to undertake hospital managers' functions should also monitor the way those functions are performed by the managers of the independent hospital, and both sets of managers should co-operate in exercising their respective discharge functions (English Code of Practice, para.31.47).

Where the RC issues a certificate barring discharge by the NR from detention or a CTO, the managers must consider holding a review (English Code of Practice, para.31.11; Welsh Code of Practice, para.27.10). In the course of such a review, the managers have to consider whether there is a risk that the patient would act dangerously to self or others. As the English Code says, this is a 'more stringent test for continuing detention' (para.31.20) since the focus of this question should be 'on the probability of dangerous acts, such as causing serious physical injury . . . not merely on the patient's general need for safety and others' general need for protection' (para.29.21). The Code then suggests that if the managers disagree with the RC and decide the answer to this question is 'no', 'they should *usually* discharge the patient, and in all cases should ensure that a full risk assessment is carried out when considering discharge' (paras.31.19–31.22).

Various key points for the hearing procedure are covered in the Codes. In addition to the RC's renewal report and other documents confirming the renewal criteria are met, written reports must be obtained from the RC, including information about any history of violence or self-harm, a full risk assessment, the history of the patient's care and treatment, and details of the care plan. A copy should be given to the patient unless this is likely to cause harm to the patient or others. The Codes also suggest that:

- the patient should be given a full opportunity, and any necessary help, to explain why he or she wishes to be discharged;
- the patient should be allowed to be accompanied by a friend or representative of his or her own choosing to help in putting his or her point of view to the panel;
- the RC and other professionals should be asked to give their views on: whether the patient's continued detention or continued SCT order is justified, and the factors on which those views are based;
- the patient and the other parties to the review should, if the patient wishes it, be able to hear each other's statements to the panel and to put questions to each other. However, the patient should always be offered the opportunity of speaking to the panel alone.

If the panel concludes that the patient ought to be discharged but arrangements for after-care need to be made, they may adjourn the panel, for a brief period, to enable a full Care Programme Approach (CPA)/care planning meeting to take place.

The managers have a common law duty to give reasons for their decision. The decision and the reasons for it should be recorded, and communicated immediately, both orally and in writing, to the patient, to the nearest relative with the patient's consent, and to the professionals concerned. At least one of the members of the panel should offer to see the patient to explain in person the reasons for the decision (English Code of Practice, paras.31.43–31.44; Welsh Code of Practice, paras.27.31–27.32). Copies of the papers relating to the review, and the formal record of the decision, should be placed in the patient's records.

4.11 ENTITLEMENT OF PATIENTS DETAINED UNDER MENTAL HEALTH ACT 1983, PART II TO TRIBUNAL REVIEW

There are essentially four ways in which a case may come before a Mental Health Tribunal. The most common is on an application by the patient. The nearest relative also has a right in certain circumstances to make an application seeking the patient's discharge. The third route is following a reference by the hospital managers. The fourth is on a reference by the Secretary of State for Health. Each is dealt with in turn.

4.11.1 Patients detained for assessment under Mental Health Act 1983, ss.2 and 4

A patient admitted for assessment under s.2 may apply once within the first 14 days of detention, extended to the next day when the tribunal office is open if it was closed on the fourteenth day (MHA 1983, s.66(1)(a) and (2)(a); see also *R (Modaresi)* v. *Secretary of State for Health* [2011] EWCA (Civ) 1359).

As noted above, a patient detained under s.4 may apply within the 72-hour period of detention authorised under s.4, albeit there will be no hearing during the 72 hours. If the s.4 detention is subsequently converted to a s.2 detention by the acquisition of a second medical recommendation, the application remains 'alive' with the seven days running from the filing of the application while subject to the s.4 detention. If there is no conversion and the patient ceases to be detained, the application is of course treated as lapsed.

The hearing must take place within seven days after receipt of the application by the tribunal office (English Rules, rule 37(1); Welsh Rules, rule 24(1)).

In *R* v. *South Thames Mental Health Review Tribunal, ex p. M* (CO/2700/97) (unreported, 3 September 1997, QBD), Collins J explained a patient's tribunal entitlement where he or she is initially detained under s.2, but then detained under s.3 before the tribunal has heard the application for discharge from s.2. The tribunal in such a case is to hear the appeal as if it were an appeal against detention under s.3, and the patient's right to apply to a tribunal under s.66(1)(b) in the first period of detention under s.3 is unaffected.

4.11.2 Patients detained for treatment under Mental Health Act 1983, s.3

A patient admitted for treatment under s.3 may apply once in the first six months of detention, once during the second six months and thereafter once in every 12-month period for which the detention is renewed (MHA 1983, s.66(1)(b), (2)(b) and s.66(1)(f), (2)(f) and s.20(2)). Patients who are transferred from guardianship to detention in hospital under s.3 may apply within six months of the transfer, and once during each period where detention is renewed. In such cases the renewal date is six months from the date of acceptance of the original guardianship application (MHA 1983, ss.66(1)(e), (2)(e) and 19(2)(d)).

If a patient applies to a tribunal while detained under s.3 but, before the hearing takes place, is made subject to a CTO, the tribunal must hear the application as if it were for discharge from the CTO. In *AA* v. *Chester and Wirral Foundation NHS Trust* [2009] UKUT 195 (AAC), Judge Rowland said this (at [59]):

> In my judgment, there are no reasons for giving section 72(1) of the 1983 Act anything other than a literal construction. A tribunal has the power – or, if the conditions of section 72(1)(c) are satisfied, a duty – to direct that a person subject to a community treatment order be discharged notwithstanding that that person made the application to the tribunal while liable to be detained under section 2 or 3. Therefore, an application to the First-tier Tribunal made by or on behalf of a person detained under section 2 or 3 of the 1983 Act does not lapse if a community treatment order is made in respect of that person before the application is determined.

Judge Rowland went on to emphasise the need for sensible co-operation between the parties and the tribunal where a patient is made subject to a CTO while an application to the tribunal is pending (at [61]):

> In particular, it will clearly be incumbent on any representative of the applicant to inform the tribunal as soon as possible whether or not the application is being withdrawn and it is also clearly incumbent on all parties to inform the tribunal whether or not a postponement of any hearing that has already been fixed will be required in the light of the change of circumstances.

Hence the general common-sense rule is that where a patient's legal status changes from s.2 to s.3, or from s.3 to a CTO or vice versa, the tribunal hears the case as if it were an application in relation to the patient's current legal status at the time of the hearing.

4.11.3 Patients who have been absent without leave

Where a detained patient absents her or himself without leave, and a report under s.21B is furnished by the RC to the managers extending or renewing detention, the patient may apply once within the period for which the detention is extended or renewed. These provisions also apply to community patients who are absent without leave, where a s.21B report is made extending their CTO (MHA 1983, s.66(1)(fa), (1)(faa), (2)(f) and (fza)).

4.12 NEAREST RELATIVE'S RIGHT TO APPLY TO THE TRIBUNAL

Where the NR has sought to discharge the patient from detention for treatment under s.3 (or from a CTO) and the RC has issued a 'barring certificate' on grounds that if discharged the patient would be likely to act dangerously to self or others, the NR may apply for a tribunal hearing within 28 days beginning with the day on which he is informed that the barring certificate has been furnished (MHA 1983, s.66(1)(g) and (2)(d)). Although NRs have the power to apply for discharge of patients detained under s.2, if a barring certificate is issued in relation to a s.2 patient, the NR acquires no right to apply to the tribunal for the patient's discharge.

Where an NR applies in response to the RC's barring certificate, the tribunal applies an additional, stricter, test in relation to assessing the lawfulness of continued detention than that which applies if a patient applies for discharge. The tribunal must discharge 'if it is not satisfied . . . that the patient, if released would be likely to act in a manner dangerous to other persons or to himself' (MHA 1983, s.72(1)(b)(iii)). This is based on the principle that the family is permitted to take responsibility (although in practice there is no duty to take any responsibility) for the health needs of their loved one, but they are not entitled to take over the role of protecting society and the patient from dangerous conduct: this is the function of the state. In R v. *Mental Health Review Tribunal for North Thames Region, ex p. Pierce* (1996) 36 BMLR 137, the patient lost her application for discharge since detention for treatment was necessary for her health under s.72(1)(b)(ii), but her mother as NR was successful in obtaining discharge on the grounds that the tribunal was not satisfied that she was likely to act dangerously to herself or to others if discharged.

Where the NR has been displaced by order of the county court on grounds of unreasonable objection to admission for treatment or guardianship or exercising the power of discharge without regard to the welfare of the patient or the public interest, he or she may apply to the tribunal once within every 12-month period during which the order remains in force (MHA 1983, s.66(1)(h) and (2)(g)). An NR displaced on grounds of unsuitability, or being too ill to act as NR, has no right to apply to the tribunal. On an application by a displaced nearest relative, the dangerousness test does not apply, and the patient will only be entitled to discharge if the usual criteria are not met (MHA 1983, s.72(1)(b)(i) and (ii)).

4.13 AUTOMATIC REFERENCES BY HOSPITAL MANAGERS

(MHA 1983, s.68; English Code of Practice, 30.34–30.38; Welsh Code of Practice, 11.34–11.35)

MHA 1983, s.68 requires the hospital managers to refer to the tribunal the case of any patient who has not applied for a hearing (other than as a s.2 patient) within six months from 'the applicable day', which is the day on which the patient was first detained, whether that was under s.2 for assessment, s.3 for treatment, or following a transfer from guardianship (MHA 1983, s.68(5)). The requirement to make referrals also applies to CTO patients (MHA 1983, s.68(1)(c)). There is no duty to refer the case of a s.2 patient to the tribunal unless the period of detention is extended beyond six months by virtue of an application being made to displace the NR under s.29, since the duty to refer does not arise until six months have elapsed since first detention without the patient making an application. As the 1981 White Paper *Reform of Mental Health Legislation* (Cm 8405, 1981), para.24, put it, the purpose of this section is 'to ensure that patients who lack the ability or initiative to make an application to a tribunal . . . have the safeguard of an independent review of their case'.

The duty to refer under the original s.68 arose where the authority to detain was renewed and three years had elapsed since the patient's case was last considered by a tribunal. The amended s.68 breaks the link between renewal and referral. Now there is a duty to refer if three years have elapsed since a tribunal last made a determination in the patient's case (the period is one year if the patient is under 18). The six-month, three-year and one-year periods can be reduced by order made under s.68A by the Secretary of State in relation to hospitals in England, or the Welsh Ministers in relation to hospitals in Wales, but no such orders have as yet been made. Patients who are absent without leave at the point at which they should be referred to the MHT must be referred on their return to hospital (MHA 1983, s.21(3)).

If there is an undetermined reference to the tribunal and the patient has changed status from s.3 to a CTO, the validity of the reference is not affected by the change of status. In *KF* v. *Birmingham and Solihull Mental Health NHS Foundation Trust* [2010] UKUT 185 (AAC), the Upper Tribunal held that:

> [A]ny movement from section 2 to section 3 or to community patient status does not affect the continuing validity of an extant and undetermined application or reference to the First-tier Tribunal. The application or reference still falls to be determined by the tribunal in accordance with the patient's status at the time of the actual hearing and subject to the relevant criteria under section 72(1)(a)–(c).

There is also a duty on the managers to refer the case of a community patient whose CTO is revoked to the tribunal 'as soon as possible after the order is revoked' (MHA 1983, s.68(7)). For further detail, see **6.3.2**.

The procedure for making a reference to the tribunal is set out at **9.3.2**. For the purposes of furnishing information for a reference under s.68, s.68(8) empowers an AC or a doctor authorised by or on behalf of the patient (a) to visit and examine the patient in private; (b) to require the production of any records relating to the detention or treatment of the patient in any hospital or to any after-care services provided for him under s.117; and (c) to inspect those records.

4.14 REFERENCES BY THE SECRETARY OF STATE FOR HEALTH OR WELSH MINISTERS

(MHA 1983, s.67; English Code of Practice, 30.39–30.41; Welsh Code of Practice, 11.36–11.37)

The case of any patient who is liable to be detained under s.2, s.3, s.4 or s.37 may be referred at any time by the Secretary of State for Health, or in Wales the Welsh Ministers, under MHA 1983, s.67. Anyone may request a reference for any reason at any time. The English Code states that: 'Anyone may request such a reference and the Secretary of State will consider all such requests on their merits' (English Code of Practice, para.30.39; see also Welsh Code of Practice, para.11.36). Guidance issued by the Department of Health on s.67 references (*Section 67 of the Mental Health Act 1983: References by the Secretary of State to the First-tier Tribunal* (2010), p.4; see also Welsh Code of Practice, para.11.37) says that in practice they are most commonly made where:

- a patient detained under s.2 misses the 14-day deadline for applying to the tribunal through no fault of their own and there is still time for a hearing to be arranged before the s.2 detention is due to expire; or
- a patient's detention under s.2 has been extended pending resolution of proceedings under s.29 to displace their nearest relative (MHA 1983 does not give patients the right to apply directly to the tribunal in these circumstances).

The guidance goes on to say that these examples do not preclude references being made under s.67 in other situations (p.5).

Details of the procedure for requesting a reference are set out at **9.3.2**. Any request should state the reasons for the request; the length of time since the patient's case was last considered by a tribunal; the length of time before a fresh application or referral can be made; and whether any decision sought falls within the tribunal's jurisdiction, as these are the matters which will be taken into account in deciding whether to make a reference. For the purposes of furnishing information in connection with a reference, any doctor or AC authorised by or on behalf of the patient may, at any reasonable time, visit the patient and examine him in private and inspect any records relating to the detention or treatment of the patient in any hospital or any after-care services provided for the patient under s.117 (MHA 1983, s.67(2)).

The potential importance of the Secretary of State's power to refer in averting breaches of ECHR, art.5(4) is underlined by the case of *MH* v. *Secretary of State for the Department of Health and others* [2005] UKHL 60.[8] MH was severely mentally disabled by Down's Syndrome. She lacked mental capacity to consent to admission. She was admitted under s.2 for assessment when her mother became ill, and she became increasingly disturbed. The plan was to assess MH's needs in hospital and then find a suitable residential placement where she could be received into guardianship under s.7 of the 1983 Act. MH's mother, as her nearest relative, objected to guardianship. Steps were taken to displace MH's mother as nearest relative by application to the county court on the grounds of unreasonable objection. Delays in those proceedings resulted in extending MH's detention under s.2 from 28 days to over two years, and since she had not applied for a tribunal hearing within the first 14 days of her s.2 detention, she had no right, herself or through a proxy, to seek review of the lawfulness of her detention as required by ECHR, art.5(4). MH's lawyers applied for a declaration of incompatibility. Baroness Hale delivered the only speech for a unanimous House of Lords, holding that there was no necessary incompatibility between ss.2 and 29(4) of the 1983 Act and art.5(4) as long as either the county court proceedings were determined swiftly or the Secretary of State referred the case to the tribunal under s.67.

The Codes of Practice now advise hospital managers 'always' to consider requesting referral by the Secretary of State where detention is extended pending a displacement decision and the patient is unable for any reason to make a request.

---

[8] This case is currently awaiting consideration by the ECtHR: see *MH* v. *United Kingdom* (11577/06) [2008] ECHR 181.

The Codes advise that managers should normally seek a reference where (English Code of Practice, para.30.41; Welsh Code of Practice, para.11.37):

- a patient's detention under s.2 has been extended under MHA 1983, s.29 pending the outcome of an application to the county court for the displacement of their nearest relative;
- the patient lacks the capacity to request a reference; and
- either the patient's case has never been considered by the tribunal, or a significant period has passed since it was last considered.

The Codes also advise hospital managers to 'consider asking the Secretary of State to make a reference in respect of any patients whose rights under ECHR, art.5(4) might otherwise be at risk of being violated because they are unable (for whatever reason) to have their cases considered by the Tribunal speedily following their initial detention or at reasonable intervals afterwards' (English Code of Practice, para.30.40; see also Welsh Code of Practice, para.11.37).

4.15 CONCLUSION

This chapter has considered the powers to detain non-offender patients in MHA 1983, Part II, the powers to remove a patient to a place of safety under ss.135 and 136, and the entitlement of patients detained under Part II and their relatives to apply for a tribunal hearing or to have their case referred to the tribunal. **Chapter 5** considers the provisions of Part III relating to the detention of mentally disordered offenders, and the entitlement of offender patients and their relatives to have the patient's detention reviewed before a Mental Health Tribunal.

Offender patients: detention, discharge and review

5.1 PATIENTS CONCERNED IN CRIMINAL PROCEEDINGS

MHA 1983, Part III provides a framework of powers whereby courts may remand or sentence mentally disordered suspects and offenders to hospital, and whereby prisoners needing treatment for mental disorder may be transferred from prison to hospital. The Codes of Practice assert that (English Code of Practice, para.33.2; Welsh Code of Practice, para.32.2):

> People who are subject to criminal proceedings have the same rights to psychiatric assessment and treatment as anyone else. Any person who is in police or prison custody or before the courts charged with a criminal offence and who is in need of medical treatment for mental disorder should be considered for admission to hospital.

Moreover, the Codes make it clear that a prison health care centre is not a hospital within the meaning of MHA 1983. As it is not a hospital and as prisoners are not detained under MHA 1983 they may not be given treatment for mental disorder without consent using the powers and second opinion safeguards in Part IV of MHA 1983 (English Code of Practice, para.33.2; Welsh Code of Practice, para.32.3).

This chapter considers the position of patients who are subject to detention under MHA 1983, Part III. Broadly speaking there are four points at which an offender's mental condition can become relevant to the decision to detain the patient in hospital: at the time of the offence; at the time of the trial; at the time of sentencing; or while the offender is in custody on remand or is serving a prison sentence.

5.2 MENTAL DISORDER AT THE TIME OF THE OFFENCE

5.2.1 Insanity defence

(Trial of Lunatics Act 1883, s.2; Criminal Procedure (Insanity) Act 1964, s.2; Criminal Procedure (Insanity and Unfitness to Plead) Act 1991 (as amended))

Criteria: Section 2 of the Trial of Lunatics Act 1883 provides for a 'special verdict' of not guilty by reason of insanity to be returned for a person charged with an offence who was insane at the time the offence was committed. (For an excellent review of the insanity defence and the defence of diminished responsibility, see R.D. Mackay, 'Mental Disability at the Time of the Offence' in L. Gostin, P. Bartlett, P. Fennell, R. Mackay and J. McHale, *Principles of Mental Health Law* (Oxford, OUP, 2010), pp.720–56.) The definition of insanity remains as laid down by Tindal CJ in the decision of the House of Lords in *McNaghten's Case* [1843–60] All ER Rep. 229 (HL). For the defence to be made out:

> It must be clearly proved that, at the time of committing the act, the accused was labouring under such a defect of reason from disease of the mind that he did not know the nature and quality of the act, or so as not to know that what he was doing was wrong.

A person must be labouring under a very severe defect of reason to be entitled to rely on the first limb of the defence, namely, not to know the nature and quality of their act (the example often given is chopping someone with an axe believing them to be a block of wood). Similarly, there must be a severe defect of reason if someone knows the nature and quality of their act (for example, killing someone), but is relying on the second limb that they did not know that the act was wrong. Professor Ronnie Mackay succeeded in persuading the Royal Court of Jersey in *Attorney-General* v. *Prior* [2001] JLR 146, to adopt a definition of insanity more in keeping with modern medical thinking. A person would be entitled to the insanity defence if:

> at the time of the offence, his unsoundness of mind affected his criminal responsibility to such a degree that the jury consider that he ought not to be found criminally responsible.

However, the *NcNaghten* rules continue to apply in England and Wales, at least for the time being.[1] The insanity defence is rarely used, and is most often used with serious offences against the person. If the offence is homicide, the defence is more likely to plead guilty to manslaughter on grounds of diminished responsibility rather than rely on the insanity defence.

Burden of proof: If the defendant raises the issue, the burden is on him to satisfy the jury on the balance of probabilities. If the issue is raised by the prosecution they must satisfy the jury beyond reasonable doubt that the defendant was insane at the time of the offence.

Procedural requirements: The Criminal Procedure (Insanity and Unfitness to Plead) Act 1991, s.1 requires that a jury shall not return a special verdict except on the written or oral evidence of two doctors, one of whom must be s.12 approved, to the effect that the person suffers from mental disorder. This followed concerns raised by earlier cases where the insanity defence was imposed when the defendant suffered from epilepsy (see *R* v. *Sullivan* [1983] 2 All ER 673 (HL)) or hypoglycaemia (as in *R* v. *Hennessy* [1989] 2 All ER 9 (CA)) rather than what psychiatrists would accept as a true mental disorder in accordance with modern principles of medicine.

---

[1] The Law Commission is reviewing the defences of insanity and automatism and issued a scoping paper in July 2012: Law Commission, *Insanity and Automatism: A Scoping Paper* (TSO, 2012).

Effects: Prior to the enactment of the Criminal Procedure (Insanity and Unfitness to Plead) Act 1991 (which was promoted as a Private Member's Bill as a result of lobbying by the Law Society) all those found 'not guilty by reason of insanity' received the equivalent of a hospital order with restrictions without limit of time. The 1991 Act introduced a more flexible and less draconian regime of disposal options, which was further amended by the Domestic Violence, Crime and Victims Act 2004. The following options are available in the Crown Court[2] following a 'special verdict'.

1. *A hospital order with or without a restriction order*: The 1991 Act originally specified that a person could be subject to an Admission Order which had the same effect as a hospital order with or without restrictions. This meant that a person subject to the special verdict could be sent to a psychiatric hospital even though he was not mentally disordered within the meaning of MHA 1983 (for example, someone with diabetes as in *R* v. *Sullivan* [1983] 2 All ER 673 (HL)). Following concerns that this breached ECHR, art.5 (see R.D. Mackay and C. Gearty, 'On Being Insane in Jersey: the Case of *A-G* v. *Jason Prior*' [2001] Crim. LR 560), the Domestic Violence, Crime and Victims Act 2004 introduced the requirement that there must be medical evidence of mental disorder of a nature or degree which justifies detention in hospital for treatment. Where a hospital order is made in respect of a patient who has been found not guilty by reason of insanity (or unfit to plead, see **5.3.1**) 'it shall be the duty of the managers of the hospital specified in the order to admit him in accordance with it' (Criminal Procedure (Insanity) Act 1964, s.5A(1)(c), as inserted by the Domestic Violence, Crime and Victims Act 2004, s.24; see also *R (DB)* v. *Nottinghamshire Healthcare NHS Trust* [2008] EWCA Civ 1354). Admission to hospital must take place within the 28-day period specified in MHA 1983, s.37(4) (*R (DB)* v. *Nottinghamshire Healthcare NHS Trust* [2008] EWCA Civ 1354). Where the offence is murder, there must be a restriction order without limit of time. The Secretary of State retains the power to grant leave to, and order the discharge of, patients who are subject to a restriction order following an insanity verdict (or a finding of unfitness).

2. *Supervision order*: A supervision order requires 'the supervised person' to be under the supervision of a social worker or an officer of a local probation board ('the supervising officer') for a period specified in the order of not more than two years. Home Office Circular 24/2005, *The Domestic Violence, Crime and Victims Act 2004: Provisions for Unfitness to Plead and Insanity*, para.16, states that 'it will usually be appropriate for an approved social worker [now approved mental health professional (AMHP)] to act as the supervising officer'. The court can make a supervision order only if satisfied that, having regard to all the circumstances of the case, the order is the most

---

[2] MHA 1983, s.37(3) allows a magistrates' court to impose a hospital order without convicting the defendant, if the court is satisfied that the accused did the act or made the omission charged as an offence.

suitable means of dealing with the case, that the supervising officer is willing to undertake supervision and that arrangements have been made for the treatment specified in the order. Treatment may be given for physical or mental disorder, but it may not be administered without consent and there is no sanction for breach. A supervision order may require the supervised person to submit to treatment with a view to the improvement of his mental condition. The court may impose such a requirement only if satisfied on the written or oral evidence of two or more registered medical practitioners, at least one of whom is duly approved, that the mental condition of the supervised person is such as requires and may be susceptible to treatment; but is not such as to warrant the making of a hospital order within the meaning of the Mental Health Act 1983.

3.   *Absolute discharge*: The court may make an order for the absolute discharge of the accused (Criminal Procedure (Insanity) Act 1964, s.5(c), as amended by the Domestic Violence, Crime and Victims Act 2004). Home Office Circular 24/2005, para.18, states that this may be used 'where the alleged offence was trivial and the accused does not require treatment and supervision in the community'.

Eligibility to apply for a tribunal hearing: Special verdict patients subject to a hospital order with or without restrictions have the same entitlement to review by the Mental Health Tribunal as other patients subject to hospital orders. Patients may apply to the tribunal once in the second six months following the making of the order, and thereafter once in every 12-month period. Persons subject to supervision orders do not have the right to seek review before a Mental Health Tribunal.

5.2.2   Diminished responsibility

(Homicide Act 1957, s.2, as amended by Coroners and Justice Act 2009, s.52)

Criteria: The accused must be suffering from an abnormality of mental functioning arising from a recognised medical condition which (a) substantially impaired his ability (i) to understand the nature of his conduct, (ii) to form a rational judgment, or (iii) to exercise self-control; and (b) provides an explanation for the defendant's conduct in that it causes, or is a significant contributory factor in causing, him to carry out that conduct.

Decision-maker: The jury (but the court will accept pleas of guilty to manslaughter on grounds of diminished responsibility except in cases where medical opinion is divided or is open to challenge) (*R* v. *Cox* (1968) Cr. App. R 130 (CA); *R* v. *Vinagre* (1979) 69 Cr. App. R 104 (CA)).

Burden and standard of proof: The defence must satisfy the jury on the balance of probabilities.

Effect: The effect of a successful plea is that a homicide conviction is reduced from murder which carries a mandatory life sentence, to manslaughter where the sentence is within the judge's discretion. However, this does not necessarily mean that a hospital order will be imposed.

5.2.3 Infanticide

(Infanticide Act 1938, s.1)

This defence only applies where a woman, by any wilful act or omission, causes the death of her child aged under 12 months. At the time of the act or omission the balance of the mother's mind must have been disturbed by her not having fully recovered from the effect of giving birth to the child or by reason of the effect of lactation consequent upon the birth of the child. No causal connection is required between the killing and the mental disturbance. Infanticide can either be charged as an offence or be used as a defence to a charge of murder.

5.3 MENTAL DISORDER AT THE TIME OF THE TRIAL

5.3.1 Unfitness to plead

(Criminal Procedure (Insanity) Act 1964, s.4 (substituted by Criminal Procedure (Insanity and Unfitness to Plead) Act 1991 (as amended), s.2)

Criteria: That the defendant is 'under a disability' such that 'it would constitute a bar to his being tried', that is, that he is unable to plead to the indictment; unable to understand the proceedings; unable to instruct a lawyer; unable to challenge a juror; or unable to understand the evidence (*R* v. *Pritchard* (1836) 7 C & P 303; *R* v. *M* [2003] EWCA Crim 3452, approved in *R* v. *Diamond* [2008] EWCA (Crim) 923, at [43]).

Decision-maker: Since the Domestic Violence, Crime and Victims Act 2004 the judge, rather than the jury, determines the issue of whether a defendant is fit to plead.

Burden and standard of proof: The issue of unfitness may be raised at the instance of the defence or otherwise (Criminal Procedure (Insanity) Act 1964, s.4(1)). If the defendant raises the issue, the burden is on him to satisfy the judge on the balance of probabilities. If the issue is raised by the prosecution, the prosecution must satisfy the judge beyond reasonable doubt that the defendant is under disability in relation to the trial. If the issue is raised by the judge and disputed by the defence, the onus will be on the prosecution.

Evidence: The accused cannot be found unfit to plead unless there is written or oral evidence to that effect by two or more doctors, at least one of whom must be approved under MHA 1983, s.12.

Effect: Section 4A(2) of the 1964 Act provides that where the accused is found unfit to plead, the trial shall not proceed. Originally under the 1964 Act, the automatic consequence of a finding of unfitness was that the court had to impose a hospital order with a restriction order without limit of time, and there was no way in which the strength of the prosecution case could be tested. The Criminal Procedure (Insanity and Unfitness to Plead) Act 1991 introduced a new procedure, the 'trial of the facts'. A full trial does not take place, but the jury hear evidence to determine whether they are satisfied beyond reasonable doubt that the defendant did the act or made the omission charged against him as an offence. If so satisfied, they deliver a verdict to that effect; if not satisfied, they are obliged to deliver a verdict of acquittal.

Where a finding of unfitness is followed by a finding that the defendant did the act or made the omission charged as an offence, the disposal options available to the Crown Court[3] are the same as those available in relation to the insanity defence (see **5.2.1** for details), which are:

1. a hospital order, with or without a restriction order;
2. a supervision order; or
3. absolute discharge.

Where the offence is murder, the court must impose a restriction order without limit of time. The Secretary of State for Justice retains the power to prevent discharge of patients who are subject to a restriction order following a finding of unfitness to plead, and such patients cannot be granted leave or transferred to a different hospital without the agreement of the Secretary of State.

Eligibility to apply for a tribunal hearing: Patients found unfit to plead and made subject to a hospital order with or without restrictions following a trial of the facts may apply to the tribunal once in the second six months following the making of the order, and thereafter once in every 12-month period. Persons subject to supervision orders do not have the right to seek review before a Mental Health Tribunal.

5.3.2   Remand for psychiatric reports

(MHA 1983, s.35)

Maximum duration of detention: 28 days with up to two further periods of 28 days for not more than 12 weeks in all.

Criteria: The court must be satisfied that:

(a)   there is reason to suspect that the accused is suffering from mental disorder (a person with a learning disability may not be remanded for reports unless the learning disability is associated with abnormally aggressive or seriously irresponsible conduct on his part); and

(b)   it would be impracticable for a report to be made on his mental condition if he were remanded on bail.

Procedural requirements: Remand by a magistrates' court or the Crown Court on the evidence of one doctor, who must be approved under MHA 1983, s.12(2) as having special experience in the diagnosis or treatment of mental disorder (MHA

---

[3]   MHA 1983, s.37(3) allows a magistrates' court to impose a hospital order without convicting the defendant, if the court is satisfied that the accused did the act or made the omission charged as an offence.

1983, ss.35(3) and 54(1)). No court can make a remand order unless it is satisfied, on the evidence of the doctor or approved clinician (AC) responsible for making the report (MHA 1983, s.35(4)) (or who would be in charge of his case) (MHA 1983, s.36(7)) or some other person representing the hospital managers, that arrangements have been made for the patient's admission to hospital within a period of seven days after the remand order has been made.

The court can extend the remand of someone remanded under s.35 in his absence (as long as he is represented in court) if it is satisfied, on the evidence of the doctor or the AC preparing the report, that a further remand is necessary in order to complete the psychiatric assessment (MHA 1983, s.35(5), (6)).

Effect: The report may be prepared by a doctor or any approved clinician, who might be a nurse, psychologist, social worker or occupational therapist. It should contain a statement of whether a patient is suffering from mental disorder identifying its relevance to the alleged offence. The report should not comment on guilt or innocence, but should include relevant social factors and any recommendations on care and treatment, including where and when it should take place and who should be responsible.

A person remanded for reports or for treatment is entitled to commission at his own expense an independent report from a doctor or any other AC, and to apply to the court for his remand to be terminated (MHA 1983, ss.35(8), 36(7)).

Eligibility for a tribunal hearing: Remand patients have no right to apply for discharge to a Mental Health Tribunal. A person remanded under s.35 is not subject to the consent to treatment provisions in MHA 1983, Part IV (MHA 1983, s.56(1)(b)). The English Code of Practice advises that where a patient remanded under s.35 is thought to be in need of medical treatment for mental disorder under Part IV of the Act, consideration ought to be given to referring the patient back to court with an appropriate recommendation, and with an assessment of whether the patient is in a fit state to attend court (para.33.29). It goes on to suggest that if there is delay in securing a court date, and depending on the patient's mental condition, consideration should be given to whether the patient meets the criteria of s.3 (para.33.30). Consequently, a patient then has a right to apply to the tribunal against detention under the civil powers and could be successful, but still remain detained under the remand power (English Code of Practice, para.33.28; Welsh Code of Practice, para.32.31). (For a critical view see P. Fennell, 'Double Detention under the Mental Health Act 1983: a Case of Extra Parliamentary Legislation' (1991) *Journal of Social Welfare and Family Law* 194.)

5.3.3 Remand for treatment

(MHA 1983, s.36)

Maximum duration of detention: 28 days with up to two further periods of 28 days for not more than 12 weeks in all.

Criteria: The court must be satisfied that:

(a)   the patient is suffering from mental disorder of a nature or degree which makes it appropriate for him to be detained in a hospital for medical treatment (a person with a learning disability may not be remanded for treatment unless the learning disability is associated with abnormally aggressive or seriously irresponsible conduct on his part); and

(b)   appropriate medical treatment is available for him (MHA 1983, s.36(1)).

Procedural requirements: A remand order may only be made by a Crown Court on the medical evidence of two doctors, one of whom must be approved under MHA 1983, s.12(2) (MHA 1983, ss.35(3) and 54(1)). No court can make a remand order unless it is satisfied, on the evidence of the doctor or AC responsible for making the report (MHA 1983, s.35(4)) (or who would be in charge of his case) (MHA 1983, s.36(7)) or some other person representing the hospital managers, that arrangements have been made for the patient's admission to hospital within a period of seven days after the remand order has been made.

Because the sentence is fixed by law, a person accused of murder cannot be remanded for treatment under s.36 (MHA 1983, s.36(2)). However, s.3(6A) of the Bail Act 1976 allows the court to impose the following conditions of bail:

(a)   that the accused must undergo examination by two doctors for psychiatric reports to be prepared; and

(b)   that he must attend an institution or place as the court directs for that purpose and comply with any other directions from the doctors.

Effect: A person remanded under s.36 is subject to the second opinion provisions in MHA 1983, Part IV (MHA 1983, s.56). As with accused persons remanded for reports, a person remanded for treatment is entitled to commission at his own expense an independent report from a doctor or any other AC, and to apply to the court for his remand to be terminated (MHA 1983, ss.35(8), 36(7)).

Eligibility to apply for a tribunal hearing: Patients remanded for treatment have no right to apply for discharge to a Mental Health Tribunal.

5.4   MENTAL DISORDER AT THE TIME OF SENTENCE

Section 157 of the Criminal Justice Act 2003 requires any court to obtain and consider a medical report before passing a custodial sentence on an offender who is or who appears to be mentally disordered within the meaning of MHA 1983. The medical report may be made orally or in writing by a doctor approved under MHA 1983, s.12. However, the obligation is not absolute and does not apply if, in the circumstances of the case, the court is of the opinion that it is unnecessary to obtain a medical report, or in any case where the sentence is fixed by law.

Where the offender appears to be mentally disordered, unless the sentence is fixed by law, the court must consider any information (whether or not it is in a report) relating to the offender's mental condition and the likely effect of a custodial sentence on the person's mental condition and on any treatment which may be available for it. Failure to obtain and consider a report does not invalidate any custodial sentence, but any court considering an appeal against sentence must obtain a medical report if none was obtained by the court below, and must consider any report obtained by it or by the court below.

5.4.1 Interim hospital order

(MHA 1983, s.38)

Maximum duration: 12 weeks in the first instance renewable for 28-day periods up to a maximum of 12 months (MHA 1983, s.38(5)).

Criteria: The court must be satisfied that the offender is suffering from mental disorder, and that there is reason to suppose that the mental disorder is such that it may be appropriate for a hospital order to be made. A person with a learning disability may not be subject to an interim hospital order unless the learning disability is associated with abnormally aggressive or seriously irresponsible conduct on his part.

Procedural requirements: An order may be made by the Crown Court or a magistrates' court on the evidence of two doctors, one of whom must be approved under MHA 1983, s.12 as having expertise in the diagnosis or treatment of mental disorder (MHA 1983, s.38(1)).

The court must be satisfied on the evidence of the AC who would have overall responsibility for the patient's case or the hospital managers that arrangements have been made for the patient's admission to hospital within 28 days (MHA 1983, s.38(4)). The court may renew an interim hospital order after the initial period of 12 weeks and at 28-day intervals thereafter up to a maximum of 12 months on the written or oral evidence of the person appointed to be the responsible clinician (RC). The court may terminate the order if, having considered the evidence of the RC, it decides to deal with the offender in some other way. The court can renew the interim order or make a full hospital order in the absence of the patient, provided he is represented in court (MHA 1983, s.38(2), (6)).

Effect: A patient under an interim hospital order is subject to the consent to treatment provisions in MHA 1983, Part IV.

Eligibility for a tribunal hearing: A patient subject to an interim hospital order is not entitled to seek review of detention before a Mental Health Tribunal. If the patient is made subject to a hospital order under s.37, he will not be entitled to apply for a tribunal hearing until the first six months following the hospital order have elapsed.

5.4.2 Hospital order

(MHA 1983, s.37)

Maximum duration: Six months, renewable for a further six months and thereafter renewable for periods of up to one year at a time.

Criteria: The court must be satisfied that:

(a)   the offender is suffering from mental disorder ('any disorder or disability of the mind') of a nature or degree making it appropriate for him to be detained in hospital for medical treatment (a person with a learning disability may not be subject to a hospital order unless the learning disability is associated with abnormally aggressive or seriously irresponsible conduct on his part); and

(b)   appropriate medical treatment is available for him.

The court must also be of the opinion, having regard to all the circumstances, including the nature of the offence and the character and antecedents of the offender, and to other available methods of dealing with him, that the most suitable method of disposing of the case is by means of a hospital order.

A magistrates' court can make a hospital order without recording a conviction if the person is suffering from mental disorder, and the court is satisfied that he committed the act or made the omission with which he is charged as an offence (MHA 1983, s.37(3)).

Procedural requirements: The Crown Court or the magistrates' court can make an order if the patient is convicted of an offence punishable with imprisonment, except in the case of murder (for which the sentence is fixed by law). Medical evidence from two doctors is required, one of whom must be approved under MHA 1983, s.12. A hospital order cannot be made unless the court is satisfied, on the evidence of the AC who would have overall responsibility for his case or the hospital managers, that arrangements have been made for the patient's admission to hospital within 28 days. Admission to the designated hospital must take place within the mandatory 28-day period specified in MHA 1983, s.37(4), and if this does not happen the hospital order ceases to have effect (*R (DB)* v. *Nottinghamshire Health-care NHS Trust* [2008] EWCA Civ 1354). Hospitals have discretion to decide whether to admit an offender under a hospital order, unless the patient has been found not guilty by reason of insanity or unfit to plead.

In some cases under the Mental Health Act 1959, mentally disordered people were sentenced to imprisonment because hospitals refused to accept them. MHA 1983, s.39 empowers a court considering making a hospital order, an interim hospital order, or a hospital direction with a restriction direction to request the Primary Care Trust (to be replaced in 2013 by clinical commissioning groups (CCGs)) or Health Authority where the person resides or last resided (or any other Health Authority or PCT/CCG which appears to be appropriate) to furnish the court with such information as they can reasonably obtain about the hospital or hospitals in their area or elsewhere where arrangements could be made for the admission of the offender. The Trust or Authority approached by the court must comply with any such request. In relation to a person who is under 18, the duty to provide information arises in relation not only to hospital orders but also to remands under s.35 or s.36 and to committals under MHA 1983, s.44. It also requires that information be provided as to the availability of accommodation or facilities designed to be specifically suitable for patients under 18 years (MHA 1983, s.39(1A)–(1B)).

Effect: A hospital order sentences a mentally disordered person to detention in hospital for treatment rather than in prison. Only the Crown Court can make a hospital order with restrictions on discharge (for the effect of restriction orders, see **5.4.4**). A magistrates' court may only make a hospital order without restrictions, or commit the offender to the Crown Court under MHA 1983, s.43 so that a restriction order can be made. The effect of a hospital order without restrictions is similar to that of admission for treatment of a non-offender under MHA 1983, s.3 (see **4.8**). Detention is renewable under s.20 by the RC furnishing a report to the hospital managers. If the patient is subject to a hospital order without restrictions, the patient's RC may send the patient on leave under s.17, transfer him under s.19 or discharge the patient under s.23, without recourse to the Ministry of Justice Mental Health Casework Section. The other important difference is that a hospital order patient cannot be discharged by his nearest relative. Treatment for mental disorder is subject to the second opinion safeguards in MHA 1983, Part IV.

MHA 1983, s.117 places a duty jointly on Health Authorities and social services authorities, in co-operation with relevant voluntary agencies, to provide after-care services for patients who have been detained under a s.37 hospital order and who cease to be detained and leave hospital. Patients are entitled to s.117 community care services free of charge (*R* v. *Manchester City Council, ex p. Stennett* [2002] UKHL 34, [2002] 4 All ER 124 (HL)). Patients who are liable to be detained under s.37 are eligible to be placed on a community treatment order (CTO) under ss.17A–17G (MHA 1983, s.17A(2), Sched.1, Part 1, para.1). Patients' rights to community care and compulsory community powers are discussed further in **Chapter 6**.

Eligibility for tribunal review: A patient subject to a hospital order without restrictions has the right to apply for discharge to the tribunal on the same basis as a patient detained under MHA 1983, s.3 except that no application is allowed within the first six months after making the order. The logic behind this is that, in contrast to patients detained under s.3, the patient's case was considered by a court when the hospital order was made. Hospital order patients or their nearest relative may apply once during the second six months, and thereafter once in every 12-month period (MHA 1983, s.66(1)(f), (2)(f); s.40(4); s.69(1)(a), Sched.1, Part 1, paras.2, 6, 9). Where the nearest relative applies to the tribunal in relation to a hospital order patient, the tribunal does not apply the 'dangerousness' criterion in s.72 since that criterion only applies if the application is made under s.66(1)(g), whereas an application in respect of a hospital order patient is made under s.69(1)(a).

Although no application to the tribunal may be made within the first six months, a hospital order patient who is not subject to a restriction order can ask the hospital managers to exercise their power of review and discharge during that period (see **4.10.3**) (MHA 1983, ss.23 and 40(3)). The hospital managers have a duty to refer the case of a hospital order patient to the tribunal if a period of three years (one year if the patient is under 18) has elapsed since his case was last considered by a tribunal, whether on his own application or otherwise (MHA 1983, s.68(6), Sched.1, Part 1, paras.2 and 2A). The Secretary of State for Health or the Welsh

Ministers may refer a hospital order patient's case to the tribunal under s.67 at any time (see **4.13** and **4.14**).

5.4.3   Guardianship order

(MHA 1983, s.37)

Maximum duration: Six months, renewable for a further six months and thereafter renewable for periods of up to one year at a time.

Criteria: The offender must be at least 16 years of age and must be suffering from mental disorder of a nature or degree warranting reception into guardianship. The court must be of the opinion, having regard to all the circumstances, including the nature of the offence and the character and antecedents of the offender, and to other methods of dealing with him, that the most suitable method of disposing of the case is by a guardianship order. This gives the court a wide discretion. A person with a learning disability may not be subject to a guardianship order unless the learning disability is associated with abnormally aggressive or seriously irresponsible conduct on his part. The court must be satisfied that the proposed guardian (a local social services authority or 'any other person') is willing to receive the offender into guardianship (MHA 1983, s.37(6)). (See also *R (Pasul Bukowicki)* v. *Northamptonshire County Council* [2007] EWHC 310 (Admin).)

Procedural requirements: The medical evidentiary requirements for making a guardianship order are virtually the same as for making a hospital order. The court enjoys powers to request information similar to those available for hospital order cases. Under MHA 1983, s.39A a court considering making a guardianship order is empowered to request the local social services authority (or any other social services authority considered by the court to be appropriate):

(a)   to inform the court whether it or any person authorised by it is prepared to receive the patient into guardianship; and

(b)   if so, to give such information as it reasonably can about how it or the other person could be expected to exercise guardianship powers.

Effect: The effect of a guardianship order is similar to that of a guardianship application under Part II (see **6.2**), except that the nearest relative has no power to discharge the patient (MHA 1983, s.40(2)). The powers of the guardian are (MHA 1983, ss.8, 40(2), (4), Sched.1, Part 1, paras.2 and 8):

(a)   to require the patient to live at a place specified by the guardian. The person may be taken and conveyed to the place of residence and may be returned there if she or he absconds;

(b)   to require the patient to attend at specified places for medical treatment, occupation, education or training. If the patient refuses to attend, the guardian is not authorised to use force to secure attendance, nor does MHA 1983 enable medical treatment to be administered in the absence of the patient's consent (although it may be given under MCA 2005, ss.5 and 6 if it is necessary to prevent harm to the patient and the patient lacks capacity to consent); and

(c)   to require access to the patient to be given at the place where he or she is living to persons detailed in MHA 1983. A refusal without reasonable cause to permit an authorised person to have access to the patient is an offence under s.129 but no force may be used to secure entry.

MHA 1983, s.18(7) confers a power to take and convey the patient to the place where s/he is required to reside, and there is a power to retake a person under guardianship who absconds from that place. The patient is not subject to the consent to treatment provisions in MHA 1983, Part IV.

Eligibility for tribunal review: The patient may apply for a tribunal hearing once within the first six months of the making of the guardianship order, and the nearest relative (who has no power to direct discharge of the order) may apply once within the 12-month period beginning with the date of the order, and once during each subsequent 12-month period (MHA 1983, s.69(1)(b)). The Secretary of State for Health (or Welsh Ministers) may refer a guardianship order patient's case to the tribunal at any time under MHA 1983, s.67 (see **4.14**). There is no duty on the local social services authority to refer a guardianship patient's case to the tribunal equivalent to the hospital managers' duty to refer the cases of detained patients under s.68.

5.4.4 Restriction order

(MHA 1983, s.41)

Maximum duration: Without limit of time.

Criteria: Where a hospital order has been made, a Crown Court may make a restriction order where it appears to the court, having regard to all the circumstances, including the nature of the offence and the character and antecedents of the offender, and the risk of his committing further offences if set at large, that a restriction order is necessary to protect the public from serious harm. The Court of Appeal in *R* v. *Birch* (1989) 11 Cr. App. R (S) 202 held that the sentencing court is required to assess the seriousness of the risk: not the risk that he will re-offend, but the risk that if he does, the public will suffer serious harm. The harm in question need not be limited to personal injury, nor need it relate to the public in general, but the potential harm must be serious, and a high possibility of the recurrence of minor offences will not be sufficient. There must be evidence of sufficient risk to the public: a risk of self-harm, even severe self-harm, will not be enough to justify a restriction order (*R* v. *Osker* [2010] EWCA Crim 955).

Procedural requirements: A magistrates' court has no power to make a restriction order, but if the criteria are met, it may commit an offender over 14 years of age to the Crown Court where a restriction order can be made. Medical evidence from two doctors is required, one of whom must be approved under MHA 1983, s.12. The evidence of one of the two doctors supporting the hospital order must have been given orally.

Effect: The effect of a restriction order is that the patient's detention is not renewed by the hospital managers. Detention carries on without limit of time. The RC is required to submit a report 'on that person' at least once a year to the Secretary of State for Justice. Treatment for mental disorder of restriction order patients who are detained in hospital is subject to the provisions of MHA 1983, Part IV and the second opinion safeguards therein. The patient cannot be granted leave of absence, transferred or discharged by the RC (or the hospital managers) without the leave of the Secretary of State for Justice (MHA 1983, s.41(3)(c)). These decisions are dealt with by the Mental Health Casework Section (MHCS) within the National Offender Management Service in the Ministry of Justice. The power of discharge may only be exercised by the Secretary of State for Justice through the MHCS, or by the Mental Health Tribunal. The rationale for the Secretary of State's powers is that 'the control of patients who have been found to be dangerous and who are not being punished, should be vested in an authority which would have special regard to the protection of the public' (Ministry of Justice, *Offender Management Caseload Statistics Bulletin* (22 July 2010), p.160).

MHA 1983, s.117 places a duty jointly on Health Authorities and social services authorities in England, in co-operation with relevant voluntary agencies, to arrange for the provision of after-care services for patients who have been detained under a hospital order with restrictions and who cease to be detained and leave hospital. In Wales the duty is on the Local Health Board and the local social services authority in co-operation with relevant voluntary agencies *to provide* (rather than arrange for the provision of) community care services. Patients are entitled to s.117 community care services free of charge (*R v. Manchester City Council, ex p. Stennett* [2002] UKHL 34, [2002] 4 All ER 124 (HL)).

Restriction order patients are ineligible to be placed on a CTO. The equivalent power in relation to a restriction order patient (with 'liability to recall' similarly at its core) is conditional discharge. Discharge of a restriction order patient may be absolute or conditional. If a patient is given an absolute discharge, both the hospital and restriction orders cease to have effect and he cannot be recalled to hospital (MHA 1983, ss.42(2), 73(3)). If a patient is conditionally discharged, the patient may, for example, be directed to live at a specified place or attend for treatment, or accept treatment under the direction of a responsible clinician. It may be a condition of discharge that the patient must accept treatment for mental disorder, but a conditionally-discharged restricted patient cannot be forced to take medication and therefore is not eligible to seek review of treatment by a second opinion doctor under MHA 1983, Part IV.

In *R (SH) v. Mental Health Review Tribunal* [2007] EWHC 884 (Admin), at [2], SH was required by a tribunal to comply with prescribed medication, which is likely to by depot for several years. He argued that this condition was unlawful since it deprived him of his right to choose whether to accept treatment. Holman J refused to quash the condition holding that, despite the existence of the condition (at [35]):

> on each occasion that SH attends, or should attend, for his fortnightly depot injection he has an absolute right to choose whether to consent to it or not. The treating doctor or nurse must, on each occasion, satisfy himself that the apparent consent is a real consent and that the independence of the patient's decision or his will has not been overborne.

Although in deciding whether to consent SH may take into account the condition, '[it] must be read as respecting and being subject to his own final choice, which must be his real or true choice' (at [37]).

The judge recommended that tribunals should in future add to a condition that the patient accept medication that this was 'subject always to his right to give or withhold consent to treatment or medication on any given occasion' (at [42]). The existence of consent is a question of fact. The fact that consent is given in the knowledge that refusal will most probably lead to recall to hospital does not render it invalid.

The nearest relative does not have the power of discharge (MHA 1983, ss.41(3), 40(4), Sched.1, Part II, paras.2 and 7). In fact, in *R (H)* v. *Mental Health Review Tribunal for the West Midlands and North West Region* [2000] MHLR 203, Longmore J held that as a matter of statutory construction, *restricted* patients (including those subject to MHA 1983, s.45A) in effect do not have nearest relatives, and the person who would be the nearest relative has no right to appeal to the tribunal if the patient is subject to a restriction order under s.41, a restriction direction under s.49 or a hospital direction with a limitation direction under s.45A (see below).

A conditionally-discharged restricted patient may be recalled to hospital by the Secretary of State for Justice at any time while the restriction order is in force (MHA 1983, s.42(3)). The Ministry of Justice *Guidance on Recall of Conditionally Discharged Restricted Patients* (2009) states that the MHCS should be notified by the RC of a conditionally-discharged patient in any case where there appears to be a risk to the public, the patient is unwilling to co-operate with supervision, or the patient needs further in-patient treatment. Non-compliance with medication could well amount to non-co-operation with supervision. Unless it is an emergency recall, in order to comply with ECHR, art.5, there must be medical evidence of mental disorder warranting confinement (*Kay* v. *United Kingdom* (1994) 40 BMLR 20).

In *R (MM)* v. *Secretary of State for the Home Department* [2007] EWCA Civ 687, the Court of Appeal held that breach of a condition was not a free-standing ground for ordering recall. The question was whether the breach enables the Secretary of State to form a proper judgment on the medical evidence that the statutory criteria for detention are established (mental disorder of a kind or degree warranting detention). Nevertheless, the Court of Appeal held that there do not have to be psychotic symptoms or the certainty of psychotic symptoms in the near future before detention for treatment could be authorised.

Eligibility for tribunal review: A patient who is made subject to a hospital order with restrictions may apply to the tribunal once in the second six months following the making of the order, and thereafter once in every 12-month period (MHA 1983, s.70).

Until 1 October 2007, when the amendment to MHA 1983, s.41(1) by MHA 2007 took effect, restriction orders could be for a fixed term rather than for an indefinite period. Since that day they are all imposed without limit of time. If a patient received a fixed-term restriction order prior to that date, and the restrictions expire, the patient becomes an unrestricted hospital order patient, and acquires an immediate right to apply to the tribunal by virtue of MHA 1983, ss.41(5) and 69(2)(a). In such a case, the hospital managers will have a duty to refer the patient's case to the tribunal under s.68 if three years have elapsed since the patient's case was last considered by a tribunal.

Reference by the Secretary of State for Justice: The Secretary of State for Justice has a discretion under s.71 to refer the case of any restricted patient to the tribunal at any time, and must refer the case of any restricted patient detained in hospital whose case has not been considered by the tribunal, whether on his own application or otherwise, within the last three years.

The case of a conditionally-discharged patient who is recalled to hospital must be referred by the Secretary of State for Justice to the tribunal immediately (*R (Rayner) v. Secretary of State for Justice* [2008] EWCA Civ 176), at least within one month of his return to hospital (MHA 1983, s.75(1)). Because the recalled patient returns to the status of restricted patient, if the tribunal decides not to discharge following the automatic referral, the patient only acquires a right to apply to the tribunal after the expiry of six months following recall. S/he may apply once during the second six months and thereafter once in every 12-month period (MHA 1983, ss.70, 75(1)).

5.4.5 Hospital direction and limitation direction ('hybrid orders')

(MHA 1983, s.45A)

Maximum duration: Indeterminate.

Criteria: These are set out in s.45A(2):

(a) that the offender is suffering from mental disorder;

(b) that the mental disorder from which the offender is suffering is of a nature or degree which makes it appropriate for him to be detained in a hospital for medical treatment; and

(c) that appropriate medical treatment is available for him.

Procedural requirements: The court must have considered making a hospital order before imposing a sentence of imprisonment (MHA 1983, s.45(1)(b)). There must be medical evidence from two doctors, one of whom must be approved under MHA 1983, s.12, and one doctor must have given oral evidence.

Effect: These disposals are known colloquially as 'hybrid orders'. Only one hybrid order was made in 2010–2011, and in 2009 there were only 16 such patients resident in hospitals.[4] The effects of a hospital direction and a limitation direction are set out in s.45B. A hospital direction has the same effect as a transfer direction under s.47; a limitation direction has the same effect as a restriction direction under s.49 (both discussed at **5.5.1**). The offender is given a prison sentence calculated in accordance with normal sentencing principles, but is directed to hospital in the first instance. Although directed initially to hospital, the offender has the legal status of prisoner rather than patient. This means that in the event of the mental disorder being successfully treated before the expiry of the prison sentence, the offender can be returned to prison to serve the remainder of the sentence.

While a person is subject to a hospital direction and a limitation direction, detention carries on without need for renewal by the hospital managers. The responsible clinician is required to submit a report 'on that person' at least once a year to the Secretary of State for Justice. If the person is still in hospital at the time of his release date (defined in MHA 1983, s.50(3) as the date he would be entitled to be released (whether unconditionally or on licence) from prison or other institution), the hospital direction remains, and s/he becomes subject to the hospital direction alone, which means having the same status as a patient detained under s.37 (known as 'notional hospital order' or 'notional s.37 patients'). Treatment for mental disorder of hospital direction and limitation direction patients who are detained in hospital is subject to the provisions of MHA 1983, Part IV and the second opinion safeguards therein.

MHA 1983, s.117 places a duty jointly on Health Authorities and social services authorities in England, in co-operation with relevant voluntary agencies, to arrange for the provision of after-care services for patients who have been detained under a hospital direction and a limitation direction and who cease to be detained and leave hospital. In Wales the duty is on the Local Health Board and the local social services authority in co-operation with relevant voluntary agencies *to provide* (rather than arrange for the provision of) community care services. Patients are entitled to s.117 community care services free of charge (*R* v. *Manchester City Council, ex p. Stennett* [2002] UKHL 34, [2002] 4 All ER 124 (HL)). Community care services are discussed in **Chapter 6**. Section 45A patients are ineligible to be placed on a CTO.

Eligibility for tribunal review: The patient may apply once within the second six-month period following the making of the hospital direction and the limitation direction, and thereafter once in every subsequent 12-month period (Department of Health, *Reference Guide to the Mental Health Act 1983* (2008), Table 22.6). If the patient ceases to be subject to the limitation direction and becomes a 'notional s.37' patient, which means that they are treated as if detained on a hospital order without restrictions (MHA 1983, s.41(5)), such patients acquire the right to apply to the tribunal, and their nearest relative also acquires a right to apply to the tribunal under MHA 1983, s.69.

---

[4]   NHS Information Centre, *Inpatients Formally Detained in Hospitals under the Mental Health Act 1983 and Patients Subject to Supervised Community Treatment, Annual Figures, England 2010/11* (2011), Table 2a; Ministry of Justice, *Offender Management Caseload Statistics Bulletin* (22 July 2010), p.163.

Reference by the Secretary of State for Justice: The Secretary of State for Justice has a discretion under s.71 to refer the case of any restricted patient (including those subject to a limitation direction) to the tribunal at any time, and must refer the case of any restricted patient detained in hospital whose case has not been considered by the tribunal, whether on his own application or otherwise, within the last three years.

5.5 MENTAL DISORDER WHILE A PRISONER IN CUSTODY

5.5.1 Transfer of sentenced prisoner

(MHA 1983, ss.47 and 49)

Maximum duration:

1. A transfer direction under s.47 where no restriction direction is made: six months, renewable for six months and thereafter for one year at a time.
2. If a restriction direction under s.49 is made: it expires on the earliest date when the offender would have been released from prison (the 'release date' as defined in MHA 1983, s.50(3)); thereafter the patient is detained as if he were under a hospital order without restrictions (known as a 'notional s.37'). Once the restrictions expire, the patient may be discharged by the RC or the hospital managers without recourse to the Ministry of Justice or by the Mental Health Tribunal. For prisoners with an indeterminate sentence, the restriction direction remains without limit of time.

Criteria: Before issuing a transfer direction the Secretary of State for Justice must be satisfied that the prisoner is:

(a) suffering from mental disorder; and
(b) the mental disorder is of a nature or degree which makes it appropriate for him to be detained in hospital for medical treatment; and
(c) that appropriate medical treatment is available for him; and
(d) having regard to the public interest and to all the other circumstances, a transfer is expedient.

Procedural requirements: The direction must be based on two medical reports, one from a doctor approved under s.12 (MHA 1983, s.54(1)). The English Code of Practice states that (English Code of Practice, para.33.31; see also Welsh Code of Practice, para.32.23):

> The need for in-patient treatment for a prisoner should be identified and acted upon quickly, and prison healthcare staff should make contact immediately with the responsible PCT.

In 2008 the (then) Mental Health Act Commission expressed its continuing concern that transfers late in the sentence were distorting mental health law by using it for primarily public protection purposes, since a transfer in such circumstances may well be seen by the prisoner as being primarily intended to extend his detention. The Commission stressed that transfer should take place as soon as is therapeutically indicated rather than being delayed until risk is the primary factor (Mental Health Act Commission, *Placed Among Strangers* (13th Biennial Report 2005–2007, TSO, 2007), pp.382–383). When a patient is transferred to hospital near the end of their sentence the hospital authorities must carefully scrutinise the medical reports to ensure that they provide a sound basis for transfer (*R (SP)* v. *Secretary of State for Justice* [2010] EWHC 1124 (Admin)).

In *R (TF)* v. *Secretary of State for Justice* [2008] EWCA Civ 1457, [2008] MHLR 370, at [31], Waller LJ expressed the hope that s.47 would only be used at the end of the sentence in 'very exceptional cases' and placed the onus on the Secretary of State 'to show that the mind of the decision-maker has focused on each of the criteria which it is necessary to satisfy if there is to be power to issue a warrant directing transfer to a hospital'.

The Ministry of Justice National Offender Management Service, *Guidance for Working with MAPPA (Multi-Agency Public Protection Arrangements) and Mentally Disordered Offenders*, para.5.8 addresses the consequences of the *TF* ruling and advises that if transfer at the end of sentence is necessary on clinical grounds:

> assessment and admission under civil powers is to be preferred, a procedure which demonstrates that the decision is clinically-led, and is not a misuse of the powers of the Mental Health Act to extend the sentence of the Court.

See also Department of Health, *Good Practice Procedure Guide: The Transfer and Remission of Adult Prisoners under s.47 and s.48 of the Mental Health Act* (2011), para.3.9–3.17.

Effect: A transfer direction without restrictions has broadly the same effect as a hospital order, except that the patient may apply to the tribunal within the first six months of the transfer. A restriction direction has broadly the same effect as a hospital order with restrictions, except that the tribunal has no power to direct discharge. The vast majority of prisoners transferred to hospital are subject to restriction directions.[5] If the Secretary of State for Justice is notified by the responsible clinician or the tribunal that an offender subject to a restriction direction no longer requires treatment in hospital, he has two options. He can either discharge an offender who would have been eligible for release on parole had he remained in prison, or he can direct that the offender be returned to prison to serve the remainder of his sentence. This means that the Secretary of State for Justice retains greater control over the duration of detention of a transferred prisoner with a restriction direction than he does over a restriction order patient.

---

[5] In 2010–2011, 430 patients were transferred from prison under MHA 1983, s.47 with s.49 restrictions and 40 patients under s.47 without restrictions. NHS Information Centre, *Inpatients Formally Detained in Hospitals under the Mental Health Act 1983 and Patients Subject to Supervised Community Treatment, Annual Figures, England 2010/11* (2011), Table 1.

To comply with ECHR, art.5 a tribunal must have the power to discharge restriction order patients if they no longer suffer from mental disorder of a kind or degree warranting confinement. Because transferred prisoners retain the legal status of prisoner until they reach their earliest release date, the Secretary of State for Justice may remit them to prison to serve out their term without breaching art.5. If in hospital when they reach their earliest release date, then the basis of their detention is mental disorder only. At that point they become notional s.37 patients and they may be discharged by the RC, the hospital managers or the tribunal if the grounds for detention are no longer met.

Treatment for mental disorder of patients transferred under s.47 with or without restrictions under s.49 who are detained in hospital is subject to the provisions of MHA 1983, Part IV and the second opinion safeguards therein.

Such patients are also entitled to s.117 after-care services free of charge (*R* v. *Manchester City Council, ex p. Stennett* [2002] UKHL 34, [2002] 4 All ER 124 (HL)). Patients transferred under s.47 without restrictions, and patients who have become notional s.37 patients when their restrictions have lapsed, are eligible to be placed on a CTO under s.17A (MHA 1983, s.17A(2), Sched.1, Part 1, para.1). Community care services and CTOs are discussed in **Chapter 6**.

Eligibility for tribunal review: Patients transferred under s.47, with or without s.49 restriction directions can apply within the first six months following transfer, once during the second six months and once in each subsequent period of 12 months (MHA 1983, s.69(2)(b)). In *R (MN)* v. *Mental Health Review Tribunal* [2008] EWHC 3383 (Admin), Plender J in an extempore judgment held that where a patient's restrictions lapse while a tribunal hearing is pending following an application under s.70 against the s.47/49 transfer, a fresh application must be made against the notional s.37 (under s.69(2)(b)).

Reference by the Secretary of State for Justice: The Secretary of State for Justice has a discretion under s.71 to refer the case of any restricted patient (including those subject to a restriction direction) to the tribunal at any time, and must refer the case of any restricted patient detained in hospital whose case has not been considered by the tribunal, whether on his own application or otherwise, within the last three years.

5.5.2 Transfer of remand or unsentenced prisoner

(MHA 1983, s.48)

Maximum duration: N/A

Criteria: The Secretary of State for Justice must be satisfied:

(a)   that the person is suffering from mental disorder of a nature or degree which makes it appropriate for him to be detained in hospital for medical treatment (Note: s.48 cannot be used to transfer a person with a learning disability unless the learning disability is associated with abnormally aggressive or seriously irresponsible conduct on his part); and

(b)   he is in urgent need of such treatment; and

(c)   appropriate medical treatment is available for him.

Procedural requirements: The same procedural requirements apply to transfer under s.48 as apply to s.47 transfers (see **5.5.1**).

Effect: Treatment for mental disorder of patients transferred under s.48 with or without restrictions under s.49 who are detained in hospital is subject to the provisions of MHA 1983, Part IV and the second opinion safeguards therein. In 2010–2011, 403 patients were transferred to hospital under s.48 with s.49 restrictions and only 10 without.

Patients who have been detained under a transfer direction with or without restrictions and who cease to be detained and leave hospital are entitled to s.117 after-care services free of charge (*R* v. *Manchester City Council, ex p. Stennett* [2002] UKHL 34, [2002] 4 All ER 124 (HL)). Patients transferred under s.48 (without a s.49 restriction direction) are eligible to be placed on a CTO. Community care services and CTOs are discussed in **Chapter 6**.

Eligibility for tribunal review: Patients transferred under s.48, with or without s.49 restriction directions, can apply within the first six months following transfer, once during the second six months and once in each subsequent period of 12 months (MHA 1983, s.69(2)(b)). If the patient is not subject to restrictions, the case may be referred to the tribunal by the Secretary of State for Health under s.67. The Secretary of State for Justice has discretion under s.71 to refer the case of any restricted patient to the tribunal at any time and must refer the case if three years have elapsed since the patient's case was last considered by the tribunal.

5.6   CONCLUSION

This chapter has considered the powers to detain offender patients in MHA 1983, Part III, in particular the powers available to the courts to send such patients to hospital. It has also considered the entitlement of those patients, and in some instances their relatives, to apply for a tribunal hearing, as well as the means by which a patient's case may be referred to the tribunal.

Chapter 6 considers the rights of patients to after-care support, the various possibilities under MHA 1983 to exercise compulsory powers over patients living in the community, and the entitlement of patients subject to compulsory community powers and their nearest relatives to have the patient's compulsory status reviewed before a tribunal.

CHAPTER 6

Community care, guardianship and community treatment orders: compulsory powers, discharge and review

The patient's circumstances after discharge from detention and the arrangements for after-care services and support are often key factors which may influence the decision made by the Mental Health Tribunal. The provision of community care services and support are also essential elements in the care of patients living in the community. This chapter begins by describing the main powers and duties of public authorities to provide community care services.[1] It then considers the power in MHA 1983, Part II to subject a patient to guardianship under s.7, the power to impose a community treatment order (CTO) under ss.17A–17G, and the entitlement of patients subject to those powers and their relatives to apply for a tribunal hearing.

6.1 COMMUNITY CARE SERVICES

(English Code of Practice, chapter 27; Welsh Code of Practice, chapter 31)

6.1.1 Care Programme Approach

All service users, whether or not they have been detained, who have been in contact with the specialist psychiatric service are entitled to be considered for support in hospital or in the community under the Care Programme Approach (CPA). The CPA requires a risk assessment, a needs assessment, a written care plan which will be regularly reviewed and a key worker (now known as a care co-ordinator). In 1996 the CPA was extended to all patients receiving care from the specialist psychiatric services (NHS Executive, *Audit Pack for Monitoring the Care Programme Approach: Background and Explanatory Notes* (HSG 96(6), NHS Executive,

---

[1] A detailed description of the law relating to community care is beyond the scope of this book. See Luke Clements and Pauline Thompson, *Community Care and the Law* (5th edn, Legal Action Group, 2011).

1996)). Under guidance issued in 2003, *Modernising the Care Programme Approach* (see Care Programme Approach Association, *The Care Programme Approach Handbook* (Chesterfield, 2003); Welsh Assembly Government, *Mental Health Policy Wales Implementation Guidance: The Care Programme Approach for Mental Health Service Users* (2003)) there were two levels of CPA, standard and enhanced. Standard CPA was for people whose mental illness was less severe or who have low risk factors or have an active informal support network. People were on enhanced CPA if their mental disorder is assessed as posing a potential risk to their own safety or to that of other people and their needs required involvement of multiple agencies.

From October 2008, new guidance has applied in England whereby the two tiers have been abolished and 'New CPA' is now available to manage 'complex and serious' cases who, according to the Department of Health guidance, should not be significantly different from those previously needing the support of enhanced CPA (Department of Health, *Refocusing the Care Programme Approach* (March 2008), p.13; see also Welsh Assembly Government, *Delivering the Care Programme Approach in Wales: Interim Policy Implementation Guidance* (July 2010)). The guidance states that:

> (New) CPA is a process for managing complex and serious cases – it should *not* be used as . . . a 'badge' of entitlement to receive any other services and benefits. Eligibility for services continues to be in accordance with statutory definitions and based upon assessment of individual need.

The guidance stresses that service providers should continue to use current local eligibility criteria to make decisions about an individual's need for secondary mental health services. The guidance then provides a list to decide if the person needs New CPA. This is the list of characteristics to consider (pp.13–14):

- severe mental disorder including mental disorder with a high degree of clinical complexity;
- current or potential risks including suicide, self-harm or harm to others;
- relapse history requiring urgent response;
- self neglect or non compliance with treatment;
- vulnerable adult for example financial or sexual exploitation, dis-inhibited behaviour, physical or emotional abuse, cognitive impairment;
- current or significant history of severe distress, instability or disengagement;
- presence of non physical co-morbidity, e.g. substance, alcohol or drug misuse or learning disability;
- multiple service provision from different agencies including housing, physical care, employment, criminal justice or voluntary agencies;
- currently/recently detained under MHA or referred to crisis or home treatment team, significant reliance on carers or has own caring responsibilities;
- experiencing disadvantage as a result of parenting responsibilities, physical health problems or disability, unsettled accommodation, employment issues when mentally ill, significant impairment of function due to mental disorder, ethnicity, sexuality or gender issues.

All services users on CTOs or guardianship should be supported by New CPA.

6.1.2 Mental Health (Wales) Measure 2010

In Wales, the Mental Health (Wales) Measure 2010 with its associated regulations and Code of Practice (Welsh Government, *Code of Practice to Parts 2 and 3 of the Mental Health (Wales) Measure* (2012)) requires that 'all individuals accepted into secondary mental health services have a dedicated care coordinator and receive a care and treatment plan which is proportionate to their clinical need' (Welsh Government, *Policy Implementation Guidance on Local Primary Mental Health Support Services and Secondary Mental Health Services for the purposes of the Mental Health (Wales) Measure 2010* (2011)). 'Secondary mental health services' are defined in s.49 of the Measure to include hospital in-patients, people receiving community care services under MHA 1983, s.117 (see **6.1.3**), and people receiving 'a community care service the main purpose of which is to meet a need relating to an adult's mental health' (see also the Mental Health (Secondary Mental Health Services) (Wales) Order 2012, SI 2012/1428 (W.178)). The definition is so constructed that, in the words of the Policy Implementation Guidance:

> in most cases, all services provided to an individual the treatment of their mental health (except those which are delivered as part of the General Medical Services contract) are, in effect secondary mental health services.

This means that all patients appearing before the MHRT for Wales must have a care co-ordinator, and a written care and treatment plan. Section 18 of the Measure lists the issues which should be addressed in the care and treatment plan. The process of drawing up the care plan and reviewing the treatment plan is governed by regulations, and Sched.2 to the regulations sets out the form which the care and treatment plan must take (Mental Health (Care Co-ordination, and Care and Treatment Planning) (Wales) Regulations 2011, SI 2011/2942 (W.318)). The care and treatment plan must record the outcomes that the provision of mental health services are designed to achieve, details of the services that are to be provided, and the actions that are to be taken with a view to achieving any outcomes specified. The planned outcomes must relate to at least one of the areas listed. These are (SI 2011/2942 (W.318), Sched.2):

(a)　accommodation;
(b)　education and training;
(c)　finance and money;
(d)　medical and other forms of treatment, including psychological interventions;
(e)　parenting or caring relationships;
(f)　personal care and physical wellbeing;
(g)　social, cultural or spiritual;
(h)　work and occupation.

It is suggested that the care co-ordinator, who now under the Welsh Measure exercises a statutory function in relation to the patient, will be an important source of evidence as to the patient's suitability for discharge, and the MHRT for Wales should always ask for the care and treatment plan.

6.1.3 Mental Health Act 1983, s.117

MHA 1983, s.117 currently places a duty jointly on Health Authorities (Primary Care Trusts in England or Local Health Boards in Wales) and local social services authorities (LSSAs), in co-operation with relevant voluntary agencies, to provide after-care services for patients who have previously been detained in hospital under the 'treatment' sections of MHA 1983 (ss.3, 37 (with or without restrictions), 45A, 47 or 48). The duty also applies in relation to patients granted leave of absence under s.17 and those living in the community subject to a CTO under s.17A. In 2013, in England Primary Care Trusts will be replaced by clinical commissioning groups (CCGs), and s.117 has been amended to place the duty on CCGs jointly with the LSSA and relevant voluntary organisations to *arrange for the provision of*, rather than provide, community care services under s.117 (Health and Social Care Act 2012, s.40) (in Wales, the joint duty to *provide* services under s.117 remains). The s.117 duty applies when the patient ceases to be detained and leaves hospital, 'whether or not immediately after so ceasing'. The significance of these words is explained by the English Code of Practice (para.27.6):

> Where eligible patients have remained in hospital informally after ceasing to be detained under the Act, they are still entitled to after-care under section 117 once they leave hospital. This also applies when patients are released from prison, having spent part of their sentence detained in hospital under a relevant section of the Act.

This enforceable duty continues until the Health Authorities and LSSAs are jointly satisfied that the person concerned is no longer in need of such services, 'but they shall not be so satisfied in the case of a community patient while he remains such a patient' (MHA 1983, s.117). Hence, patients on supervised community treatment (SCT) remain entitled to s.117 after-care services throughout the duration of their CTO.

Section 117 services are community care services within the meaning of s.46 of the National Health Service and Community Care Act 1990 (see **6.1.5**). Section 47 provides that where it appears to a local authority that any person for whom they may provide or arrange to provide community care services may be in need of any such services, the authority (National Health Service and Community Care Act 1990, s.47):

(a) shall carry out an assessment of his needs for those services; and

(b) having regard to the results of that assessment, shall then decide whether his needs call for the provision by them of any such services.

The two-stage process under s.47 of needs assessment followed by a care provision decision applies to people who are eligible for s.117 services. Local authorities may lawfully employ eligibility criteria (*R* v. *Gloucestershire County Council, ex p. Barry* [1997] 2 All ER 1 (HL)). Unlike other community care services, for which the service user may be charged, it is unlawful to charge for s.117 after-care and such services must be provided free of charge until such time as both the relevant Health Authorities and LSSAs are satisfied that they are no longer needed (*R* v. *Manchester City Council, ex p. Stennett* [2002] UKHL 34, [2002] 4 All ER 124 (HL)).

Disputes may arise as to which LSSA is responsible for providing s.117 after-care. Section 117 states that the responsible LSSA is the authority 'for the area in which the person concerned is resident or to which is sent on discharge by the hospital in which he was detained'. The Department of Health (DH) issued revised guidance on ordinary residence in 2011 (*Ordinary Residence: Guidance on the Identification of the Ordinary Residence of People in Need of Community Care Services, England* (London, 2011); paras.182–189 refer to s.117).

In *R* v. *Mental Health Review Tribunal, ex p. Hall* [1999] 3 All ER 132, the court made it clear that the responsible Health Authorities and LSSAs are those for the area in which the person was resident before being detained in hospital, even if the person does not return to that area on discharge. Taking account of the decision in *Hall*, the DH Guidance notes (para.185): 'If no such residence can be established, the duty falls on the authority where the person is to go on discharge from hospital'. The guidance goes on to say that (para.189):

> Disputes arising in connection with section 117 of the 1983 Act cannot be referred to the Secretary of State or Welsh Ministers for determination under section 32(3) of the 1948 Act. If such a dispute could not be resolved locally, it would be necessary to involve the courts.

The issue was further considered in *R (M)* v. *Hammersmith and Fulham LBC and others* [2010] EWHC 562 (Admin) (upheld on appeal in *R (Hertfordshire County Council)* v. *London Borough of Hammersmith and Fulham* [2011] EWCA Civ 77), where the patient receiving s.117 services moved to a new area and was subsequently detained under a new s.3 detention. As Jones puts it (R.M. Jones, *Mental Health Act Manual* (15th edn, London, Sweet & Maxwell, 2012), p.488):

> Apart from a situation where authorities agree to a transfer of responsibility for providing s.117 services, the only occasion where responsibility would change is where the patient who is subject to s.117 moves to a new area and is subsequently detained under one of the provisions listed in subs.(1). Such an admission would trigger the duty under this section and the rulings in *Hall* and *M* mean that the relevant health and social care bodies would be the health and social services bodies for the area where the patient resided at the time of the subsequent admission.

This remains a good summary of the law. However, the Court of Appeal decision in *R (Sunderland City Council)* v. *South Tyneside Council* [2012] EWCA Civ 1232, reversing [2011] EWHC 2355 (Admin)), has made it necessary to qualify Professor

110

Jones' statement slightly to the effect that a person's residence may change if he is admitted informally in a new area and loses his home so that he ceases to have any other available residence. In such a case, unless the person is to be regarded as having no residence, there is no alternative to viewing him for s.117 purposes as resident in the hospital. Lloyd LJ, delivering the judgment of the court, emphasised that 'no residence is a last resort, an ultimate default position, which should not be held to apply except in extreme and clear circumstances' (at [46]).

Identification of the relevant authorities is important since the availability of s.117 after-care will be a significant factor which may influence a tribunal's decision as to whether discharge is appropriate. This is clearly recognised in the English Code (English Code of Practice, para.27.7; see also Welsh Code of Practice, paras.31.7 and 31.11):

> When considering relevant patients' cases, the Tribunal and hospital managers will expect to be provided with information from the professionals concerned on what after-care arrangements might be made for them under s.117 if they were to be discharged. Some discussion of after-care needs, involving LSSAs and other relevant agencies, should take place in advance of the hearing.

The English Code advises that where a tribunal or hospital managers' hearing has been arranged for a patient who might be entitled to after-care under MHA 1983, s.117, the hospital managers should ensure that the relevant Health Authorities and LSSAs have been informed. The authorities (para.27.9):

> should consider putting practical preparations in hand for after-care in every case, but should in particular consider doing so where there is a strong possibility that the patient will be discharged if appropriate after-care can be arranged. Where the Tribunal has provisionally decided to give a restricted patient a conditional discharge, the PCT and LSSA must do their best to put after-care in place which would allow that discharge to take place.

The question of when the authorities' obligations under s.117 should actually be put into effect for a patient who is still subject to detention has been considered by the courts in a number of cases (see e.g., *R* v. *Ealing District Health Authority, ex p. Fox* [1993] All ER 170; *R* v. *Mental Health Review Tribunal, ex p. Hall* [1999] 3 All ER 132; *R (oao W)* v. *Doncaster MBC* [2003] EWHC Admin 192), when it was suggested that planning for after-care should, if practicable, take place before a tribunal hearing, so that the authorities can comply with their s.117 duty if the patient is discharged by the tribunal. However, it was also recognised that it would be wasteful of limited resources for authorities to have to plan and make arrangements in cases where the application is unlikely to succeed. These judgments were considered by the Court of Appeal in 2004 (*W* v. *Doncaster MBC* [2004] EWCA Civ 378) when Scott Baker J said (at [51]):

> It is therefore necessary to focus on the after-care the respondent was expected to put into place and see why it did not happen. Although the section 117 duty does not bite on local authorities or health authorities until after the tribunal decision, they do not at that point

start entirely from scratch. Most such authorities will be faced fairly frequently with circumstances in which they are expected to exercise their section 117 duty to help to rehabilitate mental patients within the community. It is reasonable to suppose therefore that they have procedures in place for coping with situations of this kind. Also, they certainly have the *power*, in appropriate cases, to start making plans before the tribunal sits. Kennedy LJ in *Hall* referred to them as plans in embryo. Once the tribunal has made its decision it will be a case of tailoring their procedures to meet the needs of the particular case.

6.1.4   Definition of after-care services

There is no clear definition in MHA 1983 as to what after-care services consist of for the purposes of s.117. The courts have consistently adopted the definition given by Beldam LJ in *Clunis* v. *Camden and Islington Health Authority* [1997] EWCA Civ 2918 (approved in *R* v. *Manchester City Council, ex p. Stennett* [2002] UKHL 34, at [9]), as follows:

> After-care services are not defined in the Act. They would normally include social work support, support in helping the ex-patient with problems of employment, accommodation or family relationships, the provision of domiciliary services and the use of day centre and residential facilities.

In practice, the services required should be planned within the framework of the Care Programme Approach and the multi-disciplinary meetings which take place within that framework.[2] In relation to assessing a patient's need for after-care services, the English Code of Practice advises (at para.27.13):

> A thorough assessment is likely to involve consideration of:
>
> - continuing mental healthcare, whether in the community or on an out-patient basis;
> - the psychological needs of the patient and, where appropriate, of their family and carers;
> - physical healthcare;
> - daytime activities or employment;
> - appropriate accommodation;
> - identified risks and safety issues;
> - any specific needs arising from, for example, co-existing physical disability, sensory impairment, learning disability or autistic spectrum disorder;
> - any specific needs arising from drug, alcohol or substance misuse (if relevant);
> - any parenting or caring needs;
> - social, cultural or spiritual needs;
> - counselling and personal support;
> - assistance in welfare rights and managing finances;
> - the involvement of authorities and agencies in a different area, if the patient is not going to live locally;

---

[2]   See DH, *Refocusing the Care Programme Approach: Policy and Positive Practice Guidance* (March 2008). For a list of people who should be involved in after-care planning, see English Code of Practice, para.27.12. The Welsh Code of Practice states that after-care planning must take place 'in full consultation with other professionals involved' (para.31.9).

- the involvement of other agencies, for example the probation service or voluntary organisations;
- for a restricted patient, the conditions which the Secretary of State for Justice or the Tribunal has imposed or is likely to impose on their conditional discharge; and
- contingency plans (should the patient's mental health deteriorate) and crisis contact details.

It is clear, therefore, that after-care services are intended to address both the patient's healthcare needs and social care needs, and include (where necessary) the provision of accommodation, assistance in sorting out entitlement to and claiming welfare benefits, help with managing finances or finding employment, help in dealing with problems in family relationships and providing support for carers. But it is left to local discretion to decide the level of services to be provided and which authority (health or social services) is responsible for providing (or arranging) specific services.

6.1.5   Other community care services

In addition to the obligations imposed by s.117, there is also a duty on LSSAs to assess the needs of any individual in their area who 'may be in need' of community care services under s.47 of the National Health Service and Community Care Act 1990, and to provide services to meet any assessed needs. The LSSA will therefore be obliged (either under a combination of s.47 of the NHS and Community Care Act 1990 and MHA 1983, s.117 for those to whom s.117 applies, or under s.47 alone for those who fall outside s.117) to provide whatever services are identified as necessary by the s.47 assessment, although it has discretion in determining the level and precise nature of the services to be provided, taking account of resource constraints (*R* v. *Gloucestershire County Council, ex p. Barry* [1997] AC 584; *R (McDonald)* v. *Royal Borough of Kensington and Chelsea* [2011] UKSC 33; *R (KM)* v. *Cambridgeshire County Council* [2012] UKSC 23).

Although the duty to assess is on the local authority alone, the relevant Health Authority should also be involved in the assessment process for patients being discharged from MHA detention, since the subsequent duty to provide after-care services under s.117 is a joint duty on both Health Authorities and LSSAs.

The point at which the assessment duty is triggered for those currently detained who at some point 'may be in need' of community care services has also been considered by the courts (see e.g. *W* v. *Doncaster MBC* [2004] EWCA Civ 378). In *R (B)* v. *Camden LBC and Camden and Islington Mental Health and Social Care Trust* [2005] EWHC 1366 (Admin), it was held that (at 66]–[67]):

> In my judgment, the words 'a person who may be in need of such services' refer to a person who may be in need at the time, or who may be about to be in need. A detained patient who is the subject of a deferred conditional discharge decision of a tribunal, which envisages his conditional discharge once section 117 after-care services are in place, is a person who 'may be in need of such services', since if such services are available to him he will be discharged and immediately need them. . . .

However, the duty under section 47 does not arise until it 'appears' to the local authority that a person may be in need, and it cannot appear to it that he may be in need unless it knows of his possible need. It is presumably for this reason that the Community Care (Delayed Discharges etc) Act 2003 was enacted. It follows that section 47 does not impose an obligation on a local authority to monitor a patient detained in hospital in case he should at some later time be in need. The decision of the local authority under section 47(1)(b) whether his needs call for the provision of services falls to be made by reference to the result of the assessment it has carried out. It follows that section 47 cannot require the local authority to monitor the situation of a patient to consider providing for his changed needs.

In the more recent case of a person with learning disabilities serving a prison sentence appearing before the Parole Board (*R (NM)* v. *London Borough of Islington and others* [2012] EWHC 414 (Admin)), it was held (at [77]–[78]):

The words 'may be in need' are in the present tense and do not import a flavour of coverage of possible needs which may arise in the future . . . In context, the word 'may' is apt because it indicates that there has to appear to the relevant local authority a significant possibility that the person in question might have a present need for community care services to be provided to him by that local authority and it is that possibility which then has to be investigated by means of the assessment under section 47(1)(a).

However, in a number of situations – such as release from mental hospital as contemplated in *R (B)* v. *Camden LBC*, discharge from hospital as in *R* v. *Berkshire County Council, ex p. P* and release from prison as in *R* v. *Mid Glamorgan CC, ex p. Miles* – it may be sufficiently clear that a person is likely in the very near future to be present in the area of the local authority and, when they are, may then be in need of community care services, so that the obligation of assessment under section 47(1)(a) arises before the person actually arrives.

In this case, the claimant had argued that arts. 19 and 26 of the UN Convention on the Rights of Persons with Disabilities (CRPD, see **1.4**) provide rights of access to services and independent living. However, the judge concluded that there was not, at the present time, a basis to argue either that CRPD had any free-standing status in domestic law or that rights under the European Convention on Human Rights (ECHR) should necessarily be interpreted in accordance with the CRPD.

6.1.6 Support for carers

All carers of people with disabilities, including those with mental health problems, (regardless of the level of care they provide, or intend to provide) have the right to have their views taken into account by the relevant LSSA when it is considering how best to make provision for a disabled person. When undertaking a community care assessment under s.47 of the National Health Service and Community Care Act 1990, the LSSA must (amongst other things) (Community Care Assessment Directions 2004 (LAC (2004) 24)):

- consider whether the person has any carers and, if so, also consult them if the authority 'thinks it appropriate';

- take all reasonable steps to reach agreement with the person being assessed and, where they think it appropriate, any carers of that person, on the community care services which they are considering providing to meet the person's needs.

Certain carers who provide (or intend to provide) a substantial amount of care on a regular basis have the right to a 'carer's assessment' of their own needs for support in sustaining their caring role (under the Carers (Recognition and Services) Act 1995, extended by the Carers and Disabled Children Act 2000 and the Carers (Equal Opportunities) Act 2004). Such carers can refuse an assessment – but even if they do so, the law requires that their 'ability to manage' their caring role must nevertheless be taken into account (Disabled Persons (Services, Consultation and Representation) Act 1986, s.8), and the fact that they have refused such an assessment should not be 'used as a reason to exclude the carer from assisting with care planning' (Community Care Assessment Directions 2004 (LAC (2004) 24), para.2.2).

The Carers and Disabled Children Act 2000 extended the rights of carers, to include the right to support services to address their own needs, and for these services to be made available by way of direct payments and 'vouchers'. The Carers (Equal Opportunities) Act 2004 imposed a statutory duty on the LSSA to inform carers of their rights to be consulted and for their own needs to be assessed, and introduced a requirement that carers' assessments consider whether the carer works or wishes to work and/or is undertaking, or wishes to undertake, education, training or any leisure activity. The assessment should therefore consider whether the carer is willing and able to carry on providing care, or the same level of care, and should assess any risks to the sustainability of the caring role, including health risks to the carer and how caring affects their work, education or leisure activity.

In *Coleman* v. *Attridge Law* (C-303/06) [2008] All ER (EC) 1105, ECJ (Grand Chamber), the European Court of Justice (ECJ) ruled that adverse treatment of a carer could constitute unlawful discrimination. This concept of 'associative discrimination' in relation to disabled people has now been recognised in the Equality Act 2010 (see Equality Act 2010, s.13). The Equality Act 2010, s.149 also extends the current duty on public bodies (such as local authorities and the NHS) to ensure that their policies and practices do not have an adverse impact on disabled (and other) persons. This duty includes an obligation to ensure that policies and practices are designed to eliminate discrimination, harassment and victimisation and to advance equality of opportunity and foster good relations. This includes an obligation to consider the impact of their policies and practices because of the concept of 'associative' discrimination.[3]

---

[3] See Luke Clements *et al.*, *The Equality Act 2010 and Carers*, available at **www.lukeclements.co.uk/resources/files/PDF%2004.pdf**.

6.2 GUARDIANSHIP

(MHA 1983, s.7; English Code of Practice, chapter 26; Welsh Code of Practice, chapter 6)

Maximum duration: Six months, renewable for six months and thereafter renewable at 12-monthly intervals.

Criteria: The patient must be 16 or over and suffering from mental disorder of a nature or degree warranting reception into guardianship. In addition, reception into guardianship must be necessary in the interests of the patient's welfare or for the protection of others (MHA 1983, s.7(2)).

Procedural requirements: An application may be made by an approved mental health professional (AMHP) or the patient's nearest relative (NR) (MHA 1983, s.11(1)). (See also Mental Health (Hospital, Guardianship and Treatment) (England) Regulations 2008, SI 2008/1184 and Mental Health (Hospital, Guardianship, Community Treatment and Consent to Treatment) (Wales) Regulations 2008, SI 2008/2439 (W.212).) Two medical recommendations are necessary, one of which must be from a medical practitioner approved under MHA 1983, s.12, as having special experience in the diagnosis or treatment of mental disorder (MHA 1983, s.7(3)). The nearest relative may block a guardianship application (MHA 1983, s.11(4)) but unreasonable objection will be grounds for displacement of the NR by the county court under MHA 1983, s.29.

Effects: The effect of reception into guardianship under s.7 is similar to that of a guardianship order under s.37 (see **5.4.3**). Three powers are conferred on the guardian (MHA 1983, s.8(1)):

1. to require the patient to live at a place specified by the guardian. The person may be taken and conveyed to the place of residence and may be returned there if she or he absconds;
2. to require the patient to attend at specified places for medical treatment, occupation, education or training. If the patient refuses to attend, the guardian is not authorised to use force to secure attendance, nor does MHA 1983 enable medical treatment to be administered in the absence of the patient's consent;
3. to require access to the patient to be given at the place where he or she is living to persons detailed in MHA 1983. A refusal without reasonable cause to permit an authorised person to have access to the patient is an offence under s.129, but no force may be used to secure entry.

MHA 1983, s.18(7) confers a power to take and convey the patient to the place where s/he is required to reside, and there is a power to retake a person under guardianship who absconds from that place. Guardianship patients are not subject to the provisions of MHA 1983, Part IV which allow treatment without consent of detained patients subject to a system of second opinion safeguards. Guardianship patients are entitled to the Care Programme Approach (see **6.1.1**) (Department of Health, *Refocusing the Care Programme Approach* (March 2008), p.14).

Eligibility to apply for a tribunal hearing: Guardianship patients have the right to apply to the tribunal once during the first six months following acceptance of the guardianship application, once within six months of the furnishing of the first renewal report, and once within 12 months of each subsequent renewal report under s.20(6) (MHA 1983, s.66(1)(c), (f) and s.66(2)(c), (f)). Patients who are transferred from guardianship to hospital may apply within six months of the transfer, and once during each period where detention is renewed. In such cases the renewal date is six months from the date of acceptance of the original guardianship application (MHA 1983, ss.66(1)(e), (2)(e) and 19(2)(d)).

The NR of a guardianship patient does not have a right to apply to the tribunal, as the NR can direct discharge of the patient from guardianship, and discharge cannot be 'barred' (MHA 1983, s.25 which allows an NR's discharge order to be barred on grounds of likely dangerousness to self or others, only applies to patients who are liable to be detained (s.25(1)) and to CTO patients (s.25(1A))). A displaced NR has a right to apply within 12 months of the displacement order (and once within each subsequent 12 months) if displaced under s.29(1)(c) on grounds of unreasonable objection to the making of an application for guardianship, or under s.29(1)(d) as having attempted to discharge the patient without due regard to the welfare of the patient or the protection of the public (MHA 1983, s.66(1)(h), (2)(g)). The Secretary of State for Health or Welsh Ministers may refer a guardianship patient's case to the tribunal under MHA 1983, s.67 (for a full discussion of such references see **4.14**). There is no duty on LSSAs to refer guardianship cases to the tribunal equivalent to the hospital managers' duty under s.68.

6.3 COMMUNITY TREATMENT ORDERS

(MHA 1983, s.17A; English Code of Practice, chapters 25, 29; Welsh Code of Practice, chapter 30)

Maximum duration: Six months, renewable for six months and thereafter renewable at 12-monthly intervals.

Criteria: To be eligible for supervised community treatment (SCT) and hence be made the subject of a community treatment order (CTO), the patient must be liable to be detained in hospital under MHA 1983, s.3 or, if a Part III patient, be subject to a hospital order, a hospital direction (after the limitation direction has expired), or a transfer direction without restrictions. SCT is also available for patients treated as being subject to s.3 or subject to an unrestricted hospital order or transfer direction, following transfer from Northern Ireland, Scotland, the Isle of Man or the Channel Islands (MHA 1983, s.17A(2), Sched.1, Part 1, para.1; see also English Code of Practice, para.25.4; Welsh Code of Practice, para.30.7).

The patient's responsible clinician (RC) must be of the opinion that:

(a)   the patient is suffering from mental disorder (any disorder or disability of the mind) of a nature or degree which makes it appropriate for him to receive medical treatment;

(b)   it is necessary for his health or safety or for the protection of other persons that he should receive such treatment;

(c)   subject to his being liable to be recalled, such treatment can be provided without his continuing to be detained in a hospital;

(d)   it is necessary[4] that the responsible clinician should be able to exercise the power to recall the patient to hospital; and

(e)   appropriate medical treatment is available for him.

A person with a learning disability cannot be detained under s.3 or s.37 unless the learning disability results in abnormally aggressive or seriously irresponsible conduct on his or her part. Such patients, being ineligible for detention under s.3 or s.37, are also ineligible for a CTO.

Procedural requirements: The RC may not make a CTO without a written statement from an AMHP agreeing with the RC's opinion that it is appropriate to make the order (MHA 1983, s.17A(1); see also Mental Health (Hospital, Guardianship and Treatment) (England) Regulations 2008, SI 2008/1184, and Mental Health (Hospital, Guardianship, Community Treatment and Consent to Treatment) (Wales) Regulations 2008, SI 2008/2439 (W.212)). When considering an order the RC must give priority to the risk of deterioration, and the risk of non-compliance with medication if the patient were not to remain in detention. When considering whether a person should be liable to recall under s.17E, the RC must (MHA 1983, s.17A(6)):

> in particular, consider, having regard to the patient's history of mental disorder and any other relevant factors, what risk there would be of a deterioration of the patient's condition if he were not detained in a hospital (as a result, for example, of his refusing or neglecting to receive the medical treatment he requires for his mental disorder).

Effects: A patient who is subject to SCT is known as a 'community patient'. While subject to SCT, the s.3 or s.37 order authorising the patient's original detention is effectively suspended unless and until the CTO is revoked. MHA 1983, s.17B requires that a CTO must 'specify conditions to which the patient is to be subject'. There are two 'mandatory conditions', which are set out in s.17B(3). They are:

(a)   a condition that the patient make himself available for examination under MHA 1983, s.20A; and

(b)   a condition that, if it is proposed to give a certificate under MHA 1983, Part IVA in his case, he make himself available for examination so as to enable the certificate to be given.

---

[4]   The Mental Health Bill 2006 said 'It is necessary for the patient's health or safety or for the protection of others', but MHA 2007 simply says 'necessary'.

Any other conditions (such as residence or supervision) must be agreed between the RC and the AMHP. The only limitation on the scope of the discretionary conditions is that the RC and AMHP must agree that they are 'necessary or appropriate' for (MHA 1983, s.17B):

(a) ensuring that the patient receives medical treatment;
(b) preventing risk of harm to the patient's health or safety;
(c) protecting other persons.

Recall: A community patient subject to a CTO may be recalled to any hospital (not necessarily the responsible hospital)[5] if in the RC's opinion:

(a) the patient requires medical treatment in hospital for his mental disorder; and
(b) there would be a risk of harm to the health or safety of the patient or to other persons if the patient were not recalled to hospital for that purpose.

A patient may also be recalled for breach of a mandatory condition of a CTO, although if the above criteria are met it is not necessary for there to be a breach of condition if recall is to take place.

The power of recall is exercisable by notice in writing to the patient, which is sufficient authority for the managers of that hospital to detain the patient. A patient who has been recalled under MHA 1983, s.17(4) or s.17E can be taken and conveyed to hospital by any AMHP, officer on the staff of the hospital, any constable or by any person authorised in writing by the responsible clinician or the hospital managers. The RC is responsible for co-ordinating the recall, which is designed to provide a means to respond to evidence of relapse or high risk behaviour before it becomes critical and leads to the patient or other people being put at risk (English Code of Practice, para.25.47; Welsh Code of Practice, para.30.54).

Recalling a community patient means that the patient may be detained in a hospital for up to 72 hours immediately following return to hospital, but the CTO is not automatically revoked. A separate decision under s.17F is necessary to revoke a CTO. The RC may revoke a CTO by order in writing if of the opinion that the conditions for detention under s.3(2) are met in respect of the patient. An AMHP must agree with that opinion and that it is appropriate to revoke the order. If a CTO is revoked, the patient reverts to detained patient status and is treated for the purposes of renewal of detention as if they had been admitted for treatment on the date of the order being revoked (MHA 1983, s.17G).

The RC may 'release' the patient at any time during the 72 hours, in which case the patient remains subject to the CTO (MHA 1983, s.17F(5), (7)). If the CTO has not been revoked by the end of the 72-hour period and the patient is still in hospital, he must be released. Again, the patient remains subject to the CTO (MHA 1983, s.17F(6), (7)). 'Released' means 'released from that detention' (MHA 1983, s.17F(8)(b)), it does not mean that the patient is discharged from the CTO or from

---

[5] MHA 1983, s.17E(3) provides that: 'The hospital to which a patient is recalled need not be the responsible hospital'.

hospital. The patient remains liable to s.17E recall. If a recalled patient whose CTO has not been revoked remains in hospital as an informal patient, s/he may not be prevented from leaving by using the holding power under MHA 1983, s.5 since this is prohibited by s.5(6) for community patients. If the patient in such a case is to be prevented from leaving hospital, this must be done by recall. A community patient can be recalled to a hospital even though he is already in the hospital at the time when the power of recall is exercised (MHA 1983, s.17E(4)).

6.3.1 Treatment of community patients

Treatment of detained patients without consent is governed by MHA 1983, Part IV and the second opinion safeguards therein. Part IVA (ss.64A–64K) deals with the treatment of patients subject to CTOs who are living in the community (community patients). It authorises 'relevant treatment' (medicines for mental disorder or electro-convulsive therapy (ECT)) to be given to a community patient who has not been recalled to hospital. Part IVA permits treatment in the community of a community patient if (MHA 1983, ss.64C, 64D and 64G):

(a) the treatment is immediately necessary and the patient is capable and consents to the treatment;

(b) the treatment is immediately necessary, the patient lacks capacity and there is consent from someone authorised under MCA 2005 to make decisions on the patient's behalf;

(c) the patient lacks capacity and force is not necessary to secure compliance; or

(d) emergency treatment needs to be given, using force if necessary, to a patient who lacks capacity.

Safeguards are provided in the shape of a 'certificate requirement' from a second opinion doctor appointed for the purposes of Part IVA. The certificate requirement only applies to s.58 or s.58A type treatment, namely, treatment to which s.58 or s.58A would have applied at the time it was given including medication and ECT. Since s.299 of the Health and Social Care Act 2012 came into force, a second opinion appointed doctor (SOAD) certificate is not required if the approved clinician (AC) in charge of the patient's treatment certifies that the patient is capable of consenting and has consented to the relevant treatment (MHA 1983, s.64C(4A), inserted by Health and Social Care Act 2012, s.299). The AC cannot give a certificate of capacity and consent if the treatment is ECT and the patient is under 18. If the treatment is medicines for mental disorder, a certificate is not required until the expiry of one month from the date the CTO was made (MHA 1983, s.64B(4)). If the CTO is made before a detained patient has been receiving medicine for three months, the period during which the certificate must be provided is extended for the duration of that three month-period, since s.58 would only apply to medicines after three months had elapsed since the first time medicines were given in that period of detention.

A certificate is not required where the treatment is 'immediately necessary' and the patient has capacity and consents. Nor is one required if the patient lacks capacity to consent, the treatment is 'immediately necessary' and there is consent from a person exercising powers under a lasting power of attorney or from a deputy appointed by the Court of Protection. The test of immediate necessity depends on the treatment. In a case where the treatment is medicine for mental disorder, treatment is immediately necessary if (MHA 1983, s.64C(5)):

(a) it is immediately necessary to save the patient's life; or
(b) it is immediately necessary to prevent a serious deterioration of the patient's condition and is not irreversible; or
(c) it is immediately necessary to alleviate serious suffering by the patient and is not irreversible or hazardous; or
(d) it is immediately necessary, represents the minimum interference necessary to prevent the patient from behaving violently or being a danger to himself or others, and is not irreversible or hazardous.

If the treatment is ECT, treatment is immediately necessary if (MHA 1983, s.64C(6)):

(a) it is immediately necessary to save the patient's life; or
(b) it is immediately necessary to prevent a serious deterioration of the patient's condition and is not irreversible.

No certificate is required where emergency treatment is given under s.64G (MHA 1983, s.64B(3)). The conditions for giving emergency treatment under s.64G are as follows:

1. When giving the treatment, the person giving it must have taken reasonable steps to assess capacity and must reasonably believe that the person lacks capacity, or if under 16 lacks competence to consent to it.
2. The treatment must be immediately necessary according to the criteria set out above in relation to medicines and ECT, respectively.
3. If it is necessary to use force to give the treatment, the treatment must be given in order to prevent harm to the patient *and* the use of force must be proportionate to the likelihood of harm and the seriousness of harm.

Although the English Code emphasises that MHA 1983, s.64G does not authorise forcible treatment aimed at preventing harm to others (para.23.17), such treatment may be authorised under the common law doctrine of necessity, as enunciated by Hale LJ (as she then was) in *Munjaz* v. *Merseycare NHS Trust and others* [2003] EWCA Civ 1306, at [46], where she said:

> There is a general power to take such steps as are reasonably necessary and proportionate to protect others from the immediate risk of significant harm. This applies whether or not the patient lacks the capacity to make decisions for himself.

121

Section 62A applies where the patient is recalled under s.17E or has the CTO revoked under s.17F. On recall to hospital, a patient may be given treatment which would otherwise require a certificate under s.58 or s.58A (medicines or ECT) on the basis of a certificate given by a SOAD under Part IVA, but only until a certificate under Part IV can be arranged. Hence, second opinion doctors giving Part IVA certificates are expected to authorise in advance treatment which may be given forcibly if the patient is recalled or has the CTO revoked. However, s.62A(6) and (6A) allow continuation of any treatment, or of treatment under any plan if the AC in charge of treatment considers that the discontinuance of the treatment, or of treatment under the plan, would cause serious suffering to the patient.

6.3.2 Review of CTOs by the Mental Health Tribunal

Eligibility to apply for a tribunal hearing: A community patient's case may come before the tribunal on an application by the patient or the nearest relative, following referral by the hospital managers under s.68 or by the Secretary of State or Welsh Ministers under s.67.

A community patient who was placed on a CTO from detention under MHA 1983, s.3 is entitled to apply to the tribunal once within the first six months, once within the second six months, and thereafter once within each subsequent period of 12 months (MHA 1983, s.66(1)(ca), (fza), (2)(ca), (fza)). If a patient applies for a tribunal while detained under s.3, but before the hearing takes place is made subject to a CTO, the tribunal hears the application as if it were for discharge from the CTO. In *AA* v. *Chester and Wirral Foundation NHS Trust* [2009] UKUT 195 (AAC), Judge Rowland said this (at [61]):

> [P]arties need to co-operate sensibly with each other and the First-tier Tribunal if a patient is made the subject of a community treatment order while an application to the tribunal is pending. In particular, it will clearly be incumbent on any representative of the applicant to inform the tribunal as soon as possible whether or not the application is being withdrawn and it is also clearly incumbent on all parties to inform the tribunal whether or not a postponement of any hearing that has already been fixed will be required in the light of the change of circumstances.

Hence, there is a duty on all parties to keep the tribunal informed of the position when the patient's legal status has changed.

If the patient was placed on a CTO from a hospital order made by a court under s.37, the patient does not acquire a right to apply until six months have elapsed from the date of the hospital order being made (MHA 1983, s.69(4)). The patient may, however, ask the managers to exercise their power of discharge under s.23(2)(c) during that time. Other Part III patients who were not given a hospital order by a court but are treated as if they had been given an unrestricted hospital order ('notional s.37s') and are placed on a CTO have the right to apply within the first six months of the CTO (Department of Health, *Reference Guide to the Mental Health Act 1983* (London, 2008), Tables 22.3 and 22.9). If the CTO is revoked under s.17F, the patient has the right to apply to the tribunal within six months following the date of revocation (MHA 1983, s.66(1)(cb), (2)(cb)).

Nearest relative applications: The nearest relative of a patient subject to a CTO may direct discharge of a community patient from the CTO provided the patient has been placed on the CTO from s.3 detention, and 72 hours notice has been given to the managers of the responsible hospital (MHA 1983, ss.23(1A), (2)(c), 25). The direction for discharge may be barred by the RC on grounds that the patient, if discharged, would be likely to act in a manner dangerous to self or to others. The NR has a right to apply to the tribunal within 28 days of being informed that the RC's 'barring certificate' has been issued (MHA 1983, s.66(1)(g), (2)(d)), and the tribunal must discharge if not satisfied that the patient if discharged from the CTO would be likely to act in a manner dangerous to self or to others (MHA 1983, s.72(1)(c)(v)). If the patient was placed on the CTO from detention under s.37 following a hospital order made by a court, the NR has no power to direct discharge but does have the right to apply to the MHT once in the second six months following the making of the hospital order. The relatives of other Part III patients who were not given a hospital order by a court but are treated as if they had been given an unrestricted hospital order ('notional s.37s') and are placed on a CTO have the right to apply at any time within the first six months of the CTO (Department of Health, *Reference Guide to the Mental Health Act 1983* (London, 2008), Tables 22.3 and 22.9). In such cases, the dangerousness criterion is not applied by the tribunal in assessing entitlement to discharge.

References to the tribunal: The duty of hospital managers to refer patients' cases to the tribunal under MHA 1983, s.68 applies to CTO patients. If the patient was placed on the CTO from detention under s.3, the hospital managers must refer the case at the end of the first six months beginning with the day on which the patient was admitted for treatment (or for assessment if there was a preceding s.2 detention), and thereafter if three years have elapsed since his case was last considered by a tribunal. In *KF, MO and FF* v. *Birmingham and Solihull NHS Mental Health Foundation Trust* [2010] UKUT 185 (AAC), [2011] AACR 3, a three-judge panel approved *AA* v. *Chester and Wirral Foundation NHS Trust* [2009] UKUT 195 (AAC), and decided that a reference made while a patient was detained under s.3 did not lapse when the patient was made the subject of a CTO.

If the patient was placed on a CTO from detention under s.37 following a hospital order made by a court, the managers of the responsible hospital must refer the patient's case if three years have elapsed since the patient's case was last considered by a tribunal.

The English Rules governing tribunal procedure provide for a decision on a reference under s.68 to be made without a hearing in the case of a CTO patient over 18 if:

(a)   the patient has stated in writing that s/he does not wish to attend or be represented at a hearing of the reference and the tribunal is satisfied that the patient has the capacity to decide whether or not to make that decision; or

(b)   the patient's representative has stated in writing that the patient does not wish to attend or be represented at the hearing of the reference (see Tribunal Procedure (First-Tier Tribunal) (Health, Education and Social Care Chamber) Rules 2008, SI 2008/2699 (as amended), rule 35(3)).

If the CTO is revoked, the hospital managers must refer the patient's case to the tribunal 'as soon as possible after the order is revoked' (MHA 1983, s.68(7)).

In 2010 Deputy Chamber President Judge Hinchliffe issued guidance on s.68(7) references to deal with the situation where a person's CTO is revoked, but they are then shortly afterwards placed on a new CTO. The guidance states that:[6]

> After careful consideration of the overriding objective, and to enable the tribunal to deal with its cases proportionately, I have decided that following a reference under section 68(7), if the patient is subsequently placed on a new CTO, the 68(7) reference will be treated as having lapsed, and no further action will be taken by the tribunal in relation to it . . . Accordingly, if a CTO patient is recalled and the CTO is revoked under section 17F, Hospital Managers must continue to refer cases to the tribunal pursuant to s.68(7) – but *must then notify the tribunal immediately if the patient is placed on a new CTO*. Following such notification the referral will be treated as having lapsed, the parties should be notified, and the file will be closed unless there are other outstanding references or applications, in which case consideration will be given to the management or, consolidation and listing of any continuing proceedings. [emphasis in original]

In *PS* v. *Camden and Islington NHS Foundation Trust* [2011] UKUT 143 (AAC), the patient had her CTO revoked and the managers referred the case to the MHT under s.68(7), but shortly afterwards a new CTO was made and the patient was returned to the community. The First-tier Tribunal judge followed the above policy and decided that s.68(7) referrals should generally be treated as lapsed if, before the hearing, the patient is again discharged from hospital back on to a CTO. However, he agreed to treat a letter from the applicant's solicitors protesting about this as a fresh application by the patient. In the Upper Tribunal, Judge Jacobs held that the referral did not lapse and found the policy to be unlawful. He accepted the authority of *KF, MO and FF* v. *Birmingham and Solihull NHS Mental Health Foundation Trust* [2010] UKUT 185 (AAC), [2011] AACR 3, and *AA* v. *Chester and Wirral Foundation NHS Trust* [2009] UKUT 195 (AAC), saying (at [15]): 'Given that the legislation places a patient whose community treatment order has been revoked in the same position as any other patient detained under section 3, the reasoning in those cases governs this case'.

It had been suggested that the reason for the policy of treating s.68(7) referrals as lapsing on the making of a new CTO was that patients were reluctant to co-operate and participate in such hearings. Judge Jacobs suggested that an appropriate solution might be 'to arrange block hearings of community treatment references on the limited information that it is able to obtain'. Such a procedure has now been introduced in England by the changes to the rules described above, allowing for paper hearings in such cases.

---

[6]   **www.mhrt.org.uk/Documents/News/68_7_Guidance_CTO_22July10.pdf**.

The Secretary of State for Health or Welsh Ministers may at any time refer a CTO patient's case to the tribunal under MHA 1983, s.67 (for a full discussion of such references, see **4.14**).

6.4 CONCLUSION

This chapter has considered patients' entitlement to community care support and after-care services, the powers in MHA 1983, Part II to subject patients to guardianship under s.7 or a community treatment order under ss.17A–17G, and the entitlement of patients subject to those provisions and their relatives to apply for a tribunal hearing. **Chapters 7** and **8** deal with the powers and duties of tribunals relating to non-offender and offender patients, respectively.

CHAPTER 7

Tribunal powers and duties in relation to unrestricted patients and community patients

The powers of the tribunal in any case depend on the provision of MHA 1983 under which the patient is detained. The tribunal's powers in relation to unrestricted patients (patients who are not subject to a restriction order, a restriction direction or a limitation direction), those subject to guardianship, and community patients are set out in MHA 1983, s.72. Powers in relation to restriction order patients are contained in s.73, and in relation to restriction direction patients in s.74. Finally, s.75 sets out the tribunal's powers when considering applications and references concerning conditionally-discharged restricted patients. This chapter deals with the tribunal's powers in relation to unrestricted, guardianship and community patients under s.72.

The role and functions of Mental Health Tribunals are discussed in **Chapter 2**. In essence, the tribunal's task is to determine whether at the time of the hearing, the criteria justifying detention, guardianship or a community treatment order (CTO) continue to be met. Any challenges to the lawfulness of decisions to detain, subject to guardianship, or impose a CTO in the first place, and the lawfulness of decisions to renew compulsion, continue to be matters to be dealt with in the High Court by way of judicial review or *habeas corpus* (*R* v. *Hallstrom and another, ex p. W* (1985) 2 BMLR 54, [1985] 3 All ER 775; and *R* v. *North West Thames Mental Health Review Tribunal, ex p. Cooper* (1990) 5 BMLR 7). Although the tribunal has different powers in relation to restricted and unrestricted patients, the burden and standard of proof to be applied in relation to each group are the same, as described below. The one exception is in relation to patients subject to guardianship, where the burden rests with the patient to establish entitlement to discharge (MHA 1983, s.72(4)).

7.1 BURDEN OF PROOF

For the first 40 years of its existence the Mental Health Review Tribunal (MHRT) operated under a reverse of the normal common law presumption that it is for those carrying out the detention to justify it, rather than for the detainee to justify his or her freedom (see e.g. Lord Atkin in *Liversidge* v. *Anderson* [1942] AC 206, at 245, where he said that 'in English law every imprisonment is prima facie unlawful, and it is for the person directing the imprisonment to justify his act'). Prior to November 2001, patients would only be entitled to discharge if they could satisfy the tribunal that they were no longer suffering from mental disorder of a nature or degree warranting confinement. This faced patients with the considerable burden of establishing a negative, the absence of mental disorder of a nature or degree making detention for medical treatment appropriate. In a series of cases decided prior to the coming into force of HRA 1998, the courts emphasised the importance of this reverse burden of proof. (See e.g. *R* v. *Canons Park Mental Health Review Tribunal, ex p. A* [1994] 2 All ER 659 (CA). The reverse burden was also emphasised in *Perkins* v. *Bath District Health Authority; R* v. *Wessex Mental Health Review Tribunal, ex p. Wiltshire County Council* (1989) 4 BMLR 145 (CA); and *R* v. *Merseyside Mental Health Review Tribunal, ex p. K* [1990] 1 All ER 694, (1989) 4 BMLR 60 (CA).) The European Court of Human Rights (ECtHR) case law also contained suggestions that the burden of proof might be incompatible with European Convention on Human Rights (ECHR) rights (see in particular, *James Kay* v. *United Kingdom* (Application 17821/91), Decision of 7 July 1993).

In *R (H)* v. *London North and East Region Mental Health Review Tribunal (Secretary of State for Health intervening)* [2001] 3 WLR 512 (CA),[1] the first declaration of incompatibility granted under HRA 1998, the Court of Appeal held that the positioning of the burden of proof under ss.72 and 73 on the applicant to satisfy the tribunal of the absence of detainable mental disorder was incompatible with ECHR, art.5.

The Government introduced a remedial order to rectify the incompatibility. Under the amended s.72(1)(b) a patient is entitled to discharge if the tribunal is not satisfied (MHA 1983, s.72(1)(b) as amended by the Mental Health Act 1983 (Remedial) Order 2001, SI 2001/3712, and MHA 2007, s.4(8)(a), Sched.1, para.14):

(i)   that he is then suffering from mental disorder or from mental disorder of a *nature or degree* which makes it appropriate for him to be *liable to be detained* in hospital for medical treatment; or

(ii)   that it is necessary for the health or safety of the patient or for the protection of other persons that he should receive such treatment; or

(iia)   that appropriate medical treatment is available for him; or

(iii)   in the case of an application by [the nearest relative following the barring of a

---

[1]   See also *Lyons* v. *Scottish Ministers* (unreported, First Division of Scottish Court of Session, 17 January 2002).

discharge order], that the patient, if released, would be likely to act in a manner dangerous to himself or to other persons.

The tribunal must discharge if not satisfied that any *one* of conditions (i), (ii) or (iia) is met or, in the case of a nearest relative application following a barring certificate, if not satisfied that condition (iii) is met (i.e. if not satisfied that *all* relevant conditions are met).

In *R (N)* v. *Mental Health Review Tribunal (Northern Region)* [2005] EWCA Civ 1605, 88 BMLR 59 (CA), Richards LJ acknowledged that the burden of proof is on the detaining authority to satisfy the tribunal that the conditions of detention are met. His Lordship went on to say that (at [87]):

> The existence of the burden is unaffected by the fact that aspects of the tribunal's procedures are inquisitorial in nature (for example, the requirement of a medical examination by the medical member of the tribunal and the power to require the attendance of witnesses and to call for further information).

The English Code of Practice emphasises this too (para.32.4; similar wording is used in Welsh Code of Practice, para.26.3):

> It is for those who believe that a patient should continue to be detained or remain an SCT patient to prove their case, not for the patient to disprove it. They will therefore need to present the Tribunal with sufficient evidence to support continuing liability to detention or SCT.

In many cases the tribunal will be able to rely on evidence put before them by the parties and that evidence will be cogent. However, as Collins J put it in *R (X)* v. *Mental Health Review Tribunal* [2003] EWHC 1272 (Admin), at [25]–[30] (albeit in this case concerning a restricted patient, but still relevant in unrestricted cases):

> the Tribunal will inevitably, and particularly in a case involving the release of someone who has committed a very serious offence, have regard to whether there is any danger to the public, and in undertaking its task, it must of necessity be concerned that it has before it all relevant information which will enable it to reach the correct decision in the circumstances of the individual case.
>
> The Tribunal will normally rely upon the material that is put before it by the responsible bodies: on the one hand the authority and [where relevant] the Secretary of State . . . ; and on the other, such material and such reports as the patient chooses to present before the Tribunal.
>
> But the Tribunal must clearly have to consider in every case whether there is a gap in the evidence which it requires to be filled in order to enable it to reach the right decision.

Hence, the responsible authority needs to produce cogent evidence to justify continued compulsion, but the tribunal still retains important inquisitorial powers and those powers may be used to gather evidence to supplement that revealed by examination and cross-examination by the parties. In this sense the proceedings must be viewed as a hybrid between adversarial and inquisitorial.[2]

7.2 STANDARD OF PROOF

The question of the standard of proof to be applied, initially dismissed by Ackner LJ in *R* v. *Mental Health Review Tribunal, ex p. Hayes* (unreported, CA Civil Division, 9 May 1985), as 'an academic' question of little concern to the courts, has now been clarified by case law. In *R (N)* v. *Mental Health Review Tribunal (Northern Region)* [2005] EWCA Civ 1605, 88 BMLR 59 (CA), Richards LJ, delivering the judgment of the Court of Appeal, affirmed that the standard of proof was the balance of probabilities, which in relation to matters of fact means that the court (or tribunal) must be satisfied that the occurrence of the event is more likely than not. The standard was to be flexibly applied. As Richards LJ put it (at [62]):

> Although there is a single civil standard of proof on the balance of probabilities, it is flexible in its application. In particular, the more serious the allegation or the more serious the consequences if the allegation is proved, the stronger must be the evidence before a court will find the allegation proved on the balance of probabilities. Thus the flexibility of the standard lies not in any adjustment to the degree of probability required for an allegation to be proved (such that a more serious allegation has to be proved to a higher degree of probability), but in the strength or quality of the evidence that will in practice be required for an allegation to be proved on the balance of probabilities.

Richards LJ went on to say that 'the seriousness of the consequences if a matter is proved is nonetheless a factor to be taken into account when deciding in practice whether the evidence is sufficiently strong to prove that matter on the balance of probabilities' (at [70]).

As to the question whether a particularly high standard of probability is required to meet the requirements of s.72, Richards LJ said that 'cogent evidence will in practice be required in order to satisfy the tribunal, on the balance of probabilities, that the conditions for continuing detention are met. But we would not put it any higher than that' (at [72]).

The Court of Appeal held that the standard of balance of probabilities applies to all the questions under s.72 (at [101]):

> the question under section 72(1)(b)(i) whether the person is suffering from a mental disorder 'of a nature or degree which makes it appropriate for him to be liable to be detained in a hospital for medical treatment', is a mixed question of fact and judgment or evaluation. The nature and degree of the mental disorder is a question of fact and is accepted to be susceptible to proof on the balance of probabilities. There is a certain artificiality in applying a standard of proof to that question but not to the related question whether the nature and degree of the disorder make detention appropriate.

---

[2] For an interesting discussion of these issues see J. Cooper and H. Davis, 'Is there a Burden of Proof in Mental Health Cases?' (2011) *Journal of Mental Health Law* (Spring) 5.

The court considered that the tribunal's task would be made easier if it approached all the issues by reference to the standard of proof on the balance of probabilities, 'whilst recognising that in practice the standard of proof will have a much more important part to play in the determination of disputed issues of fact than it will generally have in matters of judgment as to appropriateness and necessity' (at [103]).

7.3 DISCRETION TO DISCHARGE

In respect of non-restricted patients, the tribunal has a general discretion to discharge a patient from liability to detention or guardianship in any case under MHA 1983, s.72(1), which states that the tribunal 'may in any case direct that the patient be discharged'. The Act used to specify factors to be taken into account in exercising this discretion, such as the likelihood of medical treatment alleviating or preventing deterioration of the patient's condition, but these provisions have been repealed (MHA 1983, s.72(2), repealed by MHA 2007, s.4(8)). Where the tribunal exercises the discretion to discharge it must give reasons. Where satisfied that there has been risk to self or to others, the tribunal will have to consider and spell out what treatment is considered necessary and satisfy itself that this would be available without the need for the patient to remain liable to be detained (*R (East London and City Mental Health NHS Trust)* v. *Mental Health Review Tribunal* [2005] EWHC 2329 (Admin), at [19]–[20] (Collins J)).

Section 72(3A) provides that nothing in s.72(1) requires a tribunal to direct the discharge of a patient just because it thinks it might be appropriate for the patient to be discharged (subject to the possibility of recall) under a CTO. If the tribunal considers a CTO may be appropriate, rather than direct discharge in the exercise of discretion, the tribunal may recommend that the responsible clinician (RC) consider a CTO, and may (but need not) further consider the patient's case if the RC does not make an order.

7.4 DUTY TO DISCHARGE UNDER MENTAL HEALTH ACT 1983, S.72

The circumstances in which the tribunal comes under a duty to discharge detained patients and CTO patients are set out in MHA 1983, s.72(1). The circumstances where it has a duty to discharge guardianship patients are found in s.72(4).

7.4.1 Duty to discharge Mental Health Act 1983, s.2 patients

Section 72(1)(a)(i)–(ii) provide that the tribunal *must* discharge a patient admitted under s.2 if it is not satisfied *either*:

(i)   that he is then suffering from mental disorder or from mental disorder of a nature or degree which warrants detention in hospital for assessment (or for assessment followed by medical treatment) for at least a limited period; or

(ii) that his detention is justified in the interests of his own health or safety or with a view to the protection of others.

The criteria for discharge correspond with the criteria for admission. The words used in s.72(1)(a)(i) and in s.72(1)(b)(i) in relation to other detained patients are 'not satisfied that he is *then* suffering', which make it clear that the tribunal must consider the patient's condition at the time of the hearing. The concept of mental disorder which applies to this provision includes learning disability, but in this case without the need for the disability to be accompanied by abnormally aggressive or seriously irresponsible conduct on the patient's part. Learning disability is defined in MHA 1983, s.1(4) as 'a state of arrested or incomplete development of the mind which includes significant impairment of intelligence and social functioning'.

The terms 'nature or degree' in relation to mental disorder are disjunctive. In other words, a person can have a detainable mental disorder which although not currently exhibiting symptoms of a degree justifying detention, nevertheless is of such a serious nature that detention is warranted (*R* v. *Mental Health Review Tribunal for the South Thames Region, ex p. Smith* (1998) 47 BMLR 104). In relation to mentally ill patients detained under s.2, the patient will usually have been admitted because the illness has been manifesting itself in symptoms of a degree justifying detention, and the purpose of the detention may well be to assess (or reassess) the true nature of the mental disorder. However, a patient may have been diagnosed with a disorder whose nature might justify detention, but it might have been some time since the patient had been in hospital or in contact with the secondary psychiatric service so the purpose of admitting for assessment might be to reassess either the nature or the degree of the disorder. In criterion (ii), 'in the interests of his own health or safety' is an alternative to 'the protection of other persons'. The tribunal may decide not to discharge the patient if only one of the grounds (own health *or* own safety *or* the protection of others) is fulfilled.

7.4.2 Duty to discharge patients detained under Mental Health Act 1983, s.3 or s.37

Section 72(1)(b) provides that the tribunal has a duty to discharge a patient detained under ss.3 or 37 if it is *not* satisfied:

(i) that he is then suffering from mental disorder or from mental disorder of a nature or degree which makes it appropriate for him to be liable to be detained in a hospital for medical treatment; or

(ii) that it is necessary for the health or safety of the patient or for the protection of other persons that he should receive such treatment; or

(iia) that appropriate medical treatment is available for him; or

(iii) in the case of an application by the nearest relative following the barring of a discharge order, that the patient, if released, would be likely to act in a manner dangerous to other persons or to himself. (NB This provision does not apply to patients detained under s.37.)

If the tribunal is not satisfied that all relevant grounds apply, it is under a duty to discharge. The tribunal is under a duty to give reasons for its decision, whether the decision is to discharge or not. Case law (see *Bone* v. *Mental Health Review Tribunal* [1985] 3 All ER 330; *R* v. *Mental Health Review Tribunal, ex p. Clatworthy* [1985] 3 All ER 699, 703; *R* v. *Mental Health Review Tribunal, ex p. Pickering* [1986] 1 All ER 99, 104 (Forbes J)) has established that reasons must not be mere rehearsals of the statutory criteria, but they must address each of the issues in s.72(1)(b)(i)–(iii), where relevant. They must be adequate and intelligible, and must reasonably be said to deal with the substantial points that have been raised. It has to be possible to read from the reasons the issue to which they are directed. Where there is a conflict of evidence the reasons have to reveal why the tribunal had accepted the evidence of one party and not the other. The key question to ask was whether the tribunal 'has provided the parties with sufficient material to enable them to know that the tribunal has made no error of law in reaching its finding of fact?'.

In *R (Ashworth Hospital Authority)* v. *Mental Health Review Tribunal for West Midlands and Northwest Region* [2002] EWCA Civ 923, the Court of Appeal upheld Stanley Burnton J's decision to quash (as *Wednesbury*[3] irrational) the tribunal's direction to discharge the patient immediately where the preponderance of the medical evidence was against discharge, and the tribunal's reasons showed that it had not given adequate attention to the need for and availability of after-care support. The court held that reasons must deal with the entirety of the tribunal's decision and not merely whether there is mental disorder of the relevant nature or degree and whether it is safe to discharge. Dyson LJ held that where the tribunal is required to resolve a difference of opinion between experts as to whether the patient should be discharged it is important that the tribunal should state which, if any, of the expert evidence it accepts and which it rejects, giving reasons. The reasons must at least indicate the reasoning process by which the tribunal has decided to accept some and reject other evidence. In this case, the reasons given for deciding to accept the evidence of one doctor and reject that of the other experts were 'wholly inadequate'. Moreover, the tribunal was required to give reasons for not adjourning to see whether adequate after-care arrangements could be made, or for not making an order for deferred discharge.

Each of the grounds of discharge will now be considered in turn.

---

[3] *Associated Provincial Picture Houses* v. *Wednesbury Corporation* [1948] 1 KB 223. '*Wednesbury* irrational' has been summarised by Lord Diplock as: 'So outrageous in its defiance of logic or accepted moral standards that no sensible person who had applied his mind to the question to be decided could have arrived at it': *Council of Civil Service Unions* v. *Minister for the Civil Service* [1985] AC 374, at 410.

7.4.3   Mental Health Act 1983, s.72(1)(b)(i)

Not satisfied . . . that the patient is then suffering from mental disorder or from mental disorder of a nature or degree which makes it appropriate for him to be liable to be detained in a hospital for medical treatment.

Mental disorder

MHA 1983, s.1(2) provides a broad definition of mental disorder as 'any disorder or disability of the mind'. For the purposes of s.72(1)(b), mental disorder does not include learning disability unless that disability is associated with abnormally aggressive or seriously irresponsible conduct on the patient's part (MHA 1983, s.1(2A)(a), (2B)(c)). The question of what might be abnormally aggressive or seriously irresponsible conduct (the 'conduct requirement') is discussed at **3.7.3**.

One issue for the tribunal in relation to learning disabled patients may well be the extent to which there must be recent evidence of abnormally aggressive or seriously irresponsible conduct in order for the tribunal to be satisfied that the conduct requirement is met in the patient's case. The main case law of relevance to this issue is *R (P)* v. *Mental Health Review Tribunal (East Midlands and North East Region)* [2002] EWCA Civ 697, which, although it relates to a restricted patient with a diagnosis of psychopathic disorder under the previous MHA definition, is still relevant here. The issue was whether the patient could still be suffering from psychopathic disorder even though there had been no recent abnormally aggressive or seriously irresponsible conduct. It was not in dispute that P suffered from psychopathic disorder at the time of his index offence in 1992 of manslaughter of a young man whom he had ferociously assaulted. But there had been no abnormally aggressive or seriously irresponsible conduct for some years. Pill LJ said this (at [23] and [26]):

> The extent to which abnormally aggressive or seriously irresponsible conduct now occurs may throw light on whether there is a psychopathic disorder, but the disorder may still exist, even if there has been no such conduct for several years.
>
> I have no difficulty in accepting that the Tribunal were entitled to decide that a disorder which admittedly existed in 1992 still existed in 2000, even though, because of successful management of the condition, no abnormally aggressive or seriously irresponsible conduct has occurred for several years.

Thorpe LJ applied this ruling in relation to learning disability in *Lewis* v. *Gibson* [2005] EWCA Civ 587, where he said (at [31]):

> Although those observations were made in relation to psychopathic disorder that 'results in' aggressive or irresponsible conduct, in my judgment they apply equally to severe mental impairment that is 'associated with' abnormally aggressive or seriously irresponsible conduct. To make a balanced assessment of the patient's present state some regard must be had to the past history and the future propensity. A conclusion based only on the recent past, which might represent a transient phase of quiescence, would be superficial.

Therefore it may be difficult to argue that the conduct requirement is not met in relation to a patient with a learning disability even if there is no recent evidence of abnormally aggressive or seriously irresponsible conduct.

'Nature or degree which makes it appropriate for him to be liable to be detained in hospital for medical treatment'

The patient must be discharged if the tribunal is not satisfied that he is then suffering from mental disorder of a nature or degree which makes it appropriate for him to be liable to be detained in hospital for treatment. The terms 'nature or degree' in relation to mental disorder are disjunctive. In other words, a person can have a mental disorder which although not currently exhibiting symptoms of a degree justifying detention, nevertheless is of a nature that it is appropriate for him to be liable to be detained (*R* v. *Mental Health Review Tribunal for the South Thames Region, ex p. Smith* (1998) 47 BMLR 104).

Note here that the mental disorder must be of a nature or degree which makes it appropriate for the patient to be *liable to be detained* in hospital, not necessarily of a nature or degree making detention appropriate. While cases like *R* v. *Canons Park Mental Health Review Tribunal, ex p. A* [1995] QB 60 (CA); *Reid* v. *Secretary of State for Scotland* [1999] 2 WLR 28 (HL); and *Reid* v. *United Kingdom* (2003) 37 EHRR 9 show a trend towards requiring tribunals to apply discharge criteria which mirror the admission criteria in order to guarantee compliance with ECHR, art.5(4), this is not so of detention under MHA 1983, s.3 or s.37. The phrase 'liable to be detained' was retained from the Mental Health Act 1959 and introduced in MHA 1983 as a result of arguments that the tribunal should not be obliged to discharge someone who was on s.17 leave if it is satisfied that the patient still needs the discipline of liability to recall although not requiring to be actually detained in hospital. The wording adopted means that a patient cannot claim entitlement to discharge in cases where the tribunal considers it appropriate for the patient to remain liable to be detained and therefore liable to recall in order to ensure that s/he continues to accept medication.

In *R (DR)* v. *Merseycare NHS Trust* [2002] EWHC 1810 (Admin), the patient was receiving no in-patient treatment while on leave, but was receiving treatment in hospital as an out-patient. Wilson J held that the only relevant question to renewal, which could only take place if treatment in hospital was necessary, was whether a significant component of the treatment plan for the claimant included treatment in hospital. That treatment did not have to be as an in-patient. In effect 'in hospital' was deemed to be the same as 'at hospital'. In *R (CS)* v. *Mental Health Review Tribunal* [2004] EWHC 2958 (Admin), [2004] MHLR 355, the patient was residing at her home on s.17 leave on condition that she attend weekly sessions with her psychologist and attended ward rounds once per month. The purpose of the ward round requirement was to give the patient the necessary motivation and encouragement to progress in the community. Pitchford J held that the MHRT had acted lawfully in declining to discharge on the grounds that some treatment in hospital was still required. Cases like *DR* and *CS*, where prolonged use was made of s.17 leave, are less likely to occur since the changes introduced by MHA 2007. MHA 1983, 17(2A) now requires an RC, before sending a patient on s.17 leave for more than seven consecutive days, to first consider placing the patient on a CTO under s.17A.

Patients who are currently asymptomatic but who are at risk of relapse

In *R* v. *London and South West Mental Health Review Tribunal, ex p. Moyle* [1999] MHLR 195, Latham J considered that the correct approach in the case of a patient with a history of relapsing if he ceased medication was to ask the question:

> Whether the nature of that illness is such as to make it appropriate for him to be liable to be detained in a hospital for medical treatment. Whether it is appropriate or not will depend upon an assessment of the probability that *he will relapse in the near future if he were free in the community*. [emphasis added]

Judge Levenson applied this test in *CM* v. *DH NHS Foundation Trust* [2011] UKUT 129 (AAC), at [12]. CM was a restricted patient who had been recalled to hospital three times in the past, not as a result of deterioration in his mental state or because of non-compliance with medication, but as a result of his chaotic lifestyle and his consumption of illicit drugs. The tribunal had concluded that there was a risk that CM's 'chaotic lifestyle, continued consumption of drugs, and failure to keep appointments with his supervisors will *eventually* lead to non-compliance with his medication' (at [22]). Judge Levenson held that the tribunal's decision was made in error of law and must be set aside because 'there was no real evidence to support its view that non-compliance with medication and the risk of consequent relapse *in the near future* would probably occur, [and] because it did not establish that in these circumstances it had complied with the "least restriction principle"' (at [27]). Finally, Judge Levenson held that 'continued detention for the purposes of avoiding a chaotic lifestyle or drug taking or the absence of drug counselling is not permitted by law on the facts of this case'. For these reasons the decision was quashed and a rehearing ordered. The assessment of the probability of relapse in the near future on the balance of probabilities is likely to be a highly subjective exercise. Where the nature of the illness is deemed severe, a great deal will depend on the cogency of evidence that the patient is likely to relapse in the near future.

In *R (H)* v. *Mental Health Review Tribunal North and North East London Region* [2001] EWCA Civ 415[4] (the burden of proof / declaration of incompatibility case) Lord Phillips MR suggested that the issue of the asymptomatic patient who is at risk of relapse might be resolved by recourse to the principle of proportionality when he said this (at [33]):

> A patient is detained who is unquestionably suffering from schizophrenia. While in the controlled environment of the hospital he is taking medication, and as a result of the

---

[4]   Elias J followed this approach in *R (Secretary of State for the Home Department)* v. *Mental Health Review Tribunal* [2002] EWHC 1128 (Admin), at [24].

medication is in remission. So long as he continues to take the medication he will pose no danger to himself or to others. The nature of the illness is such, however, that if he ceases to take the medication he will relapse and pose a danger to himself or to others. The professionals may be uncertain whether, if he is discharged into the community, he will continue to take the medication. We do not believe that Article 5 requires that the patient must always be discharged in such circumstances. The appropriate response should depend upon the result of weighing the interests of the patient against those of the public having regard to the particular facts. Continued detention can be justified if, but only if, it is a proportionate response having regard to the risks that would be involved in discharge.

Under the ECtHR case law, for detention on grounds of unsoundness of mind to be lawful, the mental disorder must be of a kind or degree warranting compulsory confinement. The ECtHR has repeatedly held (most recently in *X* v. *Finland* [2012] ECHR 1371, at [151]) that:

> detention of an individual is such a serious measure that it is only justified where other, less severe measures have been considered and found to be insufficient to safeguard the individual or public interest which might require that the person concerned be detained. That means that it does not suffice that the deprivation of liberty is executed in conformity with national law but it must also be necessary in the circumstances.

In other words, the detention must be a proportionate response. In *Stojanovksi* v. *Macedonia* (unreported, ECtHR, 22 October 2009), a case where the domestic court considering discharge had been influenced more by the fears of the villagers than by the medical opinion of the detaining hospital that the applicant was ready for discharge, the court held his continued confinement to contravene ECHR, art.5(4) because it was 'manifestly disproportionate to his state of mind at that time' (para.36).

The principle of proportionality is implemented by the requirement that detention must be necessary in the interests of the patient's health or safety or for the protection of others, and the precondition of detention for treatment in MHA 1983, s.3(2)(c) that the treatment which the patient needs cannot be provided unless he is detained.

In *DL-H* v. *Devon Partnership NHS Trust and Secretary of State for Justice* [2010] UKUT 102 (AAC), Judge Jacobs expressed the view that introducing the concept of proportionality into the application of MHA 1983, ss.72 and 73 could (at [27]):

> divert attention from the wording of the legislation and bring with it connotations that are not appropriate in the mental health context. The tribunal must discharge the patient unless detention for treatment is necessary for the patient's health or safety or for the protection of others. The legislation authorises detention by reference to the twin requirements of treatment and protection moderated by the word 'necessary'. That is a demanding test and provides ample protection for the patient without the need for any additional consideration of proportionality.

Professor Richard Jones is emphatic that (*Mental Health Act Manual* (15th edn, London, Sweet & Maxwell, 2012), p.398):

Although when making a determination under this section the tribunal must consider the proportionality which the patient's mental state and needs bear to the steps proposed by the responsible clinician, there is no requirement in Article 5 that detention must be proportionate. Article 5 protects against arbitrary detention; it does not incorporate any additional requirement of proportionality.

There may not be an express requirement of proportionality in ECHR, art.5 itself, but it is clear from the ECtHR case law that detention will only be lawful if it is strictly necessary to safeguard the individual or public interest which might require that the person concerned be detained (see *X* v. *Finland* [2012] ECHR 1371, at [151], and the cases cited there).

7.4.4 Mental Health Act 1983, s.72(1)(b)(ii)

Not satisfied . . . that it is necessary for the health or safety of the patient or for the protection of other persons that [the patient] should receive such treatment.

The tribunal must discharge if it is not satisfied that the treatment is necessary for the health *or* safety of the patient *or* for the protection of other persons. If it is necessary for one of these reasons, that will be enough to justify continued detention, provided the other grounds for detention, including the availability of appropriate treatment test, have been met. 'Necessary' means necessary and not desirable, and such an interpretation is essential to comply with ECHR (*Reid* v. *Secretary of State for Scotland* [1999] 1 All ER 481, at 504 (Lord Clyde)). 'For the protection of other persons' is a lower threshold than the requirement to make a restriction order: that restrictions are necessary to 'protect the public from serious harm'. The treatment might be necessary to protect one other person, for example a family member, and the harm need not be physical but could be psychological or emotional (*R* v. *North London Mental Health Trust, ex p. Stewart* (1996) 39 BMLR 105; English Code of Practice, para.4.8).

With decisions about entitlement to discharge under s.72(1)(b)(i) or (ii), the availability of after-care support and the availability of some levers to ensure compliance will often be crucial factors in the tribunal's decision that the risk posed by the patient to his own health or safety or to other people can safely be managed in the community. If the tribunal does not consider itself under a duty to discharge under either of these provisions but considers it might be appropriate for the patient to be discharged into the community under a CTO, it may, under s.72(3A), recommend that the RC consider whether to make a CTO; and may (but need not) further consider the patient's case if the RC does not make a CTO. Section 72(3A), it will be remembered, states that 'Subsection (1) above does not require a tribunal to direct the discharge of a patient just because it thinks it might be appropriate for the patient to be discharged (subject to the possibility of recall) under a community treatment order'.

7.4.5 Mental Health Act 1983, s.72(1)(b)(iia)

> Not satisfied . . . that appropriate medical treatment is available.

It is impossible to disagree with Professor Richard Jones' one line note on this provision in his *Mental Health Act Manual*, where he says that 'It will be difficult for a patient to successfully challenge a RC's assertion that this test is satisfied' (*Mental Health Act Manual* (15th edn, London, Sweet & Maxwell, 2012), p.405). Medical treatment is extremely broadly defined in MHA 1983, s.145(1) which states that: 'medical treatment includes nursing, psychological intervention and specialist mental health habilitation, rehabilitation and care'. Section 3(4) provides that references to appropriate medical treatment are references to medical treatment which is appropriate in the patient's case, taking into account the nature and degree of the mental disorder and all other circumstances of his/her case. Section 145(4) provides that 'Any reference in this Act to medical treatment, in relation to mental disorder, shall be construed as a reference to medical treatment the purpose of which is to alleviate, or prevent a worsening of, the disorder or one or more of its symptoms or manifestations'.

Treatment for mental disorder and the availability of appropriate treatment are discussed at **3.11**. As noted there, the English Code of Practice says this, *inter alia*, about appropriate treatment (paras.6.16–6.17; see also Welsh Code of Practice, paras.4.15–4.16):

> Appropriate medical treatment does not have to involve medication or individual or group psychological therapy – although it very often will. There may be patients whose particular circumstances mean that treatment may be appropriate even though it consists only of nursing and specialist day-to-day care under the clinical supervision of an approved clinician, in a safe and secure therapeutic environment.
>
> Simply detaining someone – even in a hospital – does not constitute medical treatment.

Although nursing and care, without more, can be treatment as long as it has one of the purposes set out in s.145(4), in *MD* v. *Nottinghamshire Healthcare Trust* [2010] UKUT 59 (AAC), the contention was made on behalf of the patient that detention in hospital without the possibility of reduction of the risk posed by the patient was mere containment ('simply detaining someone') and not appropriate treatment. Judge Jacobs, dismissing this argument, said (at [34]):

> The treatment has to be appropriate, but it need not reduce the risk. Section 145(4) provides that it is sufficient if the treatment is for the purpose of preventing a worsening of the symptoms or manifestations. That envisages that the treatment required may not reduce risk. It is also sufficient if it will alleviate but one of the symptoms or manifestations, regardless of the impact on the risk posed by the patient.

The First-tier Tribunal had concluded that the patient had been ([25]–[26]):

> engaging in and benefiting from the specialist nursing care and 'milieu' therapy on the ward . . . nursing and specialist day-to-day care under clinical supervision of an approved

clinician, in a safe and secure therapeutic environment with a structured regime . . . the language of Code paragraph 6.16.

Judge Jacobs held that the distinction between containment and treatment and the definition of 'available' and 'appropriate' were 'matters of fact and judgment for the tribunal . . . [which] is an expert body and . . . has to use that expertise to make its findings and exercise its judgment' (at [48]). The line between treatment and containment would only be crossed 'if there was no prospect of the patient progressing beyond milieu' while in this case 'there was the potential for the milieu to benefit the patient in both the short and longer term' (at [35]) (although the concept of 'milieu therapy' was not further defined).

In *DH-L* v. *Devon Partnership NHS Trust* [2010] UKUT 102 (AAC), Judge Jacobs returned to the issue of availability of appropriate treatment. Here he had to consider the reasons given by the tribunal for finding that appropriate treatment was available to the patient, who had a personality disorder and was not engaging with the nursing staff or the offer of anger management, among other interventions. The tribunal's reasons were (at [34]):

> We accept the opinion of Dr Parker that continued treatment in hospital provides alleviation or prevention of a deterioration in his condition. Appropriate medical treatment is available on C Ward with the hope that he will begin to engage in treatment.

Judge Jacobs held that the tribunal's reason were inadequate, as they were too general to deal with the issue and ignored evidence to the contrary. He identified that the availability of appropriate treatment test 'produces the danger that a patient for whom no appropriate treatment is available may be contained for public safety rather than detained for treatment'. In his view this could be resolved by adopting the following approach (at [33]):

> The solution lies in the tribunal's duty to ensure that the conditions for continued detention are satisfied. The tribunal must investigate behind assertions, generalisations and standard phrases. By focusing on specific questions, it will ensure that it makes an individualised assessment for the particular patient.
>
> What precisely is the treatment that can be provided?
> What discernible benefit may it have on this patient?
> Is that benefit related to the patient's mental disorder or to some unrelated problem?
> Is the patient truly resistant to engagement?
>
> The tribunal's reasons then need only reflect what it did in the inquisitorial and decision-making stages.

While in this case the tribunal's reasons were found to be inadequate, in general where a patient, who might if discharged pose a risk to self or to others, is being nursed in a structured environment and is receiving milieu therapy which still has the potential to benefit him in the short or the long term, appropriate treatment will be available, and that patient will be highly unlikely to achieve discharge on the basis of s.72(1)(b)(iia). It is important to note that 'medical treatment need not be the *most* appropriate treatment that could ideally be made available' (English Code of Practice, para.6.12, emphasis added; see also Welsh Code of Practice, para.4.11).

7.4.6   Mental Health Act 1983, s.72(1)(b)(iii)

> In the case of an application by [the nearest relative following the barring of a discharge order, not satisfied] that the patient, if released, would be likely to act in a manner dangerous to other persons or to himself.

Where the nearest relative (NR) of a patient detained under MHA 1983, s.3 applies for discharge under s.23, and a barring certificate is issued under s.25, the NR acquires a right to apply to the tribunal for the patient's discharge under s.66(1)(g). In such a case the tribunal must discharge if it is satisfied that the patient would not, if discharged, be likely to act in a manner dangerous to self or to others. The 'dangerousness criterion' is much narrower than the criteria in s.72(1)(b)(ii), and there must be a likelihood, not a mere possibility, of physical or psychological danger to self or others. In *R* v. *Mental Health Review Tribunal for North Thames Region, ex p. Pierce* (1996) 36 BMLR 137, the patient lost her application for discharge since detention for treatment was necessary for her health, but her mother was successful in obtaining discharge on the grounds that the patient was not likely to act dangerously to herself or to others.

This discharge criterion only applies in relation to s.3 cases, not to patients detained under s.37. The nearest relative of a s.37 patient has a right to apply to the tribunal with the same frequency as the patient under s.69(1)(a), but the criterion in s.72(1)(b)(iii) is not applicable in such cases.

7.5   PATIENTS SUBJECT TO COMMUNITY TREATMENT ORDERS

Section 72(1)(c) requires the tribunal to direct the discharge of a community patient if it is not satisfied of any one of the following:

(i)   that he is then suffering from a mental disorder or mental disorder of a nature or degree which makes it appropriate for him to receive medical treatment; or

(ii)   that it is necessary for his health or safety or for the protection of other persons that he should receive such treatment; or

(iii)   that it is necessary that the responsible clinician should be able to exercise the power under s.17E(1) to recall the patient to hospital; or

(iv)   that appropriate medical treatment is available for him; or

(v)   in the case of an application by the nearest relative following barring of a discharge order, that the patient, if discharged, would be likely to act in a manner dangerous to other persons or to himself.

It is difficult for a community patient to challenge (i), (ii) and (iv). A patient is most likely to achieve discharge on his own application by relying on ground (iii), that it is not necessary for the RC to have the power of recall, an argument which may succeed if the patient has been complying with medication in the community for a substantial period without need for recall.

Section 72(1A) requires that when determining whether it is necessary that the RC should have the power of recall, the tribunal must:

> in particular, consider, having regard to the patient's history of mental disorder and any other relevant factors, what risk there would be of a deterioration of the patient's condition if he were to continue not to be detained in a hospital (as a result, for example, of his refusing or neglecting to receive the medical treatment he requires for his mental disorder).

A patient is not entitled to seek review of specific conditions attached to the CTO before the tribunal. That will only be possible by judicial review. Nor does the tribunal have the power to vary, set aside or discharge conditions – unlike a tribunal considering the case of a conditionally-discharged restricted patient. (See the comments of Brenda Hale in *Mental Health Law* (5th edn, London, Sweet & Maxwell, 2010): 'Another curiosity is that, unlike their powers in relation to conditionally-discharged restricted patients, the tribunal have no powers to alter the condition to which a community patient is subject'.)

7.6 PATIENTS SUBJECT TO GUARDIANSHIP

Tribunals have a general discretion to discharge a guardianship patient in any case, and must so direct if satisfied:

(a)   that the patient is not then suffering from mental disorder; or
(b)   that it is not necessary in the interests of the welfare of the patient, or for the protection of other persons, that the patient should remain under guardianship.

Unlike patients detained in hospital there is no specification as to the nature or degree of the mental disorder. In criterion (b), 'the interests of the welfare of the patient' is wider than the corresponding term 'for the health or safety of the patient' which is applicable to detained patients.

It should be noted that the burden of proof in relation to guardianship remains on the patient. There will be an issue of compatibility with ECHR, art.5(4) if the new powers under MHA 1983, s.18(7) to take and convey a person to a place of required residence and to return them there are used in ways which amount in effect to a deprivation of liberty. In relation to people under guardianship who are not subject to sufficient control to be deprived of their liberty, there are equally compelling arguments for removing the reverse burden of proof.

In *R (SC)* v. *Mental Health Review Tribunal* [2005] EWHC 17 (Admin) (a case concerning a conditionally-discharged restricted patient, but of relevance to a tribunal's consideration of guardianship), Munby J said that when concerned with the exercise by state authorities of compulsory powers in relation to persons suffering from mental disorder, increased vigilance is called for in reviewing whether ECHR has been complied with (at [54]). The judge accepted that tribunal decisions in relation to conditionally-discharged restricted patients could engage art.8 and art.6 as the patient could be required to reside at a specified place, to comply with the directions of the RC and could be recalled to hospital. If civil rights and obligations under art.8 are engaged, any interference with private life upheld by the tribunal must be in accordance with law, which must be foreseeable in its effects, and the tribunal is acting as an independent and impartial tribunal for the purposes of art.6. In such a situation where the state is interfering with private life, it is submitted that it should be for the state to bear the burden of justifying the interference.

7.7 DISCHARGE ON A FUTURE DATE

(MHA 1983, s.72(3))

The tribunal may direct the discharge of a patient on a future date specified in the direction. The power is not available for restricted patients (*Grant* v. *Mental Health Review Tribunal* (1986) *The Times*, 28 April). In *R* v. *Mental Health Review Tribunal for North Thames Region, ex p. Pierce* (1996) 36 BMLR 137, Harrison J held that s.72 operates in the following way:

> The tribunal deals first with the principle whether or not to direct discharge. If (i), the patient is not suffering from mental disorder of a nature or degree making treatment in hospital appropriate, or (ii), detention is not necessary in the interests of his health or safety or for the protection of others, applies, they are obliged to direct discharge. If not, they have to decide whether to direct discharge in the exercise of their discretion. Having decided whether or not to direct discharge, the tribunal has to decide whether that discharge should be immediate or should be delayed under s.72(3).

Reasons for directing discharge on a future date would include allowing time to set up community support. Discharge on a future date means that the discharge takes place on that date, whether or not the services are in place. In *R (H)* v. *Ashworth Hospital Authority and others* [2002] EWCA Civ 923, the Court of Appeal held that the tribunal must give careful consideration to the likelihood that the services will be available within that time (at [68]):

> if the tribunal is in doubt as to whether suitable after-care arrangements will be made available, it is difficult to see how they can specify a particular date for discharge. In cases of doubt, the safer course is to adjourn. On the facts of the present case, the Tribunal could not reasonably have assumed that the services would be provided as soon as H was discharged into the community.

For that reason alone the Court of Appeal held the tribunal's decision to be *Wednesbury* unreasonable.

In *DN* v. *Northumberland Tyne and Wear NHS Foundation Trust* [2011] UKUT 327 (AAC), the patient's representative had argued that he would benefit from a deprivation of liberty procedure under MCA 2005, which could impose a condition requiring him to be accompanied at all times in order to prevent him buying or acquiring alcohol. Not having the power to delay discharge other than to a fixed date, the tribunal declined to direct discharge deferred until suitable arrangements could be made. Judge Jacobs directed a rehearing because the tribunal's reasons had not addressed the arguments based on MCA 2005.

If a patient is made subject to a CTO during the period for which the discharge is delayed, the CTO ends on the discharge being implemented (*MP* v. *Mersey Care NHS Trust* [2011] UKUT 107 (AAC)).

In *CNWL NHS Foundation Trust* v. *H J-H* [2012] UKUT 210 (AAC), Mrs H's appeal to the tribunal for discharge from her CTO was heard on 15 March 2012. The tribunal ordered her deferred discharge on 15 June 2012. The tribunal gave the Trust permission to appeal to the Upper Tribunal. The appeal was heard on 13 June and dismissed by Judge Jacobs. The First-tier Tribunal agreed with Mrs H's representative that a deferred discharge would be better than an immediate discharge, expressing the hope that in the meanwhile the RC would consider reducing the level of her medication. The tribunal considered the possible effect that this might have, saying: 'if that happens and she reacts adversely to it, then no doubt the appropriate action can be taken' (at [6]). The Trust argued that the decision to discharge was irrational. This argument was rejected. They further argued that the decision to delay discharge should be set aside. Judge Jacobs rejected this argument also (at [18]):

> The tribunal was deferring to allow an opportunity for the responsible clinician to reduce Mrs H's medication. That might make it more bearable for her; she had complained about the side-effects. It cannot be read as a deferral so that her medication would be reduced in order to make her ready for release. It is not consistent with the way it expressed itself.

The power to direct discharge on a future date, like the power to adjourn, cannot be used to give the patient's condition an opportunity to improve such that discharge might be warranted at that future date (*R* v. *Nottingham Mental Health Review Tribunal, ex p. Secretary of State for the Home Department* (1988) *The Times*, 12 October (CA)).

Judge Jacobs gave the following guidance as to how detaining authorities might proceed in the event of the patient's condition deteriorating before her discharge took effect (*CNWL NHS Foundation Trust* v. *H J-H* [2012] UKUT 210 (AAC), at [22]):

> An authority's powers have to be considered at two stages: (i) before the discharge takes effect; and (ii) thereafter. As to (i), the community treatment order remains in force until the discharge takes effect. Until then, a patient remains liable to have her medication changed and to be recalled to hospital. As to (ii), it is possible to detain a patient immediately following discharge. Theoretically, that could be under section 2. In practice, it would almost certainly be under section 3.

Although the decision of a tribunal to terminate detention makes further detention under that authority unlawful, it does not necessarily prevent a fresh application being made for detention or guardianship. In *R (Von Brandenburg (aka Hanley))* v. *East London and the City Mental Health NHS Trust* [2003] UKHL 58, the House of Lords rejected the argument that the test for compulsory admission following discharge by a tribunal had to be based on a 'material change of circumstances'. Instead what was necessary was that the approved social worker (now approved mental health professional (AMHP)) had to have information which had not been available to the tribunal. Lord Bingham of Cornhill said that (at [10]):

> An [AMHP] may not lawfully apply for the admission of a patient whose discharge has been ordered by the decision of [an MHRT] of which the [AMHP] is aware unless the [AMHP] has formed the reasonable and bona fide opinion that he has information not known to the tribunal which puts a significantly different complexion on the case as compared with that which was before the tribunal.

In such a case the AMHP may properly apply for the admission of a patient, subject of course to obtaining the required medical recommendations, notwithstanding a tribunal decision directing discharge.

7.8 POWER TO MAKE RECOMMENDATIONS

(MHA 1983, s.72(3)(a)–(b) and s.72(3A))

In cases where the tribunal does not direct the discharge or delayed discharge of a s.2 patient or a patient who is liable to be detained, it has power under s.72(3)(a)–(b) to recommend leave of absence, transfer to another hospital or into guardianship, 'with a view to facilitating his discharge on a future date', and to reconsider the case in the event of the recommendation not being complied with. The power applies not only to patients detained under s.3 and s.37 but also to s.2 patients, but does not apply to guardianship patients. Nor is the power available for restricted patients (*Grant* v. *Mental Health Review Tribunal* (1986) *The Times*, 28 April), although extra-statutory recommendations may be considered by the Secretary of State for Justice (discussed at **8.1.5**). In respect of s.3 and s.37 patients there is the additional power to recommend that the responsible clinician consider the making of a CTO, and there is the power (but no obligation) to reconvene if no order is made (MHA 1983, s.72(3A)).

It should be noted that these are the only express powers to make recommendations which the tribunal has been granted under MHA 1983. There is no power to make other recommendations, such as changes of medication (it has been said that these could be confusing and dangerous for those who have to implement tribunals' decisions: L. Blom-Cooper, A. Grounds, H. Hally and E. Murphy, *The Case of Jason Mitchell: Report of the Independent Inquiry* (Duckworth, 1996), chapter 9).

That said, in practice representatives do seek (and sometimes obtain) extra-statutory recommendations to assist their client's progress towards eventual discharge.

In *R (H)* v. *Mental Health Review Tribunal* [2002] EWHC 1522 (Admin), Stanley Burnton J held that the power to make recommendations is expressly qualified. There is no power to make recommendations with a view to anything other than facilitating future discharge. Where discharge is not in contemplation, ECHR does not require the tribunal to give reasons for not making recommendations. The applicant was detained under s.3 in an institution remote from his mother's home. The tribunal found that the patient continued to require detention and that this could only be provided in conditions of high security. The applicant argued that the tribunal had breached ECHR, art.8 because it had failed to make a recommendation in relation to the patient that he live at or nearer home, and had failed to give reasons for that failure. Stanley Burnton J held that there was no evidence to justify making a recommendation of transfer. In those circumstances the absence of any reasons was wholly explicable.

The fact that a tribunal has made a recommendation with funding implications does not mean that the NHS commissioning bodies are obliged to fund it. In *R (F)* v. *Oxfordshire Mental Healthcare NHS Trust* [2001] EWHC Admin 535, the tribunal recommended transfer to a regional secure unit in Manchester where the patient's parents lived and where she wanted to go, rather than the Oxford unit with which the Trust contracted for its secure psychiatric provision. The Manchester placement would necessitate a costly extra-contractual referral. The applicant sought judicial review of the Trust's refusal to fund the Manchester placement, arguing that her rights to family life under art.8 were engaged and the Trust's funding forum had attached insufficient weight to the opinion of her current responsible medical officer (RMO) who was in favour of Manchester. Sullivan J held (at [76]–[80]) that the forum was not obliged, as a matter of either proportionality or rationality, to accept the RMO's view. Fairness required that the claimant should have the opportunity to tell the forum in writing why resources should be allocated to her. If art.8 was engaged, a balancing act had to be carried out under art.8(2), taking into account the effect on other patients (at [80]):

> Decisions on funding affect lives, not just liberty. That is a good reason not to judicialise them. They are agonisingly difficult decisions, and they will not be made any easier or better by being encumbered with legalistic procedures.

This decision reflects the courts' long-standing reluctance to embroil themselves in issues about resource allocation. Nevertheless, decisions with recommendations are appealable.

In England, the tribunal rules (English Rules, rules 42 and 45) state that a decision with recommendations is a decision which disposes of the proceedings and therefore may be set aside if it is in the interests of justice to do so and some procedural irregularity has occurred. In *RN* v. *Curo Care* [2011] UKUT 263 (AAC), the patient's representative claimed that the tribunal judge stated at the outset that the tribunal would not be making a recommendation for a CTO, and invited her to consider what other position she might adopt. It was argued that reaching a firm conclusion (as opposed to a provisional opinion), and preventing the patient from arguing to the contrary, was a breach of natural justice and the right to a fair hearing. Whether or not this had occurred, the tribunal's failure to give reasons for not making the requested recommendation amounted to an error of law. The Upper Tribunal acknowledged that if, in the circumstances of the case, a recommendation were impossible or not a realistic possibility, there would be no point in setting aside the decision. However, 'this was not a case where the evidence showed that a CTO would never become a realistic option in the foreseeable future' (at [8]). Judge Jacobs held that the tribunal can make a CTO recommendation not only if it considers that the criteria are satisfied (here it did not) but also in order to trigger consideration of future steps that could be taken to move the patient towards eventual release. The tribunal's reasons did not address why it had not made a recommendation, and thus deprived the patient of having those steps considered. The decision was set aside and remitted to a differently constituted panel.

In *RB* v. *Nottinghamshire Healthcare NHS Trust* [2011] UKUT 73 (AAC), the patient appealed against the tribunal's decision not to reconvene to consider his case further on the grounds that the reasons given were inadequate. The sequence of events was this. The tribunal made its recommendation of transfer to a specified institution on 12 August 2009 and set a target date to reconvene of 12 December 2009. On 28 October 2009 the respondent wrote to RB's solicitor saying that a 'gate-keeping assessment' had been requested and the solicitors were given to believe that it would not take place until mid-January 2010. They therefore requested that the tribunal postpone reconvening until after that date. The tribunal decided on 14 December not to reconvene. Their reasons were: (i) the gate-keepers had not completed their assessment and there was no purpose in reconvening; (ii) a reconvened hearing would not be proportional to the issue in the case and would run counter to the overriding objective set out in rule 2 of the English Rules (SI 2008/2699) both the tribunal and the parties are required to follow; and (iii) the patient could always apply for another tribunal when the results of the gate-keeping assessment were known. In the Upper Tribunal, Judge Jacobs said this about recommendations (at 16):

> I make no criticism of the tribunal's original decision to make a recommendation. I am sure it was made for the best of reasons and I have no information on the thinking that led to it. The experience of this case may, though, provide a useful lesson for the future. It is surely undesirable to give a patient false hope. The first question is whether to make a recommendation at all. The more obvious the recommendation, the more likely it is that the authority will consider it anyway. So recommendations are likely to be made in those cases where the authority has not considered the possibility or would be unlikely to do so. If the tribunal does make a recommendation, it has to take account of the tenuous nature of its control. This makes it essential to consider very carefully the timescale and the directions that the tribunal might give in order (i) to apply its moral pressure on the authority and (ii) to be fully informed by the time it has to decide whether to reconvene. It may, for example, be appropriate for the tribunal to direct that a progress report be

provided shortly before a specified date so that it can decide if there is any practical purpose in reconvening. Finally, the tribunal has to decide whether to reconvene. In making that decision, it has to decide what practical value this would serve. It has no power to enforce the recommendation and is not reconvening for that purpose. It has the power to embarrass the authority into explaining its thinking or, possibly, into compliance. But it has to make a judgment on what it can practically achieve, if anything. That is where the issue of proportionality comes in. It may be that that is what the tribunal had in mind in its reference to proportionality.

Judge Jacobs criticised the tribunal for failing to inquire into the reasons why the assessment had been delayed when it was 'clear that the authority did not accept the tribunal's recommendation' (at [17]), indicating that it was unwilling or unlikely to comply. Although he held the tribunal's reasons for deciding not to reconvene to be clearly inadequate, Judge Jacobs felt that it would be pointless to set the decision aside after such a long delay when 'any hearing would realistically be limited to obtaining an explanation. After so long, applying moral pressure is unlikely to have any effect' (at [17]).

If the tribunal does reconvene, in *Mental Health Review Tribunal* v. *Hempstock* (1997) 39 BMLR 123, Kay J held that the tribunal has all the powers at the time of further consideration that it had originally. It can order immediate discharge, or future discharge. Although the circumstances in which the tribunal might exercise the power might be rare, the powers were available for consideration.

7.9 CONCLUSION

This chapter has dealt with the powers of the tribunal in relation to patients detained under MHA 1983, Part II, patients subject to guardianship or a CTO, and unrestricted patients subject to MHA 1983, Part III. **Chapter 8** considers the powers of the tribunal under s.73 in relation to patients subject to restriction orders, under s.74 for patients subject to restriction directions and under s.75 in relation to conditionally-discharged restricted patients.

CHAPTER 8

Tribunal powers and duties in relation to restricted patients

The tribunal's powers in relation to patients who are subject to restrictions are more limited than the powers which it enjoys in relation to unrestricted patients. The powers in relation to restriction order patients are set out in MHA 1983, s.73; those in relation to restriction direction patients are contained in s.74. The main difference between these sections is that the tribunal has power under s.73 to discharge patients subject to restriction orders, but their powers under s.74 in relation to restriction direction patients are confined to notifying the Secretary of State for Justice as to the patient's eligibility for discharge.

Under the Mental Health Act 1959, the tribunal had no power to discharge any restricted patient, and could only advise the Home Secretary, who retained the ultimate power of discharge. In *X* v. *United Kingdom* (1981) 4 EHRR 181, a case involving a restriction order patient, this was held to be a breach of ECHR, art.5(4), which requires judicial review of sufficient scope 'to enable enquiry to be made whether, in the case of detention of a mental patient, the reasons which initially justified the detention continue thereafter to subsist'. The judicial review must be carried out by a court with the power to order discharge if those reasons no longer subsist. The Government enacted MHA 1983, s.73 to give effect to this judgment, conferring on the tribunal the power to direct discharge.

This power to discharge was not extended to restriction direction patients, because their primary legal status is that of prisoner, not patient, and until their release date (as defined in MHA 1983, s.50(3)), they remain subject to their prison sentence. If they are still in hospital at the time of their release date, they become notional s.37 patients and their rights in relation to the tribunal are the same as those of unrestricted hospital order patients. Notional s.37 patients may be discharged by their responsible clinician (RC) (or the hospital managers) without recourse to the Secretary of State for Justice, or by the tribunal. If a restriction direction patient is a life prisoner, or subject to an indeterminate sentence for public protection (IPP), his sentence will be prolonged beyond the tariff period until the Parole Board is satisfied that he may be released on grounds that he is no longer dangerous.

8.1 TRIBUNAL'S POWER TO DISCHARGE A RESTRICTION ORDER PATIENT

In cases involving restricted patients, tribunals have no overriding discretion to discharge. A tribunal may only direct discharge when it is satisfied that the relevant statutory criteria for discharge are met. One of the circumstances where a restricted patient's case must be referred to a tribunal is following recall to hospital by the Secretary of State for Justice. Here, the tribunal's function is to consider the justification for detention at the time of the hearing, not whether the recall was justified at the time it took place. However, events prior to recall may be relevant to the decision as to whether the patient currently meets the criteria for continued detention. In *R* v. *Merseyside Mental Health Review Tribunal, ex p. Kelly* (1997) 39 BMLR 114, the patient had been recalled after a number of criminal allegations were made against him. Proceedings were not taken in relation to these allegations and he denied them. The medical evidence of his responsible medical officer (RMO) assumed that he was guilty and concluded that it was difficult to assess the risk presented by the patient, given his denials. Keene J concluded that it was:

> unfair procedurally for the tribunal to prevent cross-examination of the RMO about the factual basis for his conclusions and to prevent evidence being led by the applicant on the same topic. If that factual basis could not be tested in that way, one can only wonder how it was that the applicant would be able to conduct his case in a proper manner with any prospect at all of success.

The only statutory powers available to a tribunal in relation to restriction order patients are to direct either absolute discharge or conditional discharge (immediate or deferred). A tribunal may make non-statutory recommendations in relation to leave of absence or transfer to another hospital, often at a lower level of security, and the Secretary of State for Justice has indicated that these will be considered. However, it is for the Secretary of State to decide whether to act upon those recommendations, and there is no power to reconvene if they are not followed. Recommendations in cases of restricted patients are discussed further at **8.1.5**.

8.1.1 Duty to direct absolute discharge

Section 73(1)(a) requires the tribunal to direct the discharge of the patient if it is not satisfied:

(i)   that he is then suffering from mental disorder or from mental disorder of a nature or degree which makes it appropriate for him to be liable to be detained in a hospital for medical treatment; or

(ii) that it is necessary for the health or safety of the patient or for the protection of other persons that he should receive such treatment; or

(iia) that appropriate medical treatment is available for him.

If the tribunal is not satisfied that any one of the above conditions is met the patient is entitled to discharge, and the tribunal must then consider whether s/he is entitled to be discharged absolutely or conditionally. If the tribunal is satisfied that it is not appropriate for the patient to remain liable to be recalled to hospital for further treatment, it must discharge absolutely. The effect of an absolute discharge is that both the hospital order and the restriction order are discharged, and if the patient is to be detained in hospital subsequently a fresh application under MHA 1983, Part II will be needed (s.73(3)).

If the tribunal is satisfied that the power of recall is necessary, it must discharge conditionally.

Even if a tribunal is not satisfied that a patient is mentally disordered at the time of the hearing, it must direct conditional discharge unless satisfied that it is not appropriate for the patient to remain liable to recall (*R* v. *Merseyside Mental Health Review Tribunal, ex p. K* [1990] 1 All ER 694, (1989) 4 BMLR 60 (CA)). In order for an absolute discharge to be lawful, there must be an express finding that it is not appropriate for the patient to remain subject to recall for further treatment. In *R (Secretary of State for the Home Department)* v. *Mental Health Tribunal* [2001] EWHC Admin 849, Pill LJ said (at [25] and [26]):

> The possible consequences for the safety of members of the public and the patient, when an order of absolute discharge is made, are such that the question of liability to be recalled must be dealt with expressly. . . . The failure to deal with the requirement of section 73(1)(b) is a flaw fatal to the tribunal's decision.

Reasons for preferring absolute discharge to conditional discharge should be given, and such decisions are open to challenge by the Secretary of State (*R (Secretary of State for the Home Department)* v. *Mental Health Review Tribunal* [2005] EWCA Civ 1616).

8.1.2 Duty to direct conditional discharge

Section 73(2) requires the tribunal to direct conditional discharge where it is satisfied that the patient needs to be subject to recall but is not satisfied that any one of the following criteria are met: (a) that the patient has mental disorder of the requisite nature or degree; or (b) that detention is necessary for the health or safety of the patient or for the protection of others; or (c) that appropriate treatment is available.

In *Secretary of State for the Home Department* v. *Mental Health Review Tribunal for Wales* [1986] 1 WLR 1170, [1986] 3 All ER 233, it was held that a tribunal must be satisfied that the patient should be released from hospital before directing conditional discharge. In *R (Secretary of State for the Home Department)* v. *Mental Health Review Tribunal* [2002] EWCA Civ 1868, [2003] MHLR 202, the tribunal had decided to direct a conditional discharge of the patient, PH, subject to suitable accommodation being identified. The Secretary of State sought judicial review, arguing that there could be no 'discharge' in law without release from detention, and the tribunal should have held that the effect of the conditions was that PH remained detained. The Court of Appeal proceeded on the basis that this proposition of law was correct, but declined to reverse the tribunal's conclusion that PH would not be deprived of his liberty.

Since the PH ruling there have been three first instance decisions on the issue of whether a patient's conditional discharge is unlawful because they are being discharged to conditions amounting to a deprivation of liberty. In *R (Secretary of State for the Home Department)* v. *Mental Health Review Tribunal* [2004] EWHC 219 (Admin), Collins J upheld a challenge by the Home Secretary to a decision to discharge a patient to a 24-hour staffed hostel which he would only be able to leave under escort. Collins J held that the fact of the patient's consent made no difference to the conclusion that he was deprived of his liberty. Since this would amount to a deprivation of liberty rather than a discharge, the tribunal had no jurisdiction to make such an order. In *R (G)* v. *Mental Health Review Tribunal* [2004] EWHC 2193 (Admin), it was held that a condition of residence in a rehabilitation flat within the hospital grounds could be a deprivation of liberty. Collins J held that the lack of any changes in regime or accommodation led inexorably to the conclusion that there was a deprivation of liberty. In *IT* v. *Secretary of State for Justice* [2008] EWHC 1707 (Admin), Bean J considered the effect of the Court of Appeal's decision in *PH*, and said (at [17]):

> This is a curious area of human rights jurisprudence, in which the Secretary of State prays Article 5 of the ECHR in aid of an argument that a patient should be detained in hospital. The ratio of the *PH* case, in my view, is that the MHRT acts ultra vires if it imposes conditions which amount to a transfer from one state of detention to another. Restrictions on liberty of movement do not amount to deprivation of liberty; the distinction between the two is one of fact and degree; and among other matters the duration of the measures in question is relevant.

On the facts of the case Bean J held that the transfer was not to conditions amounting to 'detention by another name' (at [18]).

The case of *Secretary of State for Justice* v. *RB* [2010] UKUT 454 (AAC) merits some detailed consideration. RB was 75 years old and suffered from a persistent delusional disorder. He had been sentenced to a restriction order in 1999, following conviction for indecent assault. The evidence was that he could be cared for in a location with less security than a mental hospital, but that his transfer to that institution would need to be subject to conditions, including a condition that he should have only escorted access to the community. The Upper Tribunal considered the effect of this case law, and concluded that, although it should exercise caution, it was not bound by the Court of Appeal decision in *PH*, 'because it did not purport to decide the relevant point. We are not formally bound by the successive decisions of the High Court, because we are exercising a jurisdiction of equivalent status for these purposes' (at [47]). The tribunal concluded that (at [54] and [55]):

> we do not think that we are bound by the Court of Appeal decision in *PH* or the High Court cases which followed it, to hold (contrary to our clear view as to the effect of section 73) that the validity of the conditions proposed by the First-tier Tribunal depended solely on whether or not they amounted to detention. A tribunal's finding that a care home, not

being a hospital, is an appropriate place for a patient's accommodation, subject to conditions, is enough to give them jurisdiction (and indeed require them) to direct conditional discharge.

On the other hand, a qualified *PH* principle holds good. A tribunal cannot conditionally discharge a person with conditions that amount to detention in a hospital for treatment. That is not because the detention would be an assault on the patient's human rights but because a finding that such conditions are necessary would be inconsistent with the premise upon which any conditional discharge under section 73 must be based which is that the tribunal is not satisfied as to the matters mentioned in section 72(b)(i), (ii) or (iia).

The Upper Tribunal concluded that the patient could lawfully be discharged to a care home, but not a hospital under the following conditions:

1. That he resides at the care home;
2. That he abides by the rules of that institution;
3. That he does not leave the grounds of [the care home] except when supervised;
4. That he accepts his prescribed medication;
5. That he engages with social supervision;
6. That he engages with medical supervision.

These conditions are clearly capable of reaching a degree and intensity to amount to a deprivation of liberty, but in comparison with remaining in hospital they would represent clear progress for the patient to a less restrictive setting. The Secretary of State appealed, and the Court of Appeal granted the appeal.

Arden LJ said this (*Secretary of State for Justice* v. *RB* and *Lancashire Care NHS Foundation Trust* [2011] EWCA Civ 1608, at [66]):

> I conclude a tribunal cannot rely on the patient's best interests as a ground for ordering conditional discharge on terms that involve a deprivation of liberty. This is more particularly so if the detention would not be for the purpose of any treatment. However, the position is to some degree mitigated by the fact that the Secretary of State has powers of transfer in an appropriate case. The Secretary of State could well be at risk of judicial review if he does not make an appropriate decision to exercise his powers of transfer.[1]

The Upper Tribunal's decision in *RB* had been carefully crafted to enable the patient to make some progress to a less restrictive environment. Arden LJ dismissed Bean J's earlier references to the irony of ECHR, art.5 being used to block such progress, and effectively placed control over any conditional discharge into a care setting where the level of control might potentially amount to a deprivation of liberty in the hands of the Secretary of State for Justice.

8.1.3 Conditions

A conditionally-discharged patient must abide by any conditions laid down by the tribunal or imposed subsequently by the Secretary of State for Justice (MHA 1983,

---

[1] Note that the Secretary of State cannot direct transfer to a setting which is not registered to receive detained patients, although s.17 leave would of course be possible.

s.73(4)(b)). Although, as we have seen, conditions may not impose control sufficient in degree and intensity to amount to a deprivation of liberty (if they do there will be no discharge), both the Secretary of State and the tribunal have wide discretion to impose conditions. The Secretary of State has the power 'from time to time' to vary any conditions and to direct an absolute discharge at any time (ss.73(5), 73(8) and 42(2). These provisions are applied to hospital direction and limitation direction patients and to transfer direction and restriction direction patients by s.74(6)). A patient who is conditionally-discharged may be recalled to hospital by the Secretary of State (ss.73(4)(a) and 42(3)). The rationale of the power of recall rests on the opportunity to detect any deterioration in the patient's condition and to intervene before any further offence is committed.

It should be noted that the tribunal is not obliged to lay down specific conditions when it makes its order for conditional discharge. However, in practice it is unlikely that a patient will be conditionally-discharged without conditions being imposed either by the tribunal or by the Secretary of State. The usual conditions imposed relate to supervision, residence and acceptance of medical treatment. Conditions may be imposed requiring patients to stay away from specified locations or submit to testing for illicit substances. In *R* v. *Mental Health Review Tribunal for London North and East Region, ex p. Lawrence* (CO/4399/99, unreported, 1999), the tribunal had imposed a condition of submission to testing for illicit drugs. The tribunal conceded that it had insufficient evidence on which to conclude that such a condition was necessary, and had failed to give adequate reasons for imposing it.

Since conditionally-discharged patients may be subject to a condition that they accept treatment, they are not subject to the second opinion provisions in MHA 1983, Part IV. In *R (SH)* v. *Mental Health Review Tribunal* [2007] EWHC 884 (Admin), SH was required by a tribunal to comply with prescribed medication, which is likely to by depot for several years (at [2]). He argued that this condition was unlawful since it deprived him of his right to choose whether to accept treatment. Holman J refused to quash the condition, holding that, despite the existence of the condition (at [35]):

> on each occasion that SH attends, or should attend, for his fortnightly depot injection he has an absolute right to choose whether to consent to it or not. The treating doctor or nurse must, on each occasion, satisfy himself that the apparent consent is a real consent and that the independence of the patient's decision or his will has not been overborne.

Although in deciding whether to consent SH may take into account the condition, '[it] must be read as respecting and being subject to his own final choice, which must be his real or true choice' (at [37]). The judge recommended that tribunals should in future add to a condition that the patient accept medication that this was 'subject always to his right to give or withhold consent to treatment or medication on any given occasion' (at [42]). The existence of consent is a question of fact. The fact that consent is given in the knowledge that refusal will most probably lead to recall to hospital does not render it invalid.

The Ministry of Justice 2009 *Guidance on Recall of Conditionally Discharged Restricted Patients* states that the Mental Health Casework Section (MHCS) should be notified by the RC about a conditionally-discharged patient in any case where there appears to be a risk to the public, the patient is unwilling to co-operate with supervision, or the patient needs further in-patient treatment. Non-compliance with medication would amount to non-co-operation with supervision. A conditionally-discharged patient may be recalled to hospital by the Secretary of State for Justice at any time while the restriction order is in force but, unless it is an emergency recall, in order to comply with ECHR, art.5, there must be medical evidence of mental disorder warranting confinement (see *Kay* v. *United Kingdom* (1994) 40 BMLR 20).

In *R (MM)* v. *Secretary of State for the Home Department* [2007] EWCA Civ 687, the Court of Appeal held that breach of a condition was not a free-standing ground for ordering recall. The question was whether the breach enables the Secretary of State to form a proper judgment on the medical evidence that the statutory criteria for detention are established (mental disorder of a kind or degree warranting detention). Nevertheless, the Court of Appeal held that there do not have to be psychotic symptoms or the certainty of psychotic symptoms in the near future before detention for treatment could be authorised. The case of a conditionally-discharged patient who is recalled to hospital must be referred by the Secretary of State for Justice to a Mental Health Tribunal within a month of his return to hospital (MHA 1983, s.75(1)(a)).

8.1.4 Deferred conditional discharge

Once a decision has been taken to direct a conditional discharge, the tribunal can defer the direction until such arrangements that appear to the tribunal to be necessary for the discharge have been made to its satisfaction (MHA 1983, s.73(7)). The power to defer a conditional discharge differs significantly from the power to delay a discharge in the case of a non-restricted patient (see **7.7**). Where a tribunal delays the discharge of an unrestricted patient, it makes an order for discharge which is to take effect at a specified date in the future; discharge must be effected on or before that date, irrespective of whether arrangements for the patient's care have been completed. By contrast, where a tribunal considering the case of a patient subject to a restriction order defers a direction for his conditional discharge, it postpones the coming into effect of the discharge direction until arrangements are made to its satisfaction. Once those arrangements have been made, the tribunal office should be informed, and provided they are approved by a tribunal judge, the patient's conditional discharge can be directed without a further hearing.

The tribunal may only direct deferred conditional discharge if it is satisfied that the patient is entitled to it on the statutory criteria. As Judge Jacobs put it in *DC* v. *Nottinghamshire Healthcare NHS Trust and the Secretary of State for Justice* [2012] UKUT 92 (AAC) (at [26]):

the tribunal cannot exercise the power in section 73(7) unless it finds that the patient should not be detained but should be subject to recall and it formulates a direction, including conditions for discharge, that can take effect if the necessary arrangements can be made.

A tribunal may not defer discharge on the basis that the patient will in the near future improve sufficiently to be entitled to discharge. In *Secretary of State for the Home Department* v. *Mental Health Review Tribunal for the Mersey Regional Health Authority* [1986] 1 WLR 1170, [1986] 3 All ER 233, it was held that the tribunal cannot defer a conditional discharge until arrangements are made for admission to another hospital.

The difficulty with the power of deferred conditional discharge is that it can result in an impasse where the tribunal suggests conditions which for one reason or another are not met by the relevant authorities. The key European Court of Human Rights (ECtHR) case on this is *Johnson* v. *United Kingdom* (1997) 27 EHRR 296. Johnson was found by three tribunals (in 1989, 1990 and 1991) not to be suffering from mental disorder, but his conditional discharge was deferred until a suitable hostel could be found. However, no hostel was found, and he was finally released following a tribunal hearing in 1993. The court held that there had been a breach of ECHR, art.5(1). The court rejected the argument that a finding by an expert authority that a person is no longer suffering from the form of mental illness which led to his confinement must inevitably lead to his immediate and unconditional release into the community. This would be an unfortunate curtailment of the expert authority's discretion to assess, part of the 'margin of appreciation' left to the national authorities. Nevertheless, discharge must not be unreasonably delayed, and there must be safeguards, including remedies of a judicial nature to ensure that discharge is not unduly delayed.

The leading British case on this issue is now the decision of the House of Lords in *R (H)* v. *Secretary of State for the Home Department* [2003] UKHL 59, which concerned a patient with a diagnosis of paranoid psychosis. He had a tribunal hearing in June which was adjourned until December 1999 at the latest for a full care plan to be drawn up for the patient's conditional discharge. The consultant forensic psychiatrist of the North London Forensic Service, which provided psychiatric services on behalf of the authority, took the view, shared by all his colleagues, that 'a proposed conditional discharge . . . direct into the community was clinically inappropriate, and unsafe'. He was willing to admit the appellant to his medium secure unit, but he and his colleagues declined to supervise the appellant as named forensic psychiatrist on conditional discharge. Transfer to the secure unit in question was precluded by the Home Secretary withholding consent.

The tribunal reconvened on 3 February 2000, and directed the applicant's deferred conditional discharge. The tribunal expressed itself satisfied that the patient was not then suffering from mental disorder of a nature or degree which made it appropriate for the patient to be liable to be detained in a hospital for medical treatment. The tribunal was also satisfied that, if suitable after-care arrangements could be put in place, it would not be necessary in the interests of the patient's health or safety or for the protection of others that he should receive such treatment. The tribunal considered that the patient should remain liable to recall. However, because of the risk factors involved, the tribunal deferred the discharge until suitable arrangements could be made for after-care supervision in the community.

Further unsuccessful attempts were made by the Health Authority to find a psychiatrist willing to supervise the appellant but without success and his detention continued. The House of Lords held that in order to ensure compatibility with ECHR, art.5(4) a decision to defer conditional discharge should be treated as a provisional decision, and the tribunal should monitor progress towards implementing it so as to ensure that the patient is not left 'in limbo for an unreasonable length of time'. The tribunal should meet after an appropriate interval to monitor progress in making these arrangements if they have not been put in place. Once the arrangements have been made, the tribunal can direct a conditional discharge without a further hearing. If problems arise with making arrangements to meet the conditions, the tribunal may:

(a) defer for a further period;
(b) amend or vary the proposed conditions;
(c) order conditional discharge without specific conditions, thereby making the patient subject to recall; or
(d) decide that the patient remain detained in hospital for treatment.

The s.117 authorities had not been able to find a psychiatrist who considered that H could be safely supervised in the community. The House of Lords held that the duty of the Health Authority, whether under MHA 1983, s.117 or in response to the tribunal's order of deferred conditional discharge, was to use its best endeavours to procure compliance with the conditions laid down by the tribunal. This it had done. It was not subject to an absolute obligation to procure compliance and was not at fault in failing to do so. It had no power to require any psychiatrist to act in a way which conflicted with the conscientious professional judgment of that psychiatrist. Thus, the appellant could base no claim on the fact that the tribunal's conditions were not met. The following passage from the English Code of Practice reflects this ruling that the duty of the Health Authority and local social services authority (LSSA) is not absolute, but a duty to use best endeavours (para.27.9):

> Where the Tribunal has provisionally decided to give a restricted patient a conditional discharge, the PCT and LSSA must do their best to put after-care in place which would allow that discharge to take place.

In *R (W)* v. *Doncaster Metropolitan Borough Council* [2003] EWHC 192 (Admin), Stanley Burnton J held that the authority's duty was, before actual discharge, to endeavour to put in place the arrangements required by the tribunal as conditions of a conditional discharge, or which the tribunal required to be satisfied before a deferred discharge took effect, or which the tribunal provisionally decided should be put in place.

In *DC* v. *Nottinghamshire Healthcare NHS Trust and the Secretary of State for Justice* [2012] UKUT 92 (AAC), Judge Jacobs emphasised that MHA 1983, s.73(7) may not be used to bypass the detention and discharge conditions by employing it as 'a device for gathering information that it needs'. Nor might the tribunal bypass difficulties in formulating conditions for discharge by using s.73(7) to gather the information it needs to decide whether a conditional discharge would be possible or what conditions might be appropriate (at [28]):

> The proper approach in all three circumstances is to adjourn for the information to be obtained. It is only permissible to use section 73 when (a) it is able to find, on the balance of probabilities, that the patient should not be detained but should be subject to recall, and (b) it has drafted the conditions for the discharge.

As for the duty of the authorities under s.117, Judge Jacobs said that although the duty under s.117 does not arise until the tribunal has made its decision,[2] that did not justify the tribunal using s.73(7) to gather information about after-care. Where such information was needed, there was no reason in principle why a tribunal may not adjourn for enquiries to be made about the type of support that might be provided (at [29]).

8.1.5 Recommendations

The practice of entertaining recommendations in cases involving restricted patients was begun 25 years ago when Douglas Hogg, then Minister at the Home Office, which at the time had responsibility for these matters, made the following statement to Parliament (*Hansard* HC Deb., vol. 121, col. 261 (28 October 1987)):

> Any such recommendation received by the Home Office is acknowledged, and any comments are offered which can usefully be made at that stage. Correspondence with the tribunal is copied to the patient's responsible medical officer since it is for this officer to consider the recommendation in the first instance. If the responsible medical officer submits a proposal based on a tribunal's recommendation, full account is taken of the tribunal's views. At any subsequent hearing of the case, the statement which the Home Office provides will explain the outcome of any recommendation which the tribunal has made.

It is unlawful for the tribunal to adjourn solely for the purpose of the exercise of this non-statutory advisory role (*R (Secretary of State for the Home Department)* v. *Mental Health Review Tribunal* [2000] MHLR 209).

In *R (RA)* v. *Secretary of State for the Home Department* [2002] EWHC 1618 (Admin), Crane J stated that the Secretary of State has the following duties:

- to respond with reasonable promptness to recommendations by a tribunal and to requests by a RMO (now RC);

---

[2] See, however, English Code of Practice: 'Although the duty to provide after-care begins when the patient leaves hospital, the planning of after-care needs to start as soon as the patient is admitted to hospital' (para.27.8). See also Welsh Code of Practice, para.31.7.

- not to obstruct or cause unreasonable delay to the implementation of a tribunal decision; and
- to follow recommendations made by a tribunal in the absence of sound reasons or new circumstances.

In view of the fact that a patient's prospects of a conditional discharge are often low to non-existent because, for example they have not yet experienced unescorted leave or they remain on a secure ward, it is unsurprising that representatives of restricted patients frequently seek extra-statutory recommendations in respect of, for example, leave or transfer. In 2012, in *EC* v. *Birmingham and Solihull Mental Health NHS Trust* [2012] UKUT 178 (AAC), two restricted patients challenged the tribunal's refusal to make recommendations. The first applicant did not ask the tribunal to discharge, but did apply for a recommendation that he be granted leave outside the hospital. The tribunal indicated at the outset that it would not be recommending leave, and refused to allow the representative to ask the RC any questions about leave. The other applicant had asked at the outset, before any evidence was heard, for a recommendation of transfer to another hospital. The tribunal judge had indicated that he would not look favourably on this request. In both cases the patients sought to appeal, and applied for leave from the Upper Tribunal to seek judicial review. Both applications were rejected by the Upper Tribunal. Judge Rowland held that a patient had no right to challenge a tribunal's decision to refuse to make an extra-statutory recommendation as to his future care or treatment. In his view, the Minister's written answer (at [21]):

> cannot rationally be thought . . . to create any expectation that the making of a recommendation will be considered by the [tribunal] in all cases or in any particular case. Nothing in the written answer implies that the Secretary of State expects there to have been consideration of a recommendation in every case or in every case of a particular type. If that had been intended, no doubt legislation would have been introduced suitably to amend the 1983 Act and so provide.

Judge Rowland went on to say this (at [24]):

> [T]here can be no right to an opportunity to invite a tribunal to act beyond its powers and it is sufficient explanation for not making an extra-statutory recommendation that the patient is not entitled to one. Even if not expressly stated in the formal statement of reasons, that explanation can normally be implied. Although the First-tier Tribunal can in practice make a recommendation if it wishes to do so, it is, I suggest, inappropriate to talk in terms of it having a 'power' to do so. It has no *legal* power to make an extra-statutory recommendation and can never be compelled to do so.

Judge Rowland noted that there was inconsistency between tribunals as to when and whether it was appropriate to make recommendations, considering this to be 'inevitable' in the absence of formalisation. However, he declined to express any view as to when recommendations should or should not be made, confining himself to deprecating the practice, 'if some panels are routinely spending a great deal of time considering issues not necessary for the exercise of their statutory functions for no better reason than that a party has asked them to do so' (at [35]).

8.2 PATIENTS SUBJECT TO RESTRICTION DIRECTIONS OR HOSPITAL DIRECTIONS WITH LIMITATION DIRECTIONS

(MHA 1983, ss.47/49, ss.48/49 and s.45A)

Patients transferred from prison to hospital, including those transferred under s.48 and those subject to MHA 1983, s.45A, have the right to apply to the tribunal. Where a patient has been transferred from prison to a hospital under a restriction direction, or is detained under a hospital direction and limitation direction, the tribunal is not empowered to order his discharge. This is because, technically, the patient is still subject to his prison sentence and thus any decision regarding his discharge must be taken by the Secretary of State for Justice.

The legislation gives the final decision to the Secretary of State for Justice as to whether the patient is discharged from the section, or remains in hospital as a detained patient, or is remitted to prison. The tribunal approaches such cases as if the patient were subject to the provisions of ss.37/41, in that it applies the criteria set out in s.73 to each case. If it is satisfied that the criteria for an absolute or a conditional discharge are met, the tribunal is then guided by the provisions of s.74. By reason of s.74(1)(a) the tribunal must notify the Secretary of State of its finding. The position is then as follows:

- *Section 48 patients* (i.e. most commonly, patients transferred while awaiting trial): If the absolute discharge criteria have been met, the Secretary of State must direct a return to prison. If the conditional discharge criteria have been met, the Secretary of State must direct a return to prison, unless the tribunal has recommended that the patient remain in hospital. Such a recommendation would be made if the tribunal feared relapse on return to prison (MHA 1983, s.74(1)(b) and (4)). The patient will remain detained in hospital until remitted to prison by the Secretary of State under MHA 1983, s.53, discharged by the Secretary of State under s.42(2), or the justification for his underlying detention expires (*R (Abu Rideh)* v. *Mental Health Review Tribunal* [2004] EWHC 1999 (Admin)).
- *Section 47 and 45A patients* (i.e. patients transferred after conviction): If the absolute discharge criteria have been met, the tribunal can then go on to direct such a discharge provided the Secretary of State serves notice of his/her agreement within the following 90 days. In the absence of such notice, the hospital must send the patient back to prison at the end of the 90-day period. The Secretary of State is most likely to agree if the patient is nearing his earliest date of release from the prison sentence that was imposed (MHA 1983, s.74(2)). If the conditional discharge criteria have been met, the tribunal can go on to direct a conditional discharge if the Secretary of State serves notice of

his/her agreement within the following 90 days. In the absence of such a notice, the hospital must transfer the patient back to prison (at the expiry of the 90 days), unless the tribunal has recommended that if the patient's conditional discharge is not approved by the Secretary of State, the patient should remain in hospital (MHA 1983, s.74(2), (3)).

8.2.1 Position of life prisoners and prisoners subject to an indeterminate sentence for public protection

Life sentence prisoners, or prisoners subject to an indeterminate sentence for public protection (IPP), may be transferred under MHA 1983, ss.47 and 49 and detained in hospital irrespective of tariff for as long as the RC believes that medical treatment in hospital is necessary, subject of course, to review by the tribunal, which may find that the criteria for detention in hospital under MHA 1983 are no longer met. Where that happens, the patient will be remitted to prison unless the tribunal recommends that s/he remain in hospital. If the tariff date has passed, the patient/prisoner will have automatic access to the Parole Board, whether s/he remains in hospital or is remitted to prison. Release can only be ordered by the Parole Board and will be on licence and subject to probation supervision. The life sentence prisoner will be on licence for life, whereas the IPP prisoner, while the sentence is indefinite, may apply to the Parole Board after 10 years on licence for the lifting of the licence (see National Offender Management Service, *Guidance for Working with Multi-Agency Public Protection Arrangements and Mentally Disordered Offenders* (2009), para.3.4).

Benjamin and Wilson v. *United Kingdom* (2003) 36 EHRR 1, involved two sex offenders serving discretionary life sentences who had been transferred to hospital and were detained under ss.47 and 49. They applied to the ECtHR on the grounds of breach of ECHR, art.5(4), since the tribunal's powers were limited to recommending to the Secretary of State that he should direct discharge, unlike ss.37/41 restricted patients where the tribunal has the power to discharge. In agreeing with the applicants that the tribunal's limited powers were insufficient for the tribunal in this instance to be viewed as 'a court' for the purposes of art.5(4), the ECtHR held as follows (at [36]):

> In this case, the power to order release lay with the Secretary of State, even though he may have been under some constraints of administrative law as regarded the situations in which he could or could not depart from a policy that had created legitimate expectations. The ability of an applicant to challenge a refusal by the Secretary of State to follow his previous policy in the courts would not remedy the lack of power of decision in the Tribunal. Article 5(4) presupposes the existence of a procedure in conformity with its provisions without the necessity to institute separate legal proceedings in order to bring it about. Similarly, although both parties appear to agree that the Secretary of State, following entry into force of the Human Rights Act 1998, would not be able lawfully to depart from the Tribunal's recommendation, this does not alter the fact that the decision to release would be taken by a member of the executive and not by the Tribunal. This is not a

matter of form but impinges on the fundamental principle of separation of powers and detracts from a necessary guarantee against the possibility of abuse.

In *R (D)* v. *Secretary of State for the Home Department* [2002] EWHC 2805 (Admin), [2003] MHLR 193, Stanley Burnton J held s.74(3) to be incompatible with ECHR, art.5 in relation to a discretionary life prisoner. At the time, a discretionary life prisoner who was detained in hospital after the penal tariff element of the sentence had been served had no statutory right to apply to the Discretionary Lifer Panel of the Parole Board, or to require the Secretary of State to refer his case to the Parole Board. The patient's case would not come before the Parole Board if the tribunal was persuaded that the patient should no longer be liable to be detained, but recommended that he should remain in hospital if not discharged. Hence, although the tribunal was satisfied that mental health detention was no longer necessary, the patient would not be discharged from MHA 1983 detention, and would not be eligible to seek review of detention before the Parole Board. This breached the right to review of detention under art.5(4). Section 74(5A) was introduced (by the Criminal Justice Act 2003, s.295) to rectify this incompatibility. Section 74(5A)(a) provides that, where the tribunal have made a recommendation that a restriction direction or limitation direction patient remain in hospital if not conditionally discharged, the fact that the restriction direction or limitation direction remains in force does not prevent the making of an application or reference to the Parole Board by or in respect of him or the exercise by him of any power to require the Secretary of State to refer his case to the Parole Board.

Section 74(5A)(b) provides that if the Parole Board make a direction or recommendation by virtue of which the patient would become entitled to be released, any restriction or limitation direction ceases to have effect 'at the time when he would become entitled to be so released'.

8.3 POWERS OF THE TRIBUNAL IN RELATION TO CONDITIONALLY-DISCHARGED PATIENTS

MHA 1983, s.75 gives the right to conditionally-discharged patients to apply to a Mental Health Tribunal. The tribunal has the power to change the conditions, or to discharge absolutely. The tribunal may vary any condition by which the patient must abide or impose a new condition (MHA 1983, s.75(3)(a)). Thus, the tribunal may change a condition in accordance with a change in the patient's circumstances or remove a condition if it is no longer necessary. In *R (SC)* v. *Mental Health Review Tribunal* [2005] EWHC 17 (Admin), Munby J agreed that decisions under s.75 could engage arts.6 and 8. This means that any interference with private life authorised by the tribunal must be in accordance with law, which must be foreseeable in its effects, and that the tribunal is acting as an independent and impartial tribunal for the purposes of art.6. While Munby J accepted that arts.6 and 8 were engaged, he dismissed the application on the grounds that, whilst s.75(3) lays down no criteria for the exercise of the discretion it bestows, it was sufficiently foresee-able in it effects. Munby J said that tribunals exercising the s.75(3) power (at [57]):

> will need to consider such matters as the nature, gravity and circumstances of the patient's offence, the nature and gravity of his mental disorder, past, present and future, the risk and likelihood of the patient re-offending, the degree of harm to which the public may be exposed if he re-offends, the risk and likelihood of a recurrence or exacerbation of any mental disorder, and the risk and likelihood of his needing to be recalled in the future for further treatment in hospital. The Tribunal will also need to consider the nature of any conditions previously imposed, whether by the Tribunal or by the Secretary of State, . . . the reasons why they were imposed and the extent to which it is desirable to continue, vary or add to them.

In *RH* v. *South London and Maudsley NHS Foundation Trust* [2010] UKUT 32 (AAC), Judge Mark Rowland followed Munby J's approach in *SC* holding that (at [26]–[27]):

> [E]vidence of current mental disorder is not actually required in all cases. Nonetheless, I would accept that the mere existence of current, or possible future, mental disorder is not enough to justify the continuation of a restriction order. The First-tier Tribunal must also have regard to the seriousness of any risk of harm to others.
> However, manslaughter may, and murder must, be punished by a sentence of life imprisonment. It therefore cannot be regarded as surprising that a restriction order imposed in a case of manslaughter arising out of a deliberate killing – in this case, two deliberate killings – should remain in force for as long as that person continues to be subject to what the First-tier Tribunal here called 'vulnerabilities', even if that has the effect that, in some cases, it will remain in force for life. In this case, the First-tier Tribunal regarded the risk of harm to others to be sufficiently serious to justify the continuation of the restriction order. Reading its decision as a whole against the background of the evidence before it and a proper understanding of the law, there can be no doubt as to why it reached that conclusion or that the decision was one it was entitled to reach. Accordingly, I dismiss this appeal.

The tribunal's general statutory role is to review the justification for detaining the patient or for otherwise restricting his liberty. Only in exceptional circumstances will the tribunal be likely to conclude that its duty is to impose upon the patient conditions more restrictive than those already imposed by the Secretary of State for Justice or by a previous tribunal. The tribunal may direct that the restriction order, limitation direction or restriction direction is lifted. If so, the patient will then cease to be liable to be detained under the relevant hospital order, hospital direction or transfer direction and will not be subject to recall to hospital. (The power to lift a limitation direction or restriction direction is added to MHA 1983, s.75(3) by MHA 2007, s.41.)

8.4 CONCLUSION

This chapter has explained the powers of the tribunal under s.73 in relation to patients subject to restriction orders, under s.74 for patients subject to restriction directions, and under s.75 in relation to conditionally-discharged restricted patients. These cases often raise acute issues in relation to public protection and risk management, and in such cases the Ministry of Justice takes an active part in the proceedings where it is thought necessary to protect the public.

CHAPTER 9

Tribunal procedure: pre-hearing procedure

The procedures to be followed by Mental Health Tribunals were substantially altered on 3 November 2008 with the creation of separate procedural rules for the First-tier Tribunal (Health and Social Care Chamber) (Mental Health) in England (Mental Health Tribunal (MHT)) and the Mental Health Review Tribunal for Wales (MHRT for Wales). These rules are made under the Tribunals, Courts and Enforcement Act 2007 and MHA 1983 (as amended by MHA 2007) respectively. The new separate procedural rules for the respective tribunals reflect many of the principles set out in the Civil Procedure Rules 1998, SI 1998/3132 with a strong emphasis on case management and directions from salaried tribunal judges in England and the MHRT Chairman in Wales. This chapter considers the rules governing pre-hearing procedures. The responsible authority's statement and the accompanying reports continue to play a pivotal role in the process, and these are considered in **Chapter 10**, while **Chapter 11** deals with procedures relating to the hearing itself. Many of the provisions of the new rules in England and Wales are based on the Mental Health Review Tribunal Rules 1983 SI 1983/942 ('MHRT Rules 1983', now repealed), and much of the case law on those rules remains relevant.

9.1 RULES AND PRACTICE DIRECTIONS

9.1.1 Introduction

The tribunal procedure rules (and in England, Practice Directions) relating to Mental Health Tribunals were introduced at **2.5**. There are three relevant sets of rules:

- Tribunal Procedure (First-tier Tribunal) (Health, Education and Social Care Chamber) Rules 2008, SI 2008/2699 ('English Rules');
- Mental Health Review Tribunal for Wales Rules 2008, SI 2008/2705 (W.17) ('Welsh Rules');
- Tribunal Procedure (Upper Tribunal) Rules 2008, SI 2008/2698 ('UT Rules').

9.1.2 The overriding objective

The MHT, the MHRT for Wales, and the Upper Tribunal are each required, in exercising any power or interpreting and applying any rule or Practice Direction, to seek to give effect to the overriding objective (English Rules, rule 2(3); Welsh Rules, rule 3(3); UT Rules, rule 3(3)), a concept taken from the Civil Procedure Rules 1998. The English Rules and the UT Rules state that the overriding objective is to deal with cases 'fairly and justly'; the Welsh Rules say 'fairly, justly, efficiently and expeditiously' (English Rules 2008, rule 2(1); Welsh Rules 2008, rule 3(1); UT Rules, rule 2(1)).

Each set of rules provides a non-exclusive list of what dealing with a case in accordance with the overriding objective entails (English Rules 2008, rule 2(2); Welsh Rules 2008, rule 3(2); UT Rules, rule 2(2)):

(a)   avoiding unnecessary formality and seeking flexibility in the proceedings;
(b)   ensuring, so far as practicable, that the parties are able to participate fully in the proceedings;
(c)   using any special expertise of the tribunal effectively; and
(d)   avoiding delay, so far as compatible with proper consideration of the issues.

The Welsh Rules leave out a fifth element which the English and UT Rules place at the top of the list, namely, 'dealing with the case in ways which are proportionate to the importance of the case, the complexity of the issues, the anticipated costs and the resources of the parties' (English Rules, rule 2(2)(a); UT Rules, rule 2(2)(a)). Since the list of what is entailed by the overriding objective is inclusive rather than exclusive, the MHRT for Wales may consider that this fifth element is part and parcel of dealing with cases fairly, justly, efficiently and expeditiously (English Rules, rule 2(1); Welsh Rules, rule 3(1)).

Since the tribunals must seek to give effect to the overriding objective when they exercise any power under the Rules or interpret any rule or Practice Direction (English Rules, rule 2(3); Welsh Rules, rule 3(3); UT Rules, rule 2(3)), when seeking directions representatives may usefully refer to the overriding objective. For instance, where there is an issue about the nature or degree of the mental disorder, it could be argued that an adjournment to enable an independent opinion to be obtained is necessary to achieve justice, and to be proportionate to the complexity of the issues, the importance of the case, and the anticipated cost. Although this might cause some delay, this could be argued to be no more than is compatible with proper consideration of the issues. (See, however, the obiter comment by Upper Tribunal Judge Jacobs in *MD* v. *Nottinghamshire Health Care NHS Trust* [2010] UKUT 59 (AAC), at [46].)

The English Rules and the UT Rules each put an obligation on the parties (a) to help the tribunal to further the overriding objective; and (b) to co-operate with the tribunal generally (see **9.2.1** for the definition of 'parties') (English Rules, rule 2(4); UT Rules, rule 2(4)). The Upper Tribunal (in *Dorset Healthcare NHS Foundation Trust* v. *MH* [2009] UKUT 4 (AAC)) has interpreted this as requiring (at [13]):

parties to cooperate and liaise with each other concerning procedural matters, with a view to agreeing a procedural course promptly where they are able to do so, before making any application to the tribunal. This is particularly to be expected where parties have legal representation. Parties should endeavour to agree disclosure issues without the need for the tribunal to make a ruling. However, even where a direction from the tribunal may be required . . . it will assist the tribunal to further the overriding objective if the parties can identify any directions they are able to agree, subject to the approval of the tribunal. Where they are unable to agree every aspect, this liaison will at least have the advantage of crystallising their positions, and more clearly identifying the issue(s) upon which the tribunal will have to rule.

The Welsh Rules do not include equivalent provision because it was felt that placing an obligation on a detained patient to co-operate with the tribunal was undesirable.

Communications from HM Courts and Tribunals Service (HMCTS) to tribunal representatives in England make frequent reference to the obligation to further the overriding objective and to co-operate. For example, representatives are directed, on receipt of the report of the responsible clinician (RC) in restricted cases, to complete and return within 10 days a questionnaire, HQ2, aimed at identifying, as early as possible, cases that would benefit from early judicial intervention and case management. Representatives are reminded that (HMCTS, *Mental Health Tribunal Stakeholder Bulletin* (April 2012)):[1]

> parties must help the tribunal to further the overriding objective, which includes avoiding delay and dealing with cases in ways that are proportionate to the complexity and costs involved. Parties must also co-operate with the tribunal generally, and we see this important process as part of the way in which parties can assist the tribunal in targeting its case-management resources on those cases that most need it.

To that end parties are urged to complete the questionnaire, and failure to comply 'may result in the tribunal exercising such powers, and imposing such sanctions, as are provided for under the Rules'.

9.2 PARTIES AND THEIR REPRESENTATIVES

9.2.1 Parties

'Party' means (a) the patient; (b) the responsible authority; (c) any person making a reference seeking approval for the removal of an 'alien' patient under MHA 1983, s.86 (the Secretary of State for Justice in restricted cases, the Secretary of State for Health in English unrestricted cases, and the Welsh Ministers in Welsh unrestricted cases); and (d) any other person who makes an application (or in Wales a reference) (English Rules, rule 1(3); Welsh Rules, rule 2(1)). The 'other person' could be the nearest relative, but only if he made the application. The responsible authority is defined as: (a) the hospital managers if the patient is detained in hospital; (b) the

---

[1] HMCTS, 'Mental Health Tribunal Stakeholder Bulletin April 2012', **www.mentalhealthlaw.co. uk/File:MHT_Stakeholder_Bulletin_April_2012.pdf**.

responsible local social services authority (LSSA) for a guardianship patient; or (c) the managers of the responsible hospital for a community patient (English Rules, rule 1; Welsh Rules, rule 2; for definitions of these terms, see MHA 1983, ss.34(1) and 145).

The English Rules refer only to parties, but allow the tribunal to give a direction adding a person to the proceedings as a 'respondent' (English Rules, rule 9(2)). It appears this rule is more relevant to jurisdictions other than mental health in the First-tier Tribunal. The equivalent provision in the Welsh Rules allows the MHRT for Wales to give a direction adding a person, not as a respondent, but as an 'interested party' (Welsh Rules, rule 12(2)). Parties have extensive rights which are not extended to interested parties or respondents. The right of a party to receive documents is considered in more detail at **10.10**, and entitlement to attend the hearing is considered at **11.3.1**.

The English and Welsh Rules require the tribunal to give notice of the proceedings to specified persons (English Rules, rule 33; Welsh Rules, rule 16; see **9.4.1**) who may in consequence of receiving such notice either attend and take part in a hearing to such extent as the tribunal considers proper or provide written submissions to the tribunal (English Rules, rule 36(2); Welsh Rules, rule 26 makes provision for the tribunal to issue a direction allowing such participation). They do not have the same entitlement as parties such as to receive copies of any reports lodged with the tribunal or to receive the decision notice.

It should be noted that a victim is not a party to the tribunal proceedings. The Domestic Violence, Crime and Victims Act 2004 provides that victims of some sexual or violent offences are entitled to be informed of any tribunal proceedings held in respect of an offender who has received a hospital order with or without a restriction order and to make representations on certain matters. It will be open to a tribunal to consider whether a victim ought to be notified of proceedings on the grounds that he or she should have an opportunity to be heard (English Rules, rule 33(e); Welsh Rules, rule 16(e)). The tribunal in England has issued guidance on handling representations from victims (HMCTS, *Practice Guidance on Procedures concerning Handling Representations from Victims in the First-tier Tribunal (Mental Health)* (1 July, 2011), see **10.8.1**).[2]

The tribunal may substitute a party if the wrong person was named as a party or substitution becomes necessary because of a change in circumstances (English Rules, rule 9(1); Welsh Rules, rule 12(1)). This would happen, for example, if a detained patient is transferred to a hospital with different managers.

9.2.2 Representatives

Any party may appoint a representative, and there is no need for that person to be legally qualified. However, a representative must not be (a) liable to be detained; (b)

---

[2]   Available at **www.justice.gov.uk/guidance/courts-and-tribunals/tribunals/mental-health/ index.htm**.

subject to guardianship; (c) subject to a community treatment order under MHA 1983; or (d) a person receiving treatment for mental disorder at the same hospital or registered establishment as the patient (English Rules, rule 11(1); Welsh Rules, rule 13(1)). 'Legal representative' means 'a person who, for the purposes of the Legal Services Act 2007, is an authorised person in relation to an activity which constitutes the exercise of a right of audience or the conduct of litigation within the meaning of that Act' (English Rules, rule 1; Welsh Rules, rule 1 is materially the same). In practice this means solicitors, barristers and legal executives, but not trainee solicitors, paralegals or others.

The representative's name and address must be sent to the tribunal. In England, the Rules require this to be sent to the other parties also, and stipulate that if the representative is a legal representative, this step must be carried out by the representative (English Rules, rule 11(2); Welsh Rules, rule 13(2)). Anything permitted or required to be done by or provided to a party (under Rules, a direction or, in England, a Practice Direction), other than signing a witness statement, may be done by or provided to the representative of that party (English Rules, rule 11(3), (4)(a); Welsh Rules, rule 13(3)). The tribunal (and, under the English Rules, the other parties) must (a) assume that the representative continues to act as such until notified to the contrary by the representative or the party (English Rules, rule 11(4)(b); Welsh Rules, rule 13(4)(a)); and (b) provide the representative with documents for the party, and need not provide these also to the party (English Rules, rule 11(4)(a); Welsh Rules, rule 11(4)(b)).

Both English and Welsh Rules provide for a party to be accompanied by someone whose details have not been notified to the tribunal as the representative (English Rules, rule 11(5); Welsh Rules, rule 13(6)). Their role is considered at **11.3.1**.

It is usual for only the patient to be represented. The Secretary of State for Justice may be represented in cases involving restricted patients, for example when the RC supports discharge but there is a perceived high risk to the public. The responsible authority is also legally represented on only rare occasions. The RC almost invariably appears only as a witness, but the responsible authority could appoint the RC as its representative (by notifying the tribunal in advance as required by the Rules) (*R (Mersey Care NHS Trust* v. *Mental Health Review Tribunal* [2003] EWHC 1183 (Admin)). The difference would be that, rather than merely being a witness, the RC could be allowed to question witnesses and sum up (English Code of Practice, para.32.28; Welsh Code of Practice, para.26.27). In *R (S)* v. *Mental Health Tribunal* [2012] MHLO 164 (UT), the RC acted as representative but the whole clinical team was excluded while the patient gave evidence (see **11.5.8**). When referring the case for a rehearing (for other reasons) the Upper Tribunal suggested that the responsible authority may wish to arrange for (legal) representation in order that the representative might be present and therefore know what the patient would say in evidence (para.28).

9.2.3   Appointment of patient's representative by tribunal

There are two circumstances in which the tribunal may appoint a legal representative for the patient.

1.   The first is where the patient has stated that he does not wish to conduct his own case or that he wishes to be represented (English Rules, rule 11(7)(a); Welsh Rules, rule 13(5)(b)(i)). This would apply, for example, if the patient selects the option 'I would like a solicitor to be appointed on my behalf' on the English tribunal application form (the Welsh form only suggests that the patient can be sent a list of solicitors). The patient could change his mind after the representative has been appointed, for instance by instructing someone else.

2.   The second circumstance is where the patient lacks the capacity to appoint a representative but the tribunal believes that it is in the patient's best interests for the patient to be represented (English Rules, rule 11(7)(b); Welsh Rules, rule 13(5)(b)(ii)). In light of the requirements of art.5(4) of the European Convention on Human Rights (ECHR) it is likely, in the absence of any special circumstances, that the tribunal will make an appointment in cases of incapacity (see *Megyeri* v. *Germany* (13770/88) [1992] ECHR 49). Capacity is considered further at **13.3.3**.

The Welsh Rules explicitly state that the tribunal cannot appoint a representative if the patient has himself already made an appointment (Welsh Rules, rule 13(5)(a)). The English tribunal follows the same approach in practice.

Although a party can appoint anyone as a representative (subject to the restrictions set out in **9.2.2**), the tribunal may only appoint a *legal* representative for the patient. In addition, it is the practice of the Tribunal Secretariat only to appoint members of the Law Society Mental Health Accreditation Scheme (see **13.1**).

9.3   APPLICATION OR REFERENCE

9.3.1   Making an application

An application may be made by the patient, or the nearest relative (NR), in the circumstances described in **Chapters 4** and **5**. Additionally, a donee of a 'health and welfare' lasting power of attorney or a deputy appointed by the Court of Protection, with the necessary authority to act for the patient in relation to health and welfare decisions, may make an application on the patient's behalf (see Department for Constitutional Affairs, *Mental Capacity Act 2005 Code of Practice* (TSO, 2007), para.13.42). The question of the patient's capacity to apply is considered at **13.3.3**.

The application must be made in writing, signed (by the applicant or any person authorised by the applicant to so do), and sent so that it is received within the statutorily-specified time (English Rules, rule 32(1); Welsh Rules, rule 14(1)). In England, the Rules allow a typed signature on an email instead of a handwritten signature (English Rules, rule 13(3A), inserted by Tribunal Procedure (Amendment) Rules 2011, SI 2011/651). The person authorised to sign on behalf of the applicant may be the person who will represent him at the hearing, or could be anyone else, such as a member of staff at the hospital.

The rules set out information which the application must, if possible, include: (a) the name and address (and in England, date of birth) of the patient; (b) if the application is made by the patient's NR, the name, address and relationship to the patient of the patient's NR; (c) the provision under which the patient is detained, liable to be detained, subject to guardianship, or a community patient; (d) whether the person making the application has appointed a representative or intends to do so, and the name and address of any representative appointed; (e) the name and address of the responsible authority in relation to the patient (English Rules, rule 32(2); Welsh Rules, rule 14(2)). There is no requirement that the applicant give reasons for the application.

There are no prescribed forms, but both the English and Welsh tribunals provide forms which are encouraged for use for applications, as they help to ensure that the necessary information is provided. The forms are available online.[3]

The current English forms were introduced with the warning (relying on the duty to assist and co-operate with the tribunal) that 'any applications or referrals received without the information requested [in the Rules] will be returned to you as incomplete unless satisfactory reasons for not providing the requested information are given at the same time as the application/referral is submitted'.[4] Although every effort should be made to provide the requested information, it is submitted that the absence of full information does not affect the validity of an application and for the Tribunal Secretariat to disregard or return an incomplete application would be unlawful and risk breaching ECHR, art.5(4) right to take proceedings and speedily obtain a decision on lawfulness of detention.

The application should be sent to the appropriate tribunal. The addresses are set out in **Appendix I**. The Tribunal Secretariat in England prefers applications to be sent by one route only, since sending duplicate applications by various routes (e.g. both by fax and post) creates extra work on receipt. Fax or email are preferable as they are quicker (an application takes effect when it is faxed (or emailed) even if the tribunal office is closed, see *R (Modaresi)* v. *Secretary of State for Health* [2011] EWHC 417 (Admin)) and it is less likely that applications will be mislaid.

There are no fees payable to the tribunal at any stage of proceedings.

9.3.2 References

References may be made under MHA 1983 or the Repatriation of Prisoners Act 1984 in the circumstances set out at **4.13** and **4.14** (see English Rules, rule 32(8);

---

[3] Available at **http://hmctsformfinder.justice.gov.uk/HMCTS/GetForms.do?court_forms_category=Mental+Health+Tribunal**; **www.mentalhealthlaw.co.uk/File:MHRT_Wales_application_form.pdf**.
[4] Circular email from Karen Early, Senior Operations Manager, HMCTS(MH), 20 August 2010.

Welsh Rules, rule 15(7)). The definition of 'applicant' in the Rules covers a person who starts proceedings by making a reference (English Rules, rule 1; Welsh Rules, rule 1).

In Wales, the provisions in relation to the content of applications apply equally to references (Welsh Rules, rule 14). In England, the Rules state that a reference must, if possible, include (a) the name and address of the person or body making the reference; (b) the name, address and date of birth of the patient; (c) the name and address of any representative of the patient; (d) the provision under which the patient is detained, liable to be detained, subject to guardianship or a community patient (as the case may be); (e) whether the person or body making the reference has appointed a representative or intends to do so, and the name and address of any representative appointed; and (f) if the reference is made by the Secretary of State, the name and address of the responsible authority in relation to the patient, or, in the case of a conditionally-discharged patient, the name and address of the RC and any social supervisor in relation to the patient (English Rules, rule 32(2A)).

There are no prescribed forms for references, but the English tribunal has produced a form for this purpose which is available online.[5]

The Department of Health has produced guidance in relation to seeking discretionary references by the Secretary of State for Health, which are most often made in s.2 cases where no application was made during the statutory timeframe or where s.2 is extended during proceedings to displace the patient's NR (*Section 67 of the Mental Health Act: References by the Secretary of State for Health to the First-tier Tribunal* (13 April 2011)). The Codes of Practice state that hospital managers should normally seek a reference in any case where (a) s.2 has been extended; (b) the patient lacks capacity to request a reference; and (c) either there has never been a tribunal or a significant period has passed since the last tribunal (English Code of Practice, para.30.41; Welsh Code of Practice, para.11.37).

The addresses where requests for references should be sent are set out in **Appendix I**. The guidance in England asks that a completed, but unsigned and undated, reference form be submitted with the request. Requests for references are readily agreed to, no doubt because the Department of Health is aware that it must ensure the operation of MHA 1983 is compliant with ECHR (see *R (MH)* v. *Secretary of State for Health* [2005] UKHL 60, at [30] (Baroness Hale)). The Welsh Ministers have not published similar guidance but a similar approach should be adopted.

9.3.3 Withdrawal

The Rules permit a party to withdraw his case in certain circumstances. An application (by the patient or NR) may not be withdrawn without the tribunal's

---

[5] Available at **http://hmctsformfinder.justice.gov.uk/HMCTS/GetForms.do?court_forms_category=Mental+Health+Tribunal**.

consent (English Rules, rule 17(2); Welsh Rules, rule 22(2)). The rules for references are different: a discretionary reference may be withdrawn without permission (English Rules, rule 17(2)(b); Welsh Rules, rule 22(4)), while a mandatory reference may not be withdrawn at all (English Rules, rule 17(3); the same can be inferred from the Welsh Rules). See **Chapters 4** and **5** for further information in relation to when references can or must be made.

The Welsh Rules require a written notice of withdrawal stating reasons (rule 22(1)). The English Rules require a written notice of withdrawal (with no requirement for reasons) at any time until disposal of the proceedings, but permit withdrawal to be sought orally at a hearing (rule 17(1)).

Requests to withdraw are routinely agreed. In England, the power to consent to a withdrawal request has been delegated to the Tribunal Secretariat if (a) it is lodged by a legal representative; (b) it is received not less than seven days before the hearing; (c) there is no concurrent application/reference; and (d) there is no reason to believe it is a 'tactical ploy' (see Practice Statement: *Delegation of Functions to Staff on or after 2 November 2010*).

The term 'tactical ploy' was introduced in *R (O)* v. *Mental Health Review Tribunal* [2006] EWHC 2659 (Admin), but the Upper Tribunal has since doubted whether it is helpful to use this terminology, concluding as follows: 'The danger of an unduly broad approach to the notion of a "tactical ploy" is that a patient might be denied what would otherwise be a legitimate opportunity to question [his] continued detention' (*KF* v. *Birmingham and Solihull Mental Health NHS Foundation Trust* [2010] UKUT 185 (AAC)). It is submitted that it is legitimate for a patient to apply to withdraw when he believes he would have a better chance of achieving his aim at a later hearing, or when he is advised that a withdrawal will trigger an immediate mandatory reference (under MHA 1983, ss.68 or 71).

One particular situation where the tribunal may be less inclined to accept a withdrawal is when it is made during the hearing. In *MB* v. *BEH MH NHS Trust* [2011] UKUT 328 (AAC), the patient did withdraw during the hearing, when the judge had informed him (before all the evidence had been heard) that a conditional discharge could not be granted. The Upper Tribunal confirmed that consent to withdrawal is a judicial act which is appealable, and in this case allowed the appeal against that decision because of the judge's 'preconceived concluded opinion'.

The tribunal must inform the parties (and in Wales, any other persons considered necessary) of the withdrawal (English Rules, rule 17(6); Welsh Rules, rule 22(3), (4)).

9.3.4   Reinstatement

In England, a party who has withdrawn his case may apply in writing to the tribunal for the case to be reinstated; the application must be received within 28 days after the date the tribunal received the withdrawal request (English Rules, rule 17(4)). In mental health cases this provision might be used where a patient withdrew his application before obtaining legal representation, and has subsequently entered a new period of eligibility. A reinstatement would allow the original application to proceed to hearing, and preserve the patient's right of application during the new period.

Reinstatement is rarely encountered in practice, as the more usual approach is simply to make a fresh application. There is no equivalent Welsh provision.

9.3.5 Transfer between jurisdictions

Under the English Rules, the power to transfer proceedings to another tribunal jurisdiction may be exercised if (a) because of a change of circumstances since the proceedings were started, the tribunal no longer has jurisdiction; or (b) the tribunal considered that the other court or tribunal is a more appropriate forum for the determination of the case (rule 5(3)(k)). For example, the tribunal would transfer a case to the MHRT for Wales if the patient applies while detained in England but is subsequently transferred to Wales.

Under the Welsh Rules, where the patient moves to England, the Chairman of the tribunal may direct that the proceedings be transferred to the First-tier Tribunal and notice of the transfer will be given to the parties and such other persons as the tribunal considers necessary (rule 23(2)).

9.3.6 Strike out

Under the English Rules, the tribunal must strike out the proceedings if the tribunal does not have jurisdiction in relation to the proceedings and does not exercise its power to transfer proceedings (rule 8(3)). There is no strike out power in the Welsh Rules (but an invalid application would be disregarded).

Ordinarily before exercising the power to strike out, the Rules require the tribunal to give the applicant an opportunity to make representations about the proposed course of action. It appears that this does not explicitly apply to mental health cases (see English Rules, rule 8(1), (5)), but natural justice may require it. The tribunal need not hold a hearing before striking out a party's case (English Rules, rule 35(4)).

The power to strike out should not be exercised in a situation where it is believed that detention may be unlawful for technical reasons. This is because (a) detention under MHA 1983 continues (even if unlawfully) until it is ended by those detaining the patient; and (b) this question of lawfulness is a matter for the High Court. In unrestricted cases the tribunal may be invited to exercise its discretion to discharge. See **13.3.6** for options available to the representative in cases of unlawful detention.

9.4 PROCEDURES ON RECEIPT OF APPLICATION OR REFERENCE

9.4.1 Notifications

There are three notices which the tribunal must give:

1. The first is notice that the application has been made. The Welsh Rules state that this must be sent to the responsible authority, the patient (where the patient is not the applicant) and, in restricted cases, to the Secretary of State for Justice (rule 14(3)), and require the tribunal to request the necessary reports at the same time (rule 15(1)). There is no specific English rule for this notification, but there is a general rule that when the tribunal receives a document (which would include an application form) from any party it must send a copy to each other party (subject to the non-disclosure rules, which are considered at **10.10**) (rule 32(3)).

2. The second notice is the formal notice of proceedings which is sent once the tribunal has received the necessary statements and reports. (See **Chapter 10** for details of the report requirements.) The following are notified in appropriate cases: (a) a private guardian; (b) the Court of Protection, where there is an extant order relating to the patient; (c) the nearest relative, unless a patient with capacity requests otherwise; (d) any authority with the right to discharge under MHA 1983, s.23(3); and (e) any other person who, in the opinion of the tribunal, should have an opportunity of being heard (English Rules, rule 33(3); Welsh Rules, rule 16).

3. Finally, the tribunal must give reasonable notice of the time and place of any hearing to the parties (and, in England, to any person notified of the proceedings). Ordinarily the notice must be no less than 14 days, or three working days in s.2 cases, but the tribunal may give shorter notice with the parties' consent or in urgent or exceptional circumstances (English Rules, rule 37(4); Welsh Rules, rule 24(3)).

Failure to notify the Ministry of Justice of cases involving restricted patients, thus preventing its involvement in proceedings as a party and exercising its role in safeguarding the public interest, will lead to a breach of natural justice and invalidate the proceedings (*R (Secretary of State for the Home Department)* v. *Mental Health Review Tribunal (Ogden as Interested Party)* [2004] EWHC 650 (Admin)). In appropriate cases, in theory, the tribunal could decide to notify an independent mental health advocate (IMHA) or other lay advocate, or to notify a victim, on the basis that they 'should have an opportunity of being heard', but this would be rare.

Notification does not confer on the person notified the status or rights of a party, in particular in relation to receipt of documents (see **10.10**). However, a person notified may have a right to attend or provide written submissions, which is considered at **11.3.1**.

9.4.2 Listing and the requirement for a 'speedy review'

ECHR, art.5(4) entitles those detained on grounds of unsoundness of mind to take proceedings by which the lawfulness of their detention will be decided speedily by a court and their release ordered if their detention is not lawful.

In relation to the time between application and hearing, the Rules only provide deadlines for two types of hearing:

1. Section 2 hearings must commence within seven days after the application is received (English Rules, rule 37(1); Welsh Rules, rule 24(1)). In practice, if the application is received on, say, a Wednesday the hearing will usually take place the following Wednesday.
2. Hearings being held as a result of a reference following the recall of a conditionally-discharged patient must commence within five to eight weeks of the reference being received (English Rules, rule 24(1); Welsh Rules, rule 24(2)).

These deadlines relate to when the hearing of the case must commence: the case could be disposed of at a later date should adjournments be necessary.

The European Court of Human Rights (ECtHR) does not specify what is meant by 'speedily' by stating that a particular time delay (three months, for example) is or is not compatible with ECHR, art.5(4). Instead, it asks whether, on the facts of the individual case, there was a failure to proceed with reasonable dispatch having regard to all the material circumstances (*Reid* v. *United Kingdom* (2003) 37 EHRR 9). In *R (C)* v. *Mental Health Review Tribunal* [2002] 1 WLR 176 (CA), the Court of Appeal held that a practice of listing all cases exactly eight weeks after application was unlawful as it made no effort to ensure that an individual application was heard as soon as reasonably practicable, having regard to the relevant circumstances of the case: the policy meant that some applications, such as C's, would not lead to the speedy decision required by art.5(4). Despite this judgment, there appears to be no documented procedure or mechanism for expediting individual cases.

When the Tribunal Secretariat receives an application or reference it aims to identify potential dates five to eight weeks ahead (in unrestricted cases) or 12 to 14 weeks ahead (in restricted cases). During the ensuing 48 hours, the Secretariat will seek to obtain the agreement of the parties on a specific date.[6] If a date cannot be agreed within this time, the tribunal will still list the case for hearing.[7]

The Justice website states that unrestricted cases usually take place within eight weeks and restricted cases within 16 weeks.[8] The official targets for the listing of hearings are as follows: 100 per cent of s.2 cases to be heard within seven days of receipt of application; 75 per cent of unrestricted cases to be heard within nine weeks (it was formerly eight weeks but this was felt to be unrealistic); 75 per cent of restricted cases to be heard within 17 weeks (see Tribunals Service, *Business Plan for 2010–11* (March 2010)). In 2010–2011, these targets were met in 99 per cent, 51

---

[6]   From mid- to late-May 2013 it is proposed that hearings will be listed not by negotiation, but using dates of availability submitted by the parties using new form HQ 1 (HM CTS, Note to all MHT stakeholders from Neil Skelton, 11 March 2013).
[7]   See **www.justice.gov.uk/tribunals/mental-health/making-an-appeal**.
[8]   See **www.justice.gov.uk/tribunals/mental-health/hearings**.

per cent and 64 per cent of cases, respectively (Ministry of Justice and HMCTS, *Annual Tribunals Statistics, 2010–11: 1 April 2010 to 31 March 2011* (30 June 2011)).

If proceedings are delayed seriously enough to breach the art.5(4) right to a speedy determination of the case, then compensation may be payable (*R (KB)* v. *MHRT* [2002] EWHC 639 (Admin); *R (KB)* v. *MHRT* [2003] EWHC 193 (Admin)). To obtain compensation (which is relatively modest) the patient must show on the balance of probabilities that (a) he would have had a favourable decision at an earlier date if his ECHR right had been respected; and/or (b) he experienced significant frustration and distress 'of such intensity that it would in itself justify an award of compensation for non-pecuniary damage' (*R (KB)* v. *MHRT* [2003] EWHC 193 (Admin), at [64] and [73] (Stanley Burnton J)).

9.5 CASE MANAGEMENT AND DIRECTIONS

The case management powers available to Mental Health Tribunals have been given greater prominence under the 2008 Rules (English Rules, rules 5–6; Welsh Rules, rules 5–6). Rule 5(1) of the English Rules gives the tribunal the power to regulate its own procedure (subject to the Tribunals Courts and Enforcement Act 2007, any other enactment and, of course, the overriding objective). This express statement is not replicated in the Welsh Rules, but both sets of Rules permit the giving of directions at any time, on application or on the tribunal's own initiative (English Rules, rule 5(2); Welsh Rules, rule 5(1)).

9.5.1 Forms

In England, the tribunal uses the following forms:

1. Form CMR1 ('Case Management Request') has tick-boxes for the following: (a) directions; (b) postponement; (c) prohibition of disclosure of information; (d) wasted costs; (e) permission to withdraw an application; and (f) other.[9] The form seeks the exact wording of the requested direction, as this allows the STJ quickly to identify the issues and to 'cut and paste' approved directions, and the form states: 'If you do not provide a draft, the judge may refuse to consider your request'.
2. On receipt of the medical report in restricted cases the tribunal sends the representative CNL2 ('Case Notification Letter') and HQ2 ('Hearing Questionnaire').[10] The purpose of these documents is to identify cases which may

---

[9] See **http://hmctsformfinder.justice.gov.uk/HMCTS/GetForms.do?court_forms_category= Mental+Health+Tribunal**.

[10] HMCTS, *Mental Health Tribunal Stakeholder Bulletin April 2012* (17 April 2012), available at **www.mentalhealthlaw.co.uk/File:MHT_Stakeholder_Bulletin_April_2012.pdf**. The forms are available at **http://hmctsformfinder.justice.gov.uk/HMCTS/GetForms.do?court_forms_ category=Mental+Health+Tribunal**.

need the attention of an STJ, and to reduce the need for postponements and adjournments (see **9.1.2**).

In Wales there are no case management forms.

9.5.2 Obtaining and challenging directions

The procedures for seeking and issuing directions are expressed differently in the English and Welsh Rules, but the effect is much the same (English Rules, rule 6; Welsh Rules, rule 6). An application for a direction may be made in writing, or made orally during the hearing. The English Rules state that reasons must be given for the request; although this is absent from the Welsh Rules, common sense dictates that the same must apply. The tribunal may also give directions on its own initiative.

Unless there is good reason not to, the tribunal must send written notice of any direction to every party and to any other person affected by the decision.

If a party, or person given notice of the direction, wishes to challenge the direction, he may do so by applying for another direction which amends, suspends or sets aside the first direction (English Rules, rule 6(5); the same can be inferred from Welsh Rules, rule 6(1)). This is a simpler process than to apply to review or appeal the original decision, and is discussed further in **12.3.1**.

9.5.3 Types of directions

The rules specify some particular powers which may be exercised, in a non-exhaustive list which does not restrict the general power to issue directions. The English and Welsh powers are sometimes expressed differently in the Rules, and in a different order. These powers, which must be exercised by a judge (see Practice Statement: *Composition of Tribunals in relation to matters that fall to be decided by the Health, Education and Social Care Chamber on or after 18 January 2010*), allow the tribunal to:

(a) extend or shorten the time for complying with any rule, Practice Direction or direction, unless such extension or shortening would conflict with a provision of another enactment containing a time limit (English Rules, rule 5(3)(a); Welsh Rules, rule 5(2)(a)). The Welsh Rules allow this if (a) the party requiring the extension or abridgement has shown a good reason why it is necessary; and (b) the tribunal considers the extension or abridgement to be in the interests of justice. Similar considerations would apply in England also;

(b) consolidate or hear together two or more sets of proceedings or parts of proceedings raising common issues, or treat a case as a lead case (English Rules, rule 5(3)(b)). Consolidation would allow, for instance, an application and a reference to be dealt with at a single hearing. The 'lead case' provision would only apply to 'review' decisions (under English Rules, rule 47, see **12.3.4**). Consolidation of proceedings is not explicitly mentioned in the Welsh Rules, but can be achieved by case management directions;

(c)   permit or require a party to amend a document (English Rules, rule 5(3)(c); Welsh Rules, rule 5(2)(b));

(d)   permit or require a party or another person to provide documents, information or submissions to the tribunal or a party (English Rules, rule 5(3)(d); Welsh Rules, rule 5(2)(c)). The Welsh Rules explicitly state that this is subject to the 'non-disclosure' rules, and similar considerations would apply in England. See **10.10** for further details;

(e)   deal with an issue in the proceedings as a preliminary issue (English Rules, rule 5(3)(e); Welsh Rules, rule 5(2)(d)). This is considered further at **11.1.2**;

(f)   hold a hearing to consider any matter, including a case management issue (English Rules, rule 5(3)(f); Welsh Rules, rule 5(2)(e)). Again, this is considered at **11.1.2**;

(g)   decide the form of any hearing (English Rules, rule 5(3)(g); Welsh Rules, rule 5(2)(f)). The usual form of hearings is discussed at **11.5**;

(h)   adjourn or postpone a hearing (English Rules, rule 5(3)(h); Welsh Rules, rule 21(1)). This issue is considered in detail at **11.4**;

(i)   require a party to produce a bundle for a hearing (English Rules, rule 5(3)(i)). Although this appears only in the English Rules, there is nothing to prevent a similar direction being given in Wales. This is very rare in practice and would only be relevant to the most complex cases. The documentation required by the tribunal is considered in detail in **Chapter 10**;

(j)   stay proceedings (English Rules, rule 5(3)(j); Welsh Rules, rule 5(2)(h)). A stay is not defined in the Rules, but it is effectively an adjournment during which nothing need be done in relation to the proceedings.[11] For instance, proceedings might be stayed pending the determination of a legal issue (in another case) by the Upper Tribunal;

(k)   transfer proceedings between jurisdictions (English Rules, rule 5(3)(k); Welsh Rules, rule 23(2)). This is considered at **9.3.5**;

(l)   suspend the effect of its own decision until an appeal has been determined (English Rules, rule 5(3)(l); Welsh Rules, rule 5(2)(g)). In England this is worded as 'suspend the effect of its own decision pending the determination by the Tribunal or the Upper Tribunal of an application for permission to appeal against, and any appeal or review of, that decision'; in Wales, 'stay execution of its own decision pending an appeal of such decision'. Challenges to decisions are dealt with in detail at **11.7.4** and **Chapter 12**.

The Rules specify that, in relation to evidence and submissions, the tribunal may give directions as to (English Rules, rule 15; Welsh Rules, rule 18):

(i)   issues on which it requires evidence or submissions;

(ii)   the nature of the evidence or submissions it requires;

(iii)   whether the parties are permitted or requested to provide expert evidence;

---

[11]   The Glossary to the Civil Procedure Rules 1998 gives the following meaning: 'A stay imposes a halt on proceedings, apart from taking any steps allowed by the Rules or the terms of the stay. Proceedings can be continued if a stay is lifted'.

(iv) any limit on the number of witnesses whose evidence a party may put forward, whether in relation to a particular issue or generally;

(v) the manner in which any evidence or submissions are to be provided, which may include a direction for them to be given (a) orally at a hearing, or (b) by written submissions or witness statement;

(vi) the time in which any evidence or submissions are to be provided.

At the outset of the hearing, the tribunal may set out the main issues under consideration, but the power to give specific directions in relation to evidence is not often used. In particular, it would be rare for the tribunal to refuse permission for independent expert evidence to be provided if it is available (although the rule could be cited when an adjournment to obtain evidence for this purpose is not granted).

9.5.4   Failure to comply with Rules or directions

The Rules state that an irregularity resulting from a failure to comply with any requirement in the Rules or a direction (or, in England, a Practice Direction) does not of itself render void the proceedings or any step taken in the proceedings (English Rules, rule 7(1); Welsh Rules, rule 7(1)).

If a party fails to comply with a requirement, the tribunal may take such action as it considers just, which may include waiving the requirement or requiring that the failure be remedied (English Rules, rule 7(2); Welsh Rules, rule 7(2)). The Welsh Rules add that the tribunal may, and must if it considers that any person may have been prejudiced, take such steps to cure the irregularity as it thinks fit before determining the application, whether by the amendment of any document, the giving of any notice or otherwise (rule 29(2)).

In England there is a further possibility of referring the matter to the Upper Tribunal where a person fails to comply with a requirement (a) to attend at any place for the purpose of giving evidence; (b) otherwise to make themselves available to give evidence; (c) to swear an oath in connection with the giving of evidence; (d) to give evidence as a witness; (e) to produce a document; or (f) to facilitate the inspection of a document or any other thing (including any premises) (English Rules, rule 7(3)). In this respect, the Upper Tribunal has the same powers, rights, privileges and authority as the High Court (Tribunals, Courts and Enforcement Act (TCEA) 2007, s.25). This power is rarely used. An example (in the education jurisdiction) was a fine of £500 for refusal to attend the tribunal as a witness (see *CB v. Sussex County Council* [2010] UKUT 413 (AAC)).

9.5.5   Summonses

The Rules provide the tribunal with the power to issue a witness summons, either on the application of a party or on its own initiative (English Rules, rule 16; Welsh Rules, rule 19).

A summons may require a person (a) to attend as a witness at a hearing at the time and place specified in the summons; or (b) to answer any questions or produce any documents in that person's possession or control which relate to any issue in the proceedings. In relation to the former, the person must be given notice (14 days or 'such shorter period as the Tribunal may direct' in England, 'reasonable' notice in Wales) and state that the necessary expenses of a non-party will be paid and by whom. In relation to the latter, the Rules state that no person may be compelled to give any evidence or produce any document that the person could not be compelled to give or produce on a trial of an action in a court of law.

If the person has not had an opportunity to object to the summons, he may apply to the tribunal to have it varied or set aside, and the summons must explain this.

The English Rules require the summons to state the consequences of failure to comply. The Welsh Rules require the tribunal to send a copy of the summons to each party. Summonses are rarely issued, directions being more common. When reports are late, the tribunal prefers in the first instance to issue 'non-compliance' directions setting out a new deadline for submission; it is only after these have been ignored that the tribunal would normally consider a summons. Another scenario might be when no local authority is willing to take responsibility for a patient's after-care, in which case the tribunal could summons the relevant director of social services to attend to explain the authority's position.

9.5.6 Wasted costs orders

The English Rules allow the tribunal to make a wasted costs order (English Rules, rule 10; also UT Rules, rule 10). There is no Welsh equivalent.

This is a power to 'disallow, or (as the case may be) order the legal or other representative concerned to meet, the whole of any wasted costs or such part of them as may be determined in accordance with Tribunal Procedure Rules' (TCEA 2007, s. 29(4)). Wasted costs are any costs incurred by a party (a) as a result of any improper, unreasonable or negligent act or omission on the part of any legal or other representative or any employee of such a representative; or (b) which, in the light of any such act or omission occurring after they were incurred, the relevant tribunal considers it is unreasonable to expect that party to pay (TCEA 2007, s.29(5)). It is not possible for the Upper Tribunal to grant a wasted costs order against the First-tier Tribunal (*RB* v. *Nottinghamshire Healthcare NHS Trust* [2011] UKUT 135 (AAC)).

It is likely that wasted costs orders will rarely be used in the mental health jurisdiction, given that normally only one party is legally represented and that party is funded by the Legal Aid fixed fee scheme.

9.6 PUBLICITY

9.6.1 Public and private hearings

In England, the general rule is that all hearings must be held in private unless the tribunal considers that it is in the 'interests of justice' for the hearing to be held in public (English Rules, rule 38). There is no restriction on who can request that a hearing be public. In Wales, the general rule is that all hearings must be held in private unless the patient requests a public hearing and the tribunal is satisfied that it would be in the 'interests of the patient' (Welsh Rules, rule 25).

In Wales there is an explicit requirement on the tribunal to provide reasons for refusing a public hearing (Welsh Rules, rule 25(2)); this is not the case in England but it is submitted that the overriding objective and rules of natural justice require reasons.

The English 'interests of justice' test was considered in depth when Broadmoor patient Albert Haines successfully sought a public hearing. The Upper Tribunal stated that the relevant factors in deciding whether to direct a hearing in public are: (a) Is it consistent with the subjective and informed wishes of the applicant (assuming he has capacity to make an informed choice)? (b) Will it have an adverse effect on his mental health in the short or long term, taking account of the views of those treating him and any other expert views? (c) Are there any other special factors for or against a public hearing? (d) Can practical arrangements be made for an open hearing without disproportionate burden on the authority? (See *AH v. West London MH NHS Trust* [2010] UKUT 264 (AAC), at [29].)

Once these threshold tests for establishing a right to a public hearing have been satisfied, ECHR, art.6 (reinforced by arts.13 and 14 of the UN Convention on the Rights of Persons with Disabilities (CRPD)) requires that a patient should have the same or substantially equivalent right of access to a public hearing as a non-disabled person who has been deprived of his liberty; such a right can only be denied a patient if enabling that right imposes a truly disproportionate burden on the state (*AH v. West London MH NHS Trust* [2011] UKUT 74 (AAC), at [22]).

In Haines' case, having regard to these factors, the Upper Tribunal set aside the First-tier Tribunal's decision not to hold a public hearing. When the hearing took place, the patient was not discharged. (See *Re Albert Haines* (unreported, First-tier Tribunal, 30 September 2011) for the decision on discharge, and *Re Albert Haines* (unreported, First-tier Tribunal, 18 October 2011) for the reasons for publishing those reasons.) The hearing was held outside Broadmoor hospital, although the Upper Tribunal commented that in future cases a video-link to off-site premises would suffice, subject to the provision of detail on how video-link and public notification arrangements would work in practice. When Ian Brady was subsequently allowed a public hearing, it was decided that it should be held in Ashworth hospital and broadcast by video-link to a local courtroom, with no representatives of the press present in the hearing room. (See *Re Ian Brady: Decision on Media Attendance at Ashworth Hospital Hearing* (unreported, First-tier Tribunal, 6 June 2012).)

The current Welsh 'interests of the patient' test is similar to the test in rule 21 of the old MHRT Rules 1983 (where there could be a public hearing if it would not be contrary to the interests of the patient). It might be thought that this more paternalistic approach would reduce a patient's chance of obtaining a public hearing in Wales. However, the requirement to read the Rules in the context of ECHR, art.6 and CRPD, arts.13 and 14 would suggest that a similar approach to public hearings should be applied in both jurisdictions. (Notably, under the 2008 English Rules, Ian Brady was permitted a public hearing but under the old MHRT Rules 1983 permission was denied: see *Re Ian Brady* (unreported, First-tier Tribunal, 17 October 2011) and *R (Mersey Care NHS Trust)* v. *Mental Health Review Tribunal (Brady)* [2004] EWHC 1749 (Admin), respectively).

A public hearing need not be public in its entirety. The English Rules provide that the tribunal may direct that part of a public hearing be held in private (rule 38(2)) and the Welsh Rules provide for the tribunal to direct that a hearing which begins in public may continue in private (rule 25(2)). If a hearing, or part of it, is to be held in private, the tribunal may determine who is permitted to attend the hearing or part of it (English Rules, rule 38(3); Welsh Rules, rule 25(3) is similar). Exclusion of people from hearings is considered more generally at **11.3.2**.

9.6.2 Publication and contempt

It is contempt to publish information that: (a) while proceedings are active, create a substantial risk (regardless of intent) that the course of justice in the proceedings will be seriously impeded or prejudiced; or (b) whether or not proceedings are active, is intended to impede or prejudice proceedings (under Contempt of Court Act 1981, ss.1–2 and common law, respectively).

The publication of information relating to proceedings before the Mental Health Tribunal sitting in private is of itself contempt of court (Administration of Justice Act 1960, s.12).

Two specific provisions in the tribunal rules apply specifically to the publication of information:

1. The first is a general presumption that, unless the tribunal gives a direction to the contrary, information about mental health cases and the names of any persons concerned in such cases must not be made public (English Rules, rule 14(7); Welsh Rules, rule 10(1)). The same provision in the old MHRT Rules was considered by the House of Lords in a case where a high-profile patient sought to restrain publication of information about his case (*Pickering* v. *Liverpool Daily Post and Echo Newspapers* [1991] 2 AC 370 (HL)). It was held that the tribunal is a court for the purposes of the laws of contempt (Administration of Justice Act 1960, s.12(1)(b); Contempt of Court Act 1981,

s.19). It was not a contempt of court to publish the following, as publication would not disclose any information about the proceedings which ought to be kept secret: the fact that a named patient had made an application to the tribunal; information as to the date, time or place when proceedings are to be or have been heard; the fact that a patient had been discharged, either absolutely or conditionally. It was not, however, permissible to publish the evidential and other material on which the tribunal's decision was based, or, for similar reasons, the conditions, if any, imposed by the tribunal. Nevertheless, the tribunal does have discretion to permit disclosure of conditions, for example to disclose 'exclusion zone' and 'no contact' conditions to a victim (*R(T)* v. *Mental Health Review Tribunal* [2002] EWHC 247 (Admin)).

2.   The other provision is a power to make an order prohibiting the disclosure or publication of (a) specified documents or information relating to the proceedings; or (b) any matter likely to lead members of the public to identify any person whom the tribunal considers should not be identified (English Rules, rule 14(1); Welsh Rules, rule 10(2)). The Welsh Rules expressly state that this power can be exercised in relation to non-disclosure orders under the Rules, and in such other circumstances as it considers just (rule 10(3)), and, although not expressly stated, the same would apply in England (see **10.10** for details of non-disclosure orders). This power, which was not in the MHRT Rules 1983, means it is open to the tribunal to prohibit disclosure of information which would otherwise be publishable.

It is a contempt of court to use a sound recorder without permission, or to publish a recording of proceedings (see Contempt of Court Act 1981, s.9, considered in *Ross* v. *Secretary of State for Work and Pensions* (2011) UKFTT 8/8/11 (SEC)).

9.7   MEDICAL MEMBER'S EXAMINATION

The role of the medical member is dealt with at **2.4.4**. The following paragraphs describe the process followed by the medical member in carrying out the preliminary medical examination prior to a tribunal hearing.

The medical member has a duty 'so far as practicable' to examine the patient prior to the hearing and is entitled to see any case/nursing notes as well as take copies of them for the purposes of forming 'an opinion of the patient's mental condition' in relation to the application/reference (English Rules, rule 34; Welsh Rules, rule 20). The 'so far as practicable' proviso covers the situation where patients refuse to co-operate, in which case the patient's representative should (if aware of the patient's position) advise the tribunal in advance of the hearing.

All patients who apply or are referred to the tribunal will be sent an information sheet (T129) with the letter acknowledging receipt of the application or reference, explaining the purpose of the preliminary medical examination and how the information gathered by the medical member will be used by the tribunal panel.[12]

The medical member will contact the ward, Mental Health Act Administrator or care co-ordinator to make arrangements to see the patient before the hearing, explaining who he or she is, the purpose of the visit, and the proposed time and date for the preliminary examination. It is important that a detained patient is told of the visit in advance and is present on the ward when the medical member visits. If the patient is on leave of absence the ward should make arrangements for the patient to return to the ward for the medical examination. Where a patient is on a community treatment order, the Mental Health Act Administrator and care co-ordinator should assist the medical member to arrange to meet the patient either at hospital or at a mutually agreed alternative venue.

9.8 POWER TO PAY EXPENSES

In England, the tribunal may pay allowances in respect of travelling expenses, subsistence and loss of earnings to: (a) any person who attends a hearing as an applicant or witness; (b) a patient who attends a hearing otherwise than as the applicant or a witness; or (c) any person (other than a legal representative) who attends as the representative of an applicant (English Rules, rule 40). There is no equivalent provision in the Welsh Rules, although in practice both tribunals pay expenses in the same way.

A 'Witness and Nearest Relative Claim Form' is available on the Justice web-site.[13] Despite the title, and despite the broader wording of rule 40, the form and its guidance make clear that expenses will only be paid to: (a) in unrestricted cases, the nearest relative and his carer; and (b) in restricted cases, only to the person who would be nearest relative (if the patient were unrestricted) where evidence is given by that person to the tribunal.

If the tribunal summons a non-party to attend as a witness, the summons must make provision for the person's necessary expenses of attendance to be paid, and state by whom it will be paid (English Rules, rule 19(1); Welsh Rules, rule 16(2)).

9.9 CONCLUSION

This chapter has considered the pre-hearing procedures of the First-tier Tribunal (Mental Health) in England, and the MHRT in Wales. The written statement of the responsible authority and the reports of the professionals concerned with the

---

[12] See HMCTS, *Your Interview with the Tribunal Doctor: Information for Patients* (T129) (2012), available at **http://hmctsformfinder.justice.gov.uk/HMCTS/GetLeaflet.do?court_leaflets_id= 2642**.

[13] Form FD ECF, available at **http://hmctsformfinder.justice.gov.uk/HMCTS/GetForms.do? court_forms_category=Mental+Health+Tribunal**.

patient's care play a vital role in the process, and provide the tribunal panel with their first knowledge of the patient's case. These documents are the subject of **Chapter 10**.

CHAPTER 10

Tribunal procedure: statements and reports

The first impression which the members of the tribunal panel will have of the patient will come from the responsible authority's statement and reports. These provide the tribunal with a case history and up-to-date clinical and social circumstances reports. This chapter sets out the legal requirements of those required to produce statements and reports for the tribunal in relation to different categories of patients, the timescales within which the reports must be filed and the arrangements for disclosure of documents.[1]

The role of the patient's representative in ensuring that the requirements are complied with is considered at **13.3.8**. The tribunal's approach to evidence, in particular hearsay, is considered at **11.2**.

10.1 DOCUMENTS REQUIRED BY THE TRIBUNAL

In stressing the legal duties of those required to produce reports and information to the tribunal in England, the Deputy Chamber President for the First-tier Tribunal (Mental Health) has stated (Guidance Booklet T124, *Reports for Mental Health Tribunals* (HMCTS, April 2012)):

> It is in no-one's interest if cases have to be adjourned because reports are late or lack the crucial facts or the up-to-date information required, and we know that patients and their families find it very distressing and frustrating if tribunals cannot make a decision because someone has failed in their legal duty to provide all the evidence that tribunals are entitled to. It is also very unfair on those people who do provide good quality reports on time because, if a case gets adjourned, these reports may become out-of-date and updates then have to be called for.
>
> To try and help, the Senior President of Tribunals has issued a Practice Direction, which has the full force of law and is legally binding. It spells out the minimum requirements and time limits for various types of report. Compliance is compulsory and

---

[1] Further guidance can be found in Christopher Curran, Malcolm Golightley and Phil Fennell, 'Social Circumstances Reports for Mental Health Tribunals: Part 1' (2010) *Legal Action* (June) 30; Christopher Curran, Malcolm Golightley and Phil Fennell, 'Social Circumstances Reports for Mental Health Tribunals: Part 1' (2010) *Legal Action* (July) 30; Christopher Curran, Phil Fennell and Simon Burrows, 'Responsible Authority Statements for Mental Health Tribunals' (2012) *Legal Action* (March) 15.

not optional. Indeed, when reports are late or fall short of these minimum requirements – with bad consequences for patients, families, carers, doctors, nurses and other professionals – the tribunal has legal power to order remedies, sanctions and costs. But we hope that, by providing clear guidance, we can avoid such measures.

10.1.1 Standard documents

There are three main types of documents:

(a) Statements of information from the responsible authority. The 'responsible authority' is (a) the hospital managers if the patient is detained under MHA 1983 in a NHS or independent hospital; (b) the managers of the responsible hospital if the patient is a community (community treatment order (CTO)) patient; or (c) the responsible local social services authority (LSSA) if the patient is subject to guardianship (English Rules, rule 1; Welsh Rules, rule 2);

(b) Reports: the three reports which are usually required for most tribunal hearings are medical (or 'clinical'), nursing (for in-patients only) and social circumstances reports;

(c) Statements from the Ministry of Justice (in restricted cases only).

In England, the requirements for these documents are set out in a Practice Direction issued by the Senior President of Tribunals (Practice Direction: *First-tier Tribunal Health Education and Social Care Chamber: Statements and Reports in Mental Health Cases* (6 April 2012)) and explained in an official guidance booklet (Guidance Booklet T124, *Reports for Mental Health Tribunals* (HMCTS, April 2012)). The English Practice Direction sets out the required documents under the following categories: (a) in-patients; (b) community (CTO) patients; (c) guardianship patients; and (d) conditionally-discharged patients. There is a final, overlapping, category for patients aged under 18 years.

In Wales, the requirements are set in the Schedule to the Welsh Rules, which sets out only two categories: (a) conditionally-discharged patients; and (b) all other cases.

The Practice Direction and the Welsh Rules require that reports must be up to date and be written specifically for the tribunal proceedings. It is insufficient to submit old reports with a statement that the situation remains unchanged: the patient's progress and current condition should be recorded in an up-to-date report. If information is missing this should be remedied before the hearing, to avoid risking the delay that an adjournment would cause.

10.1.2 Additional documents

Special rules apply to s.2 in-patient cases. In such cases the responsible authority must also immediately send a copy of the section papers (the application for admission and the medical recommendations) (English Rules, rule 32(5); Welsh Rules, rule 15(3)).

For other types of cases, the guidance relating to the English Practice Direction sets out the following documents which must be sent if requested by the tribunal, and if they are in the possession of the responsible authority (Guidance Booklet T124, *Reports for Mental Health Tribunals* (HMCTS, April 2012)):[2]

(a) the application, order or direction that constitutes the original authority for the patient's detention or guardianship under MHA 1983, together with all supporting recommendations, reports and records made in relation to it under the Mental Health (Hospital, Guardianship and Treatment) (England) Regulations 2008, SI 2008/1184;

(b) a copy of every tribunal decision, and the reasons given, since the application, order or direction being reviewed was made or accepted; and

(c) where the patient is liable to be detained for treatment under MHA 1983, s.3, a copy of any application for admission for assessment that was in force immediately prior to the making of the s.3 application.

10.2 TIME LIMITS

The general rule is that the relevant documents must be submitted by the responsible authority to the tribunal so that they are received as soon as practicable and in any event within *three weeks* after the responsible authority received a copy of the application or reference (or, in England, from the time it made the reference) (English Rules, rule 32(6); Welsh Rules, rule 15(5)).

There are two exceptions to this general rule.

1. One exception is for s.2 cases, because the hearing must commence within seven days after the application is received:

   (a) In England, the Rules require that the responsible authority must *immediately* send the section papers and *as soon as possible* send the statement of information and reports (rule 32(5)). The Practice Direction states that the responsible authority must balance the need for speed with the need to provide as much of the specified information as possible in the time available, and states that if information is omitted because it is not available then this should be stated (Practice Direction: First-tier Tribunal Health Education and Social Care Chamber: Statements and Reports in Mental Health Cases, para.8).

   (b) In Wales, the Rules require that the responsible authority must *on receipt* from the tribunal of a request or a copy of the application, send (a) the section papers; (b) as much of the statement of information as is within the knowledge of the responsible authority and can be provided

---

[2] This is taken from Section C of the previous Practice Direction, relating to documents which should if possible be provided 'if the tribunal so directs'. The section was omitted from the current Practice Direction and transferred to the guidance.

in the time available; and (c) such of the reports as can reasonably be provided in the time available (Welsh Rules, rule 15(3)).

2.   In relation to conditionally-discharged patients:

(a)   In England the first step is that the Secretary of State for Justice, on receipt of an application, *immediately* provides the tribunal with the names and addresses of the responsible clinician (RC) and any social supervisor. Next, the person or people named are notified by the tribunal and the named RC and social supervisor must send the necessary reports to the tribunal to be received as soon as practicable and in any event within *three weeks* of the notification (English Rules, rule 32(4) (as amended)).

(b)   In Wales, the onus is on the Secretary of State to send the relevant statement of information, and reports, to the tribunal. These must be sent as soon as practicable and in any event within *six weeks* of receipt of a copy of the application or a request from the tribunal (Welsh Rules, rule 15(4)).

If the time limits are adhered to (especially in restricted cases) there may be several weeks between preparation of the reports and the hearing. If a significant period has elapsed and the situation has changed, then addendum reports should be submitted. The tribunal may issue directions in relation to late reports or the preparation of addendum reports (see **13.3.8** for details).

In restricted cases, the English Rules explicitly state that at the same time as sending the reports and statement of information to the tribunal, those documents must also be sent to the Secretary of State (rule 32(7)). There is no equivalent provision in the Welsh Rules. Time limits in relation to the Secretary of State's statement are considered at **10.7**.

An act required by the Rules or a direction (or in England, a Practice Direction) to be done on or by a particular day must be done by 5 pm on that day, but if that day is not a working day then the act is done in time if done on the next working day (English Rules, rule 12; Welsh Rules, rule 8).

If time limits are not met then the representative may seek directions to remedy the breach of the rules (see **9.5** and **13.3.8**).

10.3 STATEMENT OF INFORMATION FROM RESPONSIBLE AUTHORITY

The responsible authority which has the legal duty to provide statements and reports will usually be, for detained patients, the managers of the responsible NHS Trust, Foundation Trust, Primary Care Trust (or from April 2013, Clinical Commissioning Group (CCG)), Strategic Heath Authority, Local Health Board or Special Health Authority. For community patients, the responsible authority will be the Trust, Authority or Board for the hospital where the patient was liable to be detained immediately before the CTO was made. For patients subject to guardianship, the responsible authority is the local authority social services department. In relation to patients detained in an independent hospital or sent on a CTO from such a hospital, the responsible authority will be the person registered in respect of that registered establishment.

Although there are no prescribed forms, it is best for statements of information to be produced on a form containing the wording and paragraph lettering of the relevant Practice Direction or Schedule. In relation to this, it should be noted that the English Practice Direction sets out a separate list of required information for each category of case, whereas for brevity the text below lists the *common* requirements first, then any *additional* requirements for individual categories of case; the numbering therefore differs.

10.3.1 England

A statement of information is required for in-patients, community patients and guardianship patients, but not for conditionally-discharged patients. The following information, so far as it is within the knowledge of the responsible authority, is required in all these cases:

1. the patient's full name (and any alternative names used in their patient records);
2. the patient's date of birth, age and usual place of residence;
3. the patient's first language and, if it is not English, whether an interpreter is required and, if so, in which language;
4. if the patient is deaf, whether the patient will require the services of a British Sign Language interpreter or a relay interpreter;
5. details of the hospital at which the patient is detained (or for community and guardianship patients, the place where the patient is living);
6. the name of the patient's RC and the date when the patient came under the care of that clinician;
7. the name of any care co-ordinator appointed for the patient;
8. (except in the case of a restricted in-patient) the name and address of the patient's nearest relative or of the person exercising that function, whether the patient has made any specific requests that their NR should not be consulted or should not be kept informed about the patient's care or treatment and, if so, the detail of any such requests and whether the responsible authority believes that the patient has capacity to make such requests;
9. the name and address of any person who plays a significant part in the care of the patient but who is not professionally concerned with that care (this information is not required for guardianship patients, but would be useful in any event);
10. the name and address of any deputy or attorney appointed for the patient under MCA 2005;

11. details of any registered lasting or enduring power of attorney made by the patient;
12. details of any existing advance decisions made by the patient to refuse treatment for mental disorder.

The following additional information is required only for in-patients:

1. the date of admission or transfer of the patient to the hospital in which the patient is detained or liable to be detained, together with details of the application, order or direction that is the original authority for the detention of the patient, and details of any subsequent renewal of, or change in, the authority for detention;
2. details of any transfers between hospitals since the original application, order or direction was made;
3. where the patient is detained in an independent hospital, details of any NHS body that funds, or will fund, the placement;
4. the name and address of the LSSA and NHS body which, were the patient to leave hospital, would have the duty to provide after-care services for the patient under MHA 1983, s.117.

The following additional information is required only for community patients:

1. the name and address of the LSSA and NHS body having a duty to provide after-care services for the patient under MHA 1983, s.117.

The following additional information is required for guardianship patients:

1. where the patient is subject to the guardianship of a private guardian, the name and address of that guardian;
2. the date of the reception of the patient into guardianship, together with details of the application, order or direction that constitutes the original authority for the guardianship of the patient.

10.3.2 Wales

There are similarities with the English requirements, but the differences make it worthwhile to reproduce the Welsh requirements separately (using the original numbering). The following information is required for patients other than those who have been conditionally discharged:

1. the patient's full name (and any alternative names used in patient records);
2. the patient's date of birth and age;
3. the patient's language of choice and, if it is not English or Welsh, whether an interpreter is required;
4. the application, order or direction made under MHA 1983 to which the tribunal proceedings relate and the date on which that application, order or direction commenced;

5. details of the original authority for the detention or guardianship of the patient, including the statutory basis for that authority and details of any subsequent renewal of or change in that authority;

6. in cases where a patient has been transferred to hospital under MHA 1983, ss.45A, 47 or 48, details of the order, direction or authority under which the patient was being held in custody before his transfer to hospital;

7. except in relation to a patient subject to guardianship or after-care under supervision,[3] or a community patient, the hospital or hospital unit at which the patient is presently liable to be detained under MHA 1983, and the ward or unit on which he is presently detained;

8. if a condition or requirement has been imposed that requires the patient to reside at a particular place, details of the condition or requirement and the address at which the patient is required to reside;

9. in the case of a community patient, details of any conditions attaching to the patient's CTO under MHA 1983, s.17B(2);

10. the name of the patient's RC and the length of time the patient has been under their care;

11. where another approved clinician (AC) is or has recently been largely concerned in the treatment of the patient, the name of that clinician and the period that the patient has spent in that clinician's care;

12. the name of any care co-ordinator appointed for the patient;

13. where the patient is subject to the guardianship of a private guardian, the name and address of that guardian;

14. where there is an extant order of the Court of Protection, the details of that order;

15. unless the patient requests otherwise, the name and address of the person exercising the functions of the NR of the patient;

16. where a Local Health Board, a NHS Trust, a Primary Care Trust (or after April 2013, CCG), a NHS Foundation Trust, a Strategic Health Authority, the Welsh Ministers or the Secretary of State have a right to discharge the patient under the provisions of MHA 1983, s.23(3), the name and address of such Board, Trust, Authority, person or persons;

17. in the case of a patient subject to after-care under supervision, the name and address of the LSSA and NHS body that are responsible for providing the patient with after-care under MHA 1983, s.117, or will be when he leaves hospital;

18. the name and address of any person who plays a substantial part in the care of the patient but who is not professionally concerned with it;

19. the name and address of any other person who the responsible authority considers should be notified to the tribunal.

---

[3] Note that the Schedule has not been updated since 'after-care under supervision' ceased to exist following implementation of MHA 2007.

The following information is required (instead of the above) for conditionally-discharged patients:

1. the patient's full name (and any alternative names used in patient records);
2. the patient's date of birth and age;
3. the patient's language of choice and, if it is not English or Welsh, whether an interpreter is required;
4. the history of the patient's present liability to detention, including details of the offence or offences, and the dates of the original order or direction and of the conditional discharge;
5. the name and address of any clinician responsible for the care and supervision of the patient in the community, and the period that the patient has spent under the care and supervision of that clinician;
6. the name and address of any social worker or probation officer responsible for the care and supervision of the patient in the community and the period that the patient has spent under the care and supervision of that person.

10.3.3 Additional useful information

The following information in relation to community patients is not required by the Practice Direction, but is useful for medical members when arranging to examine the patient and view records:

1. telephone number for the patient;
2. telephone number for the care co-ordinator or community psychiatric nurse;
3. telephone number and full address of the Community Mental Health Team base.

10.4 MEDICAL (OR CLINICAL) REPORT

An up-to-date medical report (now often referred to as a clinical report, since it may not always be prepared by a medical practitioner) is required for all categories of case, namely, in-patients, community and guardianship patients, and conditionally-discharged patients.

10.4.1 England

The Practice Direction calls the medical report 'the Responsible Clinician's Report', and requires, unless not reasonably practicable, that the report be written or countersigned by the RC responsible for the patient's treatment. The report is required to be up to date, to be specifically prepared for the tribunal, and to describe the patient's relevant medical history and current presentation.

The following specific information is required:

1.   full details of the patient's mental state, behaviour and treatment for mental disorder (for community patients is added 'and relevant medical history');
2.   so far as it is within the knowledge of the person writing the report, a statement as to whether, at a time when the patient was mentally disordered, the patient has neglected or harmed themselves or threatened themselves with harm, or has harmed other persons or threatened them with harm, or damaged property or threatened to damage property, together with details of any neglect, harm, damage or threats;
3.   an assessment of the extent to which the patient or other persons would be likely to be at risk if the patient were to be discharged by the tribunal, and how any such risks could be managed effectively (for conditionally-discharged patients, reference is made to absolute discharge);
4.   an assessment of the patient's strengths and any other positive factors of which the tribunal should be aware;
5.   whether the patient has a learning disability that may adversely affect their understanding or ability to cope with the tribunal hearing, and whether there are any approaches or adjustments that the panel may consider in order to deal with the case fairly and justly.

For community patients the following additional information is required:

1.   where the case is a reference to the tribunal, an assessment of the patient's capacity to decide whether or not to attend, or be represented at, a hearing of the reference;
2.   details of the date of, and circumstances leading up to, the patient's underlying s.3 order, and a brief account of when, and why, the patient then came to be subject to a CTO;
3.   the reasons why it is necessary that the RC should be able to exercise the power under MHA 1983, s.17E(1) to recall the patient to hospital;
4.   any conditions to which the patient is subject under MHA 1983, s.17B.

For conditionally-discharged patients, the following additional information is required:

1.   details of any existing advance decisions to refuse treatment for mental disorder made by the patient;
2.   if the patient does not have a social supervisor, the RC must also provide, or arrange to be provided, as much of the social circumstances information below as can reasonably be obtained in the time available.

There is no additional information required in in-patient or guardianship cases.

The Codes of Practice state that where the patient is under the age of 18 and the RC is not a Child and Adolescent Mental Health Service (CAMHS) specialist, the hospital managers should ensure that a report is prepared by a CAMHS specialist (English Code of Practice, para.32.19; Welsh Code of Practice, para.26.11).

10.4.2 Wales

The Welsh Schedule is much less prescriptive than the English Practice Direction.

For all patients other than conditionally-discharged patients, the requirement is as follows: 'An up-to-date clinical report, prepared for the Tribunal, including the relevant clinical history and a full report on the patient's mental condition'. The Schedule also asks for the views of the responsible authority on the suitability of the patient for discharge, and the medical report should contain this information.

For conditionally-discharged patients, the requirement is: 'Where there is a clinician responsible for the care and supervision of the patient in the community, an up-to-date report prepared for the Tribunal including the relevant medical history and a full report on the patient's mental condition'.

Given the additional detail in the English Practice Direction, it should be of assistance to report writers in Wales.

10.5 NURSING REPORT

10.5.1 England

A nursing report is only required for in-patients. It must relate to the patient's current in-patient episode and include full details of the following:

1. the patient's understanding of, and willingness to accept, the current treatment for mental disorder provided or offered;
2. the level of observation to which the patient is subject;
3. any occasions on which the patient has been secluded or restrained, including the reasons why seclusion or restraint was considered to be necessary;
4. any occasions on which the patient has been absent without leave whilst liable to be detained, or occasions when the patient has failed to return when required, after having been granted leave of absence;
5. any incidents where the patient has harmed themselves or others or threatened such harm, or damaged property or threatened such damage.

The Practice Direction requires that, in all in-patient cases, a copy of the patient's current nursing plan be appended to the report. This is helpful to the tribunal, but is rarely done.

10.5.2 Wales

There is no requirement in the Schedule for a nursing report, but in practice it is usual for these to be prepared, and to cover similar ground as in England.

10.6 SOCIAL CIRCUMSTANCES REPORT

This is usually written by the patient's care co-ordinator. There is no requirement for it to be written by a social worker, so the author could be, for example, a community psychiatric nurse or occupational therapist.

10.6.1 England: general

A social circumstances report is required in all categories of case, namely, in-patients, community and guardianship patients, and conditionally-discharged patients. The following information is required in all categories of case (with exceptions and modifications noted in parentheses):

1. the patient's home and family circumstances, and the housing facilities available;
2. so far as it is practicable, and except in restricted cases, a summary of the views of the patient's nearest relative unless, having consulted the patient, the person compiling the report considers that it would be inappropriate to consult the NR (this is not one of the requirements listed for conditional discharge cases: restricted patients do not have nearest relatives);
3. so far as it is practicable, the views of any person who plays a significant part in the care of the patient but is not professionally concerned with it;
4. the views of the patient, including the patient's concerns, hopes and beliefs;
5. the opportunities for employment available to the patient;
6. what (if any) community support or after-care is being, or would be, made available to the patient, and the author's views as to its likely effectiveness were the patient to be discharged from hospital (in relation to community, guardianship or conditionally-discharged patients, the question relates to the likely effectiveness of community support if the relevant order were to continue or if it were to be discharged);
7. an assessment of the extent to which the patient or other persons would be likely to be at risk if the patient were to be discharged, and how any such risks could be managed effectively (discharge refers to discharge from hospital, the CTO, guardianship, or absolute discharge, as appropriate).

In relation to community patients, the following additional information is required:

1. an account of the patient's progress whilst a community patient, details of any conditions or requirements to which the patient is subject under the CTO, and details of any behaviour that has put the patient or others at risk.

In relation to conditionally-discharged patients, to make up for the lack of a responsible authority statement of information, the following additional information is required:

1. the patient's full name (and any alternative names used in their patient records);
2. the patient's date of birth, age and usual place of residence;
3. the patient's first language and, if it is not English, whether an interpreter is required and, if so, in which language;
4. if the patient is deaf, whether the patient will require the services of a British Sign Language interpreter or a relay interpreter;
5. the patient's home and family circumstances, and the housing facilities available;
6. the name and address of any deputy or attorney appointed for the patient under MCA 2005;
7. details of any registered lasting or enduring power of attorney made by the patient.

No additional information is required for in-patient or guardianship cases.

Note that there are additional requirements where the patient is under the age of 18 (see **10.6.2**).

10.6.2 England: patients under the age of 18

The following are the additional requirements for a social circumstances report where the patient is under 18:

1. the names and addresses of any persons with parental responsibility, and how they acquired parental responsibility;
2. which public bodies either have liaised or need to liaise in relation to after-care services that may be provided under MHA 1983, s.117;
3. the outcome of any liaison that has taken place;
4. if liaison has not taken place, why not – and when liaison will take place;
5. the details of any multi-agency care plan in place or proposed;
6. whether there are any issues as to funding the care plan and, if so, the date by which it is intended that those issues will be resolved;
7. who will be the patient's care co-ordinator following discharge;
8. whether the patient's needs have been assessed under the Chronically Sick and Disabled Persons Act 1970 (as amended) and, if not, the reasons why such an assessment has not been carried out and whether it is proposed to carry out such an assessment;
9. if there has been an assessment under the Chronically Sick and Disabled Persons Act 1970, what needs have been identified and how those needs will be met;
10. if the patient is, or has been, subject to a care order or an interim care order, the date and duration of any such order, the identity of the relevant local authority, any person(s) with whom the local authority shares parental responsibility, whether the patient is the subject of any care proceedings which have yet to be concluded and, if so, the court in which such proceedings are taking place and

the date of the next hearing, whether the patient comes under the Children (Leaving Care) Act 2000, whether there has been any liaison between, on the one hand, social workers responsible for mental health services to children and adolescents and, on the other hand, those responsible for such services to adults, and the name of the social worker within the relevant local authority who is discharging the function of the nearest relative under MHA 1983, s.27;

11.   if the patient is subject to guardianship under MHA 1983, s.7, whether any orders have been made under the Children Act 1989 in respect of the patient, and what consultation there has been with the guardian;

12.   if the patient is a ward of court, when the patient was made a ward of court and what steps have been taken to notify the court that made the order of any significant steps taken, or to be taken, in respect of the patient;

13.   whether any orders under the Children Act 1989 are in existence in respect of the patient and, if so, the details of those orders, together with the date on which such orders were made, and whether they are final or interim orders;

14.   if a patient has been or is a looked after child under s.20 of the Children Act 1989, when the child became looked after, why the child became looked after, what steps have been taken to discharge the obligations of the local authority under para.17(1) of Sched.2 to the Children Act 1989, and what steps are being taken (if required) to discharge the obligations of the local authority under para.10(b) of Sched.2 to the Children Act 1989;

15.   if a patient has been treated by a local authority as a child in need (which includes children who have a mental disorder) under s.17(11) of the Children Act 1989, the period or periods for which they have been so treated, why they were considered to be a child in need, what services were or are being made available to the child by virtue of that status, and details of any assessment of the child;

16.   if a patient has been the subject of a secure accommodation order (under s.25 of the Children Act 1989), the date on which the order was made, the reasons it was made, and the date it expired.

10.6.3 Wales

In relation to the social circumstances of patients who have not been conditionally discharged, there must be an up-to-date report dealing with:

1.   the patient's home and family circumstances, including the views of the patient's nearest relative or the person so acting;

2.   the opportunities for employment or occupation and the housing facilities which would be available to the patient if discharged;

3.   the availability of community support and relevant medical facilities;

4.   the financial circumstances of the patient.

Additionally, where the provisions of MHA 1983, s.117 may apply, the Schedule requires a proposed after-care plan in respect of the patient. It would be appropriate for this information to be contained in the social circumstances report.

In relation to conditionally-discharged patients, the following are required:

1. where there is a social worker, probation officer or community psychiatric nurse responsible for the patient's care and supervision in the community, an up-to-date report prepared for the tribunal on the patient's progress in the community since discharge from hospital;
2. a report on the patient's home circumstances.

There are no specific requirements in Wales for reports on patients under 18 years but the matters listed at **10.6.2** may be relevant and helpful to the tribunal.

10.7 MINISTRY OF JUSTICE COMMENTS

In restricted cases, the responsible authority must also send its statement and reports to the Ministry of Justice (MoJ), which must then submit a statement of any further relevant information to the tribunal (English Rules, rule 32(7); Welsh Rules, rule 15(6)). In England, the Rules specify that the information required is (a) a summary of the index offence; (b) a record of any other criminal convictions or findings recorded against the patient; (c) full details of the history of the patient's liability to detention since the restrictions were imposed; and (d) any further information considered relevant to proceedings (rule 32(7B)). The Welsh Rules do not specify the required content but the same format is adopted in practice.

The general rule is that the MoJ's statement is sent as soon as practicable but in any event within three weeks after receipt of the reports and statement of information (English Rules, rule 32(7A)(b); Welsh Rules, rule 15(6)(b)). The only exception is for cases held as a result of the recall of a conditionally-discharged patient, in which case the deadline is two weeks (English Rules, rule 32(7A)(a); Welsh Rules, rule 15(6)(a)).

The MoJ and the Mental Health Tribunal in England have published a joint protocol which sets out their respective responsibilities in relation to submission of reports and statements (see *Ministry of Justice: Tribunal Service Mental Health Guidance* (April 2009)). This includes the following:

1. If the MoJ fails to provide its response within 21 days, then the tribunal is entitled to proceed without it, so long as the tribunal is satisfied that the relevant documents were received (in this regard, an automatic email acknowledgement or fax receipt confirmation will constitute sufficient evidence).
2. The MoJ will endeavour to respond to the standard reports even if they are submitted less than 21 days before the hearing, but this may not be achievable where:

    (a)   the MoJ assessment is that the patient poses a potentially serious risk if discharged; and

    (b)   the late report increases the likelihood that the tribunal may discharge; and

    (c)   the time available does not allow the MoJ to submit a properly considered response.

3.   The MoJ may comment on supplementary, or independent, reports, but there is no obligation to do so. So long as the tribunal is satisfied that the documents were received, the tribunal may proceed without MoJ comments.

4.   The tribunal will not normally comment on reports submitted after a deferred conditional discharge decision, unless the further reports raise issues about the patient's detainability.

If there are reports without MoJ comments, or if a report writer supports discharge at the hearing contrary to the opinion in his report, the tribunal might have to adjourn. Therefore, in order to avoid unnecessary delays, this situation should be addressed as soon as possible before the hearing.

In tribunal proceedings the MoJ is unlikely to support discharge in its statement, as in such a circumstance it would be able to use its own discharge power (see **Chapter 8**).

The MoJ could obtain and submit its own expert evidence, but this would be very rare.

10.8 INFORMATION FROM OTHER SOURCES

The tribunal may receive information from other sources, such as from victims, other agencies or from patients themselves, as described below.

10.8.1 Victims

Under the Domestic Violence, Crime and Victims Act 2004, victims (following certain court disposals for certain defined 'sexual or violent' offences) have the right to make representations to the tribunal.

The Department of Health has published guidance on the subject (Department of Health, Ministry of Justice and National Offender Management Service, *Mental Health Act 2007: Guidance on the Extension of Victims' Rights under the Domestic Violence, Crime and Victims Act 2004* (17 October 2008)).[4] Both the MHT in England and the MHRT for Wales have published their own guidance, based largely on the Department of Health guidance (see *Practice Guidance on Procedures*

---

[4] Available at **www.dh.gov.uk/en/Publicationsandstatistics/Publications/PublicationsPolicy AndGuidance/DH_089408**.

concerning Handling Representations from Victims in the First-tier Tribunal (Mental Health) (1 July 2011), which supersedes previous guidance. Details of the approach adopted by the MHRT for Wales can be obtained by contacting the tribunal office).

Whether the 2004 Act applies depends on a consideration of various definitions:

1. In relation to the identification of *victims*, the tribunal guidance states: 'The definition of "victim" is taken to include any person in relation to the patient's index offence or offences who appears to the relevant local probation board to be the victim of the offence or offences. This includes a victim's family in a case where the offence has resulted in the victim's death or incapacity and in other cases where the victim's age or circumstances make it more sensible to approach a family member' (para.2). This broad definition of victim comes from the Department of Health guidance (*Guidance on the Extension of Victims' Rights under the Domestic Violence, Crime and Victims Act 2004*, paras.1.3 and 1.4).

2. The *offences* to which the 2004 Act applies are violent or sexual offences, including murder, manslaughter, kidnapping, rape and a very extensive list of other offences (Domestic Violence, Crime and Victims Act 2004, s.45).

3. The *disposals*, for the purposes of mental health cases, are restricted hospital orders or equivalent (such as restricted transfer directions) which began on or after 1 July 2005, and unrestricted hospital orders or equivalent which began on or after 3 November 2008. Transfer directions and hospital directions only come within the 2004 Act if associated with a 'relevant sentence' (defined to include a sentence of imprisonment of 12 months or more) (Domestic Violence, Crime and Victims Act 2004, s.45).

Subject to the provisions of the 2004 Act and guidance, and the application of the tribunal rules, victims are permitted to make representations to the tribunal and, in exceptional cases, to attend either in person or via a representative. In restricted cases a Victim Liaison Officer (VLO) is the conduit of information between the tribunal and the victim, and in unrestricted cases it is the hospital managers (in practice, the hospital's Mental Health Act office).

The English guidance sets out the 2004 Act's limitations in relation to the participation of victims. In particular, it states that the victim should not be encouraged to make a general 'impact statement' because the tribunal can only take account of representations in relation to (a) whether in the event of discharge the patient should be subject to conditions; and (b) if so, what those conditions should be (*Practice Guidance on Procedures concerning Handling Representations from Victims in the First-tier Tribunal (Mental Health)*, paras.4, 10). The guidance also clarifies that the Rules do not entitle the victim to see the tribunal reports (para.9) and explains that, subject to the normal tribunal rules, the expectation is that all documents (including the victim's statement) will be disclosed to the patient (para.25).

Where the 2004 Act does not apply, the guidance provides that the Tribunal Secretariat will inform the victim of the hearing date on request, so that written representations may be provided within the tribunal rules (paras.34, 35).

The guidance states that in restricted cases the victim is entitled to be informed, via the VLO (para.27):

(a) whether the patient is to be discharged and, if so, when the discharge will take effect;

(b) if a restricted patient is to be discharged, whether the discharge is to be absolute, or subject to conditions;

(c) if a restricted patient is to be discharged subject to conditions, what the conditions are;

(d) if a restricted patient has previously been discharged subject to conditions, of any variation of these conditions by the tribunal;

(e) if the restriction order is to cease to have effect by virtue of action to be taken by the tribunal, of the date on which the restriction order is to cease to have effect.

In unrestricted cases, the hospital managers will inform the victim of the relevant aspects of the outcome of the hearing (para.29).

10.8.2 MAPPA

Multi-Agency Public Protection Arrangements (MAPPA) operate under the Criminal Justice Act (CJA) 2003 in each criminal justice area in England and Wales (CJA 2003, ss.325–327B). MAPPA is not a statutory body, but rather a mechanism for information sharing, and assessment and management of risk. The 'responsible authority' is the police, prison and probation services acting jointly; 'duty to co-operate agencies', including local social services authorities and NHS Trusts, must work with the responsible authority so far as is compatible with the exercise of their own functions.

The MAPPA guidance issued by the Ministry of Justice (MAPPA Guidance 2012, version 4) states (para.26.21): 'It may be that MAPPA will have information about a patient's current risk which would be of assistance to the Tribunal, and that information should be offered to the Tribunal or to MHCS, who can incorporate it in the Secretary of State's statement.' As MAPPA is not a party there is no automatic right to make representations, but if the information is relevant then the tribunal could admit it as evidence (see **11.2, 11.3**). Alternatively, information could be passed to the RC for inclusion in his or her report if appropriate.

There are three categories of offender who come within the MAPPA framework (MAPPA Guidance, chapter 6):

1. *Category 1: registered sexual offenders*. These offenders are subject to the notification requirements in Part 2 of the Sexual Offences Act 2003.

2.   *Category 2: violent and other sexual offenders.* This means: (a) those con-
     victed of murder or the offences listed in CJA 2003, Sched.15, and who are
     subject to disposals including custodial sentences of 12 months or more and
     hospital or guardianship orders; (b) in relation to the same offences, those
     admitted to hospital or guardianship having been found to be not guilty by
     reason of insanity, or under a disability and to have done the act charged; (c)
     those subject to, or meeting the criteria for, disqualification from working
     with children.
3.   *Category 3: other dangerous offenders.* These are 'other persons who, by
     reason of offences committed by them (wherever committed), are considered
     by the responsible authority to be persons who may cause serious harm to the
     public' (CJA 2003, s.325(2)(b)).

There are three levels of MAPPA management (MAPPA Guidance 2012, chapter
7):

1.   *Level 1: ordinary agency management.* This is where the risks can be
     managed by the agency responsible for the supervision or case management
     of the offender. In the mental health context this means the Care Programme
     Approach will be adopted (MAPPA Guidance 2012, para.3.79).
2.   *Level 2: active multi-agency management.* At this level Multi-Agency Public
     Protection (MAPP) meetings are held. The guidance states that this level is
     appropriate where: (a) the offender is assessed as posing a high or very high
     risk of serious harm; (b) the risk level is lower but the case requires the active
     involvement and co-ordination of interventions from other agencies to man-
     age the presenting risks of serious harm; (c) the case has been previously
     managed at level 3 but no longer meets the criteria for level 3; or (d)
     multi-agency management adds value to the lead agency's management of the
     risk of serious harm posed.
3.   *Level 3: active enhanced multi-agency management.* These cases meet the
     level 2 criteria but the management issues (for instance, a need to commit
     significant resources at short notice or where there is a high likelihood of
     media scrutiny or public interest) require senior representation from the
     responsible authority and duty to co-operate agencies.

Further information about MAPPA, and its involvement with mentally disordered
offenders, is available in Ministry of Justice guidance documents.[5]

---

[5]   Ministry of Justice, *Guidance for Working with MAPPA and Mentally Disordered Offenders*,
available at **www.justice.gov.uk/downloads/offenders/mentally-disordered-offenders/mappa-
mental.pdf**; MAPPA Guidance 2012, version 4, available at **www.justice.gov.uk/downloads/
offenders/mappa/mappa-guidance-2012-part1.pdf**, in particular chapter 26, 'Mentally Disordered
Offenders and MAPPA'.

10.8.3 Patient

Independent reports, obtained on behalf of the patient or nearest relative, are discussed at **13.3.10**. Skeleton arguments on behalf of the patient, and written statements from the patient, are discussed at **13.5.1**.

10.9 SENDING AND DELIVERY OF DOCUMENTS

The Rules give details of the methods by which documents may be sent. Pre-paid post, hand delivery or fax are all permissible (English Rules, rule 13(1); Welsh Rules, rule 9(1)), but the tribunal in England currently encourages the use of CJSM secure email (see Jonathan Gammon, 'Criminal Justice Secure Email (CJSM)', circular letter to solicitors, 31 January 2011).[6]

If a party gives a fax number or email address, then the party must accept delivery by those means unless the party informs the tribunal and the other parties that it must not be used. It is not possible to refuse to accept delivery by pre-paid post or hand delivery (English Rules, rule 13(2), (3); Welsh Rules, rule 8(2), (3)).

The English Rules state that the recipient of a document sent electronically may, as soon as reasonably practicable after receipt, require a hard copy to be sent (English Rules, rule 13(4)). There is no equivalent Welsh provision as, at the time of writing, email is not used for sending documents in Wales.

The MHT website provides the following guidance.[7] In s.2 cases, copies of any documents should be made available at least an hour before the hearing if the patient is represented, or in sufficient time to allow an unrepresented patient to read the reports before the hearing begins. In complex cases where there are a large number of documents (beyond the standard reports) it is helpful if the parties can agree an indexed and paginated bundle which should be sent to the tribunal office in advance, preferably at least 10 days before the hearing.

10.10 DISCLOSURE OF DOCUMENTS

The general rule is that when the tribunal receives a document from any party it must send a copy to each other party (English Rules, rule 32(3); Welsh Rules, rule 15(1)), but this is subject to the non-disclosure rules which are described below. It should be noted that this general rule only applies to parties as defined in the Rules, and not to those added as respondents or interested parties (see **9.2.1**) or those notified of proceedings (see **9.4.1**).

---

[6] Details of the CJSM system are available at **www.cjsm.net**.

[7] 'Making an application', **www.justice.gov.uk/tribunals/mental-health/making-an-appeal**.

10.10.1   Non-disclosure of information in reports

The most common situation where non-disclosure is ordered is when social circumstances (or other) information is to be withheld from the patient, and the remainder of this section will describe that scenario. However, other scenarios are possible, such as non-disclosure of certain information to a nearest relative applicant. Disclosure of information to (and from) victims is considered at **10.8.1**.

The Rules allow the tribunal (and in Wales, oblige it) to give a direction prohibiting the disclosure of a document or information to a person if *both* of the following apply (English Rules, rule 14(2); Welsh Rules, rule 17(1)):

1.   The tribunal is satisfied that such disclosure would be likely to cause that person or some other person serious harm.

   When interpreting this phrase (in the context of the Data Protection Act 1998 but also likely to be relevant here) the Administrative Court decided that the question is whether there 'may very well' be a risk of harm to health even if the risk falls short of being more probable than not (*Roberts* v. *Nottinghamshire Healthcare NHS Trust* [2008] EWHC 1934 (QB)).

2.   The tribunal is satisfied, having regard to the interests of justice, that it is proportionate to give such a direction.

   In *RM* v. *St Andrew's Healthcare* [2010] UKUT 119 (AAC), there was a real risk of serious harm to the patient if the information that he was being covertly medicated were disclosed to him, but the Upper Tribunal ordered disclosure on the basis that the 'interests of justice' limb was not met. In regard to this limb, it was held that the key test to be applied is whether or not non-disclosure of the document or information would allow the patient to make an effective challenge to his detention. On the facts, without knowing that he was being covertly medicated, the patient would have been unable effectively to challenge his detention.

The test for non-disclosure is quite strict, particularly since both limbs of the test set out above must be met. Therefore a report writer may decide that it is preferable to exclude the information from the report entirely, unless it is felt that it is vital to the tribunal's deliberations.

If a report author wants information to be presented to the tribunal as evidence, but not to be disclosed to the patient, then he should put that information in a separate document marked 'Not to be disclosed to the patient without the express permission of the tribunal' and setting out reasons for non-disclosure (see English Rules, rule 14(3); Welsh Rules, rule 17(2)). The reasons should be specific, rather than general, and should not merely recite the test in the Rules.

The English tribunal asks that: 'Any application for the non-disclosure of part or all of a document or report should be made via form CMR1, enclosing an annotated copy of the report or document and full reasons'.[8] The Welsh tribunal does not have an equivalent to Form CMR1 so the reasons should be contained in a covering letter or in the document itself.

The tribunal is required to conduct proceedings as appropriate in order to give effect to any non-disclosure direction which has been given (English Rules, rule 14(4); Welsh Rules, rule 17(3)).

If the party from whom information is withheld has a representative, the 'not to be disclosed' documents or information may be disclosed to the representative if the tribunal is satisfied that (a) such disclosure would be in the interests of the party and (b) the representative will not disclose it either directly or indirectly to any other person without the tribunal's consent (and, in Wales, will not use it otherwise than in connection with the proceedings) (English Rules, rule 14(5), (6); Welsh Rules, rule 17(4), (5)). In practice, at least when the patient is represented by a law firm, an order for non-disclosure is made by the Tribunal Secretariat and the documents are disclosed to the representative automatically.

Disclosure is not usually considered judicially until the day of the hearing, but on receipt of the documents or information the representative may challenge the non-disclosure order by submitting Form CMR1 (in England) or writing to the tribunal (in Wales). It would then be considered by a salaried tribunal judge (in England) or the Chairman (in Wales). On the day of the hearing the matter can be considered as a preliminary issue by the panel (see **11.1.2**).

In the ordinary run of events the representative will want disclosure of all information to his client. This is partly so that full instructions may be taken and any inaccuracies addressed, and partly so that the client's perception will be that justice is being done openly. It will also help to maintain the relationship with the client. It is possible (unless there is a specific direction to the contrary) to inform the client that there is a document containing 'not to be disclosed' information, and to ask whether to seek disclosure. This middle ground sometimes assists to maintain the relationship with the client, but with some clients the knowledge that the representative cannot tell him everything may arouse suspicion.

The most common ground used when seeking disclosure is that the patient is aware of the information already, for instance because it is contained in another report which has been disclosed, or is contained in the medical records which have been discussed with the patient. Otherwise it is a matter of arguing that on the facts the criteria for non-disclosure are not met.

Even if the information is ultimately not disclosed to the patient, the representative may be able to take instructions on the general themes without disclosing the information itself.

It should be noted that if the information cannot be disclosed to the patient then it cannot be disclosed to an independent expert without the tribunal's permission. The tribunal is likely to agree to such disclosure on the basis that the independent expert

---

[8] See **www.justice.gov.uk/tribunals/mental-health/making-an-appeal**.

will not disclose the information. The independent report could also have a separate 'not to be disclosed' section.

10.10.2 Disclosure of medical records

Disclosure of medical records generally is governed by the Data Protection Act (DPA) 1998 and subordinate legislation (in particular, the Data Protection (Subject Access) (Fees and Miscellaneous Provisions) Regulations 2000, SI 2000/191). In the context of tribunal proceedings, however, informal agreement and the tribunal rules have a part to play also. The Department of Health has published guidance in relation to access to health records in general, including psychiatric medical records (*Guidance for Access to Health Records Requests* (22 February 2010)).[9]

Under DPA 1998, an individual is entitled to receive a copy of data held about him, subject to certain exemptions which are described below. A written request must be made, and a fee may be charged (s.7). The maximum fee is £10 for copies of wholly computerised records, or for viewing only (of computerised or manual records), and £50 otherwise (Data Protection (Subject Access) (Fees and Miscellaneous Provisions) Regulations 2000, SI 2000/191). The statutory deadline for compliance is 40 days, although 21 days is the government target.

In tribunal cases, the written request is usually made to the hospital's Mental Health Act Administrator, who consults the RC. The fee is always waived, and access is usually granted well within the statutory timeframe. Some RCs arrange with the MHA Administrator to give automatic permission to representatives of all patients applying to the tribunal unless the contrary is stated in relation to particular patients: this saves valuable time when preparing for hearings.

Under DPA 1998, health records can be withheld if either (s.7, as modified by Data Protection (Subject Access Modification) (Health) Order 2000, SI 2000/413):

(a)   disclosure is likely to cause serious harm to the physical or mental health or condition of the data subject or any other person;

(b)   disclosure would provide information about an identifiable third party.

However, disclosure is still required if any of these apply:

(i)   the third party consents;

(ii)   it would be reasonable to disclose without that consent (some guidance on reasonableness is given in the legislation, DPA 1998, s.7(6));

(iii)   the third party is a health professional who has compiled or contributed to the health record or has been involved in the care of the data subject in his capacity as a health professional.

The 'likely to cause serious harm' element of the DPA 1998 provisions is consistent with the current tribunal rules, and is considered at **10.10.1**.

---

[9]   Gateway reference 13214, available at **www.dh.gov.uk/en/Publicationsandstatistics/ Publications/PublicationsPolicyAndGuidance/DH_112916**.

By contrast, the 'third party' DPA 1998 provisions are not reflected in the tribunal rules; however, they were the subject of consideration in *Dorset Healthcare NHS Foundation Trust* v. *MH* [2009] UKUT 4 (AAC). In that case the patient sought access to information which had not been submitted to the tribunal, and which the Trust sought to withhold on 'third party' grounds. The Upper Tribunal invoked the rule which allows the tribunal to 'permit or require a party or another person to provide documents, information or submissions to the Tribunal or a party' (English Rules, rule 5(3)(d); Welsh Rules, rule 5(2)(c)), and decided that the tribunal may adjudicate where there are disputes in relation to disclosure, in order to ensure that the patient's ECHR, art.6 (fair trial) rights and the third party's art.8 (private and family life) rights are properly considered and maintained.

The Upper Tribunal set out the following guidance:

1. The starting point is that full disclosure should generally be given, so the burden is on the responsible authority to demonstrate that non-disclosure is appropriate.
2. The responsible authority may seek consent to disclosure from any third party or parties, but this may not be practical given the delay involved.
3. Ordinarily the documents can be disclosed to the solicitors subject to an undertaking not to disclose them to the client. The solicitor can then decide whether to submit a skeleton argument to the other party seeking disclosure.
4. In exceptional circumstances where a solicitor's undertaking is not acceptable, or the documents are so sensitive that they should not be disclosed to the solicitor, the responsible authority should submit a skeleton argument identifying the documents and setting out reasons for non-disclosure.
5. The other party may respond to the skeleton argument in writing.
6. If exchange of skeleton arguments does not resolve the issue, then an application should be made to the tribunal by the solicitor (if seeking disclosure of information to his client) or by the responsible authority (if seeking non-disclosure of information to the solicitor).
7. The matter could be decided by the tribunal on the hearing day as a preliminary issue or, in a more complex matter, by a single judge in advance, either on the papers or at a hearing.
8. The tribunal may require information as to the third party's views on disclosure.

Ordinarily, a solicitor must disclose all information to his client if it is material to the case; however, it is possible to agree in advance that the duty of disclosure be limited (see **13.2.4**). The undertaking mentioned at point 3 above cannot be given without the client's informed consent (or, if he lacks capacity to consent, a decision that it is in his best interests). If the solicitor obtains information (from medical records or reports) which demonstrates that his client's instructions are inaccurate, but cannot disclose that information to his client, then, depending on the circumstances, he may have to cease to act. But in most cases the patient's case can be better presented if the representative has the full information even if it cannot all be disclosed to the client.

10.10.3 Disclosure of section papers

Strictly speaking, although section papers are often stored with medical records, they are not medical records, or at least are not *merely* medical records: they are the legal papers which authorise detention or other form of compulsion.[10] Additionally, the Codes of Practice require that a copy of the section papers be made available to the patient (subject to an exception where disclosure would adversely affect the health or wellbeing of the patient or others, and to any need to remove personal information about third parties) (English Code of Practice, para.2.14; Welsh Code of Practice, para.22.4). For these reasons, the usual procedure for access to medical records, with its inherent delays, should not be applied, and access to section papers should be given immediately to representatives following a request on behalf of the patient.

One Trust has published the following policy on access to section papers (and medical records generally):[11]

> Copies of section papers will be released to the requesting solicitors following the receipt of a request which must be accompanied by the patient's written consent. These documents must be sent as soon as reasonably practicable by (a) secure fax, (b) collected in person or (c) sent by post in a double sealed envelope. Documents must not be sent to solicitors by email.

With the suggestion that documents could now be safely sent by secure email, it would be helpful if this policy were to be adopted by all responsible authorities.

10.11 CONCLUSION

The information contained in the statements and reports provided to the tribunal, in particular those relating to the patient's current mental state and on the arrangements for after-care services and support after discharge, are often key factors which may influence the tribunal's decision. This chapter has set out the legal requirements for report writers and those responsible for the delivery of the required statements and reports. **Chapter 11** describes the hearing procedures, including how the information provided will be used by the tribunal.

---

[10] See Department of Health, *Records Management: NHS Code of Practice* (5 April 2006), available at **www.dh.gov.uk/en/Publicationsandstatistics/Publications/PublicationsPolicyAnd Guidance/DH_4131747**.
[11] South London and Maudsley NHS Foundation Trust, *Guidelines for Disclosure of Section Papers and Clinical Records with respect to Patients Detained under the Mental Health Act 1983* (22 October 2010), available at **www.mentalhealthlaw.co.uk/images/SLAM_guidelines_for_ disclosure.pdf**.

CHAPTER 11

Tribunal procedure: hearing procedure

This chapter explains the Rules (and in England, Practice Directions) which apply in relation to the tribunal hearing itself. Tribunals have a wide discretion as to the conduct of proceedings. The Mental Health Tribunal (MHT) in England and the Mental Health Review Tribunal for Wales (MHRT for Wales) may, at any time, give directions regarding the conduct or disposal of proceedings, including a direction amending or suspending an earlier direction (Tribunal Procedure (First-tier Tribunal) (Health, Education and Social Care Chamber) Rules 2008, SI 2008/2699 ('English Rules'), rule 5(2); Mental Health Review Tribunal for Wales Rules 2008, SI 2008/2705 ('Welsh Rules'), rules 5(1), 6(1)), and the Rules allow the tribunal by directions to decide the form of any hearing (English Rules, rule 5(1), (2), (3)(g); Welsh Rules, rule 5(1), (2)(f)).

11.1 HEARINGS

11.1.1 Definitions and composition

Rule 1 of the English Rules and rule 2 of the Welsh Rules define a hearing as 'an oral hearing [which] includes a hearing conducted in whole or in part by video link, telephone or other means of instantaneous two-way electronic communication'. Despite this broad definition, Mental Health Tribunal hearings are almost invariably held with the panel, parties and witnesses sitting across a table in the same room. Normally hearings take place in the hospital at which the patient is detained or at the responsible hospital in community treatment order (CTO) cases. The term 'hearing' embraces the proceedings before the tribunal until it reaches its formal decision (see *R (X)* v. *Mental Health Review Tribunal* [2003] EWHC 1272 (Admin), at [40]).

A decision that disposes of proceedings or determines a preliminary issue made at, or following, a hearing must be made by a panel of three composed as follows: one judge (or in Wales, legal member) who is the presiding member, one other member who is a registered medical practitioner, and one other member who has substantial experience of health or social care matters (see, in England, Practice Statement: *Composition of Tribunals in relation to matters that fall to be decided by the Health, Education and Social Care Chamber on or after 18 January 2010*; in relation to the MHRT for Wales, MHA 1983, Sched.2, para.1 is worded similarly). The 'other' member is currently referred to as a specialist lay member. If the decision of the tribunal is not unanimous, the decision of the majority is the decision of the tribunal (First-tier Tribunal and Upper Tribunal (Composition of Tribunal) Order 2008, SI 2008/2835, art.8; there is no Welsh equivalent but the same procedure is adopted).

11.1.2 Preliminary issues

The tribunal may deal with an issue in the proceedings as a preliminary issue (English Rules, rule 5(3)(e); Welsh Rules, rule 5(2)(d)). In relation to specified preliminary and incidental matters the judge or (in Wales) the Chairman may, at any time up to the hearing, exercise the powers of the tribunal (see Practice Statement: *Composition of Tribunals in relation to matters that fall to be decided by the Health, Education and Social Care Chamber on or after 18 January 2010,* para.10; Welsh Rules, rule 4). It is possible for the tribunal to hold a preliminary hearing to consider any matter, including a case management issue (English Rules, rule 5(3)(g); Welsh Rules, rule 5(2)(e)). In particularly complex cases it may be useful to hold a preliminary hearing on a separate day to the main hearing.

The overriding objective (see **9.1.2**) and the rules of natural justice apply to preliminary issues just as they do to the main hearing itself.

Preliminary issues can include issues such as non-disclosure of evidence (see **10.10**), the order of evidence, or adjournments. If there are such issues then, prior to the hearing, the tribunal clerk should be informed by the person wishing to raise them (or the panel approached directly in the absence of a clerk). The panel will then consider whether or not to make a decision prior to the beginning of the hearing, and probably will wish to hear from the patient's representative and the responsible clinician (RC) (or someone else from the responsible authority) before making any decision.

11.1.3 Disposal without hearing

The English tribunal is not permitted to dispose of proceedings without a hearing, except for (a) decisions under Part 5 of the English Rules (correcting, setting aside, reviewing and appealing tribunal decisions: see **12.3**); (b) CTO referral cases in certain circumstances (see below); and (c) striking out a party's case for want of jurisdiction (see **9.3.6**) (English Rules, rule 35).

There is no similar provision for the MHRT for Wales, but neither was there in the old Mental Health Review Tribunal Rules 1983, and the practice under those Rules was always to hold a hearing.

Exceptions (b) and (c) above are as a result of changes made to the English Rules on 6 April 2012 (by Tribunal Procedure (Amendment) Rules 2012, SI 2012/500). The exception in relation to CTO referral cases applies where the following three conditions are met:

1. The patient is a community patient. This is defined as a patient in respect of whom a CTO is in force (MHA 1983, s.17A and s.145); therefore, the exception does not apply if (at the time it is considered) the patient has returned to hospital following revocation of the CTO.
2. The patient is aged 18 years or over.
3. Either:

   (a) the patient has stated in writing that he does not wish to attend or be represented at the hearing, and the tribunal is satisfied that the patient has 'capacity to decide whether or not to make that decision' (presumably this means capacity to *make* the decision); or
   (b) the patient's representative has stated in writing that the patient does not wish to attend or be represented at the hearing. This element of the Rules does not mention capacity but the tribunal's advice which formerly appeared on its website stated 'The patient's representative may complete the relevant form for the patient, but the decision must be made by the patient (who must have capacity to make such a decision)'.[1]

The Practice Direction now requires the RC to provide, in CTO referral cases, 'an assessment of the patient's capacity to decide whether or not to attend, or be represented at, a hearing of the reference' (Practice Direction: *First-tier Tribunal Health Education and Social Care Chamber: Statements and Reports in Mental Health Cases* (April 2012), para.15(a)). The tribunal may rely on this evidence but if it disagrees, having read the papers, then a hearing would be held.[2] The requirement for a preliminary medical examination (see **9.7**) by the medical member (if practicable) does not apply if no hearing will be held.

The RC is not a wholly independent source so reliance on his opinion arguably involves a conflict of interest, despite the tribunal's position that, as an expert witness, the RC has 'no "interest" one way or the other' (see Judge Mark Hinchliffe, 'Important Notice', 29 March 2012). There have always been situations in relation to compulsory treatment in which the outcome depended on the RC's opinion on capacity, but this is the first time that decisions in relation to the tribunal's power of review have had such input by the responsible authority.

A tribunal panel can consider approximately 10 of these paper reviews in one day. If it considers that the detention criteria are met, the decision is not to discharge. If it considers that the criteria are not or may not be met, the patient is not discharged but

---

[1] See **http://webarchive.nationalarchives.gov.uk/20120406155417/http://www.justice.gov.uk/tribunals/mental-health/hearings/legal-reps**.
[2] See Tribunal Procedure Committee, *Response to Consultation on Proposed Amendments to the Tribunal Procedure (First-tier Tribunal) (Health, Education and Social Care Chamber) Rules 2008* (February 2012).

rather a hearing is convened (Judge Mark Hinchliffe, speaking at MHLA Conference, 4 November 2012).

11.2 APPROACH TO EVIDENCE

11.2.1 Informality

As part of the overriding objective (described at **9.1.2**), tribunals must avoid unnecessary formality in their proceedings (English Rules, rule 2(2)(b); Welsh Rules, rule 2(2)(a)). However, there must be a degree of formality so, for instance, it is normal for witnesses to give evidence strictly in turn (see **11.5**). Eldergill put it succinctly as follows (Anselm Eldergill, *Mental Health Review Tribunals: Law and Practice* (London, Sweet & Maxwell, 1997), p.808): 'A distinction must be drawn between maintaining an informal atmosphere, which reassures the patient, and following a formal approach to the taking of the evidence, which is not only essential to the proper discharge of the tribunal's powers but also reassures the patient that his liberty is highly regarded'.

11.2.2 Rules of evidence

There are no formal rules of evidence. The tribunal may admit evidence whether or not (a) the evidence would be admissible in a civil trial in England and Wales; or (b) the evidence was available to a previous decision-maker (English Rules, rule 15(2)(a); Welsh Rules, rule 18(2)(a)). At the same time, it may exclude evidence that would otherwise be admissible where (a) the evidence was not provided within the time allowed by a direction or a Practice Direction; (b) the evidence was otherwise provided in a manner that did not comply with a direction or a Practice Direction; or (c) it would otherwise be unfair to admit the evidence (English Rules, rule 15(2)(b); Welsh Rules, rule 18(2)(b)). The tribunal will consider the relevance and weight of the evidence when deciding whether or not to admit it (*LN* v. *Surrey NHS Primary Care Trust* [2011] UKUT 76 (AAC)).

  Essentially, the tribunal can decide what evidence it wants to hear, including hearsay, but this is subject to the rules of natural justice. The Administrative Court has sounded a note of caution in relation to hearsay: the tribunal must have regard to the particular dangers in relying on hearsay, and be alert to mere 'institutional folklore' being given the status of established fact by constant repetition; if an incident is really fundamental to its decision, fairness may require the patient to be able to cross-examine the relevant witnesses if their evidence is to be relied upon (*R (AN)* v. *Mental Health Review Tribunal* [2005] EWHC 587 (Admin), at [129] (Munby J)). In *R* v. *Merseyside Mental Health Review Tribunal, ex p. Kelly* (1998) 39 BMLR 114, a tribunal decision was quashed where criminal conduct prior to recall of a conditionally-discharged patient was assumed in the reports to have taken place, but cross-examination was not permitted in relation to the allegations.

213

The tribunal may consent to a witness giving, or require any witness to give, evidence on oath, and may administer an oath for that purpose (English Rules, rule 15(3); Welsh Rules, rule 18(3)). A witness may believe that this would improve his credibility, and the tribunal may oblige, but this is extremely rare in practice.

11.2.3 Burden of proof

The tribunal's approach to discharge under MHA 1983, s.72 used to be that it was obliged to discharge only if positively satisfied that the detention criteria did not apply. Currently, it is obliged to discharge if it is not positively satisfied that the detention criteria do apply. The change to the legislation was made following the Court of Appeal's decision that the previous placing of the burden of proof on the patient was in breach of ECHR, art.5 (see *R (H)* v. *MHRT North and East London Region* [2001] EWCA Civ 415; Mental Health Act 1983 (Remedial) Order 2001, SI 2001/3712). The use of the term 'burden of proof' does not mean that the tribunal is entirely adversarial: it would be more accurate to say that it is partly inquisitorial, partly adversarial (see e.g., *W* v. *Egdell* [1989] EWCA Civ 13, and *MP* v. *West London Mental Health NHS Trust* [2012] UKUT 231 (AAC); see also **7.1**).

11.2.4 Standard of proof

The civil standard of proof applies, so the tribunal should apply the standard of proof on the balance of probabilities to all the issues it has to determine (*R (AN)* v. *Mental Health Review Tribunal* [2005] EWCA Civ 1605; see also **7.2**).

11.3 ATTENDANCE AT HEARINGS

11.3.1 Entitlement to attend

At most hearings, matters are simple and attendance is not a contentious subject: the patient will attend (probably with a representative), as will the RC, care co-ordinator and nurse. The rules on entitlement to attend, which are subject to the general position that the tribunal may decide who can, or cannot, attend private hearings (see **11.3.2**) are set out below.

The following classes of person have differing rights in this area:

1. Subject to the exclusion rules, each party to proceedings is entitled to attend a hearing (English Rules, rule 36(1)). This entitlement is not explicitly stated in the Welsh Rules, but the rules of natural justice and ECHR, art.6 would require it. (See **9.2.1** for the definition of 'party'.)
2. A party may be accompanied by another person whose details have not been notified to the tribunal in advance (as is required for the representative). In England, that person may act as representative or otherwise assist in presenting the party's case (English Rules, rule 11(5)). In Wales, the Rules state that

'Unless the Tribunal otherwise directs, a patient or any other party may be accompanied by such other person as the patient or party wishes, in addition to any representative that may have been appointed under this Rule, provided that such person does not act as the representative of the patient or other party' (rule 13(6)). The accompanying person could assume the role of a McKenzie friend, who may provide moral support, take notes, help with case papers, and quietly give advice on the conduct of the case.[3]

3. Other people may become entitled to attend:

(a) The English Rules provide that any person notified of the proceedings may attend and take part in a hearing to such extent as the tribunal considers proper, or provide written submissions (rule 36(2)). The persons who must be notified are listed at **9.4.1**: in particular, the Rules also allow the tribunal to provide notice of proceedings to any person who should have an opportunity of being heard (rule 33(e)).

(b) The Welsh Rules provide that the tribunal may give a direction permitting or requesting any person to attend and take part in a hearing to such extent as the tribunal considers appropriate, or to make written submissions in relation to a particular issue (rule 26).

(c) The English tribunal website states that if the patient or his representative has provided full details of the 'nearest relative or next of kin', that person will be invited to attend the hearing, and the same practice is adopted in Wales.[4]

(d) Neither an independent mental health advocate (IMHA) nor a victim has an inherent entitlement to attend. They could, however, in appropriate cases, fall within the provisions set out above. The position of IMHAs is considered further at **11.6**, and of victims at **10.8.1**.

It should be noted that the only people automatically entitled to receive copies of the reports, reasons and other documents, subject to the non-disclosure rules (see **10.10**), are the parties (English Rules, rule 32(3); Welsh Rules, rule 15(1)).

11.3.2 Exclusion rules

The exclusion rules differ according to the circumstances:

1. If a hearing, or part of it, is to be held in private, the tribunal may determine who is permitted to attend the hearing or part of it (English Rules, rule 38(3); Welsh Rules, rule 25(3) is similar).

2. The tribunal may give a direction excluding from any hearing, or part of it: (a) any person whose conduct the tribunal considers is disrupting or is likely to

---

[3] The role of a McKenzie friend in court proceedings is described in Practice Guidance, *McKenzie Friends (Civil and Family Courts)* (12 July 2010), available at **www.judiciary.gov.uk/publications-and-reports/guidance/index/mckenzie-friends**.

[4] See **www.justice.gov.uk/tribunals/mental-health/hearings**.

disrupt the hearing; (b) any person whose presence the tribunal considers is likely to prevent another person from giving evidence or making submissions freely; (c) any person who the tribunal considers should be excluded in order to give effect to a non-disclosure direction (English Rules, rule 38(4); Welsh Rules, rule 25(4); see **10.10.1**). The English Rules have an additional category: (d) any person where the purpose of the hearing would be defeated by the attendance of that person. These rules apply both to public and to private hearings. The words 'any person' could include the patient (subject, in England, to the rules about proceeding in the patient's absence: see **11.3.4**) or in an extreme case even a representative.

3.   Additionally, the tribunal may give a direction excluding a witness from any hearing until that witness has given evidence (English Rules, rule 38(5); Welsh Rules, rule 25(5)). This may be, for instance, to receive evidence from a victim or relative without that person hearing the evidence of the other witnesses, or to allow a private interview with the patient (see **11.5.8** for further details).

11.3.3   Observing tribunals

The tribunal in England has issued guidance on this topic, which requires that requests for observers be made in advance in writing to the Deputy Chamber President or, in his absence, the principal salaried judge for a preliminary decision, and lays down guidance on the approach to take by the tribunal panel (see *Guidance for the Observation of Tribunal Hearings* (November 2009)).[5] In Wales, the request should be made to the Chairman. However, no matter whether permission has been sought or not – or granted or refused – the final decision is for the panel on the day.

Observation requests most often come from colleagues of professionals involved in the patient's care, for example, junior doctors or student nurses. Also, observation of (or representation at) four hearings is a prerequisite of the Law Society's Mental Health Accreditation Scheme (see **13.1**). The matter should be raised with the patient well before the hearing begins. If the patient does not want observers to be present then his wishes are likely to be respected. The Ministry of Justice may occasionally send observers in restricted cases, but it accepts that this is subject to the patient's consent (see *Ministry of Justice: Tribunal Service Mental Health Guidance* (April 2009), para.3.6).

The guidance mentioned above advises that observers should not be permitted to see any of the reports or documents available to the tribunal, or to take notes during the hearing (*Guidance for the Observation of Tribunal Hearings* (November 2009), paras.8.1 and 8.6).

---

[5]   Available at **www.justice.gov.uk/downloads/tribunals/mental-health/publications/Guidance ForObservationOfTribunal.pdf**.

11.3.4 Hearings in a party's absence

It may be that the patient does not wish to attend the hearing, particularly where his case has been referred to the tribunal, or it may be that he is absent without leave or in seclusion when the hearing is due to take place.

In England, the situation is that:

1. The tribunal may only proceed in a party's absence if it (a) is satisfied that the party has been notified of the hearing or that reasonable steps have been taken to notify the party of the hearing; and (b) considers that it is in the interests of justice to proceed with the hearing (English Rules, rule 39(1)).

2. Additionally, the tribunal may not proceed in the absence of the patient unless (a) the requirements in relation to the medical examination (see **9.7**) have been satisfied; and (b) it is satisfied that (i) the patient has decided not to attend the hearing, or (ii) the patient is unable to attend the hearing for reasons of ill-health (English Rules, rule 39(2)). It is not stated whether ill-health includes mental as well as physical ill-health.

In Wales, the tribunal may proceed without a party if (a) the tribunal (i) is satisfied that the party has been notified of the hearing or that reasonable steps have been taken to notify the party of the hearing; and (ii) the tribunal is not aware of any good reason for the failure to attend; or (b) the tribunal otherwise considers that it is in the interests of the patient to proceed with the hearing (Welsh Rules, rule 27).

Where the hearing proceeds in a patient's absence, the patient may or may not wish to be represented. If he has appointed a representative, that person may attend the hearing even if the patient does not (English Rules, rule 11(3); Welsh Rules, rule 13(3)). If he has not appointed a representative, it may be that the tribunal appoints a legal representative for him (see **9.2.2**).

In CTO referral cases, if the patient does not want to attend or be represented, the tribunal may proceed without a hearing at all (see **11.1.3**).

11.4 ADJOURNMENT AND POSTPONEMENT

The tribunal may adjourn or postpone a hearing at any time. Under the English Rules the power to adjourn is part of the general power to issue directions (rule 5(3)(h)). Under the Welsh Rules there is a specific rule dedicated to adjournment (rule 21), which confers a discretion on the tribunal to adjourn in order to obtain further information or for such other reason as it thinks appropriate.

The Rules do not define postponement or adjournment, but an adjournment is generally understood to be a decision made at the tribunal hearing, whereas a postponement decision is made before the hearing commences. The case law relates to adjournments but there is no reason not to apply similar principles to postponements. Both are judicial decisions, and neither has been delegated to administrative staff at the Tribunal Secretariat. By contrast, the initial process of listing a hearing, within target timeframes, is a function carried out by the Secretariat (see **9.4.2**).

The tribunal should not adjourn without giving the patient's representative an opportunity to be heard, and it should give brief reasons (*R (B)* v. *Mental Health Review Tribunal* [2002] EWHC 1553 (Admin)).

Adjournments are becoming less common. In 2008–2009, 29 per cent of listed hearings were adjourned; in 2009–2010 this reduced to 19 per cent, and in both 2010–2011 and 2011–2012 the figure was 7 per cent. A similar trend is apparent for postponements. For 2008–2009 there are no figures, but the rates decreased from 18 per cent in 2010–2011 to 13 per cent in 2010–2011 and 2011–2012. (See Ministry of Justice and HMCTS, *Annual Tribunals Statistics, 2010–11: 1 April 2010 to 31 March 2011*, 30 June 2011; Ministry of Justice and HMCTS, *Annual Tribunals Statistics, 2011–12*, 28 June 2012.)

11.4.1 Grounds for adjournment

A tribunal hearing may be adjourned or postponed for many reasons. These include obtaining further evidence, or allowing the attendance of a particular witness, the instruction of an independent expert, the appointment of a legal representative, or the attendance of an existing representative if that person is unavailable and unable to appoint a substitute.

In restricted cases there may need to be an adjournment if the Secretary of State has not been notified of the hearing or has not had the opportunity of commenting on all the reports (see *R (Secretary of State for the Home Department)* v. *Mental Health Review Tribunal (Ogden)* [2004] EWHC 650 (Admin); *R* v. *Oxford Regional Mental Health Review Tribunal, ex p. Secretary of State for the Home Department* [1988] AC 120). It is therefore incumbent on the representative, in order to avoid delay, to ensure that this sort of procedural irregularity has been dealt with prior to the hearing date.

The decision in relation to whether or not to adjourn involves the tribunal exercising its discretion, but can be appealed if it involves an error of law (see **Chapter 12**). For instance, in *R (X)* v. *Mental Health Review Tribunal* [2003] EWHC 1272 (Admin), the tribunal adjourned after hearing the evidence and submissions and (in the exceptional circumstances of the case) this was lawful, but in *R (B)* v. *Mental Health Review Tribunal* [2002] EWHC 1553 (Admin), the failure to give the patient an opportunity to make representations before adjourning resulted in a breach of natural justice.

Although the tribunal 'may regulate its own procedure' (in England, English Rules, rule 5(1)) and an adjournment or postponement may be 'for the purpose of obtaining further information or for such other purposes as it may think appropriate' (in Wales, Welsh Rules, rule 21(1)), the adjournment must relate to the tribunal's statutory function, so:

(a)   the tribunal has no power to adjourn to give an opportunity for the patient's condition to improve or to see if an improvement already made is sustained (*R v. Mental Health Review Tribunal, ex p. Secretary of State for the Home Department (Thomas)* (1988) *The Times*, 12 October, [1988] MHLO 1);

(b)   it is unlawful for the tribunal to adjourn solely for the purpose of obtaining evidence in relation to making an extra-statutory recommendation (*R (Secretary of State for the Home Department)* v. *Mental Health Review Tribunal (MW and FO)* [2000] EWHC 638 (Admin)).

In an unrestricted case where the availability of suitable after-care services is a prerequisite for the discharge criteria to be met, but the tribunal is in any doubt as to its availability, the tribunal should adjourn rather than defer discharge to a future date (see *R (Ashworth)* v. *Mental Health Review Tribunal; R (H)* v. *Ashworth* [2002] EWCA Civ 923). In a restricted case, if the tribunal has decided a conditional discharge would be appropriate but is not yet in a position to draft necessary conditions, it should adjourn for further information rather than grant a deferred conditional discharge (*DC* v. *Nottinghamshire Healthcare NHS Trust* [2012] UKUT 92 (AAC), at [28]).

11.4.2   Duration of the adjournment

The duration will depend on the reason for the adjournment and whether it is necessary to have the same panel on the subsequent occasion. The tribunal should give an indication of when the hearing will be resumed: if it is not possible to specify a date for the reconvened hearing, a date should be identified before which the hearing must take place (*R (B)* v. *Mental Health Review Tribunal* [2002] EWHC 1553 (Admin)). The tribunal must give the same notice for reconvened hearings as for the initial hearing (see **9.4.1**).

The tribunal has a duty of 'avoiding delay, so far as compatible with proper consideration of the issues' (English Rules, rule 2(2)(e); Welsh Rules, rule 3(2)(d)) and has a duty as a public authority under the Human Rights Act 1998 not to create a delay so serious as to breach ECHR, art.5(4). In *R (X)* v. *Mental Health Review Tribunal* [2003] EWHC 1272 (Admin) (Collins J), the court held that 'the tribunal should not adjourn a case unless it regards it as necessary for the purpose of doing justice and of reaching the right result in a given case, and in deciding whether it is necessary, it will have to balance the need which it perceives for the extra information against any delay that that will occasion to the determination of the appeal before it' (at [31]). The consequences of unlawful delay are considered at **9.4.2**.

11.4.3   Directions on adjournment

The tribunal's power to issue directions before the hearing has been considered at **9.5** in the context of pre-hearing procedures. Directions are also likely to be given alongside a decision to adjourn. Before postponing or adjourning any hearing, the tribunal may give such directions as it thinks fit for ensuring the prompt considera-tion of the application at a postponed or adjourned hearing (see Welsh Rules, rule 21(2); similar sentiments were expressed in *R (B)* v. *Mental Health Review Tribunal* [2002] EWHC 1553 (Admin)).

Adjournment directions should, where necessary, allow for any expert evidence to be obtained, and for experts to meet to identify and narrow any differences of opinion, before the reconvened hearing (*R (B)* v. *Mental Health Review Tribunal* [2002] EWHC 1553 (Admin)). Directions could also require a person to attend, answer questions or produce documents, and (although this is a rarely used power) a summons could be issued (see **9.5.5**).

11.4.4   Reconvening

The tribunal may be asked to reconvene after an adjournment. The Welsh Rules state that where a party requests that a hearing be reconvened, the hearing must be reconvened if the tribunal is satisfied that reconvening would be in the interests of the patient (Welsh Rules, rule 21(3)). There is no equivalent English provision but similar considerations would apply. If the tribunal decides not to reconvene, it should set out its reasons, which if inadequate could lead to an appeal (as in *RB* v. *Nottinghamshire Healthcare NHS Trust* [2011] UKUT 73 (AAC)).

Similar principles apply to reconvening after a decision with recommendations or a deferred conditional discharge decision (see **8.1.4** and **8.1.5**).

11.5   CONDUCT OF THE PROCEEDINGS

The English Rules state that, subject to statute, the tribunal may regulate its own procedure (rule 5(1)) and the Welsh Rules state that the tribunal may by directions decide the form of any hearing (rule 5(2)(f)).

This allows for much flexibility, and the order of events varies regionally. For instance, in the North East of England the default position is that the patient gives evidence first, whereas elsewhere it is normal for the patient to speak last. A common order of events is as follows: introductions, including a short statement from the patient's representative; evidence from the RC and other professional witnesses, including any independent experts; evidence from the patient and other witnesses; legal closing submissions. These stages are described in detail below. After each witness has given evidence, the tribunal is likely to have questions, and will allow any representatives to question the witness.

The role of the representative is considered in more detail in **Chapter 13**. The content of the witnesses' reports is considered at **10.1**.

11.5.1 Introductions

The tribunal clerk, or the judge (or in Wales, the president) if there is no clerk, will ensure that the seating plan is correct. The hearing normally takes place across a table, in boardroom style or similar. The tribunal panel sit at one side, the witnesses and any representatives on the other. The judge (or president) sits in the centre, with the medical member to the judge's right and the lay member to the left. The usual order of witnesses, from left to right facing the table, is as follows: RC (opposite the medical member), representative, patient, nurse, and care co-ordinator (opposite the lay member). Other people present will be placed according to whether they are witnesses or observers, and according to the size and shape of the room. Observers are considered at **11.3.3**.

The judge (or president) will introduce the panel by name, primarily addressing the patient. He will confirm the identity of the witnesses and will often ask the patient if he prefers to be known by his first name or by title and surname. He will explain the tribunal's function and its independence, and will set out the order of evidence. At this point the representative may take the opportunity to suggest any changes, for instance if the patient wishes to give evidence first or last. Usually (particularly if the case has come before the tribunal by means of a reference) the judge will invite the representative to set out briefly what the patient seeks; if this does not happen the representative may offer to do so, as knowledge of this helps to focus the tribunal's enquiry on relevant topics. The tribunal may give directions as to issues on which it requires evidence or submissions and the nature of the evidence or submissions it requires (English Rules, rule 15(1)(a), (b); Welsh Rules, rule 18(1)(a), (b)).

11.5.2 Medical member's evidence

The tribunal medical member will, if practicable, have examined the patient prior to the hearing beginning (English Rules, rule 34; Welsh Rules, rule 20), and will have given evidence about this to the panel in private (see **9.7**). It is important that the tribunal does not act on the basis of evidence known only to itself (*R (S)* v. *Mental Health Review Tribunal* [2002] EWHC 2522 (Admin)), so the judge (or sometimes the medical member) will disclose the relevant evidence to those present at the hearing. If, which would be rare, the patient disputes the medical member's account of what was said during the examination, or fresh issues are raised, then it may be necessary briefly to adjourn so that further instructions can be taken. If a factual conflict may be material to the tribunal's decision then the tribunal may need to adjourn for a new panel to be appointed (*R (S)* v. *Mental Health Review Tribunal* [2002] EWHC 2522 (Admin), at [34]).

11.5.3 Responsible authority's medical evidence

The first professional witness is invariably the responsible clinician. One approach which some tribunals adopt is for the judge to ask the RC brief questions on the statutory criteria, the medical member to ask more detailed questions on medical matters, and then the other member to ask supplementary questions. The patient's representative will be invited to ask questions also. The RC will give evidence as to the patient's mental state and treatment (the content of the medical report is set out at **10.4**).

The possibility of the RC acting as the responsible authority's representative is considered at **9.2.2**.

11.5.4 Independent evidence

If there are independent experts present to give evidence, it is common for evidence of one type to be heard at the same time so that, for instance, an independent psychiatrist would give evidence following the RC.

The instruction of independent experts is considered at **13.3.10**.

11.5.5 Nurse's evidence

Ideally, the nurse who attends the hearing will be the patient's primary nurse, who will know the patient as well as, if not better than, any other professional. The nurse will be able to give evidence about day-to-day activities, the patient's behaviour on the ward and on leave of absence, his compliance with medication, etc. (the content of the nursing report is set out at **10.5**).

The MHT in England has provided the following advice to panels in relation to nursing reports. The author of the nursing report should attend the hearing. If this is rendered impracticable by shift patterns or other good reasons, another nurse should attend and speak to the report. As a general rule, questions should relate to the report (e.g. 'patient's attitude to treatment, current observation levels, details of any seclusion or restraint imposed upon patient, any abuse of leave, and any violent incidents'). The nurse should be asked about positive as well as negative features of the patient's progress, and should not normally be involved in diagnostic issues (see *Nursing Reports: Advice to Panels from Regional Tribunal Judges* (February 2009)).

11.5.6 Care co-ordinator's evidence

The care co-ordinator, who is often a social worker but may be a community psychiatric nurse (CPN) or occupational therapist, will give evidence about the patient's family and social circumstances, and potential after-care provision (see **10.6** for further details). In s.2 cases there may have been no care co-ordinator appointed, in which case the most useful witness would be the approved mental health professional (AMHP) who made the application for detention.

When the tribunal is actively considering discharge from section to enable discharge from hospital, evidence of social circumstances is all important. It is arguably less so where the patient seeks to remain in hospital as a voluntary patient or it is common ground that discharge is not yet realistic (see *AM* v. *West London Mental Health NHS Trust* [2012] UKUT 382 (AAC)). In longer-term or restricted cases it is more common for patients to be discharged from hospital to hostel accommodation rather than independent accommodation, and it is the social worker who will provide evidence in relation to this, which can include funding issues.

11.5.7 Other evidence

The tribunal may receive evidence from family and friends, or other people known to the patient (see **11.3**) and this can be helpful in some cases. For instance, if the patient wishes to be discharged to his parents' home, then their presence to give direct evidence (as opposed to indirect evidence from the patient or other witnesses) about this possibility would be useful.

The nearest relative may appear as a witness or, if he is the applicant, may be legally represented under the Legal Aid scheme. The patient would probably be separately represented because of the possibility of a conflict of interest arising during the case.

11.5.8 Patient's evidence

Having the patient give evidence at the end allows him to hear all the evidence 'against him' before he gives his. However, it may be that he prefers to give his evidence at the beginning, for instance, if he would not cope well with hearing the evidence and wishes to leave early. This is something that should be discussed with the patient beforehand.

Usually, the patient will be guided through his evidence by his representative, whose role is to assist the patient to give his best evidence, following which the tribunal will ask further questions. If the patient requires a short break in order to consult with his representative then this is invariably permitted.

The Welsh Rules provide that at any time before the tribunal makes the final determination, the tribunal or any one or more of its members may interview the patient, which interview may take place in the absence of any other person (rule 20). There is no equivalent provision in the current English Rules, although the tribunal could take this course of action, on request, by excluding others (see English Rules, rule 38(4)(b)). Tribunals in both jurisdictions, when considering requests for a private interview, will need to be mindful of the overriding objective, as well as what the European Court of Human Rights (ECtHR) has referred to as 'the situation of inferiority and powerlessness' of detained patients (*Herczegfalvy* v. *Austria* (10533/83) [1992] ECHR 83).

11.5.9 Closing submissions

At the end of the hearing the representative (or representatives) will be given the opportunity to make closing submissions. The submissions will summarise the positive points of evidence in favour of the client's case, with reference to any relevant statutory criteria. The summing up can be quite brief. In cases where not only the patient is represented, all representatives would be able to sum up, although the patient's representative should be given the last word.

11.6 IMHA OR OTHER LAY ADVOCATE

Sometimes a lay advocate, in particular an independent mental health advocate (IMHA) appointed under MHA 1983, may wish to attend the hearing.

IMHAs are available in England and Wales for the following qualifying patients (MHA 1983, s.130C): (a) any patient detained (except under MHA 1983, ss.4, 5, 135 or 136) or liable to be detained (including conditionally-discharged patients), subject to guardianship, or subject to a CTO; (b) anyone who discusses with a doctor or approved clinician (AC) the possibility of being given s.57 treatment (psychosurgery or surgical implantation of hormones to reduce male sex drive), or anyone under 18 who discusses s.58A treatment (ECT). In Wales, the scheme has been extended to cover 'Welsh qualifying compulsory patients' (as above, with the addition of ss.4 and 5) and 'Welsh qualifying informal patients' (in-patients who are not liable to be detained but receive treatment for, or assessment in relation to, mental disorder) (MHA 1983, ss.130I, 130J).

The help available includes help in obtaining information about and understanding (a) the relevant provisions of MHA 1983; (b) any conditions or restrictions; (c) what medical treatment is given, proposed or discussed, and why; (d) the authority for it and the requirements of MHA 1983 in relation to giving it. It also includes help in obtaining information and understanding any rights which may be exercised under MHA 1983 and help (by way of representation or otherwise) in exercising those rights (s.130B). Department of Health *Reference Guide to the Mental Health Act 1983* (London, 2008) adds (para.34.11): 'But independent mental health advocacy services are not designed to take the place of advice from, or representation by, qualified legal professionals'.

The Mental Health Tribunal in England has issued guidance on this topic (see Practice Note: *Role of the Independent Mental Health Advocate in First-tier Tribunal (Mental Health) Hearings* (May 2011)). Although the guidance recognises that an IMHA could in theory be a 'representative' under the Rules, it focuses on the IMHA's role as an IMHA, and on the desirability that this does not infringe on the proper role of the representative. It states that 'In general, the role of the IMHA in relation to the conduct of the hearing would be that of ensuring, if necessary, that the patient has understood the issues, and assisting with the communication of the patient's views to the tribunal' (para.5.1.5). At the outset the judge will wish to clarify the role to be played by the IMHA or other lay advocate.

11.7   DECISION AND ITS EFFECTS

11.7.1   Announcing the decision

The tribunal may give a decision orally at the end of a hearing (English Rules, rule 41(1); Welsh Rules, rule 28(1)) and almost invariably does so. Usually, the judge (or president in Wales) states whether or not the section will be discharged and whether or not other applications (e.g. for recommendations) will be granted, but provides little or nothing by way of reasons except in the written decision notice. Rarely will a fully reasoned oral judgment be given. The decision takes effect as soon as it is announced orally.

11.7.2   Written reasons

Written reasons must be given for any decision which disposes of proceedings (defined to include a decision with statutory recommendations or a deferred conditional discharge decision) except for review or permission to appeal decisions (English Rules, rule 41(2); Welsh Rules, rule 28(2)). The tribunal may give written reasons for any other decision (English Rules, rule 41(4); although not stated in the Welsh Rules, the same applies).

Each party is entitled to receive a copy of the written reasons unless the non-disclosure provisions apply (English Rules, rule 41(2)). In England, the normal non-disclosure rules apply (see **10.10.1**). In Wales, the approach is as follows (Welsh Rules, rule 28(4)):

> Where the Tribunal considers that the full disclosure of the recorded reasons for its decision to the patient would cause the patient or any other person serious harm, the Tribunal may instead communicate its decision to him in such manner as it thinks appropriate and may communicate its decision to the other parties subject to any conditions it may think appropriate as to the disclosure thereof to the patient.

In England, the tribunal must provide to each party, as soon as reasonably practicable, a decision notice stating the decision, reasons for the decision, and notification of any right of appeal against the decision and the time within which, and the manner in which, such right of appeal may be exercised (English Rules, rule 41(2). See *Appealing to the First-tier Tribunal (Health, Education and Social Care Chamber) Mental Health Decisions* (November 2008)). The Welsh Rules are different in that they do not require notification of appeal rights, although it has been argued that the overriding objective requires this (by L.O. Gostin, P. Fennell *et al.*, *Principles of Mental Health Law* (Oxford University Press, 2010), para.16.163).

The Welsh Rules state that, subject to the rule on prohibitions on disclosure or publication, the tribunal may, where appropriate, send notice of a decision or the reasons for it to 'any person' (rule 28(6)). There is no equivalent provision in the English Rules.

The written reasons must be provided 'as soon as reasonably practicable', and within the following deadlines: in s.2 application cases, reasons must be provided at the hearing or sent within three working days after the hearing; in other cases, reasons must be sent within seven days after the hearing (English Rules, rule 41(3); Welsh Rules, rule 28(3)).

If a patient is represented, documents (including the decision notice containing the written reasons) need only be sent to the representative (English Rules, rule 11(4)(a); Welsh Rules, rule 13(3)), and tribunals have a policy of only sending documents to the representative. Therefore the representative should provide his client with the notice.

11.7.3 Provisional decisions

If a tribunal adjourns, grants a deferred conditional discharge, or makes a statutory recommendation, then the tribunal retains the power to reconvene and the proceedings continue. For Legal Aid purposes, the matter has not yet concluded (see **14.4**). In contrast, there is no power to reconvene following a decision by the tribunal to make an *extra-statutory* recommendation.

Where the tribunal makes a decision with statutory recommendations, the decision may specify any period at the expiration of which the tribunal will consider the case further in the event of those recommendations not being complied with (Welsh Rules, rule 28(5)). The same procedure should be adopted with deferred conditional discharge decisions and with adjournments (see **11.4**).

When the tribunal reconvenes it has the same powers as at the original hearing (see *R* v. *Mental Health Review Tribunal, ex p. Hempstock* [1997] EWHC 664 (following recommendations); *R (IH)* v. *Secretary of State for the Home Department* [2003] UKHL 59 (following deferred conditional discharge)). For instance, the tribunal may have recommended a CTO at the first hearing but decide to discharge at the next, or if it proves impossible to implement a deferred conditional discharge the conditions may be varied or the decision to discharge reversed.

11.7.4 Extent to which decision is binding

Each tribunal must apply its mind to the matters before it in each case; it cannot avoid that by merely following a previous tribunal's decision, even if there has been no change of circumstances, although it may pay due regard to it (*R* v. *South West Thames Mental Health Review Tribunal, ex p. Demetri (No. 1)* [1997] COD 44 (CA)).

A tribunal's judicial decision to discharge the section must be respected by those who are responsible for the patient's care. In *R (von Brandenburg)* v. *East London and City MH NHS Trust* [2003] UKHL 58, Lord Bingham held that (at [10]):

> An [AMHP] may not lawfully apply for the admission of a patient whose discharge has been ordered by the decision of a mental health review tribunal of which the [AMHP] is aware unless [he] has formed the reasonable and bona fide opinion that he has information not known to the tribunal which puts a significantly different complexion on the case as compared with that which was before the tribunal.

If the responsible authority believes that the tribunal's decision is unlawful then, rather than re-sectioning the patient, the proper course of action would be to seek a stay/suspension of the tribunal's decision pending an appeal (*R (Ashworth)* v. *MHRT; R (H)* v. *Ashworth* [2002] EWCA Civ 923). In England, the tribunal may suspend the effect of its own decision pending the determination of an application for permission to appeal against, and any appeal or review of, that decision (English Rules, rule 5(3)(l)). Similarly, the MHRT for Wales may stay execution of its own decision pending an appeal of such decision (Welsh Rules, rule 5(2)(g)).

11.8 CONCLUSION

This chapter has set out the rules and procedures relating to the conduct of Mental Health Tribunal hearings in both England and Wales, including the arrangements for announcing the tribunal's decision and providing written reasons. **Chapter 12** considers the rights of patients and others to challenge a decision of the MHT in England or the MHRT for Wales.

CHAPTER 12

Challenging a decision

The Tribunal Procedure (First-tier Tribunal) (Health, Education and Social Care Chamber) Rules 2008, SI 2008/2699 ('English Rules') require the tribunal to inform the parties in writing of the decision, the reasons, and their rights to challenge the decision of the tribunal. This chapter explains those rights of challenge and the different rights which exist in Wales (under the Mental Health Review Tribunal for Wales Rules 2008, SI 2008/2705 ('Welsh Rules')). The lawfulness of every tribunal decision should be considered, and advice provided accordingly. The representative's role in relation to this, and more generally, is considered further in **Chapter 13**. This chapter deals with the tribunal and court procedures in relation to challenging tribunal decisions.

Appeals on a point of law from decisions of the Mental Health Tribunal (MHT) in England or the Mental Health Review Tribunal for Wales (MHRT for Wales) (referred to collectively in this chapter as 'the first instance tribunal') are heard by the Administrative Appeals Chamber of the Upper Tribunal (UT). The Upper Tribunal also has a judicial review jurisdiction similar to that of the Administrative Court. The procedure of the Upper Tribunal is regulated by the Tribunal Procedure (Upper Tribunal) Rules ('UT Rules') 2008, SI 2008/2698. Additionally, the First-tier Tribunal in England has a power to 'review' its own decisions in limited circumstances.

12.1 BACKGROUND

Prior to the Tribunals, Courts and Enforcement Act (TCEA) 2007, a tribunal could not revisit its decision. Therefore, the only way to challenge a decision was by judicial review, or the rarely used and now non-existent 'appeal by way of case stated', in the Administrative Court (part of the High Court). If the tribunal recognised the error of its ways, it would concede the point at the earliest opportunity.

TCEA 2007 introduced procedures by which most decisions can be challenged within the tribunal system itself. An appeal can be made from the first instance tribunal to the Upper Tribunal on a point of law, and additionally the Upper Tribunal can hear judicial review cases (First-tier Tribunal and Upper Tribunal (Chambers) Order 2010, SI 2010/2655, art.10). Permission to appeal is required, but if the first instance tribunal refuses permission then the Upper Tribunal can grant it. In England (but not in Wales) there is an intermediate stage whereby, before considering permission to appeal, the first instance tribunal must consider whether or not to exercise the power to 'review' its own decision.

This new appeal (and review) system is the primary method of challenging a first instance tribunal decision, and is dealt with in detail at **12.2** to **12.4**. Judicial review, whether by the Upper Tribunal or Administrative Court, is still relevant in a small minority of cases and is considered separately at **12.5**.

In the Administrative Court, only barristers (or solicitors or legal executives with civil higher court rights) may appear as representatives. There is no such restriction in relation to Upper Tribunal proceedings, where essentially the same rules relating to representation apply as apply to first instance hearings. However, in practice, it is still usual for counsel to be instructed.

12.2 BASIS OF AN APPEAL

12.2.1 Grounds for appeal

An appeal to the Upper Tribunal can only succeed if the relevant decision of the first instance tribunal involved the making of an error on a point of law (TCEA 2007, s.11).

Permission to appeal may be given if there is a realistic prospect that the decision was erroneous in law (i.e. there is an arguable case) or if there is some other good reason to give permission (e.g. the law needs to be clarified) (see *Smith* v. *Cosworth Casting Processes Ltd* [1997] EWCA Civ 1099, cited in *TR* v. *Ludlow Street Healthcare Ltd* [2011] UKUT 152 (AAC)).

The issue on appeal is whether the tribunal did its job properly: whether (a) the tribunal asked itself the correct legal questions; (b) it made findings of fact that were rationally based on the evidence; (c) it answered the legal questions appropriately given its findings of fact; (d) it gave the parties a fair hearing; and (e) it provided adequate reasons (*JLG* v. *Managers of Llanarth Court* [2011] UKUT 62 (AAC), at [3]).

Some examples of issues which have led to appeals are:

(i)   lack of clarity on whether the tribunal had jurisdiction to hear the case (*DP* v. *Hywel DDA Health Board* [2011] UKUT 381 (AAC));

(ii) a tribunal member reaching a firm concluded opinion before hearing all the evidence, as opposed to a merely provisional view (*RN* v. *Curo Care* [2011] UKUT 263 (AAC); *MB* v. *BEH MH NHS Trust* [2011] UKUT 328 (AAC));

(iii) inadequate reasons when deciding to accept the evidence of one expert witness over another (*BB* v. *South London and Maudsley NHS Foundation Trust* [2009] UKUT 157 (AAC));

(iv)   inadequate reasons when addressing the statutory criteria (*CM* v. *Derbyshire Healthcare NHS Foundation Trust* [2011] UKUT 129 (AAC)).

In a complex case the representative may prefer to instruct counsel to draft the grounds of appeal.

12.2.2   Appealable decisions

Under TCEA 2007 any decision, except certain 'excluded decisions', can be appealed (s.11(1)). However, it may be that an excluded decision is challengeable by way of judicial review (discussed at **12.5**).

Excluded decisions, where relevant to mental health, are (s.11(5)):

1.   decisions of the First-tier Tribunal (a) to review, or not to review, an earlier decision of the tribunal; (b) to take no action, or not to take any particular action, in the light of a review of an earlier decision of the tribunal; (c) to set aside an earlier decision of the tribunal;[1] or (d) to refer, or not to refer, a matter to the Upper Tribunal;

2.   decisions of the First-tier Tribunal that are set aside following a review (including a decision set aside after proceedings on an appeal have been begun);

3.   decisions of a description specified in an order made by the Lord Chancellor (although none have been so specified).

The First-tier Tribunal's power of 'review' mentioned above (which is different to judicial review) is explained at **12.3.4**.

Interlocutory decisions – those made between the original tribunal application or reference and the final determination of the case – may be appealed (see *LS* v. *London Borough of Lambeth* [2010] UKUT 461 (AAC)). However, such appeals are discouraged by the Upper Tribunal on the basis that they disrupt proceedings, produce inefficiency, increase costs, and are capable of being used for tactical purposes: the preference is for challenges to be considered at the end of proceedings (*RM* v. *St Andrew's Healthcare* [2010] UKUT 119 (AAC); see also *TR* v. *Ludlow Street Healthcare Ltd* [2011] UKUT 152 (AAC)).

12.3   POWERS OF THE FIRST INSTANCE TRIBUNAL

12.3.1   Challenging directions

Although it is possible to apply for permission to appeal against a direction, it will usually be more appropriate simply to challenge the direction by applying for another direction which amends, suspends or sets aside the first direction (English

---

[1]   With one exception: in England, the First-tier Tribunal can 'review' its own previous decision to set aside, but the most it can do in consequence is to correct accidental errors in the decision or in a record of the decision (TCEA 2007, s.9(1), (9)).

Rules, rules 6(5), 5(2); Welsh Rules, rule 6(1) is worded similarly). The tribunal may treat an application for permission to appeal as an application for another direction (*Dorset Healthcare NHS Foundation Trust* v. *MH* [2009] UKUT 4 (AAC), at [17] and [19]). Directions are discussed at **9.5**.

12.3.2 Correction of slips

The tribunal may at any time correct any clerical mistake or other accidental slip or omission in a decision, direction or any document produced by it, by sending notification of the amended decision or direction, or a copy of the amended document, to all parties (English Rules, rule 44(a); Welsh Rules, rule 29(1)). The English Rules add that the tribunal may also make any necessary amendment to any information published in relation to the decision, direction or document (English Rules, rule 44(b)).

The English Tribunal Secretariat has been given the delegated power to correct clear and obvious clerical mistakes, or other clear and obvious accidental slips or omissions, in any document recording a decision or direction of the tribunal; as this is an administrative decision, within 14 days of the decision being sent, the receiving party may apply for the decision to be considered by a judge (Practice Statement: *Delegation of Functions to Staff on or after 2 November 2010*).

The power to correct is rarely invoked. Examples of its use are (a) where the written reasons contain many spelling and grammatical errors and the representative sends it back for correction before forwarding it to the client; and (b) where the tribunal accidentally fails to record a recommendation in a prison transfer case to the effect that the patient should not be remitted to prison.

12.3.3 Setting aside for procedural reasons

The English tribunal may set aside (quash) a decision which disposes of proceedings, or part of such a decision, and remake the decision or the relevant part of it, if the tribunal considers that it is in the interests of justice to do so and any of the following apply (English Rules, rule 45(1), (2)):

(a)   a document relating to the proceedings was not sent to, or was not received at an appropriate time by, any party or a party's representative;

(b)   a document relating to the proceedings was not sent to the tribunal at an appropriate time;

(c)   a party, or a party's representative, was not present at a hearing related to the proceedings;

(d)   there has been some other procedural irregularity in the proceedings.

The party asking for the power to be exercised must make a written application so that it is received no later than 28 days after the date on which the tribunal sent notice of the decision to the party (English Rules, rule 45(3)). This can be done using Form P9 which is available on the Justice website alongside guidance notes.[2]

There is no equivalent power in the Welsh Rules, but some of the procedural defects would amount to an error of law which could be appealed.

12.3.4 Review and permission to appeal

A person seeking permission to appeal on a point of law must make a written application to the tribunal for permission to appeal (English Rules, rule 46(1); Welsh Rules, rule 30(2)). The application must set out (a) the decision to which it relates; (b) the alleged error(s) of law; and (c) the result sought (English Rules, rule 46(5); Welsh Rules, rule 30(4)). In England, this can be done on Form P10 which is available on the Justice website alongside guidance notes.[3]

The appeal must be sent so that it is received no later than 28 days after the tribunal sent written reasons to the party making the application (English Rules, rule 46(2); Welsh Rules, rule 30(2)). The English Rules add two other (later) events which trigger the time limit: notification of amended reasons for, or correction of, the decision following a review; and notification that an application for the decision to be set aside has been unsuccessful (if the original application to set aside was made on time) (rule 46(2), (3)). The tribunal has a discretion to extend the time limit. An extension must be sought if the application for permission is sent late (English Rules, rules 46(4), 5(3)(a)); Welsh Rules rules 30(3), 5(2)(a)).

In England (but *not* in Wales) the first step is the possibility of a 'review' of any decision which is not an excluded decision (TCEA 2007, s.9). On receiving an application for permission to appeal, the tribunal must first consider, taking into account the overriding objective, whether to review the decision (English Rules, rule 47). In this context, 'to review' does not mean 'to look at again'; rather, it means (having looked at it again) that the tribunal 'is satisfied that there was an error of law in the decision' (rule 49(1)). The possible outcomes of a review are to (a) correct accidental errors in the decision or in a record of the decision; (b) amend reasons given for the decision; (c) set the decision aside; or (d) take no action (TCEA 2007, s.9(4)). If a decision is set aside, the tribunal must either re-decide the matter (usually by referring it to a normally constituted three-person panel) or refer it to the Upper Tribunal for it to decide (s.9(5), (6)). The tribunal must notify the parties in writing of the outcome of the review and of any appeal rights (English Rules, rule 49(2)). If any action is taken without notice then any party may apply for such action to be set aside and the decision to be reviewed again, and the decision notice must state this (rule 49(3)). It is only appropriate for the First-tier Tribunal to exercise its review powers where there has been a 'clear error of law'; where the legal points are contentious the case should be allowed to proceed to the Upper Tribunal (*R (RB)* v.

---

[2] Available at **http://hmctsformfinder.justice.gov.uk/HMCTS/GetForms.do?court_forms_num =&court_forms_title=&court_forms_category=Mental+Health+Tribunal**.
[3] Available at **http://hmctsformfinder.justice.gov.uk/HMCTS/GetForms.do?court_forms_num =&court_forms_title=&court_forms_category=Mental+Health+Tribunal**.

First-tier Tribunal (Review) [2010] UKUT 160 (AAC)). Although review decisions are decisions on points of law, and although the tribunal issues to its members a 'periodic digest of common errors made to learn from the experience of colleagues who are faced with difficult legal questions' (see *Senior President of Tribunals' Annual Report* (February 2012)), no information on review decisions is made public for the benefit of patients or their representatives.

The next step in England (if the tribunal either decides not to review the decision, or having reviewed it decides not to take any action in relation to the decision, or part of it) and the only step in Wales, is the consideration of whether or not to give permission to appeal (English Rules, rule 47(2); Welsh Rules, rule 30(5); TCEA 2007, s.11). The tribunal must send to the parties as soon as practicable: (a) a record of its decision; and (b) if the tribunal has refused to grant permission, reasons for such refusal and notification and details of the right to make an application to the Upper Tribunal (Welsh Rules, rule 30(5)). The tribunal can grant permission on limited grounds, but must give reasons for refusing the other grounds (English Rules, rule 47(3), (4); Welsh Rules, rule 30(6)).

The original tribunal panel is not involved in the review/appeal process. Rather, decisions on whether to review or grant permission to appeal are made by single judges – in practice, the principal judge or a salaried tribunal judge in England, or the Chairman of the MHRT for Wales. It is not unlawful, and may be considered to be beneficial, for judges to consider applications for permission to appeal from, or to seek review of their own decisions (see *AA* v. *Cheshire and Wirral Partnership NHS Foundation Trust* [2009] UKUT 195 (AAC)).

12.4 APPEALS TO THE UPPER TRIBUNAL

12.4.1 Upper Tribunal Rules

The UT Rules, to a large extent, mirror the Rules of the English First-tier Tribunal which have been discussed in previous chapters. Part 1 (Introduction) and Part 2 (General powers and provisions) of the Rules follow the same numbering, and usually the same wording: (1) Citation, commencement, application and interpretation; (2) Overriding objective and parties' obligation to co-operate with the Upper Tribunal; (3) Alternative dispute resolution and arbitration; (4) Delegation to staff; (5) Case management powers; (6) Procedure for applying for and giving directions; (7) Failure to comply with rules, etc.; (8) Striking out a party's case; (9) Addition, substitution and removal of parties; (10) Orders for costs; (11) Representatives; (12) Calculating time; (13) Sending and delivery of documents (including non-disclosure); (14) Use of documents and information; (15) Evidence and submissions; (16) Summoning or citation of witnesses and orders to answer questions or produce documents; (17) Withdrawal. In rule 20 there is a power to pay expenses and allowances.

There are changes where appropriate. For instance, under UT Rules, rule 5, as well as being able to suspend the effect of its own decision pending appeal, the Upper Tribunal may also suspend the effect of the first instance tribunal's decision. Another example is in rule 7 where the English Rules provide for a case to be referred to the Upper Tribunal when a person has failed to comply with a requirement imposed by the tribunal: rule 7 of the UT Rules provides for the Upper Tribunal to exercise its powers (under TCEA 2007, s.25) as if the requirement had been imposed by the Upper Tribunal (see **9.5.4**).

The parties are the same as in the original proceedings (UT Rules, rule 1) (see **11.3.1**). In appeals the person taking the case is the 'appellant' (in judicial reviews he is the 'applicant'). The other parties are 'respondents'.

When (pre-TCEA 2007) the route of appeal against a tribunal decision was to the Administrative Court, the Mental Health Review Tribunal was the respondent, and often it took an active part in proceedings. Now, on appeal, the first instance tribunal is not a party at all. The responsible authority is a respondent, but usually does not get involved. The relevant Secretary of State may also be a respondent, but may also choose not to take an active part. This often leaves only the patient being represented in Upper Tribunal cases. The Upper Tribunal has stated that it is 'extremely unsatisfactory for public authority respondents to make no submission at all' but recognised the obvious financial reason for this occurring (*RH* v. *South London and Maudsley NHS Foundation Trust* [2010] UKUT 32 (AAC)). Partly to remedy this situation, the Upper Tribunal may require the tribunal whose decision is the subject of proceedings to provide reasons for the decision, or other information or documents in relation to the decision or any proceedings before that tribunal (UT Rules, rule 5(3)(n)), although this is rarely done (see *CT* v. *Secretary of State for Defence* [2009] UKUT 167 (AAC), at [41]).

12.4.2 Appeal procedure

Application for permission: An application for permission to appeal can only be made to the Upper Tribunal once the first instance tribunal has refused permission, and must be made within one month of the notice of refusal being sent. If the application is out of time (perhaps because the applicant only recently obtained legal representation) the application must request that the Upper Tribunal exercise its power to extend time. If permission to appeal was refused by the first instance tribunal because that application was out of time, the Upper Tribunal may only extend time if it is in the interests of justice to do so (UT Rules, rule 21(2), (3)(b), (6), (7)).

The application must state (a) the name and address of the appellant; (b) the name and address of the representative (if any) of the appellant; (c) an address where documents for the appellant may be sent or delivered; (d) details (including the full reference) of the decision challenged; (e) the grounds on which the appellant relies; and (f) whether the appellant wants the application to be dealt with at a hearing. It must include a copy of the written reasons and notice of refusal of permission to appeal (UT Rules, rule 21(4), (5)).

This can be done using Form UT3 ('Application for permission to appeal to an Upper Tribunal judge and notice of appeal form for mental health cases (England)') or Form UT8 ('Application for permission to appeal to an Upper Tribunal judge and notice of appeal form against decisions of the Mental Health Review Tribunal Wales') as appropriate. Both forms, together with notes for appellants (UT3 Notes and UT8 Notes) and guidance leaflet UT304 ('Appealing against a decision of the Health, Education and Social Care Chamber of the First-tier Tribunal (Mental Health) (Appeals from decisions of the First-tier Tribunal)'), are available on the Ministry of Justice website.[4]

If the Upper Tribunal refuses permission to appeal, it must send written notice of the refusal and of the reasons for the refusal to the appellant (UT Rules, rule 22(1)).

If the Upper Tribunal gives permission to appeal it must send notice of its decision, and reasons for any limitations or conditions on permission, to the parties, together with any documents sent by the appellant (UT Rules, rule 21(2)). The Upper Tribunal may then, with the consent of all parties, determine the appeal without obtaining any further response; although, on appeal from the Welsh tribunal, the appellant may then apply for such a decision to be reconsidered at a hearing (UT Rules, rule 21(2)(c), (3), (4)).

Notice of appeal: Where it is required, the next step is the notice of appeal. Where the Upper Tribunal gave permission, the application for permission to appeal normally stands as the notice of appeal, unless it orders otherwise (UT Rules, rules 22(2)(b), 23(1)(c)); however, where the first instance tribunal gave permission the appellant must send the notice of appeal to the Upper Tribunal so that it is received within one month after the date that notice of permission was sent to him, subject to the usual discretion for applications out of time (UT Rules, rule 23(1), (2), (5)). The notice of appeal must contain the same information and documents as an application for permission to appeal, together with the case reference number and the notice of permission to appeal. The Upper Tribunal then sends the notice to all respondents (UT Rules, rule 23(3), (4), (6)).

Responses: The next two procedural steps are the responses to the notice of appeal and the appellant's reply (UT Rules, rules 24, 25). Subject to any direction given by the Upper Tribunal, any respondent may provide a written response which, subject to the usual provisions for extending time, must be received within one month of the notice of appeal or notice of permission to appeal. The Upper Tribunal will then send a copy to the other parties (UT Rules, rule 24(2), (3), (4), (5)). Similarly, the appellant may provide a written reply to any such response, which must be received within one month after the response was sent. The Upper Tribunal will then send a copy to the other parties (UT Rules, rule 25(1), (2), (3)).

---

[4] See **http://hmctsformfinder.justice.gov.uk/HMCTS/GetForms.do?court_forms_category= Upper%20Tribunal%20Administrative%20Appeal%20Chamber**.

Hearing: The Upper Tribunal may make any decision without a hearing, but must have regard to any view expressed by any party when deciding whether to hold a hearing (UT Rules, rule 34). When a hearing is held, each party is entitled to attend subject to the exclusion rules (UT Rules, rules 35, 37(4)). The period of notice must be at least 14 days prior to the hearing except with the parties' consent or in urgent or exceptional cases (UT Rules, rule 36). Hearings must be held in public unless the Upper Tribunal directs otherwise (UT Rules, rule 37(1), (2)). The hearing can take place in a party's absence on the same grounds as for the English tribunal (UT Rules, rule 38). The Upper Tribunal may dispose of proceedings by way of a consent order without holding a hearing (UT Rules, rule 39).

Decision: The decision may be given orally at a hearing but in any event the final decision notice and notification of rights of review or appeal must be sent as soon as practicable; written reasons must be sent at the same time, unless the decision was by consent or the parties consented to there being no reasons (UT Rules, rule 40(1), (2), (3)).

12.5 JUDICIAL REVIEW

12.5.1 Grounds for judicial review

Judicial review is a procedure by which the courts review the decisions of public bodies. A judicial review claim can be based on any of the following grounds:[5]

1. *illegality:* decision-maker (a) acting ultra vires; (b) unlawfully delegating power or fettering discretion; (c) taking into account irrelevant considerations;
2. *irrationality*;
3. *procedural impropriety:* (a) failure to give each party to a dispute an opportunity to be heard; (b) bias; (c) failure to conduct a consultation properly; (d) failure to give adequate reasons; (e) legitimate expectation;
4. *breach of European law:* (a) European Convention on Human Rights (ECHR); (b) EU law.

The majority of judicial reviews of tribunal decisions have been on the basis of inadequate reasons.

12.5.2 Judicial review by Upper Tribunal

The Upper Tribunal has power to grant the following kinds of relief: mandatory orders, prohibiting orders, quashing orders, declarations and injunctions (TCEA

---

[5] The headings are taken from Alexander Horne and Gavin Berman, *Judicial Review: A Short Guide to Claims in the Administrative Court*, House of Commons Library Research Paper 06/44 (28 September 2006) available at **www.parliament.uk/documents/commons/lib/research/rp2006/rp06-044.pdf**.

2007, s.15(1)). When such relief is sought in a mental health case, the Upper Tribunal has the function of deciding the application only if four conditions are met (s.18):

1. The application does not seek anything other than those forms of relief mentioned above, permission for such relief, a financial award (under TCEA 2007, s.16(6)), interest or costs. In this regard, the main remedy which the Upper Tribunal cannot give is a declaration of incompatibility under HRA 1998.
2. The application does not call into question anything done by the Crown Court.
3. The application falls within a class specified in a direction. In mental health cases, the only direction (Practice Direction: *Upper Tribunal: Judicial Review Jurisdiction* [2009] 1 WLR 327) relates to challenges to First-tier Tribunal 'review' decisions where:

   (a) there is no right of appeal to the Upper Tribunal; and
   (b) the decision is not an excluded decision (by being a decision of a description specified in an order made by the Lord Chancellor).

4. The Upper Tribunal presiding judge is a High Court or Court of Appeal judge or such other person as may be agreed between the Lord Chief Justice and the Senior President of Tribunals.

If the conditions are not met then the Upper Tribunal must by order transfer the application to the High Court (TCEA 2007, s.18(3)). There are similar provisions for the transfer of proceedings from the High Court to the Upper Tribunal in appropriate cases (see Senior Courts Act 1981, s.31A, inserted by TCEA 2007, s.19).

As there is no equivalent direction for Wales as is mentioned at point 3 above, an application for judicial review of a decision of the MHRT for Wales should be made to the High Court. From there it could be transferred to the Upper Tribunal if it appeared to the High Court to be 'just and convenient' to do so (Senior Courts Act 1981, s.31A).

The Upper Tribunal rules dealing with judicial review are similar to the rules for judicial review in the Administrative Court (UT Rules, rules 27–33A (Part 4)). An application must be made promptly and, unless any other enactment specifies a shorter time limit, received no later than three months after the date of the decision, action or omission to which the application relates; however, when a first instance tribunal decision is under challenge, the time limit is one month from the date the written reasons, or the notification that a (timely) application to set aside had been refused, were sent (rule 28(2), (3)).

The required contents of the application, and the required documents, are set out in the Rules (see rule 28(4), (6)) and Form JR1 ('Judicial review claim form,

England and Wales') should be used for this purpose. It is available on the Ministry of Justice website together with notes for guidance.[6]

A person who wishes to take part in proceedings has 21 days within which to provide an acknowledgement of service (UT Rules, rule 29). Form JR2 ('Judicial review – acknowledgment of service form') is designed for this purpose.[7]

The Upper Tribunal then sends its decision on permission following which the applicant may apply within 14 days for the decision to be reconsidered at a hearing (rule 30(1), (4), (5)).

Following receipt of the notice of the grant of permission, any person who wishes to contest the application or support it on additional grounds has 35 days to provide detailed grounds (rule 31).

The procedure concerning hearings and decisions is largely the same as for appeals (see **12.4.2**). One exception is that the period of notice in judicial reviews must be at least two working days, rather than the usual fortnight (rule 36(2)(b)).

12.5.3 Judicial review by the Administrative Court

The Administrative Court would judicially review a first instance tribunal decision when the applicant seeks a declaration of incompatibility under HRA 1998 (see Practice Direction: *Upper Tribunal: Judicial Review Jurisdiction* [2009] 1 WLR 327). In other circumstances the Upper Tribunal would usually be the appropriate forum. A declaration of incompatibility is made under HRA 1998, s.4 where the court is satisfied that a provision of primary legislation is incompatible with an ECHR right; this can lead to Parliament making legislative changes.

Legislative changes have resulted from three declarations of incompatibility in the mental health arena. The burden of proof at tribunal hearings when considering discharge from the detaining sections is no longer on the patient (see *R (H)* v. *MHRT North and East London Region* [2001] EWCA Civ 415 (which led to MHA 1983, s.72 being amended)). A transferred prisoner, after a successful tribunal, is now statutorily entitled to a Parole Board hearing even if he remains in hospital following the tribunal hearing (*R (D)* v. *Secretary of State for the Home Department* [2002] EWHC 2805 (Admin); MHA 1983, s.74). Finally, a patient can now apply to the county court for an unsuitable nearest relative to be displaced (*R (M)* v. *Secretary of State for Health* [2003] EWHC 1094 (Admin); MHA 1983, s.29).

---

[6] See http://hmctsformfinder.justice.gov.uk/HMCTS/GetForms.do?court_forms_category=Upper%20Tribunal%20Administrative%20Appeal%20Chamber.

[7] See http://hmctsformfinder.justice.gov.uk/HMCTS/GetForms.do?court_forms_category=Upper%20Tribunal%20Administrative%20Appeal%20Chamber.

12.6   CHALLENGING UPPER TRIBUNAL DECISIONS

12.6.1   Upper Tribunal's powers in relation to its own decisions

The Upper Tribunal, like the English First-tier Tribunal, has the following options (UT Rules, rules 42–45): (a) correcting clerical mistakes and accidental slips or omissions; (b) setting aside, for procedural defects, a decision which disposes of proceedings; (c) on an application for permission to appeal, considering first whether to 'review' its decision and secondly whether to grant permission to appeal.

It can only 'review' its own decision if (a) when making the decision the Upper Tribunal overlooked a legislative provision or binding authority which could have had a material effect on the decision; or (b) subsequent to the Upper Tribunal's decision, a court has made a decision which is binding on the Upper Tribunal and which, had it been made before the Upper Tribunal's decision, could have had a material effect on the decision (rule 45(1)).

12.6.2   Judicial review of Upper Tribunal decisions

Judicial review of an Upper Tribunal decision which is unappealable (for instance, the Upper Tribunal's refusal of permission to appeal to itself) is available where the 'second-tier appeal' criteria apply (i.e. if the case raises an important point of principle or practice or there is some other compelling reason for the court to hear it) (see *R (Cart)* v. *Upper Tribunal* [2011] UKSC 28). This course of action would be rare in practice.

12.6.3   Appeals to the Court of Appeal and beyond

Appeals on points of law from the Upper Tribunal or Administrative Court are made to the civil division of the Court of Appeal. Permission to appeal must be sought from the lower court; if it is refused then it must be sought from the Court of Appeal.

The criteria for appeals from the Upper Tribunal are that permission may only be granted if the relevant court or tribunal considers that (a) the proposed appeal would raise some important point of principle or practice; or (b) there is some other compelling reason for the Court of Appeal to hear the appeal (Appeals from the Upper Tribunal to the Court of Appeal Order 2008, SI 2008/2834).

The criteria for appeals from the Administrative Court are that permission may only be given where the relevant court (a) considers that the appeal would have a real prospect of success; or (b) there is some other compelling reason why the appeal should be heard (Civil Procedure Rules 1998, rule 52.3(6)).

Appeals from the Court of Appeal are to the Supreme Court. When domestic remedies have been exhausted, an application may be made to the European Court of Human Rights.

12.7 TREATING ONE TYPE OF APPLICATION AS ANOTHER

In the First-tier Tribunal, presumably because of the confusing array of routes to challenge a decision, the tribunal may treat an application for a decision to be corrected, set aside or reviewed, or for permission to appeal against a decision, as an application for any other of those things (English Rules, rule 50). The Upper Tribunal has similar powers in relation to challenges to its own decisions (UT Rules, rule 48).

Additionally, in relation to Upper Tribunal proceedings:

1.   If an appeal is made to the Upper Tribunal which should have been a judicial review, the Upper Tribunal can treat the appeal as an application for permission to apply for judicial review, and waive the requirement to serve the first instance tribunal (which is normally a requirement of judicial review) (see *Dorset Healthcare NHS Foundation Trust* v. *MH* [2009] UKUT 4 (AAC), at [8]).

2.   Similarly, if an application is made for judicial review which should have been an appeal, the Upper Tribunal can treat it as an application for permission to appeal, and waive the requirement to apply for permission from the first instance tribunal before coming to the Upper Tribunal (which is normally a requirement of an appeal) (see *TR* v. *Ludlow Street Healthcare Ltd* [2011] UKUT 152 (AAC), at [1]).

12.8 CONCLUSION

This chapter has summarised the different routes and processes available in England and Wales to challenge tribunal decisions, but further detail is beyond the scope of this book. Those involved in pursuing such appeals may need to consult other sources (see e.g., Edward Jacobs, *Tribunal Practice and Procedure* (2nd edn, Legal Action Group, 2011)).

CHAPTER 13

Tribunal representation

Although any party to a tribunal hearing may be represented, this chapter focuses on the representation of patients. The importance of tribunal representation has been underlined by the High Court:

> Mental health law is difficult enough today. Reading the report of a psychiatrist, identifying its areas of weakness, commissioning evidence from the appropriate expert to challenge it, and representing a client at a tribunal requires expert professional skills born, as we have said, of education and practical experience. It is not like going down to the magistrates' court as a duty solicitor, arduous though those duties are. In the fairly near future the demands made on skilled solicitors in this field are going to increase exponentially.[1]

The European Court of Human Rights (ECtHR) has described the unique 'situation of inferiority and powerlessness' of patients detained in hospital (*Herczegfalvy* v. *Austria* (10533/83) [1992] ECHR 83). This situation requires a unique approach to representation and advocacy and it is imperative that patients' representatives conduct themselves in exemplary fashion.

While the previous parts of this book should be useful to anyone involved in the tribunal process, this chapter (and **Chapter 14** on Legal Aid) will primarily be of use to patients' representatives.

The Law Society operates a Mental Health Accreditation Scheme, which incorporates a Code of Practice (reproduced at **Appendix G**); it has also published a Practice Note for Mental Health Tribunal representation (reproduced at **Appendix F**). The Mental Health Lawyers Association, the professional association of mental health lawyers, has issued a Code of Conduct (**Appendix H**). Additional guidance is found in the Solicitors Regulation Authority Code of Conduct, and its Professional Ethics Helpline, as well as the Legal Services Commission's peer review guidance. This chapter begins by explaining the key points from these important guidance documents, before proceeding to give more detailed step by step guidance on Mental Health Tribunal representation.

---

[1] See *R* v. *Legal Aid Board, ex p. Duncan and Mackintosh* [2000] EWHC Admin 294, at [571]–[572] (Brooke LJ). The judge had in mind the coming into force of the Human Rights Act 1998 and what became MCA 2005 and MHA 2007.

13.1 LAW SOCIETY'S MENTAL HEALTH ACCREDITATION SCHEME

In 1982, Legal Aid was extended to representation of patients before Mental Health Review Tribunals. In 1984, when automatic references were introduced in MHA 1983, the Law Society established a Mental Health Review Tribunal Panel. This was to provide a quality benchmark for representation, while ensuring that referred patients, some of whom would lack the capacity to appoint a representative, could be allocated a competent representative. The appointment of representatives is considered at **9.2**.

The Panel has since been renamed the 'Mental Health Accreditation Scheme', although members are still often called 'panel members'. Members of the scheme agree to be bound by the Law Society's Code of Practice for mental health work (see **13.2.1**) and to abide by the Law Society's Practice Note on Mental Health Tribunal representation (see **13.2.2**).

The Mental Health Accreditation Scheme is intended to assist patients and others to find a representative who has successfully completed a selection process to become accredited as competent to provide advice, assistance and representation at Mental Health Tribunals. There is no requirement that members of the scheme be legally qualified. Full details are set out on the Law Society website.[2] The benefits of membership include the following:

1. The tribunal will only appoint legal representatives who are Accreditation Scheme members, and others (such as hospital MHA Administrators) may take the same approach when assisting patients to find a representative.
2. Under the Legal Aid contract, only Accreditation Scheme members are permitted to perform the role of category supervisor. Supervisors may supervise up to six caseworkers.
3. It is a requirement of the Legal Aid contract that advocacy at high secure hospitals must be carried out by Accreditation Scheme members (see **14.4.2**).
4. In November 2012, the Legal Services Commission announced that mandatory accreditation for all tribunal representatives is to be a requirement for all future publicly funded mental health contracts.[3]

The following are the requirements of membership:

1. Agreement to abide by the Code of Conduct in relation to preparing cases personally (see **13.2.1**).
2. Attendance at a two-day course provided by a Law Society-accredited provider.

---

[2] See **www.lawsociety.org.uk/productsandservices/accreditation/accreditationmentalhealth review tribunal.page**.

[3] Legal Services Commission, 'Mandatory accreditation for representatives in Mental Health', available at **www.justice.gov.uk/legal-aid/quality-assurance/accreditation**. This announcement followed the 2011 Joint Report of the Administrative Justice and Tribunals Council (AJTC) and Care Quality Commission (CQC) recommending that the Commission accelerate its work to require this; see AJTC/CQC, *Patients' Experiences of the First-tier Tribunal (Mental Health)* (March 2011), p.16.

3. Completion of an application form demonstrating observation of or representation at four tribunal hearings (one s.2, one s.3 or s.37, one restricted, and one other of any type) by providing written case reports which are used in the assessment.

4. Satisfactory performance at interview. Interviews are carried out by assessors appointed by the Law Society and are designed to test the candidate's knowledge and suitability in relation to representing patients at tribunals. Part of the interview is based on multiple-choice questions and scenarios which are given to the candidate before the interview begins. The candidate may consult books or notes.

5. Payment of a membership fee which at the time of writing is £500 plus VAT. The trend has been for the Law Society's fee to increase while the Legal Services Commission's reimbursement decreases. The reimbursement of £73.44 will cease altogether from April 2013.[4]

13.2 SOURCES OF GUIDANCE

This section sets out some key points from the guidance documents referred to above which are directly relevant to the representation of patients. The various sources of guidance relate not only to ethical but also to competent conduct. All representatives should be familiar with and have regard to these guidance documents.

13.2.1 Law Society Code of Practice for Mental Health

Members of the Mental Health Accreditation Scheme have agreed to follow the scheme's Code of Practice. In December 2011 it was converted from an undertaking beginning with the words 'I undertake that', which partly explains the lack of a main verb in the current Code of Practice. The Code is reproduced at **Appendix G**.

The promise personally to prepare and present the case is important, as this continuity helps build up a rapport between patient and representative, and will put the patient more at ease when the tribunal takes place. It is poor practice for a representative to meet the patient for the first time on the day of the hearing other than in exceptional circumstances.

13.2.2 Law Society Practice Note

The Law Society's Practice Note *Representation before Mental Health Tribunals* (19 May 2011) is reproduced in **Appendix F** and is considered, where relevant,

---

[4] Legal Services Commission, 'Accreditation contribution scheme update' (23 March 2012), available at **www.justice.gov.uk/legal-aid/quality-assurance/accreditation**.

throughout this chapter. For ease of reference, its main headings and sub-headings are reproduced below.

1. Introduction: Who should read this practice note? What's the issue?
2. The right to legal advice and representation before the tribunal: The role of the hospital; Independent Mental Health Advocates; Facilitating referrals; Change of solicitor; Appointing a representative.
3. Communication with the client: Initial contact with the client; Client care letters.
4. Taking instructions: Clients with capacity; Clients without capacity.
5. Your duties towards your client: Duty to act in the best interests of clients; Conflicts between instructions and the best interests of clients; Duty of confidentiality.
6. Good tribunal practice: Avoiding delay at the tribunal; Independent reports; Witnesses; Interpreters; Documents; Applications for postponements; Withdrawing an application to the tribunal; Other codes of conduct.
7. Representing children and young people before the tribunal.
8. More information: Professional conduct; Legal and other requirements; Further products and support; Status of this practice note; Terminology in this practice note; Acknowledgements.

13.2.3 Mental Health Lawyers Association Code of Conduct

The Mental Health Lawyers Association (MHLA) is the professional association of mental health lawyers in England and Wales and is recognised by the Law Society as a special interest group. The majority of Mental Health Tribunal lawyers are members. Members of the Association must be members of the Law Society's Mental Health Accreditation Scheme, or actively seeking membership of it, and must also agree to abide by the MHLA's own Code of Conduct.[5] This important Code is set out in **Appendix H**.

The introduction to MHLA Code of Conduct for representatives stresses:

> In representing hospital inpatients, particularly those detained by the state against their will, legal representatives carry out an important function for a civilised society. It is therefore important that the highest ethical and professional standards are adhered to.

The Code sets out guidance on quality of service; making appointments; behaviour on the ward; disputes over representation; seeking clients; gifts; and hospital procedures. The term 'representative' includes solicitors, legal executives, and any solicitors' staff who represent clients. In acknowledging that the MHLA is a representative body rather than a regulatory body, the Code encourages any complaints about poor practice to be made to the Solicitors Regulation Authority (SRA) or to the Institute of Legal Executives (ILEX). The MHLA does, however, have a complaints procedure for members.

Feedback about members, or queries about the Code of Conduct, can be addressed to the Association's administrator.[6]

---

[5] See **www.mhla.co.uk/about/code-of-conduct**.
[6] See **www.mhla.co.uk/contact**.

244

13.2.4 Solicitors Regulation Authority's Code of Conduct

All solicitors and their employees must abide by the SRA Code of Conduct 2011, which is available online.[7]

The Code of Conduct is based on 'outcomes-focused regulation', in that it looks at outcomes rather than prescribing rules to follow. Where relevant to mental health, however, the new Code is largely the same as the previous 2007 version.

There are 10 mandatory principles, the first six of which are the most relevant for our purposes: (1) uphold the rule of law and the proper administration of justice; (2) act with integrity; (3) not allow your independence to be compromised; (4) act in the best interests of each client; (5) provide a proper standard of service to your clients; (6) behave in a way that maintains the trust the public places in you and in the provision of legal services.

Two of the important concepts in the Code are Outcomes (abbreviated in the Code to 'O') and Indicative Behaviours ('IB'). The former are mandatory and must be achieved in order to comply with the principles; the latter are non-mandatory but specify the kind of behaviour which may establish compliance.

Chapter 4 (Confidentiality and disclosure) contains the following:

O(4.1)   you keep the affairs of clients confidential unless disclosure is required or permitted by law or the client consents;

O(4.2)   any individual who is advising a client makes that client aware of all information material to that retainer of which the individual has personal knowledge;

IB(4.4) where you are an individual who has responsibility for acting for a client or supervising a client's matter, you disclose to the client all information material to the client's matter of which you are personally aware, except when:

(a)   the client gives specific informed consent to non-disclosure or a different standard of disclosure arises;

(b)   there is evidence that serious physical or mental injury will be caused to a person(s) if the information is disclosed to the client;

(c)   legal restrictions effectively prohibit you from passing the information to the client, such as the provisions in the money-laundering and anti-terrorism legislation; . . .

The precursor to O(4.1) in the old rules was in materially the same terms, but its guidance listed 'exceptional circumstances' in which the duty of confidentiality did not apply (Solicitors' Code of Conduct 2007, rule 4). One exception was: 'You may reveal confidential information to the extent that you believe necessary to prevent the client or a third party committing a criminal act that you reasonably believe is likely to result in serious bodily harm' (Guidance note 12). The list was illustrative, not exhaustive, so it was relatively clear that breaching confidentiality in order to prevent serious self-harm or suicide could be justifiable. However, there are no exceptions listed in the current Code. It is submitted that the same exceptions should be applied in practice and, if practicable, the representative should contact the SRA

---

[7]   See **www.sra.org.uk/solicitors/handbook/code/content.page**.

Professional Ethics Helpline (see **13.2.5**) and take a careful note of their agreement to the proposed course of action.

The provision in IB(4.4) for accepting consent to non-disclosure would allow a representative to follow the *Dorset* procedure for receiving confidential third party information without disclosing it to the client (see **10.10**). The provision in relation to legal restrictions would cover tribunal directions on non-disclosure (again, see **10.10**).

Chapter 5 (Your client and the court) contains the following:

O(5.1)   you do not attempt to deceive or knowingly or recklessly mislead the court;

O(5.2)   you are not complicit in another person deceiving or misleading the court;

IB(5.2)   drawing the court's attention to relevant cases and statutory provisions, and any material procedural irregularity;

IB(5.7)   [not] constructing facts supporting your client's case or drafting any documents relating to any proceedings containing: (a) any contention which you do not consider to be properly arguable; or (b) . . .

An example of the potential to mislead the court in the mental health context would involve the client who tells the representative that he does not take his medication, or does take illegal drugs, but wants to tell the tribunal the opposite in the hope of achieving discharge. However, a mental health patient's instructions may genuinely vary over time, as his mental condition changes, so inconsistent statements may not necessarily indicate deceit.

It would be rare, or perhaps inconceivable, that to argue for a patient's discharge would be considered not to be 'properly arguable' in terms of IB(5.7) (see Law Society's Practice Note: *Representation before Mental Health Tribunals* (30 September 2011), section 4).

13.2.5   SRA Professional Ethics Helpline

The SRA helpline provides advice on the SRA Handbook and Code of Conduct and how solicitors can ensure compliance. The helpline telephone number, which can be called from 9 am to 5 pm, Monday to Friday, is 0870 606 2577. You should take a careful note of your conversation with them and any advice given.

13.2.6   Legal Services Commission peer review guidance

Peer review is a quality assessment scheme developed by the Institute of Advanced Legal Studies for the Legal Services Commission (LSC).

The possible ratings are: (1) excellence; (2) competence plus; (3) threshold competence; (4) below competence; and (5) failure in performance. Ratings 4 and 5 are effectively both failures, and will lead to further peer review assessments. Repeated failure leads to removal of the Legal Aid contract.

Peer review is an important process, not only because of the implications of failure, but also because it promotes a quality service, so will be covered below in some depth. Further details are available on the LAA (Legal Aid Agency) website.[8]

Peer reviewers, who are solicitors with experience in the relevant area of law, consider a sample of a firm's files and write a detailed report of positive and negative points. This is done by requesting 20 files and marking 15 of these using the 'Peer review civil criteria' form, which is available on the LAA website.[9] The form contains questions on communication with the client, the advice given and the work or assistance carried out, with the answers being 'yes' or 'no', a mark from 1 to 5 reflecting the ratings above, or 'not applicable'. An overall mark is then given with any further necessary comments on the firm's performance in the matter.

The LSC has issued Peer Review guidance documents, which are updated from time to time.[10] The current document is 'Improving your quality: Mental Health' (3rd edn, April 2011). In its Preface the following are identified as common 'major concerns':

1. Relevant section or detention papers not being seen or examined.
2. Medical records not being examined, or no evidence to support the assertion that they had been examined.
3. No evidence of written advice specifically tailored to the client's situation; that is complete reliance on standardised correspondence.
4. No evidenced attempt to check the Tribunal decision for legality.
5. Where there is a conflict of interest demonstrated on a file, for example by acting for a party opposing discharge as well as for an applicant patient seeking discharge.
6. In cases where the Nearest Relative had the power to discharge the client from section where no attempt had been made:

    (a) to identify the Nearest Relative with the client;
    (b) discuss with the client the Nearest Relative's powers;
    (c) to seek the client's consent to contact the Nearest Relative.

The guidance is organised into 16 numbered chapters. The chapter headings are shown below, followed by a brief précis of the contents. It is worthwhile reading the document in full.

1. *Are files organised and legible?* The guidance talks of the quick 'pick up' test for another adviser who may have to consider the file at short notice, and suggests transcribing all illegible handwritten notes.
2. *Were the advisers selected to be involved in the matter appropriate?* There should be evidence of comprehensive instructions, case analysis, thorough preparation, and advice on the merits of the case prior to the hearing. Inexperienced advisers should be subject to frequent and thorough file review.
3. *Was the initial contact with the client timely?* Record when and how initial

---

[8] See www.justice.gov.uk/legal-aid/quality-assurance/audits/peer-review.
[9] See www.justice.gov.uk/downloads/legal-aid/auditing/clacivilpeerreviewcriteria-oct10.pdf.
[10] See www.justice.gov.uk/legal-aid/quality-assurance/quality-guidance.

contact was made, and visit the patient within two days for s.2 and urgent cases and otherwise within seven days; explain any delays to the client. Delays at this stage could leave the patient feeling isolated and could delay the tribunal hearing.

4. *Are clients who are detained in hospital visited sufficiently regularly to obtain instructions and inform them of progress?* It is likely that several visits will be required prior to the hearing in order to establish a rapport and to take full instructions, although every patient is different. A client's instructions, clarity and capacity may change throughout the file. Full attendance notes should be kept, and usually follow-up letters sent.

5. *Has the client been advised of the merits of their case?* This is a difficult issue in some mental health cases, but where possible the client should be advised, and that advice updated to reflect changes in the case; otherwise, the reasons for not providing this advice should be noted on the file.

6. *Are letters and information sheets used appropriately?* Clients should be informed of the objectives agreed, issues involved, steps to be taken, and progress made. Any standard letters should be tailored to the client's case. If the client is unable to receive correspondence, this should be noted on the file and consideration should be given to further meetings.

7. *Has the client been advised about the powers and the procedure of the Tribunal?* This advice, together with likely timescales, should be provided in person and by letter. The guidance recommends information sheets tailored to the client's section.

8. *Have the fundamental issues of the case been analysed appropriately as the case progresses?* Lack of analysis can lead to incorrect or inappropriate advice, lack of preparation work, drift and possibly negligence. Records should be read as soon as possible to identify the key issues, and instructions, reports and the outcome of enquiries from third parties should be analysed.

9. *Has the adviser promptly considered the use of independent experts to assist the client's case?* The file should note the issues involved and the types of independent evidence that have been considered. Early instruction can reduce any delays in proceedings. The guidance sets out criteria which may be noted on the file as justification for instruction of psychiatrists, and suggests suitable questions for inclusion in letters of instruction.

10. *Has communication been established with third parties who may be able to assist the client?* Where appropriate, contact should be made with the MHA Administrator, records department, tribunal, nearest relative, responsible clinician (RC), social worker, Ministry of Justice, independent mental health advocate (IMHA), previous advisers and advisers acting on parallel matters. The guidance recommends a checklist to ensure that all relevant third parties have been contacted. This is considered in detail at **13.3.5**.

11. *Have the necessary nursing, medical and, if appropriate, Social Services or Community Health Team, records been obtained and considered?* Failing to

check section papers may prolong unlawful detention and amount to negligence. Medical records contain vital information to assist in preparation of the client's case, and should be viewed at an early stage and subsequently close to the tribunal hearing. The client's instructions should be confirmed in a follow-up letter.

12. *Have the client's Tribunal reports and statements been considered promptly on receipt?* If the reports do not meet the requirements of the Practice Direction or Rules, consideration should be given to seeking directions. If reports are late, directions should be sought. The client should be advised on reports, and victim statements and procedures (see **10.8.1**), and instructions taken promptly following receipt. Receipt of reports will lead to consideration of obtaining independent evidence, and may require further action to be taken.

13. *Has there been thorough preparation for Tribunal hearings?* Failure to prepare is likely to lead to an unfocused approach, a poorly presented case, fundamental issues being missed, and ineffective cross-examination. The case objective and action to be taken should be kept under continuous review, particularly after significant events. A case analysis or skeleton argument should be prepared before the hearing. Pre-hearing discussions should be held with the client, and the agreed approach confirmed with the client.

14. *Have all necessary referrals been made in an appropriate way?* Clients with mental health problems are more likely than others to have other significant legal problems, such as with welfare benefits, debt, housing and crime. Referral to the IMHA service can be made for non-legal issues. These problems may be raised by the client, or be apparent from reports or discussions with third parties. The guidance suggests including questions on these potential problems in any initial questionnaire.

15. *Have the necessary steps been taken to represent children under 18 years at the Tribunal?* Children are especially vulnerable if detained in hospital. The law is more complicated in some respects, with different requirements under MHA 1983, interaction with the Children Act 1989, MCA 2005 and common law, and the possible involvement of other professionals and legal advisers (see **13.4**). One member of the tribunal panel will be on their specialist Child and Adult Mental Health Services (CAMHS) panel (see **2.4.5**), and an adviser of sufficient experience should be allocated to the case.

16. *Have adequate steps been taken to explain the Tribunal's written reasons; their adequacy; the right of review and appeal together with confirmation of the client's current legal status?* Consideration should be given to a further attendance on the client in relation to the decision, particularly if he remains in hospital. The final letter should enclose the written decision, explaining the reasons rather than merely reciting them, and advise on legality and prospects of appeal. Advice should be given on further options, such as an application to the hospital managers, or on after-care, as appropriate.

13.3 LIFE OF A FILE

Each case is different, but the following are procedural steps (addressed to 'you' as the patient's representative) which take place in most cases. You will be introduced to your client and will arrange to see him promptly. After the meeting you will, if instructed to do so, apply to the tribunal. You will then carry out initial preparatory work, contact third parties and check the section papers. As soon as possible, you will read the reports and medical records, consider the instruction of independent experts, and take full instructions. After representing the patient at the hearing, you will explain the decision to the client, and consider the lawfulness of the decision.

These steps are considered in more detail below.

13.3.1 Introduction to client

There are several ways by which you may be introduced to a new client:

1. The most likely route of obtaining a new client is a telephone call from the client himself. He may have been aware of you through the hospital's list of solicitors' firms or through a personal recommendation from another patient, or he may be a previous client. It is important to ensure that you appear in the hospital's list of solicitors and that the details held are correct.
2. The tribunal may appoint a legal representative in the two circumstances discussed at **9.2.2**. It is the practice of the tribunal only to appoint members of the Law Society's Mental Health Accreditation Scheme.
3. You may also receive a referral from a third party, such as a family member or friend. You should make it clear to family members that it is the patient who will be your client, and bear in mind the confidentiality rules.

The Joint Report of the Administrative Justice and Tribunals Council (AJTC) and Care Quality Commission (CQC), *Patients' Experiences of the First-tier Tribunal (Mental Health)* (March 2011) recommended that (p.16):

> Hospital managers should ensure that staff are aware that it is inappropriate to recommend lawyers to patients. While hospital staff should help patients to apply to the tribunal and to find a lawyer, referrals should be made by providing patients with a list of local lawyers who have a Legal Services Commission (LSC) contract for mental health work, preferably those who are members of the Law Society's Mental Health Tribunal Panel, to enable them to choose a lawyer who has been accredited as providing a competent standard of representation.

It is inappropriate to give gifts to members of staff, or to loiter on wards handing out cards or gifts. It is unethical to pay referral fees to members of staff for introductions to new clients. See the Law Society's Practice Note (**13.2.2**) and Mental Health Lawyers Association's Code of Conduct (**13.2.3**) for guidance on conduct issues.

13.3.2   First visit to client

The first visit should take place promptly after the initial introduction to the client. The peer review guidance (chapter 3) suggests within two days for s.2 and urgent cases and otherwise within seven days. To ensure that deadlines are not missed, basic information such as section type and start date should be obtained immediately.

The approach will depend on the individual client. The Law Society Practice Note puts it as follows (at section 3), you should:

> be alert to, and seek to overcome, communication challenges which the client faces, including those arising from:
>
> - lack of capacity or use of medication
> - hearing difficulties
> - learning difficulties
> - language barriers or other cross-cultural issues
>
> present information in a clear and straightforward manner, avoiding complicated forms and overly legalistic language.

The first visit will probably take around an hour, very much depending on the client and the case; in any event, the client must be put at ease and not rushed. The meeting should be held in a private room, out of earshot of anyone else.

It is important to find out at an early stage what the client wants to achieve. This will allow you to provide advice on the legal possibilities, and will provide a focus for the remainder of the meeting. Common objectives, the viability of which will depend on the legal status of the client, include: (a) discharge from section in order to leave hospital and continue treatment at home; (b) discharge from section to remain in hospital on a voluntary basis until accommodation is located; (c) conditional discharge, deferred until accommodation is located; (d) transfer back to prison; (e) transfer to another, lower-security hospital; (f) discharge from section in order to leave hospital and cease all treatment.

In a tribunal case, it is fundamentally important to work out the patient's eligibility dates for applications to the tribunal, and the dates of any forthcoming mandatory reference. The patient may know the date his section began, but you may need to check this with the nursing staff or Mental Health Act Administrator. This will allow you to advise on whether or not the client is eligible to apply, and whether it would be advisable to apply straightaway or wait until further into the eligibility period.

You may find that an 'initial interview questionnaire' assists in the first meeting. It can help to structure the meeting, and can ensure that you remember to obtain all necessary information and to provide the necessary advice. However, care must be taken that it is not followed so rigidly that the meeting takes on an over-formal character. The Legal Services Commission used to carry out audits based on its 'transaction criteria': these criteria may assist in considering what to include in a questionnaire.[11] Its current peer review guidance may also assist (see **13.2.6**). The Law Society Practice Note adds that you should advise clients about the strengths and weaknesses of the case, timescales, tribunal powers and hearing procedures (section 3.1).

The following are some issues that should be discussed at the first interview:

- Home address: what sort of accommodation this is (rented, owned, council, Housing Association, family, etc.); whether or not it is available to return to.
- Family and friends: contact details; whether client is content for you to contact them.
- Identity of nearest relative (NR): whether that person is considered likely to want to exercise the power of discharge, and whether client wants that person to know about his case.
- Identity of professionals involved in the case: responsible clinician, care co-ordinator, primary nurse, general practitioner, etc.
- Whether the client has any leave of absence and, if so, what type (unescorted, escorted, community, hospital grounds), for what duration, what happens during leave, how it goes, etc.
- The section under which the client is detained and the date it commenced.
- The date of the admission to hospital and, if different, the date detention began.
- The circumstances of admission: whether the client was taken from home, transferred from prison, etc. If an offender patient: details and date of the index offence, bearing in mind the sensitivity of the subject.
- The diagnosis: whether or not the client is aware of the diagnosis, and whether or not he agrees with it.
- Treatment: what treatment is being provided, including medication, psychological input, occupational therapy, family therapy, etc.; whether the client would agree to continue treatment if discharged from section.
- If the client has other ongoing or recent legal matters (e.g. criminal, housing, family) the details of the relevant solicitors.
- Whether the client has applied, or wishes to apply for a Mental Health Tribunal hearing and, if so, when.
- Whether or not the client has applied, or wishes to apply for a hospital managers' hearing.

If you have been instructed at the last minute, perhaps in a s.2 case or having been appointed by the tribunal, the reports may already be available, in which case you should obtain them and take instructions at the first meeting if possible.

You will need to ask the client to sign a form of authority. A 'general' form of authority is best as the single document can suffice for obtaining access to medical records and any other purpose. It could be worded along these lines:

---

[11]   See **www.mentalhealthlaw.co.uk/Transaction_criteria**.

> I, [name] of [address], authorise you to disclose any information about me, including medical and other records, and information in relation to my benefits position, to [name of solicitors].

If the client wishes you to represent him but is unwilling to sign the form, the hospital may refuse to provide access to medical records. In these circumstances, if the client lacks capacity to instruct you (see **13.3.3**) you could ask to be appointed by the tribunal and seek a direction ordering disclosure of relevant medical and other records.

The other form which needs to be completed is the Legal Aid form, currently Form CW1&2(MH). The rules surrounding the completion of this form are considered in detail at **14.7**.

It is possible to pay for an interpreter or signer as a disbursement under the Legal Aid scheme (see **14.8.2**). If necessary, one should be present for all meetings with the client. The tribunal will arrange an interpreter, free of charge, for the hearing (English Code of Practice, para.32.36; Welsh Code of Practice, para.26.24).

13.3.3   Consideration of capacity

You should keep this issue under review during the case. In all areas of life, including detention under MHA 1983, a person is assumed to have capacity unless it is established that he lacks capacity to make the decision in question (MCA 2005, s.1(2)). Assessment of a client's capacity is a decision which you can usually make yourself, although if in doubt you could obtain expert evidence.

The test of litigation capacity is 'whether the party to legal proceedings is capable of understanding, with the assistance of proper explanation from legal advisers and experts in other disciplines as the case may require, the issues on which his consent or decision is likely to be necessary in the course of those proceedings' (*Masterman-Lister* v. *Brutton & Co.* [2002] EWCA Civ 1889). The question is to be judged by reference to MCA 2005 tests (*V* v. *R* [2011] EWHC 822 (QB)). The threshold for capacity to apply to the tribunal is not a demanding one (see *R (MH)* v. *Secretary of State for the Department of Health* [2005] UKHL 60).

The issue of capacity has been considered by the Upper Tribunal (in *AA* v. *Cheshire and Wirral Partnership NHS Foundation Trust* [2009] UKUT 195 (AAC)), and is addressed in the Law Society's Practice Note (see **13.2.2**). Your approach to what the client informs you, or asks you to do, will depend on your assessment of his capacity to provide instructions:

1.   If your client has capacity you must follow his instructions (even if they are inconsistent or unhelpful) unless (a) they are as a result of duress or undue influence; (b) they are not properly arguable; or (c) they would place you in conflict with professional rules. To seek discharge at a tribunal will almost always be properly arguable. The rules on confidentiality (see **13.2.4**) apply without modification.

2.   If your client lacks capacity then:

(a) Unless you can take instructions from a personal welfare attorney acting under a registered health and welfare lasting power of attorney or a deputy appointed by the Court of Protection to make relevant personal welfare decisions for the client, you should ask to be appointed by the tribunal (see **9.2.3**). You should give appropriate weight to the client's wishes and feelings, particularly if he is close to having capacity; however, if he is unable to express wishes and feelings, you should ensure the tribunal has the necessary material and should consider the least restrictive alternative, but should not automatically argue for discharge. It may be that the patient has capacity to give instructions on some issues but not others. There is no provision for a litigation friend such as the Official Solicitor to become involved in tribunal proceedings, so the solicitor takes on a similar 'best interests' role.

(b) In relation to confidentiality, the original Law Society Guidelines for Legal Representatives[12] stated that 'the solicitor's duty of confidentiality is replaced by a duty to act in the client's best interests, in cases where the client becomes incapacitated and therefore cannot give or withhold consent to the disclosure of information'. The current Practice Note does not address the issue, but it is submitted that the earlier advice is correct.

13.3.4 Application to tribunal

You must ensure that you are aware of the relevant eligibility periods, and that you submit the application on time.

Do not rely on anyone else to submit the application. If you are told that an application has already been made, discuss this with the tribunal office and submit an application if one has not been received. This is especially important in s.2 cases where the patient may only apply during the first 14 days of detention (MHA 1983, s.66(2)(a)) or, if the tribunal is closed on the fourteenth day, on the next working day thereafter (*R (Modaresi)* v. *Secretary of State for Health* [2011] EWCA Civ 1359).

The forms and procedure are discussed at **9.3.1**.

13.3.5 Initial preparatory work and discussions with third parties

You should send a detailed confirmation of instructions letter, setting out the client's instructions, your advice, and the steps it was agreed that you would take on the client's behalf. If it is not appropriate to send a letter to the client, for instance because he cannot read it or it would distress him in some way, then you should keep a file note explaining the situation.

---

[12] The Law Society Mental Health and Disability Committee, 'Mental Health Review Tribunals: Guidelines for Legal Representatives', The Law Society, 1998. See **www.mentalhealthlaw.co.uk/ Law_Society_guidance**.

You may also need to make initial contact with the following, either by letter or by telephone or both:

1. *The tribunal*: to find out if an application has been made or if another solicitor is on record, or to submit the patient's application. It makes sense to do this first, so that the Legal Aid 'Level 2' can begin (see **14.4.3**).

2. *Nursing staff*: on the day of the first meeting, it may be that you can communicate with the nursing staff (e.g. the ward manager or your client's named nurse) and obtain useful initial information about the patient's case. This should only be done after seeing the patient, having explained the situation to him and obtained his consent.

3. *Mental Health Act Administrator*: to inform him, where relevant, that you represent the patient; that an application to the tribunal has been made; that the patient also seeks a hospital managers' hearing; that you require access to records; that you require a copy of the section papers.

4. *Responsible clinician*: to obtain, if possible, a brief outline of his opinion on the case, so that you can provide early advice to the patient prior to reports being received; to ask for an invitation to any Care Programme Approach (CPA) or s.117 meeting which is held in advance of the tribunal hearing; to raise any specific issues that the patient has asked you to raise. In restricted cases, it may be that the RC is supportive of the patient's application, any resistance subsequently coming from the Ministry of Justice.

5. *Ministry of Justice*: if appropriate, in restricted cases only, for example to find out the progress of any community leave application.

6. *Nearest relative*: to explain the NR's rights, tailored to the situation in the case (for instance, the right to object to s.3 admission, or the right to order discharge from s.2 or s.3, or the ability to delegate his functions to another person); to find out whether he wishes to exercise any of his powers; to obtain background information about the case. It is vitally important in all unrestricted cases to identify the nearest relative and, where the patient permits this, to contact him at the earliest opportunity.

7. *Family members or friends*: to obtain background information about the case, and to find out whether any would be useful witnesses at the tribunal. Family and friends can provide useful evidence which may, for instance, corroborate the patient's version of disputed events.

8. *Other advisers*: Lay advocates (see **11.6**), previous representatives and advisers acting on parallel matters: for information in relation to the patient's case.

The duty of confidentiality prevents you from contacting third parties such as family members if the client instructs you not to; however, if the client lacks capacity in this area, you will need to make a decision based on his best interests (see **13.3.3**).

Contact with third parties is useful not only at the outset of the case but also throughout. For instance, as the nurse attending the hearing is sometimes not the author of the nursing report, it could be useful to talk to the nurse prior to the hearing.

Chapter 10 of the peer review guidance (**13.2.6**) deals with communication with third parties.

13.3.6 Checking the legality of section papers

In every civil case the section papers should be checked for lawfulness. It should be possible to view the papers immediately after the first attendance (see **10.10.3**).

An aide memoire or tick-box form could be drawn up from the following information:

1. The correct forms should be used, although it is the wording rather than the layout that is important. (The English forms are contained in Mental Health (Hospital, Guardianship and Treatment) (England) Regulations 2008, SI 2008/1184, and the Welsh forms in Mental Health (Hospital, Guardianship, Community Treatment and Consent to Treatment) (Wales) Regulations 2008, SI 2008/2439 (W.212).)

2. The forms must be signed.

3. In s.3 cases the hospital (at which 'appropriate treatment' is available) should be stated in the medical recommendations (Department of Health *Reference Guide to the Mental Health Act 1983* (London, 2008), para.2.90; see also the statutory forms (A7 and A8 in England, and HO4 and HO7 in Wales)).

4. In ss.2 and 3 cases, at least one doctor must be approved under s.12 and unless that doctor has previous acquaintance with the patient, the other doctor must, if practicable, have previous acquaintance (MHA 1983, s.12(2)). If neither doctor has previous acquaintance, the application form should give reasons for this.

5. The medical recommendations must be signed on or before the date of the application (s.12(1)).

6. There must be no more than five clear days between the two medical recommendations (s.12(1)), e.g. if the first is on Wednesday, the second can be on the following Tuesday but no later.

7. The AMHP must have personally seen the patient within the period of 14 days ending on the date of the application (s.11(5)), or in the previous 24 hours for emergency (s.4) applications (s.4(5)).

8. The application gives authority to 'take and convey' the patient to hospital (s.6(1)):

    (a) in emergency (s.4) cases, within the period of 24 hours beginning with the time of the medical examination, or the application, whichever is later; and

    (b) in other cases, within the period of 14 days beginning with the date of the second medical examination (note: not necessarily the date of the recommendation).

9.   In s.2 cases, the person (if any) appearing to be the nearest relative should, if practicable, be informed (s.11(3)). In s.3 cases, the person (if any) appearing to be the NR should, if it is reasonably practicable and would not involve unreasonable delay, be consulted (s.11(4)). In these latter cases it is particularly important to check whether or not the correct person was identified as the NR, as in some cases an error may lead to unlawful detention.

10. In emergency (s.4) cases which are converted to s.2, the second medical recommendation must be received within 72 hours of admission (s.4(3)).

11. The regulations on conflicts of interest must not be breached (see Mental Health (Conflicts of Interest) (England) Regulations 2008, SI 2008/1205 and Mental Health (Conflicts of Interest) (Wales) Regulations 2008, SI 2008/ 2440 (W.213), discussed in Department of Health *Reference Guide to the Mental Health Act 1983* (London, 2008) and in English Code of Practice, chapter 7; Welsh Code of Practice, chapter 3).

The Care Quality Commission has published a guidance note which gives examples of errors in each of these overlapping categories: (a) errors which lead to unlawful detention; (b) errors so minimal as not to lead to unlawful detention; and (c) errors which are rectifiable within 14 days of admission (see Care Quality Commission, *Scrutinising and Rectifying Statutory Forms for Admission under the Mental Health Act 1983* (October 2008); some errors may be rectified under MHA 1983, s.15).

In appropriate cases where unlawful detention or other compulsion is suspected and having taken instructions, you should consider sending a letter of claim as a precursor to judicial review and/or habeas corpus proceedings and a claim for damages for false imprisonment and breach of ECHR, art.5. In a complex case you may wish to consult counsel. The defendant could be the hospital and/or the local authority, depending on the defences available and who was at fault (see *TTM* v. *LB Hackney* [2011] EWCA Civ 4).

The tribunal is only concerned with the detention criteria at the time of the hearing, rather than the underlying lawfulness of detention (*R (von Brandenburg)* v. *East London and the City Mental Health Trust* [2003] UKHL 58) (see **9.3.6**).

In criminal cases you should obtain a copy of the hospital order, transfer warrant, or other authority for detention in hospital.

13.3.7   Viewing medical and other records

The medical records should be viewed for the first time as soon as possible after receiving initial instructions, as they provide useful background information on which further instructions can be taken. Procedures vary from hospital to hospital: some provide access to the computer system, others provide redacted photocopies of records, printouts of computerised records or access to a handwritten file. Access to medical records is considered at **10.10.2**.

In s.2 cases it is particularly important to read the records at the first opportunity, as the reports may arrive just before the hearing but are invariably largely based on the records. If instructions can be taken on the records, it will speed up the process when reports are served.

If the patient disputes the factual accuracy of reports, then the corresponding entries in the records should be checked to see whether they are consistent with the patient's side of the story.

The medical records should be read again just before the hearing, particularly if there has been a long lapse of time between the reports and the hearing, so that the representative is not surprised by any oral evidence about recent events.

13.3.8 Obtaining reports and directions

The rules set out timeframes within which the reports should be served: generally, three weeks from the relevant person being notified by the tribunal, or six weeks in Welsh conditional discharge recall cases, or as soon as possible in s.2 cases (see **10.2**). The due date can be calculated by taking the date on the tribunal's acknowledgement letter (which is sent at the same time as the relevant person is notified) adding two working days for service, and adding three or six weeks as appropriate.

Directions may need to be sought in relation to various matters:

1. The rules on timeframes for submission of reports are not always observed, so the representative should keep a note of the due date and, when it has passed, ask the tribunal to issue directions that the reports be provided (English Rules, rule 5(3)(d); Welsh Rules, rule 5). Bearing in mind the date of application and the date, or likely date, of the hearing, the representative should propose an appropriate deadline for the reports to be submitted. The power to grant 'non-compliance' directions, where there has been no application to extend or shorten the time for providing reports (English Rules, rule 5(3)(a)), has been delegated in England by the tribunal judiciary to Secretariat administrative staff (see Practice Statement: *Delegation of Functions to Staff on or after 2 November 2010*; English Rules, rule 4) and such directions may be produced on the tribunal's own initiative. Unfortunately, their widespread use without enforcement can lead to the perception that deadlines are simply being extended.

2. The clinical, social circumstances, and nursing reports must adhere to the requirements for their content (Practice Direction: *First-tier Tribunal Health Education and Social Care Chamber: Statements and Reports in Mental Health Cases* (April 2012), and the Schedule to the Welsh Rules) (see **Chapter 10**). If reports are inadequate, and it is felt that full reports would be of more assistance to the patient's case (for instance, if further information on after-care facilities would help the tribunal) then the representative could seek directions to remedy this.

3. If there are reports marked 'not to be disclosed' then it is likely that you will

wish to argue that the information should be disclosed (see **10.10**). If this is refused then you can apply again as a preliminary issue on the day of the hearing.

4.   Occasionally there can be difficulties and delays in obtaining permission to view medical records. If initial instructions are taken soon before the tribunal hearing, access may need to be gained before the hospital procedures can run their course. In these situations, the tribunal can be asked to issue a direction requiring that immediate and unredacted access be given to the records (see **10.10**).

See **9.5** above for further information in relation to directions.

13.3.9   Subsequent visits to client throughout case

The number of visits will depend on the nature of the case and the client. Some clients, even in complex cases, will refuse to discuss reports or records in detail or at all. Some will have very limited understanding of their contents, or indeed the tribunal process generally. In most cases, however, it should still be possible to discuss the general themes. Some people have short attention spans so repeated visits may be necessary to discuss just one report. In any case, regular contact is necessary as the client's mental state may change throughout the case.

When the medical records have been viewed, or reports have been received, the patient should be seen promptly to discuss the contents. Take detailed notes of the instructions (for example, any factual disputes) so that you can review them later in preparation for the hearing.

The client should be advised on merits as the case progresses; a key time is likely to be when all tribunal reports have been received. When the hearing is approaching, he should be reminded about the tribunal procedure and the role of the medical member.

13.3.10   Consider the instruction of independent experts

You should consider the merits of instructing independent experts in every case. A note of the decision should be recorded on file. If an expert is not instructed, then this note will show that you have considered it, which assists on peer review. If an expert is instructed, the note will demonstrate to the Legal Aid Agency your justification for the expenditure, which is particularly important when exceptional claims are submitted (see **14.8**). Chapter 9 of the peer review guidance (**13.2.6**) sets out some reasons which can justify the instruction of experts. It also lists questions for use in letters of instruction.

Challenges to the expert evidence of the responsible authority can be considered in three categories. First, challenges to the factual basis for the expert opinion: for instance, it may be that the patient disputes incidents, and if the patient's version of events were true then the expert opinion would not be valid. Secondly, challenges to the expert opinion itself, for example in relation to diagnosis: where clinical judgment is to be challenged, the best method is to use independent expert evidence. Thirdly, challenges to the conclusions drawn from that expert opinion, for example the conclusions in relation to management of risk or the continuation of the section.

The type of expert instructed will depend on the type of case. Most often the responsible clinician is a consultant psychiatrist, and it would be appropriate to instruct a psychiatrist of similar status and specialism to challenge his medical evidence. In offender cases it should be a forensic psychiatrist. The clinician instructed should be senior, usually a consultant, or an expert in his field. When arguing for a non-statutory recommendation for transfer from high secure hospitals the doctor at the potential receiving hospital could be instructed. An independent social worker could be instructed to consider the patient's social circumstances and to research potential after-care options. In some cases, such as those involving personality disorder, it may be appropriate to instruct a psychologist. In others, expertise in learning disabilities, old age psychiatry or CAMHS may be required.

Independent doctors and approved clinicians (see **3.3**) are entitled at any reasonable time to visit the patient and examine him in private and may require the production of and inspect any relevant records (MHA 1983, s.76); to refuse to allow this would amount to the criminal offence of obstruction (MHA 1983, s.129). These statutory provisions do not apply to other independent experts, but access to the patient and his records is not normally problematic.

If the report is favourable to the client's case and the client agrees to its disclosure, it should be sent promptly to the tribunal. Guidance formerly on the tribunal website asks that it be sent no later than seven days before the hearing, and states that a salaried tribunal judge will identify cases where there is a conflict of expert evidence and may direct the experts to contact each other to understand which issues they agree on and produce reasons for issues where they disagree.[13] The duty of parties to co-operate in rule 2(4) of the English Rules includes making their experts available to comply with any directions that are given by the tribunal (*MD* v. *Nottinghamshire Health Care NHS Trust* [2010] UKUT 59 (AAC)).

If the report is unfavourable, or the client (with capacity to make the decision) does not agree to its disclosure, it should not be sent to the tribunal. If the independent expert's visit is noted in the medical records then the panel should not draw 'adverse inferences' (*MM* v. *Nottinghamshire Healthcare NHS Trust* [2013] UKUT 107 (AAC)).

The tribunal should circulate the report to all parties (English Rules, rule 32(3); Welsh Rules, rule 15(1)), but it is prudent to send it directly to the Ministry of Justice in restricted cases, to be sure that there will be time for comments to be submitted if deemed appropriate. It should also be sent to the hospital's MHA Administrator and, ideally, the RC.

The Court of Appeal has held that (*W* v. *Egdell* [1989] EWCA Civ 13):

---

[13] See **http://webarchive.nationalarchives.gov.uk/20120406155417/http://www.justice.gov.uk/ tribunals/mental-health/hearings/legal-reps**.

A consultant psychiatrist who becomes aware, even in the course of a confidential relationship, of information which leads him, in the exercise of what the court considers a sound professional judgment, to fear that such decisions may be made on the basis of inadequate information and with a real risk of consequent danger to the public is entitled to take such steps as are reasonable in all the circumstances to communicate the grounds of his concern to the responsible authorities.

So in very exceptional cases, where there is a strong public interest in disclosure, an independent expert may act lawfully in disclosing his report to others without the patient's permission, even if the patient withdraws the application.

13.3.11 Preparation for the hearing

Having gathered and considered all the evidence, and taken instructions on it, the representative must prepare for the tribunal hearing. All reports should be re-read, and the file should be reviewed, including correspondence, notes from the medical records, and the client's instructions.

You should consider what the main positive points are, so that you can focus on them in the hearing. Similarly, you should be aware of the negative points, so that you know how to deal with them when they arise. This analysis will help you to work out what you want to achieve when questioning the witnesses, and will help you to plan the questions for the patient and your own submissions.

It can help, at least initially, to write down some questions that you want to ask, and to write down what you think your submissions may be. However, do not follow this slavishly. If topics have been fully explored or questions asked already, there is no point raising them again. When you become more confident, you may prefer just to write down a list of points as an aide memoire.

Remind yourself of the statute and case law by reviewing the latest edition of Richard Jones' *Mental Health Act Manual* (currently 15th edn, Sweet & Maxwell, 2012) and other expert commentaries, particularly if there are novel or unusual points to the case. There are some useful principles from case law which are helpful to bear in mind either in cross-examination or submissions, for example, whether the nature of a relapsing disorder makes detention appropriate depends on 'an assessment of the probability that [the patient] will relapse in the near future if he were free in the community' (*R v. London and South West Regional Mental Health Review Tribunal, ex p. Moyle* [1999] MHLR 195 (Admin Court); *CM v. Derbyshire Healthcare NHS Foundation Trust* [2011] UKUT 129 (AAC)); or, for another example, in relation to the word 'necessary', the standard 'is one of necessity, not desirability' (*Reid v. Secretary of State for Scotland* [1998] UKHL 43).

It can assist to call the Tribunal Secretariat in advance to check that you and the tribunal have the same reports, and to find out the names of the panel members.

Skeleton arguments are considered at **13.5.1**, and hearsay at **11.2.2**.

13.3.12 The hearing

Advocacy is a subject all of its own, and a detailed study of the art of advocacy is outside the scope of this book.[14] However, general advice throughout the text, and the advice below, should be of some assistance.

In learning to become a good advocate, there is no substitute for observing others and being observed. Owing to the private nature of the proceedings, in comparison with, for instance, the magistrates' court, Mental Health Tribunal representatives do not as a matter of course watch each other in action. However, observation of (or representation at) four hearings is a prerequisite of Law Society's Accreditation Scheme membership (see **13.1**) and tribunal judges will normally allow an observer to be present for that purpose (see **11.3.3** for information about observing tribunals).

You should aim to arrive at least an hour before the start time. An early arrival will allow you to speak to your client to take final instructions, provide further advice, and help your client to relax. It may be that the medical examination (see **9.7**) takes place just before the hearing (although ideally it would have occurred on a separate day) which would reduce the time available. The client's objectives may have changed, or may have to change because of very recent events which shed an entirely different light on the case.

Time can usefully be spent checking the recent entries in the medical records, and in speaking to the witnesses who are to give oral evidence. This latter point is particularly important if any family or friends have turned up unexpectedly.

If there are any preliminary issues to raise with the panel, speak to the tribunal clerk or assistant at an early opportunity to let him know (see **11.1.2**). At the outset of the hearing, let the panel know what the client is seeking. This will help to focus minds, and ensure that evidence is directed at the relevant issues.

During the hearing itself, speak politely, clearly and concisely. A straightforward professional approach will be appreciated more than any rhetorical flourishes or aggressive questioning. After your cross-examination, once you have been and gone, the patient will have to continue a relationship with his clinical team.

Although you must help the patient to give his best evidence, he must not be 'coached' prior to the hearing in the answers it is thought the tribunal will want to hear. During the hearing, if possible, avoid asking your client leading questions (questions which suggest the answer which is sought) as the patient's evidence will be given more weight if he is allowed to express himself in his own words.

During the hearing, take as detailed notes as possible. These notes may be useful to refer to during the hearing, or after the hearing if it is adjourned part-heard or if the tribunal decision is being appealed.

Having obtained your client's consent, you may wish to consider making alternative submissions. For instance, a client whose instructions are that he has no mental disorder at all may agree to submissions along the following lines: 'If the panel is not in agreement with the submission that there is no mental disorder, you

---

[14] There are many books on the subject. See e.g., John Munkman, *The Technique of Advocacy* (LexisNexis, revised 2009).

must nevertheless consider the mental disorder and its nature and degree'; or, although your primary submission is for immediate discharge, you could argue in the alternative for discharge on a future date, or a recommendation, whichever is appropriate.

13.3.13 Explain the tribunal's decision to client

The tribunal will deliberate immediately after the hearing, and then the tribunal judge (or president in Wales) will usually announce the decision to the parties (English Rules, rule 41(1); Welsh Rules, rule 28(1)). In rare cases, if a violent reaction is anticipated from your client, it may be that he is not informed of the decision directly. Some reasons may be given, though full reasons will follow in writing (see **11.7**). The representative should return to the ward with the patient to discuss the hearing, the decision and its consequences.

If the patient has not been discharged, then any reasons given should be discussed. The ability to make future or immediate further applications, either to the tribunal or to hospital managers, should be explained.

If the patient has been discharged from section and wishes to leave the ward immediately then the representative should remain for a while with the patient to ensure the staff permit this (see **11.7.4**).

13.3.14 Consider written reasons

The written reasons should be received within the deadlines (see **11.7.2**) and if they are not, a complaint can be made to speed the process up. The email address for complaints is ocuhelpdesk@tribunals.gsi.gov.uk. If the patient is represented, the tribunal sends the decision to the representative and not to the patient, so the representative must do this (English Rules, rule 11(4)(a)).

The possibility of challenging the tribunal's decision on a point of law, for example the provision of inadequate reasons, should always be considered if the patient was not discharged. Usually no appeal will be made, but for peer review purposes the consideration of the possibility should be noted on the file. Any appeal must be made within 28 days of the decision being sent (English Rules, rule 45(3); Welsh Rules, rule 30(2)). For details on appeals, see **Chapter 12**.

There should usually be a final meeting with the client to discuss the written tribunal reasons and the future options and legal rights. If, in exceptional cases, this is not considered appropriate then the file should be noted accordingly to comply with the peer review guidance (see **13.2.6**).

13.4 REPRESENTATION OF CHILDREN AND YOUNG PEOPLE

It appears that the number of children (defined as persons 'under the age of eighteen' under Children Act 1989, s.105(1)) subject to detention under MHA 1983 is increasing.[15] If detained in hospital, these children are likely to be treated in specialist Child and Adolescent Mental Health Service (CAMHS) units managed by the NHS or the private sector. Geographical provision is piecemeal, with the result that children may experience significant 'separation from family, carers, friends and community or interruption of their education' (English Code of Practice, para.36.4).

In England, where a child or young person who is detained (or is subject to another order under MHA 1983) applies, or has their case referred to a tribunal, 'wherever possible' at least one of the tribunal members will be a member of the CAMHS panel (see **2.4.5**), appointed because of their special expertise relevant to the care and treatment of children and young people. There is no equivalent to the CAMHS panel in Wales. However, tribunal panels should be alert to the particular needs and vulnerabilities of child patients.

13.4.1 Other relevant legislation

Anyone involved in representing children or young people before a Mental Health Tribunal should also be familiar with other legislation and related Codes of Practice which may be relevant to the child's circumstances, including the Children Acts 1989 and 2004, MCA 2005 (in relation to those over 16 years), the Family Law Reform Act 1969, the Human Rights Act 1998 and the United Nations Convention on the Rights of the Child 1989.

13.4.2 Provisions in Mental Health Act 1983 relating to children

There is little in MHA 1983 specific to children – the relevant statutory duties relating to children are described at **4.3.3**.

Representatives should in particular be aware of the following:

- There is no lower age limit for detention, or the use of a CTO. There is a lower age limit of 16 for guardianship.
- The classification of mental disorder can encompass 'behavioural and emotional disorders of children and adolescents' (English Code of Practice, para.3.3).
- If a child is subject to an interim or a full care order the local authority will always be the child's nearest relative (MHA 1983, s.27). This is notwithstanding the fact that the local authority will continue to share parental responsibility with the child's parents (Children Act 1989, s.33(3)).
- Where a 16 or 17-year-old has capacity, they may consent (or not) to be admitted to hospital for treatment regardless of the views of any person with parental responsibility (MHA 1983, s.131(2)–(5)). The effect of this is that if

---

[15] The number of under 18s applying to the MHT increased from 960 in October 2009–September 2011, to 1,160 in October 2011–September 2012, with the greatest increase in applications (43 per cent) being for those under 16 years (Mental Health Tribunal MARTHA database).

the young person refuses admission, and the criteria for admission under MHA 1983 are met, then the young person should be detained.

- Children admitted to hospital for the treatment of mental disorder, whether informal or detained, should be accommodated in an environment which is suitable having regard to the patient's age 'subject to his needs' (MHA 1983, s.131A; see **4.3.3**). The qualification 'subject to his needs' means that there may be circumstances, for example where the young person is close to his 18th birthday, when the best place for the young person is an adult ward (English Code of Practice, paras.36.71–36.72). The duty to provide age-appropriate accommodation falls on the hospital managers.

It is also important that representatives are familiar with the detailed guidance on the care and treatment of children and young people who are subject to the provisions of MHA 1983 which is set out in the MHA Codes of Practice (English Code of Practice, chapter 36; Welsh Code of Practice, chapter 33).

13.4.3 Important factors when representing children at the tribunal

Children and young people have the same rights as other patients to apply to the tribunal and, where a period of 12 months has elapsed since the tribunal last considered a case, the hospital managers must refer the child's case to the tribunal (MHA 1983, s.68(6)). It is important that a representative is appointed at an early stage, preferably a legal representative who has experience of representing children and knowledge of CAMHS issues. Representatives should be alert to the following when representing children and young people:

1. The competence of a child under 16, or the capacity of a 16- or 17-year-old, to instruct a representative should always be determined. Where a child or young person is clearly unable to give instructions, the representative should consider whether it is appropriate to take instructions from any other person, such as the nearest relative or someone with parental responsibility. Alternatively, the representative should consider asking the tribunal to appoint him to act for the child under the tribunal rules (English Rules, rule 11(7); Welsh Rules, rule 13(5)).

2. The requirement for the tribunal to be satisfied of the responsible authority's case when the patient is detained or subject to a CTO includes the question, in s.3 cases, of whether 'appropriate' treatment is available (MHA 1983, s.72(1)(b)(iia)). This must mean in cases involving child patients that the tribunal must be satisfied that the child's accommodation in hospital is suitable for their age, subject to their needs.

3. The location of the hospital in which the detained child is being treated may result in problematic separation from family and friends. If this were the case then consideration should always be given to making a submission asking the tribunal to make a recommendation for transfer to another hospital nearer to

the child's home on the basis that this would facilitate discharge on a future date (MHA 1983, s.72(3)(a)).

4.   Establishing responsibility for planning and providing after-care for children who are detained can be problematic and cause delay, particularly as there is often a lack of co-ordination between the relevant health and social services authorities and the family. Representatives should be alert to the specific requirements in the Practice Direction for social circumstance reports to contain specific information in children's cases (see **10.6.2**) and should not delay in seeking directions from the tribunal where the reports provided do not contain this information (see **10.1.1**; there is no equivalent for Wales but the same issues are likely to be relevant).

13.5   OTHER PRACTICAL CONSIDERATIONS

13.5.1   Skeleton arguments and written statements

In complex case, where the issues are known to all parties in advance, it may be useful to serve a skeleton argument. It should contain a summary of the facts, the law, and your arguments for saying that your desired conclusion is the result of applying the facts to the law. However, it is a double-edged sword as, for instance, the client's instructions could change at the last minute so as not to reflect the contents of the skeleton argument.

Until a recent redesign, the tribunal website contained the following guidance:[16]

> The Tribunal regards it as good practice to submit a skeleton argument for cases of complexity and/or involving points of law. Skeleton arguments should contain a numbered list of points, stated in no more than a few sentences. Each point should have references to documentation that is relied on later. In the case of points of law, authorities relied on should be cited with reference to the particular pages where the principle concerned is set out.

A list of authorities to be cited should be given to the tribunal and the other parties not less than three days before the hearing and copies of any relevant ECtHR judgments provided for the tribunal.

As the first impression the panel will form of the patient will be from reading written reports from the responsible authority, it may be thought helpful in certain cases for the patient to submit a written statement of his own: however, this course of action is rarely adopted, for similar reasons as apply to skeleton arguments. The statement could address mistakes in reports or add extra information which may indicate that discharge is appropriate.

---

[16]   The current, less detailed guidance is available at **www.justice.gov.uk/tribunals/mental-health/making-an-appeal**.

13.5.2   Hospital managers' hearings

There are similarities and differences between tribunal's and managers' hearings. The similarities include:

1.   There are almost invariably three panel members.
2.   The same types of reports are prepared: clinical, social circumstances and nursing.
3.   An oral hearing will usually be held, during which the order of evidence and procedure are similar.
4.   The hospital managers have the power to discharge unrestricted patients (MHA 1983, s.23).

The differences include:

1.   There is generally no lawyer or psychiatrist on the panel, but simply lay members with one acting as chairman.
2.   A panel of three managers must be unanimous in order to discharge a patient (*R (Tagoe-Thompson)* v. *Hospital Managers of the Park Royal Centre* [2003] EWCA Civ 330).
3.   Perhaps partly because of the above points, they are less likely to discharge a patient.
4.   Although restricted patients are entitled to managers' hearings (English Code of Practice, para.31.2; Welsh Code of Practice, para.27.12), the managers have no real role in relation to discharge in such cases. Ministry of Justice permission would be required for discharge by hospital managers (MHA 1983, s.23, as modified by Sched.1) and in practice this is unheard of.
5.   There are no statutory criteria for the managers' discharge power, so they look to the Codes of Practice (English Code of Practice, chapter 31; Welsh Code of Practice, chapter 27) for their discharge tests. These reflect the tribunal's statutory criteria. Representatives should familiarise themselves with relevant chapters of the Code before representation at hospital managers' hearings.

Parallel applications to the tribunal and to the hospital managers are possible. In these circumstances, hospital managers' hearings were often seen in the past as a 'dress rehearsal' prior to the tribunal hearing, but this is less common now for the following reasons: (a) tribunals used to take many weeks to arrange even in unrestricted cases, but now take place more quickly within a relatively short number of weeks; (b) some solicitors have decided not to attend managers' hearings because of the ungenerous fixed fee Legal Aid scheme; and (c) some hospitals have a policy of ignoring applications to the hospital managers while tribunal applications are pending.

13.6 CONCLUSION

This chapter has provided detailed guidance for representatives in preparing for and presenting cases before the tribunal in both England and Wales. The contact details of those tribunals and other relevant bodies that representatives may need to contact are set out in **Appendix I**. **Chapter 14** sets out the arrangements for the provision of public funding under the Legal Aid scheme to fund the representation of patients at tribunals.

CHAPTER 14

Public funding

Over the years there has been an increase in the proportion of patients who have the benefit of legal representation at Mental Health Tribunals. The two main reasons for this have been the greater role of the tribunal after MHA 1983 came into effect and the increased availability of Legal Aid, both of which were linked to the United Kingdom being a signatory to ECHR (see **Chapter 1**). Legal Aid was initially available for preparation for (but not advocacy at) tribunal hearings, but in 1982 it was extended to cover representation at hearings. In 1994, following representations by the Law Society, entitlement to Legal Aid for representation at the Mental Health Review Tribunal was made non-means tested.

This chapter sets out an overview of the current Legal Aid provisions as they relate to representation at Mental Health Tribunals.

14.1 PUBLICLY FUNDED MENTAL HEALTH CONTRACTS

The current Legal Aid scheme for mental health work is provided through solicitors' firms, and not-for-profit organisations, who hold mental health contracts awarded following a national tender. The scheme is primarily based on fixed fees. It was run by the Legal Services Commission (LSC) until April 2013 when that body became the Legal Aid Agency (LAA), an executive agency of the Ministry of Justice.

The current contract (the Standard Civil Contract 2010) commenced on 15 November 2010 and was due to expire at the end of March 2013. In February 2013 the LSC gave notice that the contract would be extended for a further year, and that amendments would be made with effect from 1 April 2013.[1] Where relevant, the amendments are reflected in this chapter. The next contract tender will open no earlier than summer 2013.[2]

For all future publicly funded mental health contracts, it will be required (as a minimum) that all staff carrying out representation before the Mental Health Tribunal (MHT) in England or the Mental Health Review Tribunal for Wales

---

[1] See **www.justice.gov.uk/legal-aid/contracts-and-tenders/standard-civil-contract-2010**.
[2] See **www.justice.gov.uk/legal-aid/quality-assurance/accreditation**.

(MHRT for Wales) must be members of the Law Society's Mental Health Accreditation Scheme (see **13.1**).[3]

14.2   SOURCES OF INFORMATION

This chapter can only provide an overview of the Legal Aid system. The following are the main sources of information in relation to Legal Aid for Mental Health Tribunal matters:

1.   Standard Civil Contract Specification (2010) (referred to as the 'Specification'),[4] as amended, in particular:

    (a)   Section 3, 'Carrying out controlled work';

    (b)   Section 9, 'Mental health specification'.

2.   Statutory instruments made under the Legal Aid, Sentencing and Punishment of Offenders Act (LASPO) 2012, including:

    (a)   Civil Legal Aid (Financial Resources and Payment for Services) Regulations 2013, SI 2013/480 ('Financial Resources Regulations');

    (b)   Civil Legal Aid (Merits Criteria) Regulations 2013, SI 2013/104 ('Merits Regulations');

    (c)   Civil Legal Aid (Procedure) Regulations 2012, SI 2012/3098 ('Procedure Regulations');

    (d)   Civil Legal Aid (Remuneration) Regulations 2013, SI 2013/422 ('Remuneration Regulations').

3.   LAA Guidance documents:

    (a)   *Principles of Mental Health Fees* (February 2009).[5] It is expected that these will be superseded by *Contract Management: Mental Health Guidance* ('Contract Management guidance') soon after 1 April 2013.[6]

    (b)   *Legal Services Commission Manual* (or its successor).[7]

14.3   SCOPE OF LEGAL AID

Under the Category Definitions 2010, as amended,[8] and LASPO 2012, Sched.1, Part 1, the 'Mental Health Category' covers civil legal services provided in relation to matters arising under:

---

[3]   See **www.justice.gov.uk/legal-aid/quality-assurance/accreditation**.
[4]   See **www.justice.gov.uk/legal-aid/contracts-and-tenders/standard-civil-contract-2010**.
[5]   See **www.mentalhealthlaw.co.uk/File:Principles_of_MH_fees_2009.pdf**.
[6]   The Contract Management guidance was made available to the author in draft format.
[7]   See **www.lscmanual.co.uk**.
[8]   See **www.justice.gov.uk/downloads/legal-aid/civil-contracts/category-definitions-2010.pdf**.

(a) MHA 1983;

(b) Repatriation of Prisoners Act 1984, Sched, para.5(2);

(c) MCA 2005.

The category specifically includes advocacy at the MHT, MHRT for Wales, and Upper Tribunal (LASPO 2012, Sched.1, Part 3). Certain types of capacity case are included, with the possibility of exceptional funding for further types.

The category is subject to a list of excluded services, applicable to most civil Legal Aid categories (LASPO 2012, Sched.1, Part 2). This excludes various types of case such as human rights damages claims (unless there is a significant breach of Convention rights), Criminal Injuries Compensation Scheme claims and name changes. The category is also subject to category-specific exclusions: the creation of lasting powers of attorney or advance decisions under MCA 2005.

There are two types of work:

1.　'controlled' work, which covers Legal Help (for general legal advice) and Help at Court, and Controlled Legal Representation (for tribunal representation);

2.　'certificated' (or 'licensed') work, which covers Upper Tribunal challenges against decisions, and any court action such as displacement proceedings or judicial review.

Ordinarily, the client will be the patient, but Legal Aid is also available to advise a nearest relative (for instance, legal advice about his status, or tribunal representation if he is the applicant) or to advise a victim (Legal Help and Help at Court only).

14.4　'CONTROLLED' WORK

14.4.1　Matter starts

The current contract operates on a 'matter start' system which requires firms to bid for the entitlement to begin a certain number of controlled work cases per year during the operation of the contract. Unless the LAA increases a firm's allocation of matter starts (within contractual limits) the firm may only carry out work within the limit. Formerly one of the contractual key performance indicators required the firm to use 85 per cent of the allocated matter starts, but this was removed on 1 April 2013.

For each matter, there are two possible, alternative types of mental health fixed fees: tribunal and non-tribunal (in the regulations now called 'Mental Health Proceedings' and 'Mental Health – non Tribunal' respectively). The main differences between the two types of fee relate to means testing, the relevant merits test to be applied, and the fee levels.

'Certificated' work (considered at **14.6**) does not count towards the matter start limit.

14.4.2 Procurement areas

For the current contract the LSC tendered separately for work in 11 geographic areas (the 10 strategic Health Authority areas in England, plus Wales) and in the three high secure hospitals (Ashworth on Merseyside, Broadmoor in Berkshire and Rampton in Nottinghamshire). A schedule to the firm's contract sets out how many matter starts in each area it is permitted to carry out. All firms have contracts for work in at least one geographic area. Only 13 of these firms have high secure hospital (HSH) contracts, with five or six firms for each high secure hospital.

At least 70 per cent of matter starts allocated to an area must relate to clients located in the procurement area when the matter is opened; the remainder may be used in any area (Specification, para.9.7) although not in high secure hospitals unless the firm has a contract for that. For those firms with an HSH contract, 70 per cent of the HSH matter starts must relate to the hospital in the schedule but the other 30 per cent may relate to any other hospital, including one of the other HSHs (Specification, para.9.7).

Where a client is transferred to a high secure hospital, a firm without an HSH contract may continue to represent him where (a) the client wants this; (b) the firm employs an authorised litigator; (c) the firm has experience of restricted cases; (d) all tribunal representation will be by accreditation scheme members; and (e) the firm has represented the client within the previous two years or was the last firm to have represented him (Specification, para.9.8). Otherwise, such a firm may only represent at high secure hospitals as an agent of a firm with an HSH contract (Legal Services Commission, *Guidance on the Use of Agents* (10 October 2011)).

An additional requirement for HSH work is that advocates before the tribunal must be members of the Law Society's Mental Health Accreditation Scheme (Specification, para.9.6(c)) (see **13.1**).

14.4.3 Fee levels

The scheme is based on a series of fixed fees, although there is provision for 'escape fee' cases, previously known as exceptional cases, to be paid at hourly rates instead (see **14.8.1**). Detail can be found in the Specification (see para.9.56 *et seq.*), but the following is a summary:

1. The *non-tribunal fee* is paid for matters in which no tribunal application is made. This would cover such things as hospital managers' hearings or legal issues relating to complaints or provision of treatment (para.9.56). If a file begins as a non-tribunal file it only becomes a tribunal file if the patient applies to the tribunal, i.e. subsequent advice about the tribunal is not sufficient (para.9.56).
2. The *level 1 tribunal fee* covers initial advice when the client is eligible and submits or has submitted an application to the tribunal (para.9.63). It is payable even if the application was submitted before the initial visit (para.9.64).

3.	The *level 2 tribunal fee* begins once the initial advice has been given and an application has been made to the tribunal; it includes all negotiations with third parties and all preparation for the tribunal hearing (para.9.65) and is payable once the representative has carried out 30 minutes of preparation or advice or has had separate communication with other parties on legal issues (para.9.66). This is not onerous, so few files are level 1.

4.	The *level 3 tribunal fee* primarily covers representation at the tribunal and work in relation to after-care services (para.9.60). Only one level 3 fee is payable per case, but adjourned hearing fees may be payable in addition (see next point). Specifically, the level 3 fee covers visiting the client after the hearing to provide advice on eligibility periods and alternative courses of action, such as applying to the hospital managers, or, if the patient was discharged, any issues regarding compliance with treatment (para.9.25).

5.	The *adjourned hearing fee* is payable on each occasion that a hearing is adjourned, postponed or cancelled on the day at the request of the tribunal, responsible clinician (RC), or representative (where this was unavoidable), and travel costs and/or some representation costs have already been incurred (para.9.70). This would include a situation where the client withdraws on the hearing day. Where there is no effective hearing to determine the case, a level 3 fee may be claimed instead of the final adjourned hearing fee (para.9.72).

6.	A *remote travel payment* would hypothetically be made for each level of a case where a hospital at which the patient was present at any part of the case is one for which an extra fee is necessary to ensure clients' access to appropriate services (paras.9.74). No hospital has ever been designated as remote.

### 14.4.4	Means testing

There are three types of matter for the purposes of means testing:

1.	Tribunal matters are non-means tested, so even a wealthy patient would be entitled to Legal Aid for representation.

2.	Some non-tribunal matters are also non-means-tested. The LAA's position can be summarised follows: the client must be eligible to apply to the tribunal (or the supplier could not have reasonably discovered, either before or during the first attendance, that the client was ineligible to apply), the client must have sought tribunal advice, and there must have been a 'reasonable expectation' that the client would pursue a tribunal application (even though the client subsequently decides not to apply) (draft Contract Management guidance, section 2). Additionally, the sufficient benefit test for the tribunal advice must be met, and the reason for not carrying out a means test must be recorded. The 'reasonable expectation' requirement is broad enough to cover the client who specifically wants to discuss the possibility of a tribunal, or the client who

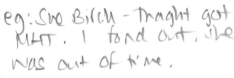

eg: Sue Birch - Thought got
MHT. I found out, she
was out of time.

simply asks to 'get out of hospital'.[9] A more natural reading of the relevant documents is that non-tribunal matters are non-means tested if the client is subject to MHA 1983 and has been advised about potential (or contemplated) tribunal proceedings but does not exercise his right to apply to the tribunal (see Financial Resources Regulations, reg.5(1)(f); Specification, paras.9.15, 9.16; LSC, *Principles of Mental Health Fees* (February 2009); LSC, *Mental Health Fee Scheme and Specification: Additional Questions and Answers following Provider Workshop Events* (17 January 2008)). It is prudent to obtain evidence of means in cases of doubt.[10]

3. All other non-tribunal matters are means tested, which usually involves an assessment of the client's income and capital.

The prescribed income and capital limits are set out in the Financial Resources Regulations. Formerly there was no need to assess income or capital if a client were in receipt of one of the 'passported' benefits listed in the Legal Aid forms; however, from April 2013 it will be necessary to assess capital in all cases (Financial Resources Regulations, reg.6). In relation to capital, the client's statement and signature on the application form will suffice except in cases of doubt (*LSC Manual*, vol. 2, Part E, section 12, para.7). However, evidence of income must be obtained. Form CW1&2MH states:

> In relation to clients detained under the Mental Health Act, you are required to attempt to obtain oral or written confirmation of the position (e.g. type of benefit received) from the ward manager or social worker where practicable.

Alternatives are to write to the hospital's Mental Health Act Administrator or the government body dealing with the relevant benefits, or to cross-refer to a social circumstances report which contains the necessary information.

14.4.5 Merits test

For non-tribunal matters and level 1 tribunal matters, the following test must be met (Specification, para 9.18; Merits Regulations, reg.32):

> there is likely to be sufficient benefit to the individual, having regard to all the circum-stances of the case, including the circumstances of the individual, to justify the cost of provision of Legal Help.

This 'sufficient benefit test' was previously described by the LSC as 'primarily a test of whether a reasonable private paying client of moderate means would pay for the legal advice and assistance' (LSC Funding Code, para.4.11). Where applicable, the test should be considered and this should be noted on the file.

---

[9] Correspondence with LSC Service Development team, 7 March 2013.

[10] The position is not entirely clear: the Costs Appeal Committee refused, on 17 October 2012, to certify a Point of Principle (which would have been a binding interpretation) which had been sought by the LSC.

The merits test in relation to level 2 and 3 tribunal matters is the question of whether it is 'reasonable in all the circumstances of the case for the individual to be provided with full representation' (Merits Regulations, reg.51). It is hard to imagine a situation where the reasonableness test (or, in relation to level 1 tribunal matters, the sufficient benefit test) would not be met in Mental Health Tribunal cases.

14.5 MATTER START BOUNDARIES AND 'ROLLING UP'

14.5.1 General rule: one matter start per problem in eligibility period

The fixed fee regime is based around a patient's periods of eligibility to make applications to the tribunal. Each time a client is newly eligible to make an application to the tribunal, he is in a new period of eligibility. Generally speaking, there can only be one matter start opened in each period of eligibility (para.9.20). It is said that the various problems are 'rolled up' into one matter. The relevant date for determining to which period a tribunal matter belongs is the date of application.

The only occasion where there can be more than one simultaneous matter start is where there is more than one 'separate and distinct legal problem'. The Specification states that, typically, separate and distinct problems arise out of different causes or events; it requires that (a) if legal proceedings were started, or other appropriate remedies pursued, for each problem it would be appropriate for such proceedings to be both issued and heard, or for other remedies to be dealt with, separately; and (b) each problem requires substantial legal work which does not address the other problem(s) (para.3.42). Substantial legal work is defined as at least (a) an additional 30 minutes of preparation or advice; or (b) separate communication with other parties on legal issues (para.3.43).

The two key questions, when considering whether multiple matter starts exist are therefore: (a) Do the client's problems relate to different periods of eligibility? and (b) Do they amount to separate and distinct legal problems?

14.5.2 Mandatory new matter starts

Where the client is detained there are certain circumstances in which an additional matter start *must* be opened. These are when there is subsequent work on a 'new legal issue' (undefined in the Specification) and one of the following events occurs (Specification, para.9.24):

(a)   owing to the passage of time, the client has a statutory entitlement to a further tribunal;
(b)   there has been a change in the client's section type;
(c)   the client is discharged, including on to a community treatment order (CTO);
(d)   the client withdraws and reapplies, where the reason for withdrawal is clearly noted on the file.

275

14.5.3 Single matter start situations

Usually, if a patient is represented in relation to several mental health problems, whether tribunal or otherwise, during one period, there is only one matter start (see Specification, para.9.21). In particular, the following are *not* considered to be separate and distinct legal issues and do not lead to separate matter starts:

1. Prior to a tribunal: attendance at hospital managers' hearings or Care Programme Approach (CPA) meetings (para.9.67).
2. Following a tribunal (paras.9.58 and 9.59):

    (a) attendance at or work in relation to s.117/CPA meetings;
    (b) work relating to a complaint arising from the client's status as a patient within the same period of eligibility; or
    (c) work following a decision with recommendations or a deferred conditional discharge.

14.5.4 Multiple matter start situations

The following are examples of situations where it is believed that there may be more than one matter start, because of either the 'period of eligibility' rule or the 'separate and distinct legal problem' rule. However, it should be noted that the specification is badly drafted and the LSC's interpretation has changed over time (usually with the effect of reducing the number of claimable matter starts) so it would be prudent to check the situation with the LAA.

1. If an informal patient is provided with advice, and subsequently he is detained and given further advice related to a tribunal application, there are two matter starts (Specification, para.9.22).
2. If there is more than one set of tribunal proceedings running concurrently, separate fees can be claimed for each (para.9.20). This could be the case, for instance, where the patient has applied to the tribunal, then a reference is made on his behalf or the nearest relative applies. (In these circumstances, the client may be well advised to withdraw his own application in order to preserve his right to apply at a later date.)
3. The 'rolling up' rules do not apply to conditionally-discharged patients (in other words, the requirement to have only one matter per eligibility period does not apply) (para.9.60). The Specification does not state whether the 'rolling up' rules apply to CTO patients, but the LAA position is that they do apply.[11]
4. Hospital managers' renewal hearings are subject to a special rule. Given two consecutive eligibility periods, the renewal process (by the RC) must take place during the final two months of the first eligibility period. For Legal Aid purposes, a renewal hearing belongs to the *first* period, even if the hearing

---

[11] Correspondence from LSC Service Development team, 10 July 2012.

276

takes place in the second (draft Contract Management guidance, section 5). Therefore, a renewal hearing will either be (a) a stand-alone matter start if there was no matter during the first period; or (b) 'rolled up' into the matter for the first period.

5.   A hospital managers' hearing, held as a result of a barring certificate, is a separate matter start from a tribunal which results from the patient's application.[12] Similarly, a tribunal held as a result of the nearest relative's application is a separate matter to a tribunal held as a result of the patient's application (Specification, para.9.34).

6.   As stated above, if a client's section type changes and there is 'subsequent work on a new legal issue' a new matter start must be begun (para.9.24). If a client's section type changes during tribunal proceedings (such as from s.2 to s.3) it is arguable that this is a separate matter. This was previously the LSC's interpretation[13] but it is no longer (per Lucy Williams, LSC Mental Health Unit, speaking at MHLA Conference, 2 November 2012).

7.   A matter start dealing with a complaint (or other ongoing non-tribunal matter) relating to a particular period of eligibility may continue into a new period of eligibility, but a separate problem in the new period will constitute a separate matter start.[14]

8.   If, while representing a patient, substantial legal work is done advising a potential nearest relative about the delegation and/or displacement procedures, there may be two matter starts, because there are two different clients.[15]

9.   Automatic references to the tribunal are treated as being separate matter starts to any other files. This is not stated in the Specification but has been the LSC's (and now LAA's) long-standing policy, the logic being that there are no eligibility periods for references and no period to 'roll up' any other matters into (per Lucy Williams, LSC Mental Health Unit, speaking at MHLA Conference, 2 November 2012).[16]

14.5.5 Exception to general rule: more than one matter start for same problem

A subsequent matter start may be opened (even where the problem is not separate and distinct) where the following applies (Specification, para.3.47):

(a)   six months have elapsed since the Legal Aid claim; or

(b)   there has been a material development or change in instructions and (unless the claim was made because the client had failed to give instructions for three months) three months have elapsed since the claim.

---

12 Correspondence from LSC Liverpool office, 27 March 2012. The LAA policy on this may change (correspondence from LSC Service Development team, 7 March 2013).
13 Correspondence from LSC Liverpool office, 16 July 2009.
14 Correspondence from LSC Liverpool office, 1 May 2009.
15 Correspondence from LSC Service Development team, 7 March 2013.
16 Also correspondence from LSC Liverpool office, 3 March 2009, 15 April 2009.

If the previous work was done by a different supplier, Legal Help may not be granted within six months of the last work done by the original provider unless: (a) there has been a material change in relevant circumstances; (b) the client has reasonable cause to be dissatisfied; (c) effective communication between the client and the original provider is not practicable because the client moved residence; or (d) the first provider has confirmed it will be making no claim (Procedure Regulations, reg.23(4)).

In such circumstances, the representative must obtain the client's permission to contact the previous provider in writing to confirm the reasons for the termination of retainer and to request a transfer or copy of the file (para.3.53), and work may not start until the file has been received and considered unless it is absolutely necessary to take steps immediately to protect the client's position or meet a court deadline (para.3.54). The full range of fees will be available to the new provider (para.9.84). From a conduct point of view, note the contents of the Mental Health Lawyers Association Code of Conduct at **13.2.3** and set out in **Appendix H.**

14.6 'CERTIFICATED' WORK

A public funding certificate is required for court work, for instance judicial reviews (in the Administrative Court or Upper Tribunal), appeals (Upper Tribunal), depriva-tion of liberty appeals (Court of Protection) and nearest relative displacement proceedings (county court).

The two types of Legal Representation are Investigative Representation (where merits of the case need to be investigated) and Full Representation (Procedure Regulations, reg.9). The means and merits tests are different from those that apply to controlled work and are set out in the relevant regulations. Upper Tribunal cases are means-tested, whereas appeals against Deprivation of Liberty Safeguards authorisations made to the Court of Protection under MCA 2005, s.21A by the detained person or the relevant person's representative are non-means-tested.

There are two types of certificates. A provider must apply to the LAA for a substantive certificate to be issued to cover work in a case. However, an emergency certificate may be issued in certain circumstances, and this may be done by the firm under its delegated functions (previously called devolved powers), without applica-tion to the LAA, if it has a contract in the relevant area of law (Specification, para.5.4).

Public funding certificates have standard wordings for proceedings, and for the costs and scope limitations which need to be extended as the case progresses. The relevant codes and wordings can be found in the *LSC Manual*; for example, MH023 is the code for an Upper Tribunal appeal.

14.7 FORMS

The main form for controlled work (tribunal and non-tribunal matters) is Form CW1&2(MH). Work under Legal Aid can commence when the client signs the form. Work in relation to tribunal matters can commence when the relevant declaration on the form is signed by 'an advisor who is one of the approved personnel of your organisation' (it no longer needs to be signed by a solicitor: just someone on an internal list of personnel approved for this purpose).

There are several forms in relation to certificated work, the main ones being:

- Form CIVAPP1, which sets out the nature of the application for funding;
- Form CIVMEANS2, financial information for clients in receipt of certain 'passporting' benefits;
- Form CIVMEANS1, financial information for other clients;
- Form CIVAPP8, to amend scope and costs limitations.

The forms are updated fairly regularly with very minor changes, but the LAA insists that the correct version must be used, so its website should be checked from time to time.[17]

It may be that the patient refuses to sign the Legal Aid form, particularly in cases where the representative has been appointed to represent a patient in a reference case. A 'protected party' is defined as 'a party or a proposed party who lacks capacity (within the meaning of MCA 2005) to conduct proceedings' (Procedure Regulations, reg.2). An application for controlled work may be made, and the form signed, on behalf of a protected party by (a) a person acting or proposing to act as the protected party's litigation friend or (b) any other person, except the proposed provider, where there is good reason why a litigation friend or proposed litigation friend cannot make the application (Procedure Regulations, reg.22). The 'other person' must have (a) sufficient connection with the protected party to ensure that he is likely to act responsibly in his interests, and (b) sufficient knowledge of the protected party, his problem and his financial circumstances, to give proper instructions (Specification, para.3.15). The rules apply in a similar way to children. Where it is not appropriate to use any of these possibilities for the application to be made on the patient's behalf and the patient will not sign the application due to his condition, the representative may annotate the form to that effect and a supervisor may sign the form (Specification, para.9.41).

---

[17] See **www.justice.gov.uk/legal-aid/make-an-application/controlled-work-applications** and **www.justice.gov.uk/legal-aid/make-an-application/civil-applications**.

14.8 PAY RATES

14.8.1 Legal fees

There are two types of hourly rates for controlled work: Legal Help (LH) rates for non-tribunal work and level 1 tribunal work, and Controlled Legal Representation (CLR) rates for levels 2 and 3 tribunal work (Specification, para.9.80). CLR rates are slightly higher, as are rates overall in London. No percentage uplift is available, including for Law Society's Mental Health Accreditation Scheme membership.

Separate hourly rates apply to certificated work, depending on whether it is High Court (or equivalent) or county court work. Certificated rates are slightly higher, and in addition a percentage uplift may be payable depending on the complexity of the case.

Certificated cases are always paid at the hourly rate, but in controlled work a fixed fee system is in operation. Separate fixed fees are payable according to which fee levels (see **14.4.3**) are reached. Hourly rates are only paid for controlled work in escape fee cases, following completion of a Form EC-CLAIM1-MH after the file has been billed as normal.

Escape fee cases are those where the hourly rate fee would amount to three times the fixed fee (or more). The comparison is between (a) the value of the file calculated using notional hourly rates (including counsel's fees at the standard rate, and travel, but excluding disbursements) (Specification, para.9.79) and (b) the total of all 'additional' fixed fee payments plus three times the 'normal' fee levels. The example calculation given in the Specification for a tribunal file with two adjourned hearings is (para.9.82):

$$(3 \times (L1 + L2 + L3)) + (2 \times \text{adjourned hearing fee})$$

Each escape fee case will be scrutinised by an LAA auditor to ensure that costs have been claimed correctly, which may reduce the value of the file to below the escape fee case level. There is an appeals procedure (see Specification, chapter 6).

The Remuneration Regulations contain the mental health fixed fees (Sched.1, Part 1, Tables 5(a) and (b)), and the hourly rates for Legal Help (Sched.1, Part 2, Table 7(a)), representation in mental health (tribunal) proceedings (Sched.1, Part 2, Table 8(d)), and licensed work (Sched.1, Part 3, Table 10(a)).

14.8.2 Experts' fees

The maximum hourly rates for experts' fees are set out in the Remuneration Regulations (Sched.5). There are no 'global' maximum figures for experts, only for their hourly rates.

In relation to the funding of an expert service of a type not listed in the Remuneration Regulations (such as social workers), the LAA will have regard to the listed rates and may require a number of quotes for provision of the service to be submitted (Sched.5, para.3).

14.9 CONCLUSION

This chapter has given a brief overview of the current Legal Aid arrangements relating to advice and representation in mental health cases. However, it is only possible to give a summary of the funding regime, which is complex and subject to interpretation and application of the Specification depending on the particular circumstances of the case. Further guidance, for example on the application of matter start rules, can be obtained from the LAA Mental Health Unit in Liverpool. Contact details are given in **Appendix I**.

Mental Health Act 1983, ss.72–77

PART V   MENTAL HEALTH TRIBUNALS

Discharge of patients

72   Powers of tribunals

(1)   Where application is made to the appropriate tribunal by or in respect of a patient who is liable to be detained under this Act or is a community patient, the tribunal may in any case direct that the patient be discharged, and –

    (a)   the tribunal shall direct the discharge of a patient liable to be detained under section 2 above if it is not satisfied –

        (i)   that he is then suffering from mental disorder or from mental disorder of a nature or degree which warrants his detention in a hospital for assessment (or for assessment followed by medical treatment) for at least a limited period; or

        (ii)   that his detention as aforesaid is justified in the interests of his own health or safety or with a view to the protection of other persons;

    (b)   the tribunal shall direct the discharge of a patient liable to be detained otherwise than under section 2 above if it is not satisfied –

        (i)   that he is then suffering from mental disorder or from mental disorder of a nature or degree which makes it appropriate for him to be liable to be detained in a hospital for medical treatment; or

        (ii)   that it is necessary for the health of safety of the patient or for the protection of other persons that he should receive such treatment; or

        (iia)   that appropriate medical treatment is available for him; or

        (iii)   in the case of an application by virtue of paragraph (g) of section 66(1) above, that the patient, if released, would be likely to act in a manner dangerous to other persons or to himself.

    (c)   the tribunal shall direct the discharge of a community patient if it is not satisfied –

        (i)   that he is then suffering from mental disorder or mental disorder of a nature or degree which makes it appropriate for him to receive medical treatment; or

        (ii)   that it is necessary for his health or safety or for the protection of other persons that he should receive such treatment; or

        (iii)   that it is necessary that the responsible clinician should be able to exercise the power under section 17E(1) above to recall the patient to hospital; or

        (iv)   that appropriate medical treatment is available for him; or

        (v)   in the case of an application by virtue of paragraph (g) of section 66(1) above, that the patient, if discharged, would be likely to act in a manner dangerous to other persons or to himself.

(1A)   In determining whether the criterion in subsection (1)(c)(iii) above is met, the tribunal shall, in particular, consider, having regard to the patient's history of mental disorder and any other relevant factors, what risk there would be of a deterioration of the patient's condition if he were to continue not to be detained in a hospital (as a result, for example, of his refusing or neglecting to receive the medical treatment he requires for his mental disorder).

(2)   [. . .]

(3)   A tribunal may under subsection (1) above direct the discharge of a patient on a future date specified in the direction; and where a tribunal does not direct the discharge of a patient under that subsection the tribunal may –

(a)   with a view to facilitating his discharge on a future date, recommend that he be granted leave of absence or transferred to another hospital or into guardianship; and

(b)   further consider his case in the event of any such recommendation not being complied with.

(3A)   Subsection (1) above does not require a tribunal to direct the discharge of a patient just because it thinks it might be appropriate for the patient to be discharged (subject to the possibility of recall) under a community treatment order; and a tribunal –

(a)   may recommend that the responsible clinician consider whether to make a community treatment order; and

(b)   may (but need not) further consider the patient's case if the responsible clinician does not make an order.

(4)   Where application is made to the appropriate tribunal by or in respect of a patient who is subject to guardianship under this Act, the tribunal may in any case direct that the patient be discharged, and shall so direct if it is satisfied –

(a)   that he is not then suffering from mental disorder; or

(b)   that it is not necessary in the interests of the welfare of the patient, or for the protection of other persons, that the patient should remain under such guardianship.

(4A)   [. . .]

(5)   [. . .]

(6)   Subsections (1) to (4) above apply in relation to references to the appropriate tribunal as they apply in relation to applications made to the appropriate tribunal by or in respect of a patient.

(7)   Subsection (1) above shall not apply in the case of a restricted patient except as provided in sections 73 and 74 below.

73   Power to discharge restricted patients

(1)   Where an application to the appropriate tribunal is made by a restricted patient who is subject to a restriction order, or where the case of such a patient is referred to the appropriate tribunal, the tribunal shall direct the absolute discharge of the patient if –

(a)   the tribunal is not satisfied as to the matters mentioned in paragraph (b)(i), (ii) or (iia) of section 72(1) above; and

(b)   the tribunal is satisfied that it is not appropriate for the patient to remain liable to be recalled to hospital for further treatment.

(2)   Where in the case of any such patient as is mentioned in subsection (1) above –

(a)   paragraph (a) of that subsection applies; but
(b)   paragraph (b) of that subsection does not apply,

the tribunal shall direct the conditional discharge of the patient.

(3)   Where a patient is absolutely discharged under this section he shall thereupon cease to be liable to be detained by virtue of the relevant hospital order, and the restriction order shall cease to have effect accordingly.

(4)   Where a patient is conditionally discharged under this section –

(a)   he may be recalled by the Secretary of State under subsection (3) of section 42 above as if he had been conditionally discharged under subsection (2) of that section; and
(b)   the patient shall comply with such conditions (if any) as may be imposed at the time of discharge by the tribunal or at any subsequent time by the Secretary of State.

(5)   The Secretary of State may from time to time vary any condition imposed (whether by the tribunal or by him) under subsection (4) above.

(6)   Where a restriction order in respect of a patient ceases to have effect after he has been conditionally discharged under this section the patient shall, unless previously recalled, be deemed to be absolutely discharged on the date when the order ceases to have effect and shall cease to be liable to be detained by virtue of the relevant hospital order.

(7)   A tribunal may defer a direction for the conditional discharge of a patient until such arrangements as appear to the tribunal to be necessary for that purpose have been made to its satisfaction; and where by virtue of any such deferment no direction has been given on an application or reference before the time when the patient's case comes before the tribunal on a subsequent application or reference, the previous application or reference shall be treated as one on which no direction under this section can be given.

(8)   This section is without prejudice to section 42 above.

74   Restricted patients subject to restriction directions

(1)   Where an application to the appropriate tribunal is made by a restricted patient who is subject to a limitation direction or a restriction direction, or where the case of such a patient is referred to the appropriate tribunal, the tribunal –

(a)   shall notify the Secretary of State whether, in its opinion, the patient would, if subject to a restriction order, be entitled to be absolutely or conditionally discharged under section 73 above; and
(b)   if the tribunal notifies him that the patient would be entitled to be conditionally discharged, may recommend that in the event of his not being discharged under this section he should continue to be detained in hospital.

(2)   If in the case of a patient not falling within subsection (4) below –

(a)   the tribunal notifies the Secretary of State that the patient would be entitled to be absolutely or conditionally discharged; and
(b)   within the period of 90 days beginning with the date of that notification the Secretary of State gives notice to the tribunal that the patient may be so discharged,

the tribunal shall direct the absolute or, as the case may be, the conditional discharge of the patient.

(3)   Where a patient continues to be liable to be detained in a hospital at the end of the period referred to in subsection (2)(b) above because the Secretary of State has not given the notice there mentioned, the managers of the hospital shall, unless the tribunal has made a recommendation under subsection (1)(b) above, transfer the patient to a prison or other institution in which he might have been detained if he had not been removed to hospital, there to be dealt with as if he had not been so removed.

(4)   If, in the case of a patient who is subject to a transfer direction under section 48 above, the tribunal notifies the Secretary of State that the patient would be entitled to be absolutely or conditionally discharged, the Secretary of State shall, unless the tribunal has made a recommendation under subsection (1)(b) above, by warrant direct that the patient be remitted to a prison or other institution in which he might have been detained if he had not been removed to hospital, there to be dealt with as if he had not been so removed.

(5)   Where a patient is transferred or remitted under subsection (3) or (4) above the relevant hospital direction and the limitation direction or, as the case may be, the relevant transfer direction and the restriction direction shall cease to have effect on his arrival in the prison or other institution.

(5A)   Where the tribunal has made a recommendation under subsection (1)(b) above in the case of a patient who is subject to a restriction direction or a limitation direction –

   (a)   the fact that the restriction direction or limitation direction remains in force does not prevent the making of any application or reference to the Parole Board by or in respect of him or the exercise by him of any power to require the Secretary of State to refer his case to the Parole Board, and

   (b)   if the Parole Board make a direction or recommendation by virtue of which the patient would become entitled to be released (whether unconditionally or on licence) from any prison or other institution in which he might have been detained if he had not been removed to hospital, the restriction direction or limitation direction shall cease to have effect at the time when he would become entitled to be so released.

(6)   Subsections (3) to (8) of section 73 above shall have effect in relation to this section as they have effect in relation to that section, taking references to the relevant hospital order and the restriction order as references to the hospital direction and the limitation direction or, as the case may be, to the transfer direction and the restriction direction.

(7)   This section is without prejudice to sections 50 to 53 above in their application to patients who are not discharged under this section.

75   Applications and references concerning conditionally discharged restricted patients

(1)   Where a restricted patient has been conditionally discharged under section 42(2), 73 or 74 above and is subsequently recalled to hospital –

   (a)   the Secretary of State shall, within one month of the day on which the patient returns or is returned to hospital, refer his case to the appropriate tribunal; and

   (b)   section 70 above shall apply to the patient as if the relevant hospital order, hospital direction or transfer direction had been made on that day.

(2)   Where a restricted patient has been conditionally discharged as aforesaid but has not been recalled to hospital he may apply to the appropriate tribunal –

   (a)   in the period between the expiration of 12 months and the expiration of two years beginning with the date on which he was conditionally discharged; and

(b) in any subsequent period of two years.

(3) Sections 73 and 74 above shall not apply to an application under subsection (2) above but on any such application the tribunal may –

 (a) vary any condition to which the patient is subject in connection with his discharge or impose any condition which might have been imposed in connection therewith; or

 (b) direct that the restriction order, limitation direction or restriction direction to which he is subject shall cease to have effect;

and if the tribunal gives a direction under paragraph (b) above the patient shall cease to be liable to be detained by virtue of the relevant hospital order, hospital direction or transfer direction.

General

76 Visiting and examination of patients

(1) For the purpose of advising whether an application to the appropriate tribunal should be made by or in respect of a patient who is liable to be detained or subject to guardianship under Part II of this Act or a community patient, or of furnishing information as to the condition of a patient for the purposes of such an application, any registered medical practitioner or approved clinician authorised by or on behalf of the patient or other person who is entitled to make or has made the application –

 (a) may at any reasonable time visit the patient and examine him in private, and

 (b) may require the production of and inspect any records relating to the detention or treatment of the patient in any hospital or to any after-care services provided for the patient under section 117 below.

(2) Section 32 above shall apply for the purposes of this section as it applies for the purposes of Part II of this Act.

77 General provisions concerning tribunal applications

(1) No application shall be made to the appropriate tribunal by or in respect of a patient under this Act except in such cases and at such times as are expressly provided by this Act.

(2) Where under this Act any person is authorised to make an application to the appropriate tribunal within a specified period, not more than one such application shall be made by that person within that period but for that purpose there shall be disregarded any application which is withdrawn in accordance with Tribunal Procedure Rules or rules made under section 78 below.

(3) Subject to subsection (4) below an application to a tribunal authorised to be made by or in respect of a patient under this Act shall be made by notice in writing addressed –

 (a) in the case of a patient who is liable to be detained in a hospital, to the First-tier Tribunal where that hospital is in England and to the Mental Health Review Tribunal for Wales where that hospital is in Wales;

 (b) in the case of a community patient, to the First-tier Tribunal where the responsible hospital is in England and to the Mental Health Review Tribunal for Wales where that hospital is in Wales;

 (c) in the case of a patient subject to guardianship, to the First-tier Tribunal where the patient resides in England and to the Mental Health Review Tribunal for Wales where the patient resides in Wales.

(4)   Any application under section 75(2) above shall be made to the First-tier Tribunal where the patient resides in England and to the Mental Health Review Tribunal for Wales where the patient resides in Wales.

Tribunal Procedure (First-tier Tribunal) (Health, Education and Social Care Chamber) Rules 2008, SI 2008/2699

PART 1   INTRODUCTION

1.   Citation, commencement, application and interpretation

(1)   These Rules may be cited as the Tribunal Procedure (First-tier Tribunal) (Health, Education and Social Care Chamber) Rules 2008 and come into force on 3rd November 2008.

(2)   These Rules apply to proceedings before the Health, Education and Social Care Chamber of the First-tier Tribunal.

(3)   In these Rules –

"the 2007 Act" means the Tribunals, Courts and Enforcement Act 2007;
"applicant" means a person who –

(a)   starts Tribunal proceedings, whether by making an application, an appeal, a claim or a reference;

(b)   makes an application to the Tribunal for leave to start such proceedings; or

(c)   is substituted as an applicant under rule 9(1) (substitution and addition of parties);

"childcare provider" means a person who is a childminder or provides day care as defined in section 19 of the Children and Families (Wales) Measure 2010, or a person who provides childcare as defined in section 18 of the Childcare Act 2006;
"disability discrimination in schools case" means proceedings concerning disability discrimination in the education of a child or related matters;
"dispose of proceedings" includes, unless indicated otherwise, disposing of a part of the proceedings;
"document" means anything in which information is recorded in any form, and an obligation under these Rules or any practice direction or direction to provide or allow access to a document or a copy of a document for any purpose means, unless the Tribunal directs otherwise, an obligation to provide or allow access to such document or copy in a legible form or in a form which can be readily made into a legible form;
"health service case" means a case under the National Health Service Act 2006, the National Health Service (Wales) Act 2006, regulations made under either of those Acts, or regulations having effect as if made under either of those Acts by reason of section 4 of and Schedule 2 to the National Health Service (Consequential Provisions) Act 2006;

"hearing" means an oral hearing and includes a hearing conducted in whole or in part by video link, telephone or other means of instantaneous two-way electronic communication;

"legal representative" means a person who, for the purposes of the Legal Services Act 2007, is an authorised person in relation to an activity which constitutes the exercise of a right of audience or the conduct of litigation within the meaning of that Act;

"mental health case" means proceedings brought under the Mental Health Act 1983 or paragraph 5(2) of the Schedule to the Repatriation of Prisoners Act 1984;

"nearest relative" has the meaning set out in section 26 of the Mental Health Act 1983;

"party" means –

(a)   in a mental health case, the patient, the responsible authority, the Secretary of State (if the patient is a restricted patient or in a reference under rule 32(8) (seeking approval under section 86 of the Mental Health Act 1983)), and any other person who starts a mental health case by making an application;

(b)   in any other case, a person who is an applicant or respondent in proceedings before the Tribunal or, if the proceedings have been concluded, a person who was an applicant or respondent when the Tribunal finally disposed of all issues in the proceedings;

"patient" means the person who is the subject of a mental health case;

"practice direction" means a direction given under section 23 of the 2007 Act;

"respondent" means –

(a)   in an appeal against an order made by a justice of the peace under section 34 of the Children and Families (Wales) Measure 2010, section 20 of the Care Standards Act 2000 or section 72 of the Childcare Act 2006, the person who applied to the justice of the peace for the order;

(b)   in an appeal against any other decision, the person who made the decision;

(c)   in proceedings on a claim under section 28I of the Disability Discrimination Act 19957, the body responsible for the school as determined in accordance with paragraph 1 of Schedule 4A to that Act or, if the claim concerns the residual duties of a local education authority under section 28F of that Act, that local education authority;

(d)   in proceedings on an application under section 4(2) of the Protection of Children Act 1999 or section 86(2) of the Care Standards Act 2000, the Secretary of State;

(da) in an application for, or for a review of, a stop order under the National Health Service (Optical Charges and Payments) Regulations 1997 –

(i) the supplier, where the Secretary of State is the applicant;
(ii) the Secretary of State, where the supplier is the applicant;

(db) in any other health service case –

(i)   the practitioner, performer or person against whom the application is made, where a Primary Care Trust or Local Health Board is, or is deemed to be, the applicant;

(ii) the Primary Care Trust or Local Health Board that served the notice, obtained the order or confirmation of the order, where any other person is the applicant; or

(e)   a person substituted or added as a respondent under rule 9 (substitution and addition of parties);

"responsible authority" means –

(a) in relation to a patient detained under the Mental Health Act 1983 in a hospital within the meaning of Part 2 of that Act, the managers (as defined in section 145 of that Act);

(b) in relation to a patient subject to guardianship, the responsible local social services authority (as defined in section 34(3) of the Mental Health Act 1983);

(c) in relation to a community patient, the managers of the responsible hospital (as defined in section 145 of the Mental Health Act 1983);

(d) in relation to a patient subject to after-care under supervision, the Primary Care Trust or Local Health Board which has the duty to provide after-care for the patient.

"restricted patient" has the meaning set out in section 79(1) of the Mental Health Act 1983;

"special educational needs case" means proceedings concerning the education of a child who has or may have special educational needs;

"Suspension Regulations" means regulations which provide for a right of appeal against a decision to suspend, or not to lift the suspension of, a person's registration as a childcare provider;

"Tribunal" means the First-tier Tribunal;

"working day" means any day except a Saturday or Sunday, Christmas Day, Good Friday or a bank holiday under section 1 of the Banking and Financial Dealings Act 1971.

2. Overriding objective and parties' obligation to co-operate with the Tribunal

(1) The overriding objective of these Rules is to enable the Tribunal to deal with cases fairly and justly.

(2) Dealing with a case fairly and justly includes –

(a) dealing with the case in ways which are proportionate to the importance of the case, the complexity of the issues, the anticipated costs and the resources of the parties;

(b) avoiding unnecessary formality and seeking flexibility in the proceedings;

(c) ensuring, so far as practicable, that the parties are able to participate fully in the proceedings;

(d) using any special expertise of the Tribunal effectively; and

(e) avoiding delay, so far as compatible with proper consideration of the issues.

(3) The Tribunal must seek to give effect to the overriding objective when it –

(a) exercises any power under these Rules; or

(b) interprets any rule or practice direction.

(4) Parties must –

(a) help the Tribunal to further the overriding objective; and

(b) co-operate with the Tribunal generally.

3. Alternative dispute resolution and arbitration

(1) The Tribunal should seek, where appropriate –

(a) to bring to the attention of the parties the availability of any appropriate alternative procedure for the resolution of the dispute; and

291

(b)   if the parties wish and provided that it is compatible with the overriding objective, to facilitate the use of the procedure.

(2)   Part 1 of the Arbitration Act 1996 does not apply to proceedings before the Tribunal.

PART 2   GENERAL POWERS AND PROVISIONS

4. Delegation to staff

(1)   Staff appointed under section 40(1) of the 2007 Act (tribunal staff and services) may, with the approval of the Senior President of Tribunals, carry out functions of a judicial nature permitted or required to be done by the Tribunal.

(2)   The approval referred to at paragraph (1) may apply generally to the carrying out of specified functions by members of staff of a specified description in specified circumstances.

(3)   Within 14 days after the date on which the Tribunal sends notice of a decision made by a member of staff under paragraph (1) to a party, that party may apply in writing to the Tribunal for that decision to be considered afresh by a judge.

5. Case management powers

(1)   Subject to the provisions of the 2007 Act and any other enactment, the Tribunal may regulate its own procedure.

(2)   The Tribunal may give a direction in relation to the conduct or disposal of proceedings at any time, including a direction amending, suspending or setting aside an earlier direction.

(3)   In particular, and without restricting the general powers in paragraphs (1) and (2), the Tribunal may –

(a)   extend or shorten the time for complying with any rule, practice direction or direction, unless such extension or shortening would conflict with a provision of another enactment containing a time limit;

(b)   consolidate or hear together two or more sets of proceedings or parts of proceedings raising common issues, or treat a case as a lead case;

(c)   permit or require a party to amend a document;

(d)   permit or require a party or another person to provide documents, information or submissions to the Tribunal or a party;

(e)   deal with an issue in the proceedings as a preliminary issue;

(f)   hold a hearing to consider any matter, including a case management issue;

(g)   decide the form of any hearing;

(h)   adjourn or postpone a hearing;

(i)   require a party to produce a bundle for a hearing;

(j)   stay proceedings;

(k)   transfer proceedings to another court or tribunal if that other court or tribunal has jurisdiction in relation to the proceedings and –

(i)   because of a change of circumstances since the proceedings were started, the Tribunal no longer has jurisdiction in relation to the proceedings; or

(ii)   the Tribunal considers that the other court or tribunal is a more appropriate forum for the determination of the case; or

(l)   suspend the effect of its own decision pending the determination by the Tribunal or the Upper Tribunal of an application for permission to appeal against, and any appeal or review of, that decision.

6. Procedure for applying for and giving directions

(1)   The Tribunal may give a direction on the application of one or more of the parties or on its own initiative.

(2)   An application for a direction may be made –

    (a)   by sending or delivering a written application to the Tribunal; or

    (b)   orally during the course of a hearing.

(3)   An application for a direction must include the reason for making that application.

(4)   Unless the Tribunal considers that there is good reason not to do so, the Tribunal must send written notice of any direction to every party and to any other person affected by the direction.

(5)   If a party, or any other person given notice of the direction under paragraph (4), wishes to challenge a direction which the Tribunal has given, they may do so by applying for another direction which amends, suspends or sets aside the first direction.

7. Failure to comply with rules etc.

(1)   An irregularity resulting from a failure to comply with any requirement in these Rules, a practice direction or a direction, does not of itself render void the proceedings or any step taken in the proceedings.

(2)   If a party has failed to comply with a requirement in these Rules, a practice direction or a direction, the Tribunal may take such action as it considers just, which may include –

    (a)   waiving the requirement;

    (b)   requiring the failure to be remedied;

    (c)   exercising its power under rule 8 (striking out a party's case);

    (d)   exercising its power under paragraph (3); or

    (e)   except in mental health cases, restricting a party's participation in the proceedings.

(3)   The Tribunal may refer to the Upper Tribunal, and ask the Upper Tribunal to exercise its power under section 25 of the 2007 Act in relation to, any failure by a person to comply with a requirement imposed by the Tribunal –

    (a)   to attend at any place for the purpose of giving evidence;

    (b)   otherwise to make themselves available to give evidence;

    (c)   to swear an oath in connection with the giving of evidence;

    (d)   to give evidence as a witness;

    (e)   to produce a document; or

    (f)   to facilitate the inspection of a document or any other thing (including any premises).

8. Striking out a party's case

(1)   With the exception of paragraph (3), this rule does not apply to mental health cases.

(2)   The proceedings, or the appropriate part of them, will automatically be struck out if the applicant has failed to comply with a direction that stated that failure by the applicant to comply with the direction would lead to the striking out of the proceedings or that part of them.

(3)   The Tribunal must strike out the whole or a part of the proceedings if the Tribunal –

(a) does not have jurisdiction in relation to the proceedings or that part of them; and

(b) does not exercise its power under rule 5(3)(k)(i) (transfer to another court or tribunal) in relation to the proceedings or that part of them.

(4) The Tribunal may strike out the whole or a part of the proceedings if –

(a) the applicant has failed to comply with a direction which stated that failure by the applicant to comply with the direction could lead to the striking out of the proceedings or part of them;

(b) the applicant has failed to co-operate with the Tribunal to such an extent that the Tribunal cannot deal with the proceedings fairly and justly; or

(c) the Tribunal considers there is no reasonable prospect of the applicant's case, or part of it, succeeding.

(5) The Tribunal may not strike out the whole or a part of the proceedings under paragraph (3) or (4)(b) or (c) without first giving the applicant an opportunity to make representations in relation to the proposed striking out.

(6) If the proceedings, or part of them, have been struck out under paragraph (2) or (4)(a), the applicant may apply for the proceedings, or part of them, to be reinstated.

(7) An application under paragraph (6) must be made in writing and received by the Tribunal within 28 days after the date on which the Tribunal sent notification of the striking out to that party.

(8) This rule applies to a respondent as it applies to an applicant except that –

(a) a reference to the striking out of the proceedings is to be read as a reference to the barring of the respondent from taking further part in the proceedings; and

(b) a reference to an application for the reinstatement of proceedings which have been struck out is to be read as a reference to an application for the lifting of the bar on the respondent from taking further part in the proceedings.

(9) If a respondent has been barred from taking further part in proceedings under this rule and that bar has not been lifted, the Tribunal need not consider any response or other submission made by that respondent and may summarily determine any or all issues against that respondent.

9. Substitution and addition of parties

(1) The Tribunal may give a direction substituting a party if –

(a) the wrong person has been named as a party; or

(b) the substitution has become necessary because of a change in circumstances since the start of proceedings.

(2) The Tribunal may give a direction adding a person to the proceedings as a respondent.

(3) If the Tribunal gives a direction under paragraph (1) or (2) it may give such consequential directions as it considers appropriate.

10. Orders for costs

(1) Subject to paragraph (2), the Tribunal may make an order in respect of costs only –

(a) under section 29(4) of the 2007 Act (wasted costs); or

(b) if the Tribunal considers that a party or its representative has acted unreasonably in bringing, defending or conducting the proceedings.

(2)   The Tribunal may not make an order under paragraph (1)(b) in mental health cases.

(3)   The Tribunal may make an order in respect of costs on an application or on its own initiative.

(4)   A person making an application for an order under this rule must –

(a)   send or deliver a written application to the Tribunal and to the person against whom it is proposed that the order be made; and

(b)   send or deliver a schedule of the costs claimed with the application.

(5)   An application for an order under paragraph (1) may be made at any time during the proceedings but may not be made later than 14 days after the date on which the Tribunal sends the decision notice recording the decision which finally disposes of all issues in the proceedings.

(6)   The Tribunal may not make an order under paragraph (1) against a person (the "paying person") without first –

(a)   giving that person an opportunity to make representations; and

(b)   if the paying person is an individual, considering that person's financial means.

(7)   The amount of costs to be paid under an order under paragraph (1) may be ascertained by –

(a)   summary assessment by the Tribunal;

(b)   agreement of a specified sum by the paying person and the person entitled to receive the costs ("the receiving person"); or

(c)   assessment of the whole or a specified part of the costs incurred by the receiving person, if not agreed.

(8)   Following an order for assessment under paragraph (7)(c), the paying person or the receiving person may apply to a county court for a detailed assessment of costs in accordance with the Civil Procedure Rules 1998 on the standard basis or, if specified in the order, on the indemnity basis.

11.   Representatives

(1)   A party may appoint a representative (whether a legal representative or not) to represent that party in the proceedings.

(2)   If a party appoints a representative, that party (or the representative if the representative is a legal representative) must send or deliver to the Tribunal and to each other party written notice of the representative's name and address.

(3)   Anything permitted or required to be done by a party under these Rules, a practice direction or a direction may be done by the representative of that party, except –

(a)   signing a witness statement; or

(b)   signing an application notice under rule 20 (the application notice) if the representative is not a legal representative.

(4)   A person who receives due notice of the appointment of a representative –

(a)   must provide to the representative any document which is required to be provided to the represented party, and need not provide that document to the represented party; and

(b)   may assume that the representative is and remains authorised as such until they receive written notification that this is not so from the representative or the represented party.

(5)   At a hearing a party may be accompanied by another person whose name and

address has not been notified under paragraph (2) but who, subject to paragraph (8) and with the permission of the Tribunal, may act as a representative or otherwise assist in presenting the party's case at the hearing.

(6) Paragraphs (2) to (4) do not apply to a person who accompanies a party under paragraph (5).

(7) In a mental health case, if the patient has not appointed a representative, the Tribunal may appoint a legal representative for the patient where –

   (a) the patient has stated that they do not wish to conduct their own case or that they wish to be represented; or

   (b) the patient lacks the capacity to appoint a representative but the Tribunal believes that it is in the patient's best interests for the patient to be represented.

(8) In a mental health case a party may not appoint as a representative, or be represented or assisted at a hearing by –

   (a) a person liable to be detained or subject to guardianship or after-care under supervision, or who is a community patient, under the Mental Health Act 1983; or

   (b) a person receiving treatment for mental disorder at the same hospital as the patient.

12. Calculating time

(1) An act required by these Rules, a practice direction or a direction to be done on or by a particular day must be done by 5pm on that day.

(2) If the time specified by these Rules, a practice direction or a direction for doing any act ends on a day other than a working day, the act is done in time if it is done on the next working day.

(3) In a special educational needs case or a disability discrimination in schools case –

   (a) if the time for starting proceedings by providing the application notice to the Tribunal under rule 20 (the application notice) ends on a day from 25th December to 1st January inclusive, or on any day in August, the application notice is provided in time if it is provided to the Tribunal on the first working day after 1st January or 31st August, as appropriate; and

   (b) the days from 25th December to 1st January inclusive and any day in August must not be counted when calculating the time by which any other act must be done.

(4) Paragraph (3)(b) does not apply where the Tribunal directs that an act must be done by or on a specified date.

13. Sending and delivery of documents

(1) Any document to be provided to the Tribunal under these Rules, a practice direction or a direction must be –

   (a) sent by pre-paid post or delivered by hand to the address specified for the proceedings;

   (b) sent by fax to the number specified for the proceedings; or

   (c) sent or delivered by such other method as the Tribunal may permit or direct.

(1A) If the Tribunal permits or directs documents to be provided to it by email, the requirement for a signature on applications or references under rules 20(2), 22(4)(a) or 32(1)(b) may be satisfied by a typed instead of a handwritten signature.

(2)   Subject to paragraph (3), if a party provides a fax number, email address or other details for the electronic transmission of documents to them, that party must accept delivery of documents by that method.

(3)   If a party informs the Tribunal and all other parties that a particular form of communication, other than pre-paid post or delivery by hand, should not be used to provide documents to that party, that form of communication must not be so used.

(4)   If the Tribunal or a party sends a document to a party or the Tribunal by email or any other electronic means of communication, the recipient may request that the sender provide a hard copy of the document to the recipient. The recipient must make such a request as soon as reasonably practicable after receiving the document electronically.

(5)   The Tribunal and each party may assume that the address provided by a party or its representative is and remains the address to which documents should be sent or delivered until receiving written notification to the contrary.

14. Use of documents and information

(1)   The Tribunal may make an order prohibiting the disclosure or publication of –

(a)   specified documents or information relating to the proceedings; or

(b)   any matter likely to lead members of the public to identify any person whom the Tribunal considers should not be identified.

(2)   The Tribunal may give a direction prohibiting the disclosure of a document or information to a person if –

(a)   the Tribunal is satisfied that such disclosure would be likely to cause that person or some other person serious harm; and

(b)   the Tribunal is satisfied, having regard to the interests of justice, that it is proportionate to give such a direction.

(3)   If a party ("the first party") considers that the Tribunal should give a direction under paragraph (2) prohibiting the disclosure of a document or information to another party ("the second party"), the first party must –

(a)   exclude the relevant document or information from any documents that will be provided to the second party; and

(b)   provide to the Tribunal the excluded document or information, and the reason for its exclusion, so that the Tribunal may decide whether the document or information should be disclosed to the second party or should be the subject of a direction under paragraph (2).

(4)   The Tribunal must conduct proceedings as appropriate in order to give effect to a direction given under paragraph (2).

(5)   If the Tribunal gives a direction under paragraph (2) which prevents disclosure to a party who has appointed a representative, the Tribunal may give a direction that the documents or information be disclosed to that representative if the Tribunal is satisfied that –

(a)   disclosure to the representative would be in the interests of the party; and

(b)   the representative will act in accordance with paragraph (6).

(6)   Documents or information disclosed to a representative in accordance with a direction under paragraph (5) must not be disclosed either directly or indirectly to any other person without the Tribunal's consent.

(7)   Unless the Tribunal gives a direction to the contrary, information about mental health cases and the names of any persons concerned in such cases must not be made public.

15. Evidence and submissions

(1)   Without restriction on the general powers in rule 5(1) and (2) (case management powers), the Tribunal may give directions as to –

   (a)   issues on which it requires evidence or submissions;
   (b)   the nature of the evidence or submissions it requires;
   (c)   whether the parties are permitted or required to provide expert evidence, and if so whether the parties must jointly appoint a single expert to provide such evidence;
   (d)   any limit on the number of witnesses whose evidence a party may put forward, whether in relation to a particular issue or generally;
   (e)   the manner in which any evidence or submissions are to be provided, which may include a direction for them to be given –

      (i)   orally at a hearing; or
      (ii)   by written submissions or witness statement; and

   (f)   the time at which any evidence or submissions are to be provided.

(2)   The Tribunal may –

   (a)   admit evidence whether or not –

      (i)   the evidence would be admissible in a civil trial in England and Wales; or
      (ii)   the evidence was available to a previous decision maker; or

   (b)   exclude evidence that would otherwise be admissible where –

      (i)   the evidence was not provided within the time allowed by a direction or a practice direction;
      (ii)   the evidence was otherwise provided in a manner that did not comply with a direction or a practice direction; or
      (iii) it would otherwise be unfair to admit the evidence.

(3)   The Tribunal may consent to a witness giving, or require any witness to give, evidence on oath, and may administer an oath for that purpose.

(4)   In a special educational needs case the Tribunal may require –

   (a)   the parents of the child, or any other person with care of the child or parental responsibility for the child (as defined in section 3 of the Children Act 1989), to make the child available for examination or assessment by a suitably qualified professional person; or
   (b)   the person responsible for a school or educational setting to allow a suitably qualified professional person to have access to the school or educational setting for the purpose of assessing the child or the provision made, or to be made, for the child.

(5)   The Tribunal may consider a failure by a party to comply with a requirement made under paragraph (4), in the absence of any good reason for such failure, as a failure to co-operate with the Tribunal, which could lead to a result which is adverse to that party's case.

16. Summoning of witnesses and orders to answer questions or produce documents

(1)   On the application of a party or on its own initiative, the Tribunal may –

    (a)   by summons require any person to attend as a witness at a hearing at the time and place specified in the summons; or

    (b)   order any person to answer any questions or produce any documents in that person's possession or control which relate to any issue in the proceedings.

(2)   A summons under paragraph (1)(a) must –

    (a)   give the person required to attend 14 days' notice of the hearing, or such shorter period as the Tribunal may direct; and

    (b)   where the person is not a party, make provision for the person's necessary expenses of attendance to be paid, and state who is to pay them.

(3)   No person may be compelled to give any evidence or produce any document that the person could not be compelled to give or produce on a trial of an action in a court of law.

(4)   A summons or order under this rule must –

    (a)   state that the person on whom the requirement is imposed may apply to the Tribunal to vary or set aside the summons or order, if they have not had an opportunity to object to it; and

    (b)   state the consequences of failure to comply with the summons or order.

17. Withdrawal

(1)   Subject to paragraphs (2) and (3), a party may give notice of the withdrawal of its case, or any part of it –

    (a)   at any time before a hearing to consider the disposal of the proceedings (or, if the Tribunal disposes of the proceedings without a hearing, before that disposal), by sending or delivering to the Tribunal a written notice of withdrawal; or

    (b)   orally at a hearing.

(2)   Notice of withdrawal will not take effect unless the Tribunal consents to the withdrawal except –

    (a)   in proceedings concerning the suitability of a person to work with children or vulnerable adults; or

    (b)   in proceedings started by a reference under section 67 or 71(1) of the Mental Health Act 1983.

(3)   A party which started a mental health case by making a reference to the Tribunal under section 68, 71(2) or 75(1) of the Mental Health Act 1983 may not withdraw its case.

(4)   A party which has withdrawn its case may apply to the Tribunal for the case to be reinstated.

(5)   An application under paragraph (4) must be made in writing and be received by the Tribunal within 28 days after –

    (a)   the date on which the Tribunal received the notice under paragraph (1)(a); or

    (b)   the date of the hearing at which the case was withdrawn orally under paragraph (1)(b).

(6)   The Tribunal must notify each party in writing of a withdrawal under this rule.

PART 3 PROCEEDINGS BEFORE THE TRIBUNAL OTHER THAN IN MENTAL HEALTH CASES

[*Omitted*]

PART 4 PROCEEDINGS BEFORE THE TRIBUNAL IN MENTAL HEALTH CASES

CHAPTER 1 Before the hearing

31. Application of Part 4

This Part applies only to mental health cases.

32. Procedure in mental health cases

(1)   An application or reference must be –

(a)   made in writing;

(b)   signed (in the case of an application, by the applicant or any person authorised by the applicant to do so); and

(c)   sent or delivered to the Tribunal so that it is received within the time specified in the Mental Health Act 1983 or the Repatriation of Prisoners Act 1984.

(2)   An application must, if possible, include –

(a)   the name, address and date of birth of the patient;

(b)   if the application is made by the patient's nearest relative, the name, address and relationship to the patient of the patient's nearest relative;

(c)   the provision under which the patient is detained, liable to be detained, subject to guardianship, or a community patient;

(d)   whether the person making the application has appointed a representative or intends to do so, and the name and address of any representative appointed;

(e)   the name and address of the responsible authority in relation to the patient.

(2A)   A reference must, if possible, include –

(a)   the name and address of the person or body making the reference;

(b)   the name, address and date of birth of the patient;

(c)   the name and address of any representative of the patient;

(d)   the provision under which the patient is detained, liable to be detained, subject to guardianship or a community patient (as the case may be);

(e)   whether the person or body making the reference has appointed a representative or intends to do so, and the name and address of any representative appointed;

(f)   if the reference is made by the Secretary of State, the name and address of the responsible authority in relation to the patient, or, in the case of a conditionally discharged patient, the name and address of the responsible clinician and any social supervisor in relation to the patient.

(3)   Subject to rule 14(2) (withholding evidence likely to cause harm), when the Tribunal receives a document from any party it must send a copy of that document to each other party.

(4)   If the patient is a conditionally discharged patient –

(a)   upon being notified by the Tribunal of an application, the Secretary of State must immediately provide to the Tribunal the names and addresses of the responsible clinician and any social supervisor in relation to the patient; and

(b)   upon being notified by the Tribunal of an application or reference, the responsible clinician and any social supervisor named by the Secretary of State under this rule must send or deliver the documents specified in the relevant practice direction to the Tribunal so that they are received by the Tribunal as soon as practicable and in any event within 3 weeks after the notification.

(5)   In proceedings under section 66(1)(a) of the Mental Health Act 1983 (application in respect of an admission for assessment), on the earlier of receipt of the copy of the application or a request from the Tribunal, the responsible authority must immediately send or deliver to the Tribunal a copy of –

(a)   the application for admission; and

(b)   the written medical recommendations on which that application was founded;

and must as soon as practicable send or deliver to the Tribunal the documents specified in the relevant practice direction.

(6)   If neither paragraph (4) nor (5) applies, the responsible authority must send or deliver the documents specified in the relevant practice direction to the Tribunal so that they are received by the Tribunal as soon as practicable and in any event within 3 weeks after the responsible authority made the reference or received a copy of the application or reference.

(7)   If the patient is a restricted patient, a person or body providing a document to the Tribunal in accordance with paragraph (4)(b) or (6) must also send or deliver a copy of the document to the Secretary of State.

(7A)   The Secretary of State must send the information specified in paragraph (7B) and any observations the Secretary of State wishes to make to the Tribunal as soon as practicable and in any event –

(a)   in proceedings under section 75(1) of the Mental Health Act 1983 (reference concerning a conditionally discharged restricted patient who has been recalled to hospital), within 2 weeks after the Secretary of State received the documents sent or delivered in accordance with paragraph (7);

(b)   otherwise, within 3 weeks after the Secretary of State received the documents sent or delivered in accordance with paragraph (7).

(7B)   The information specified in this paragraph is –

(a)   a summary of the offence or alleged offence that resulted in the patient being detained in hospital subject to a restriction order or, in the case of a patient subject to a restriction or limitation direction, that resulted in the patient being remanded in custody, kept in custody or sentenced to imprisonment;

(b)   a record of any other criminal convictions or findings recorded against the patient;

(c)   full details of the history of the patient's liability to detention under the Mental Health Act 1983 since the restrictions were imposed;

(d)   any further information in the Secretary of State's possession that the Secretary of State considers relevant to the proceedings.

(8)   If the Secretary of State wishes to seek the approval of the Tribunal under section 86(3) of the Mental Health Act 1983 (removal of alien patients), the Secretary of State must refer the patient's case to the Tribunal and the provisions of these Rules applicable to references under that Act apply to the proceedings.

33. Notice of proceedings to interested persons

When the Tribunal receives the information required by rule 32(4), (5) or (6) (procedure in mental health cases) the Tribunal must give notice of the proceedings –

(a)   where the patient is subject to the guardianship of a private guardian, to the guardian;

(b)   where there is an extant order of the Court of Protection, to that court;

(c)   subject to a patient with capacity to do so requesting otherwise, where any person other than the applicant is named by the authority as exercising the functions of the nearest relative, to that person;

(d)   where a health authority, Primary Care Trust, National Health Service trust or NHS foundation trust has a right to discharge the patient under the provisions of section 23(3) of the Mental Health Act 1983, to that authority or trust; and

(e)   to any other person who, in the opinion of the Tribunal, should have an opportunity of being heard.

34. Medical examination of the patient

(1)   Before a hearing to consider the disposal of a mental health case, an appropriate member of the Tribunal must, so far as practicable –

   (a)   examine the patient; and

   (b)   take such other steps as that member considers necessary to form an opinion of the patient's mental condition.

(2)   For the purposes of paragraph (1) that member may –

   (a)   examine the patient in private;

   (b)   examine records relating to the detention or treatment of the patient and any after-care services;

   (c)   take notes and copies of records for use in connection with the proceedings.

CHAPTER 2   Hearings

35. Restrictions on disposal of proceedings without a hearing

(1)   Subject to the following paragraphs, the Tribunal must hold a hearing before making a decision which disposes of proceedings.

(2)   This rule does not apply to a decision under Part 5.

(3)   The Tribunal may make a decision on a reference under section 68 of the Mental Health Act 1983 (duty of managers of hospitals to refer cases to tribunal) without a hearing if the patient is a community patient aged 18 or over and either –

   (a)   the patient has stated in writing that the patient does not wish to attend or be represented at a hearing of the reference and the Tribunal is satisfied that the patient has the capacity to decide whether or not to make that decision; or

   (b)   the patient's representative has stated in writing that the patient does not wish to attend or be represented at a hearing of the reference.

(4)   The Tribunal may dispose of proceedings without a hearing under rule 8(3) (striking out a party's case).

36. Entitlement to attend a hearing

(1)   Subject to rule 38(4) (exclusion of a person from a hearing), each party to proceedings is entitled to attend a hearing.

(2)   Any person notified of the proceedings under rule 33 (notice of proceedings to interested persons) may –

(a)   attend and take part in a hearing to such extent as the Tribunal considers proper; or

(b)   provide written submissions to the Tribunal.

37. Time and place of hearings

(1)   In proceedings under section 66(1)(a) of the Mental Health Act 1983 the hearing of the case must start within 7 days after the date on which the Tribunal received the application notice.

(2)   In proceedings under section 75(1) of that Act, the hearing of the case must start at least 5 weeks but no more than 8 weeks after the date on which the Tribunal received the reference.

(3)   The Tribunal must give reasonable notice of the time and place of the hearing (including any adjourned or postponed hearing), and any changes to the time and place of the hearing, to –

(a)   each party entitled to attend a hearing; and

(b)   any person who has been notified of the proceedings under rule 33 (notice of proceedings to interested persons).

(4)   The period of notice under paragraph (3) must be at least 14 days, except that –

(a)   in proceedings under section 66(1)(a) of the Mental Health Act 1983 the period must be at least 3 working days; and

(b)   the Tribunal may give shorter notice –

(i)   with the parties' consent; or

(ii)   in urgent or exceptional circumstances.

38. Public and private hearings

(1)   All hearings must be held in private unless the Tribunal considers that it is in the interests of justice for the hearing to be held in public.

(2)   If a hearing is held in public, the Tribunal may give a direction that part of the hearing is to be held in private.

(3)   Where a hearing, or part of it, is to be held in private, the Tribunal may determine who is permitted to attend the hearing or part of it.

(4)   The Tribunal may give a direction excluding from any hearing, or part of it –

(a)   any person whose conduct the Tribunal considers is disrupting or is likely to disrupt the hearing;

(b)   any person whose presence the Tribunal considers is likely to prevent another person from giving evidence or making submissions freely;

(c)   any person who the Tribunal considers should be excluded in order to give effect to a direction under rule 14(2) (withholding information likely to cause harm); or

(d)   any person where the purpose of the hearing would be defeated by the attendance of that person.

(5)   The Tribunal may give a direction excluding a witness from a hearing until that witness gives evidence.

39.   Hearings in a party's absence

(1)   Subject to paragraph (2), if a party fails to attend a hearing the Tribunal may proceed with the hearing if the Tribunal –

    (a)   is satisfied that the party has been notified of the hearing or that reasonable steps have been taken to notify the party of the hearing; and

    (b)   considers that it is in the interests of justice to proceed with the hearing.

(2)   The Tribunal may not proceed with a hearing in the absence of the patient unless –

    (a)   the requirements of rule 34 (medical examination of the patient) have been satisfied; and

    (b)   the Tribunal is satisfied that –

        (i)   the patient has decided not to attend the hearing; or

        (ii)   the patient is unable to attend the hearing for reasons of ill health.

40.   Power to pay allowances

The Tribunal may pay allowances in respect of travelling expenses, subsistence and loss of earnings to –

(a)   any person who attends a hearing as an applicant or a witness;

(b)   a patient who attends a hearing otherwise than as the applicant or a witness; and

(c)   any person (other than a legal representative) who attends as the representative of an applicant.

CHAPTER 3   Decisions

41.   Decisions

(1)   The Tribunal may give a decision orally at a hearing.

(2)   Subject to rule 14(2) (withholding information likely to cause harm), the Tribunal must provide to each party as soon as reasonably practicable after making a decision which finally disposes of all issues in the proceedings (except a decision under Part 5) –

    (a)   a decision notice stating the Tribunal's decision;

    (b)   written reasons for the decision; and

    (c)   notification of any right of appeal against the decision and the time within which, and the manner in which, such right of appeal may be exercised.

(3)   The documents and information referred to in paragraph (2) must –

    (a)   in proceedings under section 66(1)(a) of the Mental Health Act 1983, be provided at the hearing or sent within 3 working days after the hearing; and

    (b)   in other cases, be provided at the hearing or sent within 7 days after the hearing.

(4)   The Tribunal may provide written reasons for any decision to which paragraph (2) does not apply.

42. Provisional decisions

For the purposes of this Part and Parts 1, 2 and 5, a decision with recommendations under section 72(3)(a) or (3A)(a) of the Mental Health Act 1983(1) or a deferred direction for conditional discharge under section 73(7) of that Act is a decision which disposes of the proceedings.

PART 5   CORRECTING, SETTING ASIDE, REVIEWING AND APPEALING TRIBUNAL DECISIONS

43. Interpretation

In this Part –

"appeal" means the exercise of a right of appeal on a point of law under section 11 of the 2007 Act; and
"review" means the review of a decision by the Tribunal under section 9 of the 2007 Act.

44. Clerical mistakes and accidental slips or omissions

The Tribunal may at any time correct any clerical mistake or other accidental slip or omission in a decision, direction or any document produced by it, by –

(a)   sending notification of the amended decision or direction, or a copy of the amended document, to all parties; and
(b)   making any necessary amendment to any information published in relation to the decision, direction or document.

45. Setting aside a decision which disposes of proceedings

(1)   The Tribunal may set aside a decision which disposes of proceedings, or part of such a decision, and re-make the decision or the relevant part of it, if –

(a)   the Tribunal considers that it is in the interests of justice to do so; and
(b)   one or more of the conditions in paragraph (2) are satisfied.

(2)   The conditions are –

(a)   a document relating to the proceedings was not sent to, or was not received at an appropriate time by, a party or a party's representative;
(b)   a document relating to the proceedings was not sent to the Tribunal at an appropriate time;
(c)   a party, or a party's representative, was not present at a hearing related to the proceedings; or
(d)   there has been some other procedural irregularity in the proceedings.

(3)   A party applying for a decision, or part of a decision, to be set aside under paragraph (1) must make a written application to the Tribunal so that it is received no later than 28 days after the date on which the Tribunal sent notice of the decision to the party.

46. Application for permission to appeal

(1)   A person seeking permission to appeal must make a written application to the Tribunal for permission to appeal.
(2)   An application under paragraph (1) must be sent or delivered to the Tribunal so that it

is received no later than 28 days after the latest of the dates that the Tribunal sends to the person making the application –

(a)   written reasons for the decision;

(b)   notification of amended reasons for, or correction of, the decision following a review; or

(c)   notification that an application for the decision to be set aside has been unsuccessful.

(3)   The date in paragraph (2)(c) applies only if the application for the decision to be set aside was made within the time stipulated in rule 45 (setting aside a decision which disposes of proceedings) or any extension of that time granted by the Tribunal.

(4)   If the person seeking permission to appeal sends or delivers the application to the Tribunal later than the time required by paragraph (2) or by any extension of time under rule 5(3)(a) (power to extend time) –

(a)   the application must include a request for an extension of time and the reason why the application was not provided in time; and

(b)   unless the Tribunal extends time for the application under rule 5(3)(a) (power to extend time) the Tribunal must not admit the application.

(5)   An application under paragraph (1) must –

(a)   identify the decision of the Tribunal to which it relates;

(b)   identify the alleged error or errors of law in the decision; and

(c)   state the result the party making the application is seeking.

47.   Tribunal's consideration of application for permission to appeal

(1)   On receiving an application for permission to appeal the Tribunal must first consider, taking into account the overriding objective in rule 2, whether to review the decision in accordance with rule 49 (review of a decision).

(2)   If the Tribunal decides not to review the decision, or reviews the decision and decides to take no action in relation to the decision, or part of it, the Tribunal must consider whether to give permission to appeal in relation to the decision or that part of it.

(3)   The Tribunal must send a record of its decision to the parties as soon as practicable.

(4)   If the Tribunal refuses permission to appeal it must send with the record of its decision –

(a)   a statement of its reasons for such refusal; and

(b)   notification of the right to make an application to the Upper Tribunal for permission to appeal and the time within which, and the method by which, such application must be made.

(5)   The Tribunal may give permission to appeal on limited grounds, but must comply with paragraph (4) in relation to any grounds on which it has refused permission.

48.   Application for review in special educational needs cases

(1)   This rule applies to decisions which dispose of proceedings in special educational needs cases, but not to decisions under this Part.

(2)   A party may make a written application to the Tribunal for a review of a decision if circumstances relevant to the decision have changed since the decision was made.

(3)   An application under paragraph (2) must be sent or delivered to the Tribunal so that it is received within 28 days after the date on which the Tribunal sent the decision notice recording the Tribunal's decision to the party making the application.

(4)   If a party sends or delivers an application to the Tribunal later than the time required by paragraph (3) or by any extension of time under rule 5(3)(a) (power to extend time) –

    (a)   the application must include a request for an extension of time and the reason why the application was not provided in time; and

    (b)   unless the Tribunal extends time for the application under rule 5(3)(a) (power to extend time) the Tribunal must not admit the application.

49. Review of a decision

(1)   The Tribunal may only undertake a review of a decision –

    (a)   pursuant to rule 47(1) (review on an application for permission to appeal) if it is satisfied that there was an error of law in the decision; or

    (b)   pursuant to rule 48 (application for review in special educational needs cases).

(2)   The Tribunal must notify the parties in writing of the outcome of any review, and of any right of appeal in relation to the outcome.

(3)   If the Tribunal takes any action in relation to a decision following a review without first giving every party an opportunity to make representations, the notice under paragraph (2) must state that any party that did not have an opportunity to make representations may apply for such action to be set aside and for the decision to be reviewed again.

50. Power to treat an application as a different type of application

The Tribunal may treat an application for a decision to be corrected, set aside or reviewed, or for permission to appeal against a decision, as an application for any other one of those things.

APPENDIX C

Practice Direction: First-tier Tribunal Health Education and Social Care Chamber: Statements and Reports in Mental Health Cases

STATEMENTS AND REPORTS IN MENTAL HEALTH CASES IN THE HEALTH, EDUCATION AND SOCIAL CARE CHAMBER OF THE FIRST-TIER TRIBUNAL ON OR AFTER 6 APRIL 2012

1. This practice direction is made by the Senior President of Tribunals with the agreement of the Lord Chancellor in the exercise of powers conferred by section 23 of the Tribunals, Courts and Enforcement Act 2007. It applies to a "mental health case" as defined in rule 1(3) the Tribunal Procedure (First-tier Tribunal) (Health, Education and Social Care Chamber) Rules 2008. Rule 32 requires that certain documents are to be sent or delivered to the tribunal (and, in restricted cases, to the Secretary of State) by the responsible authority, the responsible clinician and any social supervisor (as the case may be). This practice direction specifies the contents of the statements and the reports that are to be sent or delivered in accordance with rule 32. It replaces the previous Practice Direction on mental health cases dated 30 October 2008 with effect from 06 April 2012.
2. In this practice direction "the Act" refers to the Mental Health Act 1983, as amended.

A.   IN-PATIENTS

3. For the purposes of this practice direction, a patient is an in-patient if they are in hospital to be assessed or treated for a mental disorder, even if treatment is being provided informally, or under a provision other than that to which the application or reference to the tribunal relates.
4. A patient is also an in-patient if they are detained in hospital through the criminal justice system, or if they have been transferred to hospital from a custodial establishment. This includes patients detained under a hospital order or removed to hospital from prison – whether or not the patient is also a restricted patient.
5. In the case of a restricted patient detained in hospital, the tribunal may make a provisional decision to order a conditional discharge. Before it finally grants a conditional discharge, the tribunal may defer its decision so that arrangements to its satisfaction can be put in place. Unless and until the tribunal finally grants a conditional discharge, the patient remains an in-patient, and so this part of the practice direction applies.
6. If the patient is an in-patient, the responsible authority must send or deliver to the tribunal the following documents containing the specified information in accordance with paragraphs 7 or 8 below, as appropriate:

    i)   Statement of Information about the Patient
    ii)   Responsible Clinician's Report
    iii) In-Patient Nursing Report [A copy of the patient's current nursing plan must be appended to the report.]
    iv) Social Circumstances Report

7.   In all cases except where a patient is detained under section 2 of the Act, the responsible authority must send or deliver to the tribunal the required documents, containing the specified information, so that the documents are received by the tribunal as soon as practicable and in any event within 3 weeks after the responsible authority made the reference or received a copy of the application or reference. If the patient is a restricted patient, the responsible authority must also, at the same time, send copies of the documents to the Secretary of State.

8.   Where a patient is detained under section 2 of the Act, the responsible authority must prepare the required documents as soon as practicable after receipt of a copy of the application or a request from the tribunal. It may be that some of the specified information will not be immediately available. The responsible authority must balance the need for speed with the need to provide as much of the specified information as possible within the time available. If information is omitted because it is not available, then that should be mentioned in the relevant document. These documents must be made available to the tribunal panel and representative at least one hour ahead of the hearing.

i) Statement of Information about the Patient

9.   The statement provided to the tribunal must, in so far as it is within the knowledge of the responsible authority, include the following up-to-date information:

    a)   the patient's full name (and any alternative names used in their patient records);
    b)   the patient's date of birth, age and usual place of residence;
    c)   the patient's first language and, if it is not English, whether an interpreter is required and, if so, in which language;
    d)   if the patient is deaf, whether the patient will require the services of a British Sign Language interpreter or a Relay Interpreter;
    e)   the date of admission or transfer of the patient to the hospital in which the patient is detained or liable to be detained, together with details of the application, order or direction that is the original authority for the detention of the patient, and details of any subsequent renewal of, or change in, the authority for detention;
    f)   details of the hospital at which the patient is detained;
    g)   details of any transfers between hospitals since the original application, order or direction was made;
    h)   where the patient is detained in an independent hospital, details of any NHS body that funds, or will fund, the placement;
    i)   the name of the patient's responsible clinician and the date when the patient came under the care of that clinician;
    j)   the name and address of the local social services authority and NHS body which, were the patient to leave hospital, would have the duty to provide aftercare services for the patient under section 117 of the Act;
    k)   the name of any care co-ordinator appointed for the patient;
    l)   except in the case of a restricted patient, the name and address of the patient's nearest relative or of the person exercising that function, whether the patient has made any specific requests that their nearest relative should not be consulted or should not be kept informed about the patient's care or treatment and, if so, the

detail of any such requests and whether the responsible authority believes that the patient has capacity to make such requests;

m) the name and address of any person who plays a significant part in the care of the patient but who is not professionally concerned with that care;

n) the name and address of any deputy or attorney appointed for the patient under the Mental Capacity Act 2005;

o) details of any registered lasting or enduring power of attorney made by the patient;

p) details of any existing advance decisions made by the patient to refuse treatment for mental disorder.

ii) Responsible Clinician's Report

10. This report must be up-to-date and specifically prepared for the use of the tribunal. Unless it is not reasonably practicable, the report must be written or countersigned by the patient's responsible clinician and must describe the patient's relevant medical history and current presentation, including:

a) full details of the patient's mental state, behaviour and treatment for mental disorder;

b) so far as it is within the knowledge of the person writing the report, a statement as to whether, at a time when the patient was mentally disordered, the patient has neglected or harmed themselves or threatened themselves with harm, or has harmed other persons or threatened them with harm, or damaged property or threatened to damage property, together with details of any neglect, harm, damage or threats;

c) an assessment of the extent to which the patient or other persons would be likely to be at risk if the patient were to be discharged by the tribunal, and how any such risks could be managed effectively;

d) an assessment of the patient's strengths and any other positive factors of which the tribunal should be aware;

e) whether the patient has a learning disability that may adversely affect their understanding or ability to cope with the tribunal hearing, and whether there are any approaches or adjustments that the panel may consider in order to deal with the case fairly and justly.

iii) In-Patient Nursing Report

11. This report must be up-to-date and specifically prepared for the use of the tribunal. In relation to the patient's current in-patient episode it must include full details of the following:

a) the patient's understanding of, and willingness to accept, the current treatment for mental disorder provided or offered;

b) the level of observation to which the patient is subject;

c) any occasions on which the patient has been secluded or restrained, including the reasons why seclusion or restraint was considered to be necessary;

d) any occasions on which the patient has been absent without leave whilst liable to be detained, or occasions when the patient has failed to return when required, after having been granted leave of absence;

e) any incidents where the patient has harmed themselves or others or threatened such harm, or damaged property or threatened such damage.

iv) Social Circumstances Report

12. This report must be up-to-date and specifically prepared for the use of the tribunal. It must include full details of the following:

   a) the patient's home and family circumstances, and the housing facilities available;
   b) so far as it is practicable, and except in restricted cases, a summary of the views of the patient's nearest relative unless (having consulted the patient) the person compiling the report considers that it would be inappropriate to consult the nearest relative;
   c) so far as it is practicable, the views of any person who plays a significant part in the care of the patient but is not professionally concerned with it;
   d) the views of the patient, including the patient's concerns, hopes and beliefs;
   e) the opportunities for employment available to the patient;
   f) what (if any) community support or after-care is being, or would be, made available to the patient, and the author's views as to its likely effectiveness were the patient to be discharged from hospital;
   g) the patient's financial circumstances (including entitlement to benefits);
   h) an assessment of the patient's strengths and any other positive factors of which the tribunal should be aware;
   i) an assessment of the extent to which the patient or other persons would be likely to be at risk if the patient were to be discharged from hospital, and how any such risks could be managed effectively.

B. COMMUNITY PATIENTS

13. If the patient is a community patient under section 17A of the Act the responsible authority must send or deliver to the tribunal the following documents, containing the specified information, so that the documents are received by the tribunal as soon as practicable and in any event within 3 weeks after the responsible authority made the reference or received a copy of the application or reference:

   i) Statement of Information about the Patient
   ii) Responsible Clinician's Report
   iii) Social Circumstances Report

i) Statement of Information about the Patient

14. The statement provided to the tribunal must, in so far as it is within the knowledge of the responsible authority, include the following up-to-date information:

   a) the patient's full name (and any alternative names used in their patient records);
   b) the patient's date of birth, age and usual place of residence;
   c) the patient's first language and, if it is not English, whether an interpreter is required and, if so, in which language;
   d) if the patient is deaf, whether the patient will require the services of a British Sign Language interpreter or a relay interpreter;
   e) details of the place where the patient is living;
   f) the name of the patient's responsible clinician and the date when the patient came under the care of that clinician;
   g) the name and address of the local social services authority and NHS body having a duty to provide after-care services for the patient under section 117 of the Act;
   h) the name of any care co-ordinator appointed for the patient;
   i) the name and address of the patient's nearest relative or of the person exercising

that function, whether the patient has made any specific requests that their nearest relative should not be consulted or should not be kept informed about the patient's care or treatment and, if so, the detail of any such requests and whether the responsible authority believes that the patient has capacity to make such requests;

j) the name and address of any deputy or attorney appointed for the patient under the Mental Capacity Act 2005;

k) details of any registered lasting or enduring power of attorney made by the patient;

l) details of any existing advance decisions made by the patient to refuse treatment for mental disorder.

ii) Responsible Clinician's Report

15. This report must be up-to-date and specifically prepared for the use of the tribunal. Unless it is not reasonably practicable, the report must be written or countersigned by the patient's responsible clinician and must describe the patient's relevant medical history and current presentation, including:

a) where the case is a reference to the tribunal, an assessment of the patient's capacity to decide whether or not to attend, or be represented at, a hearing of the reference;

b) whether the patient has a learning disability that may adversely affect their understanding or ability to cope with the tribunal hearing, and whether there are any approaches or adjustments that the panel may consider in order to deal with the case fairly and justly.

c) details of the date of, and circumstances leading up to, the patient's underlying section 3 order, and a brief account of when, and why, the patient then came to be subject to a community treatment order;

d) full details of the patient's mental state, behaviour and treatment for mental disorder, and relevant medical history;

e) so far as it is within the knowledge of the person writing the report, a statement as to whether, at a time when the patient was mentally disordered, the patient has neglected or harmed themselves or threatened themselves with harm, or has harmed other persons or threatened them with harm, or damaged property or threatened to damage property, together with details of any neglect, harm, damage or threats;

f) an assessment of the extent to which the patient or other persons would be likely to be at risk if the patient were to be discharged by the tribunal, and how any such risks could be managed effectively;

g) an assessment of the patient's strengths and any other positive factors of which the tribunal should be aware;

h) the reasons why it is necessary that the responsible clinician should be able to exercise the power under section 17E(1) of the Act to recall the patient to hospital;

i) any conditions to which the patient is subject under section 17B of the Act.

iii) Social Circumstances Report

16. This report must be up-to-date and specifically prepared for the use of the tribunal. It must include full details of the following:

a) the patient's home and family circumstances, and the housing facilities available;

b) so far as it is practicable a summary of the views of the patient's nearest relative, unless (having consulted the patient) the person compiling the report considers that it would inappropriate to consult the nearest relative;

c) the views of any person who plays a significant part in the care of the patient but is not professionally concerned with that care;

d) the views of the patient, including their concerns, hopes and beliefs;

e) the opportunities for employment available to the patient;

f) what (if any) community support or after-care is being, or would be, made available to the patient, and the author's views as to its likely effectiveness were the community treatment order to continue, or were it to be discharged;

g) the patient's financial circumstances (including entitlement to benefits);

h) an assessment of the patient's strengths and any other positive factors of which the tribunal should be aware;

i) an account of the patient's progress whilst a community patient, details of any conditions or requirements to which the patient is subject under the community treatment order, and details of any behaviour that has put the patient or others at risk;

j) an assessment of the extent to which the patient or other persons would be likely to be at risk if the tribunal were to discharge the community treatment order.

C.   GUARDIANSHIP PATIENTS

17. If the patient has been received into guardianship under section 7 of the Act, the responsible authority must send or deliver to the tribunal the following documents, containing the specified information, so that the documents are received by the tribunal as soon as practicable and in any event within 3 weeks after the responsible authority made the reference or received a copy of the application or reference:

i) Statement of Information about the Patient

ii) Responsible Clinician's Report

iii) Social Circumstances Report

i)   Statement of Information about the Patient

18. The statement provided to the tribunal must, in so far as it is within the knowledge of the responsible authority, include the following up-to-date information:

a) the patient's full name (and any alternative names used in their patient records);

b) the patient's date of birth, age and usual place of residence;

c) the patient's first language and, if it is not English, whether an interpreter is required and, if so, in which language;

d) if the patient is deaf, whether the patient will require the services of a British Sign Language interpreter or a Relay Interpreter;

e) the date of the reception of the patient into guardianship, together with details of the application, order or direction that constitutes the original authority for the guardianship of the patient;

f) where the patient is subject to the guardianship of a private guardian, the name and address of that guardian;

g) the name of the patient's responsible clinician and the date when the patient came under the care of that clinician;

h) details of the place where the patient is living;

i) the name of any care co-ordinator appointed for the patient;

j) the name and address of the patient's nearest relative or of the person exercising that function, whether the patient has made any specific requests that their nearest relative should not be consulted or should not be kept informed about the patient's care or treatment and, if so, the detail of any such requests and whether the responsible authority believes that the patient has capacity to make such requests;

k) the name and address of any person who plays a significant part in the care of the patient but who is not professionally concerned with that care;

l) the name and address of any deputy or attorney appointed for the patient under the Mental Capacity Act 2005;

m) details of any registered lasting or enduring power of attorney made by the patient;

n) details of any existing advance decisions made by the patient to refuse treatment for mental disorder.

ii) Responsible Clinician's Report

19. This report must be up-to-date and specifically prepared for the use of the tribunal. Unless it is not reasonably practicable, the report must be written or countersigned by the patient's responsible clinician and must describe the patient's relevant medical history and current presentation, including:

a) full details of the patient's mental state, behaviour and treatment for mental disorder;

b) so far as it is within the knowledge of the person writing the report, a statement as to whether, at a time when the patient was mentally disordered, the patient has neglected or harmed themselves or threatened themselves with harm, or has harmed other persons or threatened them with harm, or damaged property or threatened to damage property, together with details of any neglect, harm, damage or threats;

c) an assessment of the extent to which the patient or other persons would be likely to be at risk if the patient were to be discharged from guardianship, and how any such risks could be managed effectively;

d) an assessment of the patient's strengths and any other positive factors of which the tribunal should be aware;

e) whether the patient has a learning disability that may adversely affect their understanding or ability to cope with the tribunal hearing, and whether there are any approaches or adjustments that the panel may consider in order to deal with the case fairly and justly.

iii) Social Circumstances Report

20. This report must be up-to-date and specifically prepared for the use of the tribunal. It must include full details of the following:

a) the patient's home and family circumstances, and the housing facilities available;

b) so far as it is practicable, a summary of the views of the patient's nearest relative, unless (having consulted the patient) the person compiling the report considers that it would be inappropriate to consult the nearest relative;

c) so far as it is practicable, the views of any person who plays a significant part in the care of the patient but is not professionally concerned with that care;

d) the views of the patient, including their concerns, hopes and beliefs;

e) the opportunities for employment available to the patient;

f) what (if any) community support is being, or would be, made available to the patient, and the author's views as to its likely effectiveness were the guardianship order to continue, or were it to be discharged;

g) the patient's financial circumstances (including entitlement to benefits);

h) an assessment of the patient's strengths and any other positive factors of which the tribunal should be aware;

i) an assessment of the extent to which the patient or other persons would be likely to be at risk if the patient were to be discharged by the tribunal, and how any such risks could be managed effectively.

D. CONDITIONALLY DISCHARGED PATIENTS

21. A conditionally discharged patient is a restricted patient who has been discharged from hospital into the community, subject to a condition that the patient will remain liable to be recalled to hospital for further treatment, should it become necessary.

22. In the case of a restricted patient in hospital, the tribunal may make a provisional decision to order a conditional discharge. Before it finally grants a conditional discharge, the tribunal may defer its decision so that arrangements to its satisfaction can be put in place. Unless and until the tribunal finally grants a conditional discharge, the patient remains an in-patient, and so the in-patient part of the practice direction (and not this part) applies.

23. Upon being notified by the tribunal of an application or reference, the responsible clinician must send or deliver a responsible clinician's report, and any social supervisor must send or deliver a social circumstances report. The reports must contain the specified information and must be sent or delivered to the tribunal as soon as practicable, and in any event within 3 weeks after the responsible clinician or social supervisor (as the case may be) received the notification.

24. The responsible clinician and any social supervisor must also, at the same time, send copies of their reports to the Secretary of State.

i) Responsible Clinician's Report

25. This report must be up-to-date and specifically prepared for the use of the tribunal. Unless it is not reasonably practicable, the report must be written or countersigned by the patient's Responsible Clinician and must describe the patient's relevant medical history and current presentation, including:

a) full details of the patient's mental state, behaviour and treatment for mental disorder;

b) so far as it is within the knowledge of the person writing the report, a statement as to whether, at a time when the patient was mentally disordered, the patient has neglected or harmed themselves or threatened themselves with harm, or has harmed other persons or threatened them with harm, or damaged property or threatened to damage property, together with details of any neglect, harm, damage or threats;

c) an assessment of the extent to which the patient or other persons would be likely to be at risk if the patient were to be absolutely discharged by the tribunal, and how any such risks could be managed effectively;

d) an assessment of the patient's strengths and any other positive factors of which the tribunal should be aware;

e) details of any existing advance decisions to refuse treatment for mental disorder made by the patient;

f) whether the patient has a learning disability that may adversely affect their understanding or ability to cope with the tribunal hearing, and whether there are any approaches or adjustments that the panel may consider in order to deal with the case fairly and justly.

g) If the patient does not have a social supervisor, the responsible clinician must also provide, or arrange to be provided, as much of the social circumstances information below as can reasonably be obtained in the time available.

ii) Social Circumstances Report

26. This report must be up-to-date and specifically prepared for the use of the tribunal. It must include full details of the following:

a) the patient's full name (and any alternative names used in their patient records);

b) the patient's date of birth, age and usual place of residence;

c) the patient's first language and, if it is not English, whether an interpreter is required and, if so, in which language;

d) if the patient is deaf, whether the patient will require the services of a British Sign Language interpreter or a Relay Interpreter;

e) the patient's home and family circumstances, and the housing facilities available;

f) so far as it is practicable, the views of any person who plays a significant part in the care of the patient but is not professionally concerned with that care;

g) the views of the patient, including their concerns, hopes and beliefs;

h) the opportunities for employment available to the patient;

i) what (if any) community support or after-care is being, or would be, made available to the patient, and the author's views as to its likely effectiveness were the conditional discharge to continue, or were the patient to be absolutely discharged;

j) the patient's financial circumstances (including entitlement to benefits);

k) an assessment of the patient's strengths and any other positive factors of which the tribunal should be aware;

l) an assessment of the extent to which the patient or other persons would be likely to be at risk if the patient were to be absolutely discharged by the tribunal, and how any such risks could be managed effectively.

m) the name and address of any deputy or attorney appointed for the patient under the Mental Capacity Act 2005;

n) details of any registered lasting or enduring power of attorney made by the patient.

E. PATIENTS UNDER THE AGE OF 18

27. All the above requirements apply, as appropriate, depending upon the type of case.

28. In addition, for all patients under the age of 18, the Social Circumstances Report must state:

a) the names and addresses of any persons with parental responsibility, and how they acquired parental responsibility;

b) which public bodies either have liaised or need to liaise in relation to aftercare services that may be provided under section 117 of the Act; c) the outcome of any liaison that has taken place;

d) if liaison has not taken place, why not – and when liaison will take place;

e) the details of any multi-agency care plan in place or proposed;

f) whether there are any issues as to funding the care plan and, if so, the date by which it is intended that those issues will be resolved;

g) who will be the patient's care coordinator following discharge;

h) whether the patient's needs have been assessed under the Chronically Sick and Disabled Persons Act 1970 (as amended) and, if not, the reasons why such an assessment has not been carried out and whether it is proposed to carry out such an assessment;

i) if there has been an assessment under the Chronically Sick and Disabled Persons Act 1970, what needs have been identified and how those needs will be met;

j) if the patient is subject to or has been the subject of a care order or an interim care order, the date and duration of any such order, the identity of the relevant local authority, any person(s) with whom the local authority shares parental responsibility, whether the patient is the subject of any care proceedings which have yet to be concluded and, if so, the court in which such proceedings are taking place and the date of the next hearing, whether the patient comes under the Children (Leaving Care) Act 2000, whether there has been any liaison between, on the one hand, social workers responsible for mental health services to children and adolescents and, on the other hand, those responsible for such services to adults, and the name of the social worker within the relevant local authority who is discharging the function of the nearest relative under section 27 of the Act;

k) if the patient is subject to guardianship under section 7 of the Act, whether any orders have been made under the Children Act 1989 in respect of the patient, and what consultation there has been with the guardian;

l) if the patient is a ward of court, when the patient was made a ward of court and what steps have been taken to notify the court that made the order of any significant steps taken, or to be taken, in respect of the patient;

m) whether any orders under the Children Act 1989 are in existence in respect of the patient and, if so, the details of those orders, together with the date on which such orders were made, and whether they are final or interim orders;

n) if a patient has been or is a looked after child under section 20 of the Children Act 1989, when the child became looked after, why the child became looked after, what steps have been taken to discharge the obligations of the local authority under paragraph 17(1) of Schedule 2 of the Children Act 1989, and what steps are being taken (if required) to discharge the obligations of the local authority under paragraph 10 (b) of Schedule 2 of the Children Act 1989;

o) if a patient has been treated by a local authority as a child in need (which includes children who have a mental disorder) under section 17(11) of the Children Act 1989, the period or periods for which they have been so treated, why they were considered to be a child in need, what services were or are being made available to the child by virtue of that status, and details of any assessment of the child;

p) if a patient has been the subject of a secure accommodation order (under section 25 of the Children Act 1989), the date on which the order was made, the reasons it was made, and the date it expired.

LORD JUSTICE CARNWATH

SENIOR PRESIDENT OF TRIBUNALS

06 April 2012

Mental Health Review Tribunal for Wales Rules 2008, SI 2008/2705

PART 1 INTRODUCTION

1. Citation and commencement

These Rules may be cited as the Mental Health Review Tribunal for Wales Rules 2008 and come into force on 3rd November 2008.

2. Interpretation

(1) In these Rules –

"the Act" means the Mental Health Act 1983;
"applicant" means a person who –

(a) starts Tribunal proceedings, whether by making an application or a reference, or
(b) is substituted as a party under rule 12 (substitution and addition of parties);

"document" means anything in which information is recorded in any form, and an obligation under these Rules to provide or allow access to a document or a copy of a document for any purpose means, unless the Tribunal directs otherwise, an obligation to provide or allow access to such document or copy in a legible form or in a form which can be readily made into a legible form;
"final determination" means a decision of the Tribunal which disposes of proceedings, including a decision with recommendations or a deferred decision for conditional discharge, but a refusal of an application for permission to appeal under rule 30 (application for permission to appeal) is not a final determination;
"hearing" means an oral hearing and includes a hearing conducted in whole or in part by video link, telephone or other means of instantaneous two-way electronic communication;
"interested party" means a person added as an interested party under rule 12 (substitution and addition of parties);
"legal representative" means a person who, for the purposes of the Legal Services Act 2007, is an authorised person in relation to an activity which constitutes the exercise of a right of audience or the conduct of litigation (within the meaning of that Act);
"party" means the patient, the responsible authority, the Secretary of State (if the patient is a restricted patient), the Welsh Ministers or Secretary of State in a reference under rule 15(7) (seeking approval under section 86 of the Act) and any other person who starts a case by making an application or referring a matter to the Tribunal under the Act;
"registered person" means the person or persons registered in respect of a registered establishment;
"responsible authority" means –

(a) in relation to a patient detained under the Act in a hospital within the meaning of Part 2 of that Act, the managers (as defined in section 145 of the Act);

(b) in relation to a patient subject to guardianship, the responsible local social services authority as defined in section 34(3) of the Act;

(c) in relation to a community patient, the managers of the responsible hospital (as defined in section 145 of the Act);

(d) in relation to a patient subject to after-care under supervision, the local health board or primary care trust which has the duty to provide such after-care for the patient;

"restricted patient" has the meaning set out in section 79(1) of the Act;

"Tribunal" means the Mental Health Review Tribunal for Wales;

"working day" means any day except a Saturday or Sunday, Christmas Day, Good Friday or a bank holiday under section 1 of the Banking and Financial Dealings Act 1971.

(2) In these Rules, any reference to a rule or Schedule alone is a reference to a rule or Schedule in these Rules.

3. Overriding objective

(1) The overriding objective of these Rules is to enable the Tribunal to deal with cases fairly, justly, efficiently and expeditiously.

(2) Dealing with a case in accordance with paragraph (1) includes –

(a) avoiding unnecessary formality and seeking flexibility in the proceedings;

(b) ensuring, so far as practicable, that the parties are able to participate fully in the proceedings;

(c) using any special expertise of the Tribunal effectively; and

(d) avoiding delay, so far as compatible with proper consideration of the issues.

(3) The Tribunal must seek to give effect to the overriding objective when it –

(a) exercises any power under these Rules; or

(b) interprets any rule.

PART 2   GENERAL POWERS AND PROVISIONS

4. Preliminary and incidental matters

As regards matters preliminary or incidental to an application or reference, the chairman may, at any time up to the hearing of an application or reference by the Tribunal, exercise the powers of the Tribunal under rules 5, 6, 10, 12, 13, 14, 15, 16, 17, 21, 22, 26, 28 and 29.

5. Case management powers

(1) The Tribunal may give directions at any time in relation to the conduct or disposal of proceedings.

(2) In particular, and without restriction on the general power to give directions under paragraph (1) and any other provisions within these Rules, the Tribunal may by directions –

(a) extend or shorten the time for complying with any rule or direction (unless such extension or abridgement would conflict with a provision of an enactment containing a time limit if –

       (i)   the party requiring the extension or abridgement has shown a good reason why it is necessary; and

      (ii)   the Tribunal considers the extension or abridgement to be in the interests of justice;

(b) permit or require a party to amend a document;

(c) permit or require a party or another person to provide documents, information or submissions to the Tribunal or, subject to rule 17 (withholding documents or information likely to cause harm), a party;

(d) provide that an issue in the proceedings will be dealt with as a preliminary issue;

(e) hold a hearing to consider any matter, including a case management issue;

(f) decide the form of any hearing;

(g) stay execution of its own decision pending an appeal of such decision;

(h) stay proceedings.

(3)   Rule 6 (directions) sets out the procedures for applying for and giving directions.

6. Directions

(1)   The Tribunal may give a direction at any time, including a direction amending or suspending an earlier direction.

(2)   The Tribunal may give a direction –

(a) on the application of one or more of the parties; or

(b) on its own initiative.

(3)   An application for directions must include the reason for making that application.

(4)   An application for directions may be made either –

(a) by sending or delivering a written application to the Tribunal; or

(b) orally during the course of a hearing.

(5)   Unless the Tribunal considers that there is a good reason not to do so, the Tribunal must send written notice of any direction to every party and any other person affected by the direction.

7. Failure to comply with rules or directions

(1)   An irregularity resulting from a failure to comply with any provision of these Rules or a direction does not of itself render void the proceedings or any step taken in the proceedings.

(2)   If a party has failed to comply with a requirement in these Rules or a direction, the Tribunal may take such action the Tribunal considers just, which may include –

(a) waiving the requirement; or

(b) requiring the failure to be remedied.

8. Calculating time

(1)   An act required by these Rules or a direction to be done on or by a particular day must be done before 5pm on that day.

(2)   If the time specified by these Rules or a direction for doing any act ends on a day other than a working day, the act is done in time if it is done on the next working day.

9.   Sending and delivery of documents

(1)   Any document to be sent or delivered to the Tribunal under these Rules must be –

   (a)   sent by prepaid post or delivered by hand;
   (b)   sent by facsimile transmission to the number specified by the Tribunal; or
   (c)   sent or delivered by such other method as the Tribunal may permit or direct.

(2)   Subject to paragraph (3), a party may inform the Tribunal and all other parties that a particular form of communication (other than pre-paid post or delivery by hand) should not be used to send documents to that party.

(3)   If a party provides a facsimile transmission number, email address or other details for the electronic transmission of documents to them, that party must accept delivery of documents by that method.

(4)   Subject to paragraph (3), where any document is required or authorised by these Rules to be sent to any person it may be sent by prepaid post or delivered to the last known address of the person to whom the document is directed.

10.   Prohibitions on disclosure or publication

(1)   Unless the Tribunal gives a direction to the contrary, information about proceedings before the Tribunal and the names of any persons concerned in such proceedings must not be made public.

(2)   The Tribunal may make an order prohibiting the disclosure or publication of –

   (a)   specified documents or information relating to the proceedings; or
   (b)   any matter likely to lead members of the public to identify any person who the Tribunal considers should not be identified.

(3)   The Tribunal may use the power in paragraph (2) in order to take action under rule 17 (withholding documents or information likely to cause harm) and in such other circumstances as it considers just.

11.   Appointment of the tribunal

(1)   A person shall not be qualified to serve as a member of a Tribunal for the purpose of any proceedings where –

   (a)   that person is a member, director or registered person (as the case may be) of the responsible authority concerned in the proceedings; or
   (b)   that person is a member or director of a local health board or National Health Service trust which has the right to discharge the patient under section 23(3) of the Act; or
   (c)   the chairman or, as the case may be, president of the Tribunal considers that that person appears to have a conflict of interest or bias of opinion in respect of the patient, or any other member of that Tribunal or party to the proceedings, or has recently been involved with the medical treatment of the patient in a professional capacity.

(2)   The persons qualified to serve as president of the Tribunal for the consideration of an application or reference relating to a restricted patient shall be restricted to those legal members who have been approved for that purpose by the Lord Chief Justice after consulting the Lord Chancellor.

(3)   The Lord Chief Justice may nominate a judicial office holder (as defined in section 109(4) of the Constitutional Reform Act 2005) to exercise his functions referred to in paragraph (2).

12. Substitution and addition of parties

(1) The Tribunal may give a direction substituting a party if –

    (a) the wrong person has been named as a party; or

    (b) the substitution has become necessary because of a change in circumstances since the start of proceedings.

(2) The Tribunal may give a direction adding a person to the proceedings as an interested party.

(3) If the Tribunal gives a direction under paragraph (1) or (2) it may give such consequential directions as it considers appropriate.

13. Representatives

(1) A party may appoint a representative (whether legally qualified or not) to represent that party in the proceedings, not being a person liable to be detained or subject to guardianship or after-care under supervision or a community patient under the Act, or a person receiving treatment for mental disorder at the same hospital or registered establishment as the patient.

(2) If a party appoints a representative, that party or representative must send or deliver to the Tribunal written notice of the representative's name and address.

(3) Anything permitted or required to be done by or provided to a party under these Rules or a direction, other than signing a witness statement, may be done by or provided to the representative of that party.

(4) In the event of a representative being duly appointed –

    (a) the Tribunal and other parties may assume that the representative is and remains authorised until receiving written notification to the contrary from the representative or the represented party; and

    (b) the Tribunal must provide to the representative any document which is required to be sent to the represented party, and need not provide that document to the represented party.

(5) The Tribunal may appoint a legal representative for the patient if –

    (a) the patient has not appointed a representative; and

    (b) (i) the patient has stated that they do not wish to conduct their own case or that they wish to be represented; or

        (ii) the patient lacks the capacity to appoint a representative but the Tribunal believes that it is in the patient's best interests for the patient to be represented.

(6) Unless the Tribunal otherwise directs, a patient or any other party may be accompanied by such other person as the patient or party wishes, in addition to any representative that may have been appointed under this Rule, provided that such person does not act as the representative of the patient or other party.

PART 3 PROCEEDINGS BEFORE THE TRIBUNAL

CHAPTER 1 Before the final determination

14. Procedure for applications and references

(1) An application or reference must be made in writing, be signed (in the case of an application, by the applicant or any person authorised by the applicant to do so) and be provided to the Tribunal so that it is received within the time specified in the Act or the Repatriation of Prisoners Act 1984.

(2) An application or reference must, if possible, include –

    (a) the name and address of the patient;

    (b) in the event of an application being made by the patient's nearest relative, that person's name, address and relationship to the patient;

    (c) the provision under which the patient is detained or liable to be detained, subject to guardianship or after-care under supervision or a community patient;

    (d) whether the person making the application has appointed a representative or intends to do so, and the name and address of any representative appointed;

    (e) the name and address of the responsible authority in relation to the patient.

(3) On receipt of an application or reference, the Tribunal must send notice of the same to –

    (a) the responsible authority;

    (b) the patient (where the patient is not the applicant); and

    (c) if the patient is a restricted patient, the Secretary of State.

15. Statements, reports and documents

(1) Subject to rule 17 (withholding documents or information likely to cause harm), when the Tribunal receives a document from any party it must send a copy of that document to each other party.

(2) When the Tribunal receives an application or reference it must send to the responsible authority or the Secretary of State, as the case may be, a request for the documents and information required to be provided under paragraph (3), (4) or (5).

(3) In proceedings under section 66(1)(a) of the Act (application for admission for assessment), on the earlier of receipt of the copy of the application or receipt of a request from the Tribunal, the responsible authority must send or deliver to the Tribunal by the commencement of the hearing –

    (a) the application for admission;

    (b) the written medical recommendation or recommendations, as the case may be, of the registered medical practitioners on which the application is founded;

    (c) such of the information specified in Part A of the Schedule as is within the knowledge of the responsible authority and can reasonably be provided in the time available; and

    (d) such of the reports specified in Part B of the Schedule as can reasonably be provided in the time available.

(4) If the patient is a conditionally discharged patient the Secretary of State shall send to the Tribunal as soon as practicable, and in any event within 6 weeks of receipt by the Secretary of State of a copy of the application or request from the Tribunal, a statement which shall contain –

(a) the information specified in Part C of the Schedule, in so far as it is within the knowledge of the Secretary of State; and

(b) the reports specified in Part D of the Schedule, in so far as it is reasonably practicable to provide them.

(5) If neither paragraph (3) nor (4) applies, the responsible authority must send a statement to the Tribunal as soon as practicable, and in any event within 3 weeks of receipt by the responsible authority of a copy of the application or receipt of a request from the Tribunal, a statement which shall contain –

(a) the information specified in Part A of the Schedule, in so far as it is within the knowledge of the responsible authority;

(b) the report specified in paragraph 1 of Part B of that Schedule; and

(c) the other reports specified in Part B of the Schedule, in so far as it is reasonably practicable to provide them.

(6) If the patient is a restricted patient the responsible authority must also send the statement under paragraph (5) to the Secretary of State, and the Secretary of State must send a statement of any further relevant information to the Tribunal as soon as practicable and in any event –

(a) in proceedings under section 75(1) of the Act, within 2 weeks of receipt by the Secretary of State of the relevant authority's statement; or

(b) otherwise, within 3 weeks of receipt by the Secretary of State of the relevant authority's statement.

(7) If the Welsh Ministers or Secretary of State wish to seek the approval of the Tribunal under section 86(3) of the Act, the Welsh Ministers or Secretary of State, as the case may be, must refer the patient's case to the Tribunal and the provisions of these Rules applicable to references under the Act apply to the proceedings.

16. Notice of proceedings

When the Tribunal receives the information required by rule 15(3), (4) or (5), the Tribunal must give notice of the proceedings –

(a) where the patient is subject to the guardianship of a private guardian, to the guardian;

(b) where there is an extant order of the superior court of record established by section 45(1) of the Mental Capacity Act 2005, to that court;

(c) unless the patient requests otherwise, where any person other than the applicant is named in the responsible authority's statement as exercising the functions of the nearest relative, to that person;

(d) where a local health board, a National Health Service trust, a primary care trust, a NHS Foundation Trust, a Strategic Health Authority, the Welsh Ministers or the Secretary of State has or have a right to discharge the patient under the provisions of section 23(3) of the Act, to such board, trust, authority, person or persons; and

(e) to any other person the Tribunal may consider should have an opportunity of being heard.

17. Withholding documents or information likely to cause harm

(1) The Tribunal must give a direction prohibiting the disclosure of a document or information to a person if it is satisfied that –

(a) such disclosure would be likely to cause that person or some other person serious harm; and

(b) having regard to the interests of justice that it is proportionate to give such a direction.

(2) If a party ("the first party") considers that the Tribunal should give a direction under paragraph (1) prohibiting the disclosure of part or all of a document or of information to another party ("the second party"), the first party must –

   (a) exclude that part of the relevant document or that information from any document that will be provided to the second party; and

   (b) provide to the Tribunal the excluded part of document or information and the reason for its exclusion, in order that the Tribunal may decide whether the document or information should be disclosed to the second party or should be the subject of a direction under paragraph (1).

(3) The Tribunal must conduct proceedings as appropriate in order to avoid undermining a direction given under paragraph (1).

(4) If the Tribunal gives a direction under paragraph (1) which prevents disclosure to a party who has a representative, the Tribunal may give a direction that the document or information be disclosed to that representative if it is satisfied that –

   (a) disclosure to the representative would be in the interests of the party; and

   (b) the representative would not be likely to act contrary to paragraph (5).

(5) Documents or information disclosed to a representative in accordance with a direction under paragraph (4) must not –

   (a) be disclosed either directly or indirectly to any other person without the Tribunal's consent; or

   (b) be used otherwise than in connection with the proceedings.

18. Further evidence and submissions

(1) Without restriction on the general powers in rule 5(1) and (2) (case management powers), the Tribunal may give directions as to –

   (a) issues on which it requires evidence or submissions;

   (b) the nature of the evidence or submissions it requires;

   (c) whether the parties are permitted or requested to provide expert evidence;

   (d) any limit on the number of witnesses whose evidence a party may put forward, whether in relation to a particular issue or generally;

   (e) the manner in which any evidence or submissions are to be provided, which may include a direction for them to be given –

      (i) orally at a hearing; or

      (ii) by written submissions or witness statement; and

   (f) the time in which any evidence or submissions are to be provided.

(2) The Tribunal may –

   (a) admit evidence whether or not –

      (i) the evidence would be admissible in a civil trial in the United Kingdom; or

      (ii) the evidence was available to a previous decision maker;

   (b) exclude evidence that would otherwise be admissible where –

      (i) the evidence was not provided within the time allowed by a direction;

      (ii) the evidence was otherwise provided in a manner that did not comply with a direction; or

      (iii)   it would otherwise be unfair to admit the evidence.

(3)   The Tribunal may require any witness to give evidence on oath or affirmation, and may administer an oath or affirmation for that purpose.

19.   Summoning of witnesses and orders to answer questions or produce documents

(1)   On the application of a party or on its own initiative, the Tribunal may –

    (a) by summons require any person to attend as a witness at a hearing at the time and place specified in the summons, provided that –

       (i)   the person has been given reasonable notice of the hearing; and

       (ii) unless the person is a party to the proceedings, the summons makes provision for the person's necessary expenses of attendance to be paid, and states by whom; and

    (b) by order require any person to answer any questions or produce any documents in that person's possession or control which relate to any issue in the proceedings.

(2)   A summons under this rule must, if the person to whom it is addressed has not had an opportunity to object to it, state that the person may apply to the Tribunal to vary or set aside the summons.

(3)   When a summons is issued, the Tribunal must send a copy of the summons to each party to the proceedings.

(4)   No person may be compelled to give any evidence or produce any document that the person could not be compelled to give or produce on a trial of an action in a court of law in England or Wales.

20.   Medical examination

(1)   Before the hearing to consider the final determination, a medical member of the Tribunal must, so far as practicable –

    (a) examine the patient; and

    (b) take such other steps as that member considers necessary to form an opinion of the patient's mental condition.

(2)   For the purposes of paragraph (1) that member may –

    (a) examine the patient in private;

    (b) examine records relating to the detention or treatment of the patient and any after-care services;

    (c) take notes and copies of records for use in connection with the proceedings.

(3)   At any time before the Tribunal makes the final determination, the Tribunal or any one or more of its members may interview the patient, which interview may take place in the absence of any other person.

21.   Postponement and adjournment

(1)   The Tribunal may at any time postpone or adjourn a hearing for the purpose of obtaining further information or for such other purposes as it may think appropriate.

(2)   Before postponing or adjourning any hearing, the Tribunal may give such direction as it thinks fit for ensuring the prompt consideration of the application at a postponed or adjourned hearing.

(3) Where a party requests that a hearing postponed or adjourned in accordance with this rule be reconvened, the hearing must be reconvened if the Tribunal is satisfied that reconvening would be in the interests of the patient.

(4) Save in respect of an application under section 66(1)(a) of the Act, before the Tribunal reconvenes any hearing which has been adjourned without a further hearing date being fixed, it must give to all parties not less than 14 days' notice (or such shorter notice as all parties may consent to) of the date, time and place of the reconvened hearing.

22. Withdrawal

(1) Subject to paragraphs (2) to (3), an applicant may withdraw an application by sending to the Tribunal a written notice of withdrawal stating reasons.

(2) Before making a withdrawal under paragraph (1), the consent of the Tribunal must be obtained.

(3) Where an application is withdrawn, the Tribunal shall so inform the parties and such other persons as the Tribunal considers necessary.

(4) A reference made by the Welsh Ministers or the Secretary of State in circumstances in which they are not by the terms of the Act obliged to make a reference may be withdrawn by the Welsh Ministers or the Secretary of State, as the case may be, at any time before it is considered by the Tribunal and, where a reference is so withdrawn, the Tribunal shall inform the patient and the other parties that the reference has been withdrawn.

23. Transfer of Proceedings

(1) Where any proceedings in relation to a patient have not been disposed of by the members of the Tribunal appointed for the purpose, and the chairman is of the opinion that it is not practicable or not possible without undue delay for the consideration of those proceedings to be completed by those members, he shall make arrangements for them to be heard by other members of the Tribunal.

(2) Where a patient in respect of whom proceedings are pending moves to the jurisdiction of the First-tier Tribunal, the proceedings shall, if the chairman of the Tribunal so directs, be transferred to the First-tier Tribunal and notice of the transfer of proceedings shall be given to the parties and such other persons as the Tribunal considers necessary.

CHAPTER 2   Hearings

24. Time and place of hearings

(1) In proceedings under section 66(1)(a) of the Act the hearing of the case must start within 7 days after the date on which the Tribunal received the application.

(2) In proceedings under section 75(1) of the Act, the hearing of the case must start at least 5 weeks but no more than 8 weeks after the date that the Tribunal received the reference.

(3) Subject to paragraph (4), the Tribunal must give the parties reasonable notice, and in any event no less than 14 days' notice, of the date, time and place of any hearing (including any adjourned or postponed hearing) and any changes to the time and place of any hearing, except that in proceedings under section 66(1)(a) of the Act the Tribunal must give at least 3 days' notice.

(4) The Tribunal may give less notice than that required under paragraph (3) –

(a) with the parties' consent; or

(b) in urgent or exceptional circumstances.

25. Privacy of hearings

(1) Except where a patient requests a hearing in public and the Tribunal is satisfied that that would be in the interests of the patient, all hearings must be held in private.

(2) Where the Tribunal refuses a request for a public hearing or directs that a hearing which has begun in public shall continue in private, the Tribunal must record in writing its reasons for holding the hearing in private and shall inform the patient of those reasons.

(3) Where a hearing is held in private, the Tribunal may –

    (a) exclude particular individuals from the hearing or part of it; or

    (b) permit particular individuals to attend the hearing or part of it on such terms as it considers appropriate.

(4) The Tribunal may give a direction excluding from the hearing, or part of it –

    (a) any person whose conduct, in the opinion of the Tribunal, is disrupting or is likely to disrupt the hearing;

    (b) any person whose presence the Tribunal considers is likely to prevent another person from giving evidence or making submissions freely; or

    (c) any person who the Tribunal considers should be excluded in order to give effect to a direction under rule 17 (withholding information likely to cause harm).

(5) The Tribunal may give a direction excluding a witness from a hearing until that witness gives evidence.

26. Request to appear at and take part in a hearing

The Tribunal may give a direction permitting or requesting any person to –

(a) attend and take part in a hearing to such extent as the Tribunal considers appropriate; or

(b) make written submissions in relation to a particular issue.

27. Hearings in a party's absence

If a party fails to attend a hearing, the Tribunal may proceed with the hearing if –

(a) the Tribunal –

    (i) is satisfied that the party has been notified of the hearing or that reasonable steps have been taken to notify the party of the hearing; and

    (ii) the Tribunal is not aware of any good reason for the failure to attend; or

(b) the Tribunal otherwise considers that it is in the interests of the patient to proceed with the hearing.

CHAPTER 3   Decisions

28. Decisions

(1) The Tribunal may give a decision orally at a hearing or may reserve its decision.

(2) The Tribunal must send to each party as soon as reasonably practicable following a final determination –

    (a) a notice stating the Tribunal's decision; and

    (b) written reasons for the decision.

(3) The documents referred to in paragraph (2) must be sent –

(a) in proceedings under section 66(1)(a) of the Act, within 3 working days of the hearing; and

(b) in other proceedings, within 7 days of the hearing.

(4) Where the Tribunal considers that the full disclosure of the recorded reasons for its decision to the patient would cause the patient or any other person serious harm, the Tribunal may instead communicate its decision to him in such manner as it thinks appropriate and may communicate its decision to the other parties subject to any conditions it may think appropriate as to the disclosure thereof to the patient.

(5) Where the Tribunal makes a decision with recommendations, the decision may specify any period at the expiration of which the Tribunal will consider the case further in the event of those recommendations not being complied with.

(6) Subject to rule 10 (prohibitions on disclosure or publication) the Tribunal may, where appropriate, send notice of a decision or the reasons for it to any person.

PART 4   CORRECTING AND APPEALING TRIBUNAL DECISIONS

29.   Clerical mistakes, accidental slips or omissions and irregularities

(1) The Tribunal may at any time correct any clerical mistake or other accidental slip or omission in a decision, direction or any document produced by it, by sending notification of the amended decision or direction, or a copy of the amended document, to all parties.

(2) Any irregularity resulting from failure to comply with these Rules before the Tribunal has determined an application shall not of itself render the proceedings void, but the Tribunal may, and must if it considers that any person may have been prejudiced, take such steps to cure the irregularity as it thinks fit before determining the application, whether by the amendment of any document, the giving of any notice or otherwise.

30.   Application for permission to appeal

(1) This rule applies to an application for permission to appeal against a decision of the Tribunal on a point of law under section 78A of the Act (appeal from the Tribunal to the Upper Tribunal).

(2) A party seeking permission to appeal must send or deliver to the Tribunal a written application for permission to appeal so that it is received no later than 28 days after the date that the Tribunal sent written reasons for the decision to the party making the application.

(3) If the party sends or delivers the application to the Tribunal later than the time required by paragraph (2) or by any extension of time under rule 5(2)(a) (power to extend time) –

(a) the application must include a request for an extension of time and the reason why the application was not provided in time; and

(b) unless the Tribunal extends time for the application under rule 5(2)(a), the Tribunal must not admit the application.

(4) An application under paragraph (2) must –

(a) identify the decision of the Tribunal to which it relates;

(b) identify the alleged error or errors of law in the decision; and

(c) state the result the party making the application seeks.

(5) Upon considering the application for permission to appeal, the Tribunal must send to the parties as soon as practicable –

(a) a record of its decision; and

(b) if the Tribunal has refused to grant permission –

    (i)   reasons for such refusal; and

    (ii)   notification of the right to make an application to the Upper Tribunal for permission to appeal and the time within which, and the method by which, such application must be made.

(6)   The Tribunal may grant permission to appeal on limited grounds, but must comply with paragraph (5)(b) in relation to any grounds on which it has refused permission.

PART 5 REVOCATIONS

31. Revocations

The Mental Health Review Tribunal Rules 1983, the Mental Health Review Tribunal (Amendment) Rules 1996 and the Mental Health Review Tribunal (Amendment) Rules 1998 are revoked.

SCHEDULE 1 STATEMENTS BY THE RESPONSIBLE AUTHORITY AND THE SECRETARY OF STATE

Part A Information about patients (other than conditionally discharged patients)

1.   The patient's full name (and any alternative names used in patient records).
2.   The patient's date of birth and age.
3.   The patient's language of choice and, if it is not English or Welsh, whether an interpreter is required.
4.   The application, order or direction made under the Act to which the tribunal proceedings relate and the date on which that application, order or direction commenced.
5.   Details of the original authority for the detention or guardianship of the patient, including the statutory basis for that authority and details of any subsequent renewal of or change in that authority.
6.   In cases where a patient has been transferred to hospital under section 45A, 47 or 48 of the Act, details of the order, direction or authority under which the patient was being held in custody before his transfer to hospital.
7.   Except in relation to a patient subject to guardianship or after-care under supervision, or a community patient, the hospital or hospital unit at which the patient is presently liable to be detained under the Act, and the ward or unit on which he is presently detained.
8.   If a condition or requirement has been imposed that requires the patient to reside at a particular place, details of the condition or requirement and the address at which the patient is required to reside;
9.   In the case of a community patient, details of any conditions attaching to the patient's community treatment order under section 17B(2) of the Act.
10. The name of the patient's responsible clinician and the length of time the patient has been under their care.
11. Where another approved clinician is or has recently been largely concerned in the treatment of the patient, the name of that clinician and the period that the patient has spent in that clinician's care.
12. The name of any care co-ordinator appointed for the patient.
13. Where the patient is subject to the guardianship of a private guardian, the name and address of that guardian.
14. Where there is an extant order of the superior court of record established by section 45(1) of the Mental Capacity Act 2005, the details of that order.

15. Unless the patient requests otherwise, the name and address of the person exercising the functions of the nearest relative of the patient.
16. Where a local health board, a National Health Service trust, a primary care trust, a NHS Foundation Trust, a Strategic Health Authority, the Welsh Ministers or the Secretary of State has or have a right to discharge the patient under the provisions of section 23(3) of the Act, the name and address of such board, trust, authority, person or persons.
17. In the case of a patient subject to after-care under supervision, the name and address of the local social services authority and NHS body that are responsible for providing the patient with after-care under section 117 of the Act, or will be when he leaves hospital.
18. The name and address of any person who plays a substantial part in the care of the patient but who is not professionally concerned with it.
19. The name and address of any other person who the responsible authority considers should be notified to the Tribunal.

Part B   Reports relating to patients (other than conditionally discharged patients)

1. An up-to-date clinical report, prepared for the Tribunal, including the relevant clinical history and a full report on the patient's mental condition.
2. An up-to-date social circumstances report prepared for the tribunal including reports on the following –

    (a) the patient's home and family circumstances, including the views of the patient's nearest relative or the person so acting;
    (b) the opportunities for employment or occupation and the housing facilities which would be available to the patient if discharged;
    (c) the availability of community support and relevant medical facilities;
    (d) the financial circumstances of the patient.

3. The views of the responsible authority on the suitability of the patient for discharge.
4. Where the provisions of section 117 of the Act may apply to the patient, a proposed after care plan in respect of the patient.
5. Any other information or observations on the application which the responsible authority wishes to make.

Part C   Information about conditionally discharged patients

1. The patient's full name (and any alternative names used in patient records).
2. The patient's date of birth and age.
3. The patient's language of choice and, if it is not English or Welsh, whether an interpreter is required.
4. The history of the patient's present liability to detention including details of the offence or offences, and the dates of the original order or direction and of the conditional discharge.
5. The name and address of any clinician responsible for the care and supervision of the patient in the community, and the period that the patient has spent under the care and supervision of that clinician.
6. The name and address of any social worker or probation officer responsible for the care and supervision of the patient in the community and the period that the patient has spent under the care and supervision of that person.

Part D   Reports relating to conditionally discharged patients

1. Where there is a clinician responsible for the care and supervision of the patient in the

community, an up-to-date report prepared for the Tribunal including the relevant medical history and a full report on the patient's mental condition.

2. Where there is a social worker, probation officer or community psychiatric nurse responsible for the patient's care and supervision in the community, an up-to-date report prepared for the Tribunal on the patient's progress in the community since discharge from hospital.

3. A report on the patient's home circumstances.

4. The views of the Secretary of State on the suitability of the patient for absolute discharge.

5. Any other observations on the application which the Secretary of State wishes to make.

Summary of tribunal eligibility rules

Patients' and nearest relatives' (NRs') rights to apply to the tribunal operate in parallel with the regime of automatic and discretionary references, and with the other powers of discharge (such as by the hospital managers or Ministry of Justice, where appropriate). The table below summarises the main eligibility periods for patients and nearest relatives, and also any references that are triggered by an event such as recall. Only one application is permitted in each eligibility period, but withdrawn applications are disregarded (see Mental Health Act (MHA) 1983, s.77). Further information is set out in chapter 23 of the Department of Health, *Reference Guide to the Mental Health Act 1983* (TSO, 2008). All references are to MHA 1983.

Type of detention	Patient's application to tribunal	NR's application to tribunal
s.2	During first 14 days only (counting day of admission) (s.66(1)(a), (2)(a)), unless tribunal office is closed on 14th day, in which case the deadline is extended until the next business day (*R (Modaresi)* v. *SSH* [2011] EWCA Civ 1359).	None.
s.2 (during s.29(4) extension)	None (but Secretary of State for Health could make reference) (s.67(1)).	None.
s.4	At any time (in practice a hearing would only take place if the s.4 detention is converted to s.2) (s.66(1)(a), (2)(a)).	None.
s.3 (normal admission)	One application during first six-month period (s.66(1)(b), (2)(b)); once during subsequent six-month period, and once during each annual period thereafter (s.66(1)(f), (2)(f)).	None (but see 'barring order' below).
s.3 (transferred from guardianship to hospital under s.19)	One application during first six-month period since transfer (s.66(1)(e), (2)(e)); once during subsequent six-month period, and once during each annual period thereafter (s.66(1)(f), (2)(f)).	None (but see 'barring order' below).

Type of detention	Patient's application to tribunal	NR's application to tribunal
s.3 (following revocation of community treatment order CTO)	One application during first six-month period following revocation (s.66(1)(cb), (2)(cb)); once during subsequent six-month period, and once during each annual period thereafter (s.66(1)(f), (2)(f)). Note that the hospital managers refer the case to the tribunal upon revocation (s.68(7)).	None (but see 'barring order' below).
s.7 guardianship	One application during first six-month period (s.66(1)(c), (2)(c)); once during subsequent six-month period, and once during each annual period thereafter (s.66(1)(f), (2)(f)).	None (but the NR can discharge without 'barring order' procedure).
s.17A CTO (patient previously on s.3)	Six months beginning with the day on which the CTO was made (s.66(1)(ca), (2)(ca)); once during subsequent six-month period, and once during each annual period thereafter (s.66(1)(fza), (2)(fza)).	None (but see 'barring order' below).
s.17A CTO (patient previously Part III unrestricted patient)	Six months beginning with the day on which the CTO was made (s.66(1)(ca), (2)(ca)) (BUT no application may be made within six months of the hospital order being made) (s.69(3)–(5)); once during subsequent six-month period, and once during each annual period thereafter (s.66(1)(fza), (2)(fza)).	As for patient.
Barring order under s.25 (for s.3 or CTO patients only)	None.	Within 28 days of being informed that the report has been furnished (s.66(1)(g), (2)(d)).
NR displaced under s.29 under grounds (3)(c) or (3)(d) (and where patient becomes liable to be detained, Part II guardianship, or who is a community patient)	None.	In each 12-month period following date of order (application by *displaced* NR) (s.66(1)(h), (2)(g)).

Type of detention	Patient's application to tribunal	NR's application to tribunal
s.37 or s.51 hospital order (made by court)	No application during first six-month period (s.66(1)(b) and (2)(b) are disapplied by Sched.1, Part 1); once during subsequent six-month period, and once during each annual period thereafter (s.66(1)(f), (2)(f) (s.20 is applied by Sched.1, Part 1)).	As for patient (s.69(1)(a)).
s.37 hospital order (following revocation of CTO)	One application during first six-month period following revocation (s.66(1)(cb), (2)(cb)) (BUT no application may be made within six months of the hospital order being made) (s.69(3)–(5)); once during subsequent six-month period, and once during each annual period thereafter (s.66(1)(f), (2)(f) (s.20 is applied by Sched.1, Part 1)). Note that the hospital managers refer the case to the tribunal upon revocation (s.68(7)).	As for patient (s.69(1)(a)).
s.37 guardianship order	One application during first six-month period (s.69(1)(b)(i)); once during subsequent six-month period, and once during each annual period thereafter (s.66(1)(f), (2)(f) (s.20 is applied by Sched.1, Part 1)).	One application in each 12-month period (s.69(1)(b)(ii)).
s.37 equivalent, including: s.37/41, s.47/49, s.48/49 (after restrictions expire: s.41(5)) s.47 or s.48 transfer imposed without s.49 restrictions (ss.47(3), 48(3)) On removal from other British Isles jurisdictions under as.80B(2), 82(2), 85(2)	During first six months (unlike hospital orders made by court under s.37) (s.69(2)); during second six months, and during each 12-month period thereafter (s.66(1)(f), (2)(f) (s.20 is applied by Sched.1, Part 1)).	As for patient (s.69(1)(a)).
s.37/41 restricted hospital order	No application during first six-month period; once during subsequent six-month period, and once during each annual period thereafter (s.70).	None (restricted patients have no NR).

335

Type of detention	Patient's application to tribunal	NR's application to tribunal
s.47/49 restricted transfer from prison	One application during first six-month period (s.69(2)); once during subsequent six-month period, and once during each annual period thereafter (s.70).	None (no NR).
s.45A (before restrictions cease)	No application during first six-month period (s.69(2) was amended by MHA 2007 to remove this right); once during subsequent six-month period, and once during each annual period thereafter (s.70).	None (no NR).
Conditionally discharged (patient has not been recalled)	No application during first year after discharge, but once during second year, and once in each subsequent two-year period (s.75(2)).	None (no NR).
Conditionally discharged (patient has been recalled)	No application during first six-month period following *recall*; once during subsequent six-month period, and once during each annual period thereafter (s.70, as applied by s.75(1)). Note: (i) periods follow from recall date not admission date; (ii) the Secretary of State for Justice refers the case to the tribunal following recall (s.75(1)).	None (no NR).
AWOL patient. A report is furnished under s.21B(2) and s.21B(5) (or (5) and (6)(b)) apply. This relates to AWOL patients who are taken into custody or return after more than 28 days	One application during the period for which the detention or guardianship is renewed (s.66(1)(fa), (2)(f)) (see relevant section for subsequent rights).	None.
AWOL CTO patient. A report is furnished under s.21B(2) in respect of a community patient and s.21B(6A) (or (6A) and (6B)(b)) apply. This relates to community patients who are taken into custody or return after more than 28 days	One application during the period for which the CTO is renewed (s.66(1)(faa), (2)(fza)) (see CTO for subsequent rights).	None.

Type of detention	Patient's application to tribunal	NR's application to tribunal
s.35 remand for report	None.	None.
s.36 remand for treatment	None.	None.
s.38 interim hospital order	None.	None.
s.135 warrant to search for and remove patients	None.	None.
s.136 mentally disordered persons found in public places	None.	None.

APPENDIX F

Law Society Practice Note: Representation before mental health tribunals

*This practice note had not been updated, at the time of publication, to incorporate references to the SRA Code of Conduct 2011 (see **13.2.4**). An updated version will be available in due course on the Law Society website (**www.lawsociety.org.uk/advice/practice-notes**).*

1. INTRODUCTION

1.1 Who should read this practice note?

All legal practitioners who represent clients before the First-tier Tribunal (Mental Health) in England and the Mental Health Review Tribunal for Wales including those practitioners who are members of the Law Society's Mental Health Review Tribunal Accreditation Scheme.

This includes solicitors, legal executives, trainee solicitors and solicitors' clerks who are members of the scheme.

1.2 What's the issue?

If you are a member of the Law Society's Mental Health Review Tribunal Accreditation Scheme you are authorised to advise and represent clients who have been detained under the Mental Health Act 1983 (the MHA 1983), before the relevant tribunal (ie the Tribunal in England or the Tribunal in Wales).

Importantly, the provisions of the Mental Health Act 1983 (the MHA 1983) have been qualified by the following legislation, statutory instruments and Codes of Practice, which came into force in November 2008:

- The Mental Health Act 2007
- The Tribunal Procedure (First-tier Tribunal) (Health, Education and Social Care Chamber) Rules 2008 (for England)
- The Practice Direction on reports issued 30/10/08 (for England)
- The Mental Health Review Tribunal for Wales Rules 2008 (for Wales)
- The Mental Health Act codes of practice (different for England and Wales)

It is important that you familiarise yourself with which rules apply, depending on whether you practise in England or Wales.

For more information see 8.2 Legal and statutory requirements.

This practice note provides advice on good practice and how legal practitioners can provide effective legal advice and representation on behalf of their clients before the Tribunal. This includes advice on the following:

- how clients can access your services from hospital, including the rules regarding facilitating referrals
- what happens if the client does not have the capacity to instruct you
- what constitutes the best interests of the client
- your duty of confidentiality
- non-disclosure of documents to the client

- avoiding delay at the tribunal

Unless otherwise specified, 'Tribunal' refers both to the First-tier Tribunal (Mental Health) in England and the Mental Health Review Tribunal for Wales.

Please note that where reference is made to professional rules these are based upon the current Solicitors' Code of Conduct. This practice note will be updated to reflect the provisions of the new Solicitors' Handbook and the implementation of outcomes-focussed regulation in October 2011.

See 8.1 Professional conduct for more information.

2. THE RIGHT TO LEGAL ADVICE AND REPRESENTATION BEFORE THE TRIBUNAL

The right of access to a court is a fundamental right at common law under the European Convention on Human Rights (ECHR) and is guaranteed by Article 6 of the Convention. Moreover, Article 5(4) of the Convention further guarantees the right to legal representation.

Importantly, where an individual is detained on the grounds of mental disorder, Article 5(4) requires that effective legal representation be provided by the state, free of charge, unless there are 'special circumstances'.

'Special circumstances' do not include the fact that the detainee's prospects of release are poor or that the detainee has the means to instruct his own lawyers. Even if representation is available (whether at the detainee's or the state's expense) the state must still ensure the detainee is in fact represented unless satisfied that he or she has capacity and has made an informed choice not to be represented.

In England and Wales, public authorities will owe duties under the Human Rights Act to ensure that detained patients are represented. In practical terms this will mean that a Tribunal should consider appointing a legal representative for an unrepresented patient under rule 11(7) of the First-Tier Tribunal Rules, even where the detainee has chosen not to be represented, unless satisfied that the individual has capacity to make that choice or where the period of detention is particularly short.

To comply with Article 5(4) any legal representation that is provided must be 'effective'. That means the legal representative must be suitably qualified and experienced (although not necessarily a qualified lawyer) and must have adequate time and facilities to prepare the case, including sufficient opportunity to visit the client and take instructions.

See 8.2 Legal and statutory requirements for further details.

2.1 The role of the hospital

There is currently no duty upon hospitals to ensure that all clients who wish to be represented at the Tribunal are put in touch with a legal practitioner. The way in which hospitals assist clients to obtain legal representation varies widely.

In some, the task is undertaken by the Mental Health Act Administrator, in others by social workers or by ward staff. Section 132 of the MHA 1983 requires hospital managers to ensure that a patient understands 'what rights of applying to a tribunal are available to him in respect of his detention', which would include advice as to his right to be legally represented.

A list of mental health legal practitioners can be provided by the ward or the Mental Health Act administrator in each location. In Wales, the MHRT office in Cardiff maintains a list of accredited solicitors.

Details of firms that employ a qualified practitioner in England and Wales can be found using the Law Society's online solicitor search.

2.2 Independent Mental Health Advocates

The role of an independent mental health advocate (IMHA) is to help qualifying patients understand the legal provisions to which they are subject under the MHA 1983, and the rights and safeguards to which they are entitled. IHMA's can accompany patients to Tribunals and hospital managers' hearings and speak on their behalf. The IMHA may also assist patients to exercise their rights.

Legal practitioners can increasingly expect referrals from IMHA's, as the role of the IMHA's becomes more established. However, IMHA's are not the same as legal representatives and are not expected to take over duties currently undertaken by solicitors or other legal practitioners.

Qualifying patients must have access to an IMHA. Qualifying patients are those patients who are:

- detained under the MHA 1983, even if they are currently on leave of absence from hospital, apart from those patients detained under sections 4, 5(2), 5(4), 135 or 136
- subject to guardianship under the act; or
- a community patient.

A patient will also qualify for the assistance of an IHMA if:

- they discuss with a registered medical practitioner or approved clinician the possibility of being given a form of treatment to which section 57 applies; or
- not having attained the age of 18 years and not being a qualifying patient they discuss with a registered medical practitioner or approved clinician the possibility of being given a form of treatment to which section 58A applies.

2.3 Facilitating referrals

In your capacity as an accredited representative you may wish to facilitate referrals. You should be mindful of how you go about doing so and the following practical advice is intended to assist in this process:

You may:

- contact the Mental Health Act administrator of the hospitals in your area to express willingness to accept referrals for tribunal representation
- enquire about the procedures for appointing representatives for clients who lack the capacity to apply to the tribunal or to instruct a solicitor

You should not:

- approach clients on hospital wards without prior appointments to obtain referrals
- offer any form of remuneration for referral of work

If a patient approaches you on a ward seeking representation then you should check with the Mental Health Act administrator to ascertain whether that patient is already legally represented.

If the patient is not already represented, or the Mental Health Act administrator does not know whether or not the patient is legally represented, you are free to leave your details and invite the patient to contact you for an appointment.

You are free to take instructions immediately in emergency situations after first checking that no other legal practitioner has been approached. Examples of emergency situations include Section 2 patients where a date has already been set for a hearing or the time limit for appealing is very close.

2.4 Change of solicitor

You must not provide legal help to a client who has received legal help for the same matter from another supplier within the preceding six months. This rule is contained within the Legal Services Commission Funding Code (November 2009).

The exceptions to this are where this has been permitted under a contract or where either:

- there is a gap in time and circumstances have changed materially between the first and second occasions when the legal help was sought, eg a reconciliation which has failed
- the client has reasonable cause to be dissatisfied with the service provided by the first supplier
- the client has moved a distance away from the first supplier and communication is difficult
- the first supplier has confirmed that they will be making no claim for payment for the legal help

Where a patient requests a change of solicitor, you should record brief reasons as to why the patient is seeking to change their legal representative.

2.5 Appointing a representative

Patients may authorise a representative to act for them in the proceedings; alternatively, the Tribunal can exercise its power to appoint a representative:

- in England under Rule 11(7) of the Tribunal Procedure (First-tier Tribunal) (Health, Education and Social Care Chamber) Rules 2008 (the FTT Procedure Rules 2008)
- in Wales under Rule 13(5) of the Mental Health Review Tribunal for Wales Rules 2008 (the Tribunal (Wales) Rules 2008)

See 8.2 Legal and statutory requirements.

The tribunal may exercise this power when a patient either:

- states they want to be represented or does not want to conduct their own case
- lacks the capacity to appoint a representative but the tribunal believes that being represented is in the patient's best interests

A refusal of representation from a client with capacity cannot be overridden. See 4.1 Taking instructions from clients with capacity.

The Upper Tribunal has the power to appoint a representative for the patient under rule 11(7) of the Tribunal Procedure (Upper Tribunal) Rules 2008 (the UT Rules 2008) in the same circumstances as the Tribunal.

The MHA 1983 does not provide for a litigation friend to be appointed for a person who lacks capacity to give instructions to a representative.

There is no provision for a litigation friend to be appointed to represent the client's best interests in tribunal proceedings.

For more information see 4.2 Taking instructions from clients without capacity.

3. COMMUNICATION WITH THE CLIENT

Communicating well with clients who have mental health problems is crucial in providing effective representation. In general to communicate well, you should:

- be alert to, and seek to overcome, communication challenges which the client faces, including those arising from:
    - lack of capacity or use of medication
    - hearing difficulties

- – learning difficulties
- – language barriers or other cross-cultural issues

- present information in a clear and straightforward manner, avoiding complicated forms and overly legalistic language.

3.1 Initial contact with the client

You should make initial contact with the client in a timely manner, to take instructions and give initial advice. You should advise clients on all of the following:

- the strengths and weaknesses of their case
- timescales
- tribunal powers
- hearing procedures.

You should refer a client to another specialist legal adviser if you lack expertise on other significant issues for which they might need legal advice. Examples of common significant issues include welfare benefits, debt, housing and crime.

You should maintain regular contact with the client, and be willing to adjust the level of contact depending on the client's mental health condition. The client's clarity may change during the case as a result of changing mental health or medication.

In addition, you should aim to make contact with clients in person as much as possible, rather than relying on telephone or written communication.

3.2 Client care letters

Client care letters are especially important in the context of working with clients who have mental health problems. The general rules (set out below) apply but special care and attention may be required in this context.

Rule 2.02 of the Solicitors' Code of Conduct provides that solicitors must both:

- clearly identify the client's objectives in relation to the work to be done for them, and
- give the client a clear explanation of the issues involved and the options available to them.

See 8.1 Professional requirements for further information.

Your initial letter to the client explaining terms of business is often called the client care letter. It acts as:

- a clear record for you and the client of the instructions given and what will happen next
- a vital tool for focusing the client on the exact parameters of a retainer
- evidence against complaints of insufficient information or inadequate professional service.

You should tailor client care letters to the individual needs of the client, reflecting their communication needs and whether they are likely to be distressed by correspondence.

In the case of clients who lack capacity it may be inappropriate to send the client a client care letter. Instead, you should retain the letter on file, and go through the letter in person with the client when appropriate and as far as their comprehension allows. In this instance, you should also record the client's capacity at that time.

If an IMHA or independent mental capacity advocate (IMCA) is involved, you may wish to make them aware of the contents of the client care letter, subject to client confidentiality issues (see below).

For more information see Client care letters practice note in 8.3 Further products and support.

4. TAKING INSTRUCTIONS

4.1 Clients with capacity

The following guidance applies where a patient with capacity has instructed you directly or you have been appointed to represent them under r 11(7)(a) FTT Rules 2008 or r 13(5)(a) of the Tribunal (Wales) Rules or r 11(7)(a) UT Rules 2008, namely where the patient 'states they want to be represented or does not want to conduct their own case'. You must assume that your client has capacity unless the contrary is established (s 1(2) MCA).

The test of litigation capacity is set out in *Masterman-Lister* v. *Brutton & Co* [2003] 1 WLR 1511, namely 'whether the party to legal proceedings is capable of understanding, with the assistance of proper explanation from legal advisers and experts in other disciplines as the case may require, the issues on which his consent or decision is likely to be necessary in the course of those proceedings'.

The threshold for capacity to provide instructions is not high, and people severely affected by a mental disorder may still be able to provide instructions if you explain matters simply and clearly.

The question whether the person is able to provide instructions is a judgment that in many cases an experienced mental health advocate will be able to make themselves. If you are unable to form an opinion you should obtain expert evidence as to the client's litigation capacity by reference to the test in Masterman-Lister. It will usually be inappropriate to seek the views of the client's responsible clinician (RC) because of the risk of a conflict of interest where the client is seeking discharge against the objections of the RC. In these circumstances you should seek an opinion from an independent expert.

You must attempt to take instructions from the patient and must act in accordance with those instructions, even where they are inconsistent, unhelpful to the case or vary during the preparation of the case, or during the hearing itself. However, the fact that the client's instructions are contrary to his/her best interests may be evidence that they lack capacity.

Where you believe your client's instructions are unrealistic or contrary to their best interests you should discuss with the client an alternative and more realistic line of challenge if the initial approach chosen by the client does not appear likely to succeed.

You may only pursue this alternative line if the client agrees. Your duty to act in accordance with the client's instructions takes precedence over your duty to act in his/her best interests. See 5.2 Conflicts between instructions and the best interests of clients

This duty is subject to two exceptions. These are where you believe the client's instructions are affected by either duress or undue influence: see Rule 2.01(d) of the Solicitors' Code of Conduct 2007. In those circumstances you must not act on those instructions until you have satisfied yourself that they represent the client's wishes. If you remain concerned you may wish to ask the Tribunal to appoint you under rule 11(7) of the FTT Rules, the Tribunal (Wales) Rules or the Upper Tribunal Rules.

The Tribunal's power to appoint a solicitor under rule 11(7) was considered in *AA* v. *Cheshire and Wirral Partnership NHS Foundation Trust* [2009] UKUT 195 (AAC). Notably, the court provided the following guidance:

If appointed, the solicitor has the same duties as a litigation friend in the courts so you will exercise your judgement and advance any argument that you consider to be in the patient's 'best interests' and which will not necessarily involve arguing for discharge. In this regard you should note the following points:

- You can, and must, refuse to advance an argument which is not 'properly arguable', despite instructions to do so, consistent with the duty in the Solicitors' Code 2007, para 11.01(3): see *Buxton* v. *Mills-Owens* [2010] EWCA Civ 122, para 43. However a submission may be 'properly arguable' even if it has few, if any, prospects of success (ibid, para 43). It will depend upon the context and your judgment. Given the 'least restrictive alternative' principle in s 1(6) of the Mental Capacity Act 2005 it would be in a rare case that to seek a client's discharge in accordance with his or her express wishes would not be 'properly arguable', although it will be a matter for your judgment in each case.

- You are not permitted to advance submissions contrary to your client's instructions on the basis that you believe it to be in the client's best interests to do so. Although in *AA* v. *Cheshire and Wirral Partnership NHS Foundation Trust & Others* [2009] UKUT 195 (AAC), para 20, Judge Rowland suggested that you may, or must, advance submissions contrary to your instructions where you believe it to be in the client's best interests, the Law Society has obtained Counsel's advice which suggests that this is not a correct statement of the law.
- However, where you are instructed to take steps that you perceive to be contrary to the client's best interests you may withdraw from the case on the grounds of professional embarrassment (Solicitors' Code 2007, Rule 3). If you decide to continue to represent the client you should make sure you keep a record of the client's instructions and the advice you have given.

See 5.2 Conflicts between instructions and the best interests of clients for more information

4.2 Clients without capacity

Rule 2.01 of the Solicitors' Code 2007 and the guidance precludes you from acting for a client who lacks capacity.

Unless you are instructed by a properly authorised third party, such as a court-appointed deputy or the donee of a power of attorney, you cannot act for such a client unless the relevant Tribunal has appointed you to act under the First-tier Tribunal Rules, Tribunal (Wales) Rules or the Upper Tribunal Rules.

For further information see 2.5 Appointing a representative

However, given that you must assume your client has capacity unless the contrary is established and that the threshold for litigation capacity is a low one, it is unlikely you will be precluded from accepting instructions directly or by way of a referral unless the client manifestly lacks litigation capacity.

If, having accepted instructions, it subsequently transpires your client does lack litigation capacity, or where the client's litigation capacity is fluctuating, then the prudent course of action will be to request the Tribunal to appoint you to act for the client.

Even where a client lacks capacity their wishes and feelings are nevertheless relevant and you must still give weight to the wishes that your client expresses. The closer the patient is to having capacity, the greater the weight you must give to their wishes.

Where the client lacks the ability even to express their wishes you should:

- ensure that the tribunal receives all relevant material so that it can determine whether the criteria for continued detention are satisfied
- remember the patient's right to treatment in the least restrictive setting and alert the tribunal to possible alternatives to detention under the MHA 1983 such as Community Treatment Orders (CTOs) and Guardianship.

You should not automatically argue for discharge if you are unable to ascertain the patient's wishes.

5. YOUR DUTIES TOWARDS YOUR CLIENT

5.1 Duty to act in the best interests of clients

Solicitors must act in the legal best interests of each client, under rule 1.04 of the Solicitors Code of Conduct 2007.

This should not be confused with the best interests test under the Mental Capacity Act 2005, which encompasses wider best interests issues.

See 8.1 Professional conduct and 8.2 Legal and statutory requirements

Aspects of the duty to act in the client's best legal interests will include:

- advising clients of the likelihood of being discharged
- advising clients on possible steps towards discharge
- advising clients in respect of disclosure issues
- advocating the client's views or wishes to the tribunal
- advising on aftercare
- advising on other related issues, for example compulsory treatment provisions, alternatives to detention such as CTOs and Guardianship
- advising on the possibility and consequences of the patient withdrawing the application to the tribunal.

However this duty is subject to your overriding duty to act upon the client's instructions.

5.2   Conflicts between instructions and the best interests of clients

Where there is a conflict between the instructions you are given by the client and your judgment as to what is in the client's best interests you may be justified in acting contrary to your instructions.

5.2.1   *If the instruction is not in your client's clinical best interests*

If the client tells you to make a submission such as to seek the clients release or admit an item of evidence, then you must do so even if it is not in the client's clinical best interests if it is nevertheless in the client's best legal interests. You are concerned with the client's best legal interests, not their best clinical interests.

For example in *RM* v. *St. Andrew's Healthcare* [2010] UKUT 119 (AAC) the Upper Tribunal ruled that documents revealing the patient was being covertly medicated should be disclosed to the patient because his fair trial rights (best legal interests) required it, even though it was accepted it was likely to adversely affect his health (best clinical interests). If you make judgments based on your client's best clinical interests you will be at risk of acting in conflict with your duty to protect the client's best legal interests.

5.2.2   *If the instruction is not in your client's best legal interests (client lacking capacity)*

If the client tells you to make a submission or admit an item of evidence where that is not in the client's best legal interests then you will have to strike a balance between the prejudice that will be caused to the client's case and the weight that can appropriately be given to their wishes, bearing in mind that the closer the patient is to having capacity the greater the weight that must be attached to their wishes.

If the balance comes down in favour of protecting the client's legal interests then the solicitor can refuse to follow the client's instructions. It may be that in those circumstances a submission will not be 'properly arguable' and you are not permitted to advance it in any event, applying the test in *Buxton* v. *Mills-Owens* [2010] EWCA Civ 122, para 43.

If the client tells you not to make a submission or not to admit a piece of evidence where that is contrary to the client's best legal interests then the position is more difficult.

You are entitled to act contrary to the client's wishes in those circumstances if, having carried out the balancing exercise referred to above, you conclude that the prejudice to the client's legal interests is sufficiently grave to outweigh their instructions.

In those circumstances you should advance the submission without reservation. In *AA* Judge Rowland suggested that in such circumstances it may be appropriate for an advocate to 'raise' an argument with the Tribunal but without developing it.

However as Dyson LJ observed in *Buxton* v. *Mills-Owens*, para 45, 'if an advocate considers that a point is properly arguable, he should argue it without reservation. If he does not consider it to be properly arguable, he should refuse to argue it'.

However this is subject to a further difficulty, namely that you would not be entitled to make the submission or admit the evidence if that would involve a disclosure in breach of the client's right to legal professional privilege, which is absolute; see below, para 4.7.12.

There may be other situations not covered by this guidance. If in doubt you should seek further professional guidance from the Solicitor's Regulation Authority's Professional Ethics helpline (see 8.3 Further products and support).

5.3 Duty of confidentiality

Rule 4.0 of the Solicitors' Code of Conduct requires solicitors to keep the affairs of clients and former clients confidential except where disclosure is required or permitted by law or by the client or former client.

Exemptions to Rule 4.0 are set out in the guidance to the code. These include the ability for solicitors to reveal confidential information where:

- they believe it is necessary to prevent the client or a third party committing a criminal act that they reasonably believe is likely to result in serious bodily harm
- a child is the client and they reveal information indicating continuing sexual or other physical abuse but they refuse to allow disclosure of such information
- the client discloses abuse of a child either by themselves or by another adult, but refuses to allow any disclosure

Solicitors must consider whether the threat to the client, another person or the child, is sufficiently serious to justify a breach of the duty of confidentiality.

You should not disclose information passed to you in circumstances giving rise to a duty of legal professional privilege, which is absolute: see *R* v. *Derby Magistrates ex p B* [1996] AC 487; *L (a minor)* [1997] AC 17 (see 24B–G) and *B* v. *Auckland Law Society* [2003] 2 A.C. 736.

If you found yourself in this situation you would be entitled to consider yourself professionally embarrassed, and withdraw.

In general, where solicitors consider that they need to disclose confidential information, they should seek advice from the Solicitors Regulation Authority's Professional Ethics helpline.

See 8.3 Practice advice.

If the client discloses to the solicitor that they intend to do serious harm to themselves as this does not fall within the exceptions, guidance must be sought.

Following this, if the solicitor decides to disclose the confidential information, rather than advising the client they have been professionally embarrassed and will cease to act, they should first try to obtain the client's agreement to disclosure.

If the client does not agree, but the solicitor still feels that it is necessary to disclose the information, the solicitor should:

- inform the client that they intend to make the disclosure
- explain the client's right to withdraw instructions
- make the disclosure
- provide the client with written details of what has been disclosed to whom and why.

5.3.1 Duties of disclosure and circumstances where non-disclosure may be appropriate

Rule 4.02 of the Solicitors' Code of Conduct states that a solicitor must disclose to their client all information of which they are aware which is material to that client's matter regardless of the source of the information.

This rule does not apply where the solicitor reasonably believes that serious physical or mental injury will be caused to any person if the information is disclosed to the client.

The responsible authority (NHS Trusts and other authorities holding patients' medical records) can withhold disclosure of documents from a patient if disclosure is likely to cause serious harm to the patient or another person and it is proportionate to do so. In England, this is possible under Rule 14, Tribunal Procedure (First-tier Tribunal) (Health, Education and Social Care Chamber) Rules 2008. In Wales, this is possible under Rule 17, Mental Health Review Tribunal for Wales Rules 2008.

Under these rules, the information can be disclosed to the solicitor on the basis that they do not disclose it to anyone else, including the client. Rule 14(6) prohibits the representative from disclosing documents or the information they contain either directly or indirectly to anyone else, including the representative's client. The rule does not prohibit the representative from informing the client that the representative has a document or information that cannot be disclosed to the client, provided that the representative does not thereby indirectly disclose to the client the information which is being withheld.

This process may affect the client-solicitor relationship and be difficult for the solicitor to manage. A solicitor to whom documents are disclosed on this basis should either:

- consider requesting an earlier hearing which the client does not attend
- consider dealing with disclosure as a preliminary issue without the client on the day of the hearing.

Dorset Healthcare NHS Foundation Trust v. *MHRT* (2009) UKUT 4 (AAC) gives guidance on when a responsible authority can resist disclosure of confidential third-party information or when a solicitor wishes to disclose such information to their client.

If a solicitor requests full access to their client's medical records, the responsible authority should disclose all documents to the patient's solicitors subject to an undertaking, if necessary, not to disclose certain specific third-party documents to the patient.

If in 'exceptional circumstances' the responsible authority refuses even to disclose documents to the solicitor, they must show that it is appropriate to do so by serving a skeleton argument to the tribunal office and the Tribunal must make a ruling.

You should seek permission from the Tribunal to disclose to your client any documents disclosed to you if you consider that it may improve the prospects of a successful outcome.

You should set out your reasons for disclosure by way of a skeleton argument. In *RM* v. *St. Andrew's Healthcare* [2010] UKUT 119 (AAC) the Upper Tribunal ruled that in deciding whether disclosure should be ordered the overriding consideration must be to ensure that the patient has a fair hearing, and that this must take precedence over any concerns that disclosure will harm the patient's health. It would follow that the requirement of a fair hearing will generally override considerations of third party confidentiality.

Where a request or refusal of request is not resolved, either party can apply to the tribunal. This can be heard as a preliminary issue on the day of the hearing or in more complex cases a decision can be taken before the hearing following written or oral submissions.

The Upper Tribunal stressed the desirability of dealing with disclosure issues between the parties without the need to involve the tribunal.

Please note that the guidance above with regard to disclosure which arises from the *Dorset* case is limited to those cases where there are ongoing proceedings in the Mental Health Tribunal.

6. GOOD TRIBUNAL PRACTICE

6.1 Avoiding delay at the tribunal

The tribunals overriding objective is to deal with cases fairly and justly. This includes avoiding delay, so far as compatible with proper consideration of the issues.

These objectives are stated in Rule 2, the Tribunal Procedure (First-tier Tribunal) (Health, Education and Social Care Chamber) Rules 2008 and Rule 3 Mental Health Review Tribunal for Wales Rules 2008. This is also the case in the Upper Tribunal as stated in Rule 2, The Tribunal Procedure (Upper Tribunal) Rules 2008.

See 8.2 Legal and statutory requirements

You should take all appropriate steps to ensure that tribunal hearings are not delayed.

6.2 Independent reports

You should always consider whether it is appropriate to obtain independent evidence. Expert evidence may cover a range of issues such as diagnosis, treatment, placement and activities of daily living. You should also maintain an approved list of experts. Prompt instruction of an expert may reduce the need for adjournments of Tribunal hearings and will ensure your client has a fair hearing.

You should request independent reports as soon as possible and in restricted cases send them to the tribunal office no later than 21 days before the hearing if you would like the Secretary of State to be able to comment on the content of the report.

6.3 Witnesses

You should confirm in advance the availability of all witnesses, including experts, who are expected to attend the tribunal.

6.4 Interpreters

Hospital administration staff should notify tribunal staff of any special requirements such as the need for an interpreter for the patient. You should also identify whether an interpreter will be required at the hearing as soon as possible.

6.5 Documents

You should use your best endeavours to send all documents to the tribunal office no later than seven days before the hearing, and limit the bundle to relevant documents only.

6.6 Applications for postponements

You should avoid applications for postponements wherever possible, and only make them on the client's instructions. The tribunal frequently refuses applications for postponement especially those made at the last minute.

If you consider that a postponement is in the best interests of the client, you should advise the client accordingly, but leave the final decision to the client.

If a postponement appears unavoidable, you should apply as early as possible, setting out the reasons.

Where delay is caused by late reports from the responsible authority, solicitors should request the tribunal for directions immediately after the breach of the time limits on submission of statutory reports.

If the client lacks capacity to provide instructions, you should notify the Tribunal in writing or if or if a third party such as an attorney or a deputy is instructing you on behalf of the client, then you should discuss it with them.

6.7 Withdrawing an application to the tribunal

An application can be withdrawn at any time by the client if the tribunal accepts the withdrawal.

If the client wants to withdraw the application to the tribunal, you should notify the tribunal office immediately in writing, giving the reasons where appropriate. If the client lacks capacity to instruct you about this issue then you should notify the Tribunal office. If you are being instructed by an attorney or deputy attorney you should also discuss it with them.

Early notification allows for other cases to be rescheduled and maximises the use of the tribunal's time.

Where the withdrawal is received directly from the patient and that patient is represented, the solicitor will be approached by the tribunal and encouraged to make contact with the client to discuss the request.

The patient may apply again for a hearing within the same period of eligibility.

6.8 Other codes of conduct

6.8.1 Mental Health Lawyers Association code of conduct

The Mental Health Lawyers Association has adopted a Code of Conduct which covers: quality of service; making appointments; behaviour on the wards; disputes over representation; seeking clients; gifts; and hospital procedures.

6.8.2 NHS Mental Health Trusts codes of conduct

Some NHS Mental Health trusts and private hospitals have developed voluntary codes of conduct for solicitors. These codes ask solicitors to:

- contact the ward in advance to inform them of their intention to visit
- produce identification when visiting
- report to the ward office when visiting
- inform a member of staff if they wish to hold an informal meeting with another client whom they are visiting
- respect the operational needs of the unit/ward
- leave the ward following the completion of their appointment with a client.

Solicitors are asked not to:

- make unsolicited visits or telephone calls
- talk to or approach other patients
- hand out publicity materials
- offer gifts or money to service users other than existing clients
- offer gifts to staff.

You should find out whether there is such a code in place at the relevant hospital. If you have any concerns about the code, you should contact the relevant trust.

7. REPRESENTING CHILDREN AND YOUNG PEOPLE BEFORE THE TRIBUNAL

The tribunal has established a Child and Adolescent Mental Health Service (CAMHS) panel. Its purpose is to ensure that at least one of the tribunal members has special expertise in dealing with cases where a child is either detained under the Mental Health Act 1983 or subject to another order under the act. For the purposes of the CAMHS panel a child is treated as any person under the age of 18 at the time of the application or reference.

Although the Tribunal Rules do not make any specific provision in relation to child patients, the solicitor representing a child should always consider the following:

- the wishes and feelings of the child
- the need to ensure that the child is able to participate fully in the proceedings by, for example, requesting that the proceedings are dealt with in as informal manner as appropriate
- any legal issues that are specific to the child, eg the impact of the Children Act 1989 on decision making in relation to the child and the need to identify the child's entitlement to aftercare services under children's legislation and mental health legislation.

8. MORE INFORMATION

8.1 Professional conduct

The following sections of the Solicitors' Code of Conduct 2007 are relevant to this issue:

- Rule 2.02 – client care
- Rule 4.0 – confidentiality and disclosure
- Rule 4.02 – duty of disclosure

Please note that where reference is made to professional rules these are based upon the current Code of Conduct. This practice note will be updated to reflect the provisions of the new Handbook before the implementation of outcomes-focussed regulation in October 2011.

8.2 Legal and other requirements

- The Mental Health Act 1983 as amended by Mental Health Act 2007
- The Tribunal Procedure (First-tier Tribunal) (Health, Education and Social Care Chamber) Rules 2008
- The Practice Direction issued 30/10/08 (for England)
- The Mental Health Review Tribunal for Wales Rules 2008 (for Wales)
- The MHA codes of practice (different for England and Wales)
- Mental Capacity Act 2005
- Tribunal Procedure (Upper Tribunal) Rules 2008

8.3 Further products and support

8.3.1 Mental Health Review Tribunal Accreditation Panel

The Law Society operates the Mental Health Review Tribunal Accreditation Scheme. Solicitors and solicitors' employees who are on this scheme can, at tribunal hearings, advise and represent patients who have been detained under the Mental Health Act 1983. Only legal practitioners who meet the Law Society's strict requirements are permitted to join the scheme.

Find out more about eligibility and membership.

8.3.2   Practice Advice Line

The Law Society provides support for solicitors on a wide range of areas of practice. Practice Advice can be contacted on 0870 606 2522 from 09:00 to 17:00 on weekdays.

8.3.3   Solicitors Regulation Authority's Professional Ethics helpline

Solicitors may obtain further help on matters relating to professional ethics from the Solicitors Regulation Authority's Professional Ethics helpline (0870 606 2577) from 09:00 to 17:00 on weekdays.

8.3.4   Law Society publications

- *Assessment of Mental Capacity, 3rd ed*
- *Mental Capacity, 2nd ed*
- *Advising Mentally Disordered Offenders, 2nd ed*

8.4   Status of this practice note

Practice notes are issued by the Law Society for the use and benefit of its members. They represent the Law Society's view of good practice in a particular area. They are not intended to be the only standard of good practice that solicitors can follow. You are not required to follow them, but doing so will make it easier to account to oversight bodies for your actions.

Practice notes are not legal advice, nor do they necessarily provide a defence to complaints of misconduct or of inadequate professional service. While care has been taken to ensure that they are accurate, up to date and useful, the Law Society will not accept any legal liability in relation to them.

For queries or comments on this practice note contact the Law Society's Practice Advice Service.

8.5   Terminology in this practice note

Must – a specific requirement in the Solicitor's Code of Conduct or legislation. You must comply, unless there specific exemptions or defences provided for in the code of conduct or relevant legislation.

Should – good practice for most situations in the Law Society's view. If you do not follow this, you must be able to justify to oversight bodies why this is appropriate, either for your practice, or in the particular retainer.

May – a non-exhaustive list of options for meeting your obligations. Which option you choose is determined by the risk profile of the individual practice, client or retainer. You must be able to justify why this was an appropriate option to oversight bodies.

Legal practitioner – solicitors, legal executives, trainee solicitors and solicitors' clerks who are members of the Law Society's Mental Health Review Tribunal Accreditation Scheme.

Tribunal – either the First Tier Tribunal (Mental Health) in England, or the Mental Health Review Tribunal for Wales, depending on jurisdiction.

8.6 Acknowledgements

This practice note has been prepared by the Law Society's Mental Health and Disability Committee, which is made up of senior and specialist lawyers from across the country, who volunteer their time. Advice on certain issues has been obtained from counsel, Paul Bowen, of Doughty Street Chambers. The committee would like to thank Anthony Harbour and the Mental Health Lawyers Association for their input into the practice note.

30 September 2011

Mental Health Accreditation Scheme: Code of Practice

When representing a party in proceedings covered by the Mental Health Act 1983:

1. subject to paragraph 2, to not normally delegate the preparation, supervision, conduct or presentation of the case, but to deal with it personally
2. in each case to consider whether it is in the best interests of the client to instruct another advocate in relation to the preparation of the case
3. in addition to the provisions of the Solicitors' Code of Conduct, where it is in the best interests of my client, or becomes necessary, to instruct another advocate:

    3.1 To consider and advise the client on whom should be instructed in their best interests.

    3.2 To ensure that, save in exceptional circumstances, any advocate that is instructed will either be:

    3.2.1 another Mental Health Accreditation Scheme member, or

    3.2.2 a member of the Bar on my practice's approved counsel list who has appropriate experience of tribunal cases.

    3.3 And to obtain an undertaking from that advocate to:

    3.3.1 attend and conduct the matter personally unless an unavoidable professional engagement arises

    3.3.2 take all reasonable steps to ensure that so far as reasonably practicable a conflicting professional engagement does not arise

4. To abide by the advice and best practice issued by the Law Society in its Practice Note of 19 May 2011, which can be found on our website.

Mental Health Lawyers Association Code of Conduct

All members of the Association have agreed to adhere to the following Code of Conduct.

MHLA CODE OF CONDUCT FOR REPRESENTATIVES

In representing hospital inpatients, particularly those detained by the state against their will, legal representatives carry out an important function for a civilised society. It is therefore important that the highest ethical and professional standards are adhered to.

Status of this Code

The committee of the Mental Health Lawyers Association have adopted this Code of Conduct. Annual renewal of membership, from January 2008, will require an undertaking that the Code will be followed.

This Code is in addition to the general Codes of Conduct made by the Solicitors Regulation Authority and the Institute of Legal Executives. The MHLA is a representative body rather than a regulatory body but, where appropriate, encourages complaints to be made to the SRA and/or ILEX.

Quality of service

1. Representatives should be members of the Law Society's Mental Health Review Tribunal accreditation scheme, or actively seeking membership. The scheme is designed to demonstrate legal knowledge (through the accreditation process) and suitability (including a Criminal Records Bureau check). Unqualified representatives and/or those not on the panel must be closely supervised by a member of the scheme.
2. Representatives should always conduct themselves professionally and courteously, and strive to provide a high standard of work in both advice and representation.

Making appointments

3. Except in exceptional circumstances, representatives should contact ward staff to arrange prior appointments with clients and should arrive punctually. Ward staff should be asked to ensure that a private room will be booked.

Behaviour on the ward

4. The representative should report to ward staff on arrival, and then go straight to the appointment with his client.
5. Unplanned meetings with other existing clients should be arranged via the ward staff.

6. The representative should not loiter on the ward, hand out business cards except where requested, or otherwise approach patients who are not existing clients.
7. If approached by a patient who is not a client, the representative may give a business card for an appointment to be made, but should inform ward staff and, unless there is good reason to do so, should not accept instructions from a client who already has legal representation. The representative should consider contacting the existing solicitors to invite them to contact the patient again.

Disputes over representation

8. If there is a dispute over which firm should represent a patient, then this should be resolved via an independent third party rather than by revisiting the patient, as usually it is the more impressionable and vulnerable patients who find themselves in this situation.

Seeking clients

9. No representative is to place posters in the hospital to advertise his firm; only standard hospital/Trust/national posters are allowed. Representatives should instead ensure that they are on the hospital's list of firms and/or representatives.

Gifts

10. No gifts of any description should be given to hospital staff, including MHA administrators and nurses, or to clients or other patients.

Hospital procedures

11. Representatives will comply with any lawful hospital procedures such as those relating to searches, identification, protected meal times, and access to medical records.

General

The word 'representative' in this Code includes solicitors, legal executives, and any solicitors' staff who represent clients.

APPENDIX I

Contacts

ENGLAND: FIRST-TIER TRIBUNAL (MENTAL HEALTH)

First-tier Tribunal (Mental Health)
PO Box 8793
5th Floor
Leicester LE1 8BN
DX: 743090 Leicester 35
Secure email to tsmhapplications@hmcts.gsi.gov.uk
(or, if using CJSM, tsmhapplications@hmcts.gsi.gov.uk.cjsm.net) (details of the CJSM system are available at: **www.cjsm.net**)
General enquiries line: 0300 123 2201
Email: MHRTenquiries@hmcts.gsi.gov.uk
Complaints: ocuhelpdesk@tribunals.gsi.gov.uk
To report responsible clinician discharges: MHRCDischarges@hmcts.gsi.gov.uk
A detailed contacts list for the Tribunal Secretariat is available from the Ministry of Justice at: **www.justice.gov.uk/contacts/hmcts/tribunals/mental-health**.

WALES: MENTAL HEALTH REVIEW TRIBUNAL FOR WALES

Clerk to the Tribunal
Mental Health Review Tribunal for Wales
Crown Buildings
Cathays Park
Cardiff CF10 3NQ
Telephone: 029 2082 5328
Fax: 029 2082 6331
Email: mhrt@wales.gsi.gov.uk

UPPER TRIBUNAL

The Upper Tribunal (Administrative Appeals Chamber)
5th Floor
7 Rolls Buildings
Fetter Lane
London EC4A 1NL
DX 160042 Strand 4
Telephone (9am to 5pm): 020 7071 5662
Fax: 0870 3240028
Typetalk: 18001 020 7071 5662
Email: adminappeals@hmcts.gsi.gov.uk

REQUESTS FOR REFERENCES

In England

Department of Health
Mental Health Legislation
Area 218 Wellington House
133–155 Waterloo Road
London SE1 8UG
Fax: 020 7972 4147
Email: mentalhealthact2007@dh.gsi.gov.uk

In Wales

Head of Mental Health
Vulnerable Groups and Offenders Branch
Welsh Assembly Government
Cathays Park
Cardiff CF10 3NQ

COURT OF APPEAL

The Civil Appeals Office
Room E307
The Royal Courts of Justice
Strand
London WC2A 2LL
DX 44450 Strand
Email: civilappeals.registry@HMCS.gsi.gov.uk

MINISTRY OF JUSTICE: MENTAL HEALTH CASEWORK SECTION

Mental Health Casework Section
Ground Floor
Grenadier House
99–105 Horseferry Road
London SW1P 2DD
Telephone: 0300 047 4387 or 0300 047 4395
Ministry of Justice Switchboard: 020 3334 3555
Email: mhutribunalcorrespondence@noms.gsi.gov.uk

LEGAL AID AGENCY (FORMERLY LEGAL SERVICES COMMISSION)

LAA Mental Health Unit
Level 6
Capital Building
6 Union Street
Liverpool L3 9AF
DX: 745810 Liverpool 35
Mental health enquiry line: 0151 213 5350

DEPARTMENT OF HEALTH: MENTAL HEALTH LEGISLATION TEAM

Department of Health, Mental Health Legislation
3rd Floor
79 Whitehall
London
SW1A 2NS
Telephone: 020 7210 5359 and 020 7210 5367
Fax: 020 7210 5805
Email: mentalhealthact2007@dh.gsi.gov.uk

LAW SOCIETY

The Law Society of England and Wales
113 Chancery Lane
London WC2A 1PL
DX 56 London/Chancery Lane
Telephone: 020 7274 1222
Fax: 020 7831 0344
Practice Advice Service: 0870 606 2522
Mental Health Accreditation Scheme website:
www.lawsociety.org.uk/accreditation/specialist-schemes/mental-health/
Mental Health Accreditation Scheme email: accreditation@lawsociety.org.uk

MENTAL HEALTH LAWYERS ASSOCIATION

Website: **www.mhla.co.uk**

MENTAL HEALTH LAW ONLINE

Website: **www.mentalhealthlaw.co.uk**

SOLICITORS REGULATION AUTHORITY

The Cube
199 Wharfside Street
Birmingham B1 1RN
DX 720293 Birmingham 47
Contact centre: 0870 606 2555
Professional Ethics Helpline: 0870 606 2577

Index